The pursuit of sexual freedom and its political, philosophical and practical implications are the themes of this wide-ranging new study of seventeenth-century literature, which confronts ideological issues of sexual politics equally relevant to modern debate. The author examines the writers of the later seventeenth century in their historical context, and focuses particularly on what happens when women as well as men desire sexual freedom. In a study of the writings, notorious for their sexual candour, of the Earl of Rochester, God-haunted atheist and licensed rebel of the Restoration court, and Aphra Behn, the most prominent and most controversial woman writer of the period, the author explores some of the tensions inherent in the ideology of individual liberty as applied to the conduct of sexual relations inside and outside marriage. The works by Rochester, Behn and their contemporaries as discussed here gain much of their power from the ambivalence with which they treat the competing claims of freedom and authority, rebelliousness and security, the assertion of power and the need to love.

SEXUAL FREEDOM
IN RESTORATION LITERATURE

SEXUAL FREEDOM IN RESTORATION LITERATURE

WARREN CHERNAIK

Reader in English Literature, Queen Mary and Westfield College,
University of London

CAMBRIDGE
UNIVERSITY PRESS

Published by the Press Syndicate of the University of Cambridge
The Pitt Building, Trumpington Street, Cambridge CB1 1RP
40 West 20th Street, New York, NY 10011-4211, USA
10 Stamford Road, Oakleigh, Melbourne 3166, Australia

First published 1995

Printed in Great Britain at the University Press, Cambridge

A catalogue record for this book is available from the British Library

Library of Congress cataloguing in publication data
Chernaik, Warren L.
Sexual freedom in restoration literature / Warren Chernaik.
p.   cm.
Includes bibliographical references and index.
ISBN 0 521 46497 8 (hardback)
1. English literature – Early modern, 1500–1700 – History and criticism.
2. Sex customs in literature.
3. Literature and society – England – History – 17th century.
4. Great Britain – History – Restoration, 1660–1688.
5. Libertines in literature.   6. Liberty in literature.
I. Title.
PR437.C48 1995
820.9'3538'09032–dc20   94–19823 CIP

ISBN 0 521 46497 8 hardback

In memory of my mother, Ruth Parker Chernaik

Contents

Acknowledgements

This book is very different from the one I started to write nearly ten years ago, and during the book's extended gestation period I have had the benefit of advice and assistance from a number of friends and colleagues. When I began teaching Restoration literature to students at the University of London, no edition of any of the works of Aphra Behn was in print: I kept a dog-eared edition of *Love-Letters* on my shelf at the North Library, which my graduate students passed round, and I made up my own photocopied anthology of Behn's poems from transcriptions of the 1697 edition. Now both Rochester and Behn, virtually excluded from the canon a few years ago, are recognised as central to their age, and critical studies and editions, virtually non-existent a few years back, are crowding the library shelves. The subversive sexual content and the hostility toward authority which, in both of these authors, once kept them out of the canon have now brought them back in and assured them a responsive audience in a later age.

For advice and encouragement (and in some cases for comments on drafts of sections of the book), I am particularly grateful to Isobel Grundy, James Grantham Turner, Elaine Hobby, Valerie Rumbold, Keith Walker, Paddy Lyons, Susan Wiseman, Felicity Baker, Harold Weber, Eva Simmons, Margaret Cannon, Ken Robinson, Rob Hume, Peter Dixon and Michael Miller. Laura Chernaik made helpful comments on a draft of the introduction, and Judith Chernaik has given expert editorial advice on countless details in successive drafts. Barbara Everett, Janet Todd, James Winn and readers consulted by Cambridge University Press have convinced me that the book needed further revision when I had thought I had finished with it, and the final version is greatly improved as a result of their suggestions. My editor at Cambridge University Press, Josie Dixon, has been helpful and supportive throughout, and in preparing the manuscript I have had the invaluable clerical assistance of Sylvia Reynolds, Blanche Litwin and Sue McDaid. My research was materially assisted by a grant awarded by the British Academy and by study leave granted by my department. Much of the book was written in the British Library, and I owe a particular debt of gratitude to the staff of the North Library, who were amused by my doing research on dirty books.

Part of chapter 1 appeared, in a different form, as 'Those Whoreson Appetites: Varieties of Libertinism in Restoration Comedy', in *Comedy: Essays in Honour of Peter Dixon by friends and colleagues*, ed. Elizabeth Maslen (London, 1993); and a few sentences of chapter 2 appeared in 'The Rake's Progress', a review-essay on Jeremy Treglown's edition of Rochester's *Letters*, in *English*, 30 (1981). I have tried out much of this book in seminar papers and lectures in the last few years, and am grateful for comments I received on those occasions: the Cambridge University Restoration to Reform inter-faculty seminar; the Oxford Renaissance literature seminar; the University of Leeds, the University of Essex and the University of California, Berkeley; the Women's Studies Group 1550–1815; and the Extra-Mural Division of the University of London. I owe a particular debt of gratitude to the University of London Extra-Mural Association for inviting me to give the Charles Peake Memorial Lecture in 1990; to the National Theatre for inviting me to give platform lectures on *The Provok'd Wife* and *Venice Preserv'd* in 1981 and 1984; and to my students, undergraduate and postgraduate, at Queen Mary and Westfield College.

Introduction: the imperfect enjoyment

> This is the monstruosity in love, lady, that the will is infinite,
> and the execution confined; that the desire is boundless, and the
> act a slave to limit.
>
> *(Troilus and Cressida, III.ii.79–81)*

> How Blest was the Created *State*
>   Of *Man* and *Woman*, e're they fell,
> Compar'd to our unhappy *Fate*;
>   We need not fear another *Hell*.
>
> *(The Fall, 1–4)*

Libertinism embodies a dream of human freedom, recognised from
the outset both as infinitely desirable and as unattainable, a magical
power enabling one to overcome a sense of alienation and helplessness. The appeal of transgressive libertinism is perhaps best
embodied in the problematical figure of Don Juan, trickster, rebel,
servant of the phallus and of the ruthless amoral will, demanding a
freedom which enslaves oneself or others. Mozart's Don Giovanni,
like other libertine heroes, exploits a deep ambivalence in his victims
and in the audience, embodying their secret unacted desires, lulling
moral judgement to sleep.[1]
   With nothing to rebel against, no taboos to be transgressed,
blasphemy would lose its power to shock. It can be argued that
society creates its rebels, and that limited toleration and eventual
punishment of dissenters from the established order of family,
church and state serve as effective instruments of social control. The
youthful libertine, for all his vaunted independence, is acting out his
part in a described Oedipal scenario, and must inevitably define
himself in terms of the perceived norm he is rebelling against.
Society asserts its hegemony over the rebel by pre-empting the very
vocabulary the rebel is allowed to use. Indeed, as Foucault and
others have argued, the very conceptions of sexual norm and

deviancy serve a policing function.[2] Donna Anna and the Commendatore, in this view, create Don Giovanni in order to keep the Don Ottavios of the world in line. Yet even Foucault, who argues that the sexual instincts have no existence other than as a 'historical formation', in a universe of 'force relations' in which the controllers and the controlled are indissolubly bound together in symbiosis, recognises that the attempt by those in authority to contain rebellion often produces the very effect it seeks to preclude.[3] As I shall show in detail in examining the careers of the Earl of Rochester, Aphra Behn and other writers of the Restoration period, the dialogue between the felt need for order and the compulsion to rebel cannot be resolved in a single predictable pattern.

Nearly all accounts of libertinism as an ideology stress restlessness, dissatisfaction or a sense of incompleteness as its defining characteristic. No one woman, no one conquest, can ever satisfy, and the libertine finds himself on 'an infinite round of repetition, where each disillusionment leads to a new idealisation'.[4] The rake-hero of Restoration comedy, like Mozart's paradigmatic libertine, remains uninvolved emotionally, unperturbed by the chaos he creates around him. This accords with the Platonic theory that there must always be in love an imbalance of emotion between lover and beloved, pursuer and the object pursued.[5] It is the nature of the libertine hero to resist entanglements and responsibilities:

> Then bring my Bath, and strew my bed,
>   as each kind night returns,
> I'le change a Mistress till i'me dead,
>   and fate change me for worms.[6]

Leporello's catalogue aria, with great comic gusto, admiringly depicts his master's seductions as an infinite series – not quite ending in death, as in Hobbes's formulation and in the Rochester passage just quoted, since the prospect of extending the series keeps death at bay. With 1,003 sexual encounters – both the stuff of myth and, in its wry comic precision, the mock-heroic undercutting of myth – the sex act must inevitably become an assertion of power: one woman is more or less like all the others. But it is equally true that each time will be the first time, a fresh start: Mozart makes it clear that nothing in Elvira's or Zerlina's life will be nearly as interesting. The catalogue aria, itself an enacted seduction, in which the singer (or composer) toys with Elvira and with the opera-house audience, knowing they are in his power, is an instance of the transformative power of the erotic, made manifest in the supple, witty, expressive music.

The compulsion to secure conquest after conquest, fleeing from any possibility of a stable relationship, is in many ways a manifestation of insecurity. Psychoanalytically, it can be seen as Oedipal, with the unattainable mother as origin of a series of unsatisfactory surrogates, 'while the adversaries, deceived, fought and eventually even killed, represent the unconquerable mortal enemy, the father'.[7] Certainly the element of misogyny has always been prominent in libertine writing – quite unabashedly so in pornography, with its symbolic reduction of women to objects to be used, soiled and discarded, and more obliquely in the casual unexamined assumption, prevalent in many of the works to be discussed in this study, that women are created for the diversion of men, 'not to dwell in constantly, but only for a night and away': 'Mistresses are like Books; if you pore upon them too much, they doze you, and make you unfit for Company; but if us'd discreetly, you are fitter for conversation by 'em.'[8] The pleasures of 'Company' and 'conversation' are in this passage in *The Country-Wife* (1675) defined as male, reflecting a bonding which, in Eve Kosofsky Sedgwick's useful term, is 'homosocial', effectively excluding women: 'I tell you, 'tis hard to be a good Fellow, a good Friend, and a Lover of Women, as 'tis to be a good Fellow, a good Friend, and a Lover of Money: You cannot follow both, then choose your side' (i.i.203–6). Sedgwick in her discussion of *The Country-Wife* defines cuckoldry as 'a sexual act, performed on a man, by another man', in which a woman, third party in a triangular relationship, serves only as an object of exchange, assumed to have no intrinsic value.[9] The women in the play in their different ways all seek to resist or subvert such commodification ('Sir, you dispose of me a little before your time', ii.i.200), yet *The Country-Wife*, like a number of works we shall be considering, presents no alternative to a competitive model in which all human relationships are property relationships and 'freedom' means mastering and humiliating another: 'Now I think I am rid of her, and shall have no more trouble with her – Our Sisters and Daughters like Usurers money, are safest, when put out; but our Wifes, like their writings, never safe, but in our Closets under lock and key' (v.ii.75–8).[10] The assertion of power, literally phallocentric in *The Country-Wife*, masks a fear of impotence and reduction to a 'female' passivity, no less marked in the priapic Horner, the play's Don Juan prototype, than in the play's collection of blind and foolish cuckolds: 'Now your Sting is gone, you look'd in the Box amongst all those Women, like a drone in the hive, all upon you, shov'd and ill-us'd by 'em all' (III.ii.10–12).

As we shall see in subsequent chapters, the ideology of libertinism in seventeenth-century England places a pre-eminent emphasis on competition, presupposing a zero-sum game. In every transaction, the assertion of freedom by one participant means the deprivation of freedom for another: in a world where betrayal is the norm, the sex act itself becomes predatory. C. B. Macpherson has argued persuasively that the Hobbesian competitive model of man, so influential in the later seventeenth century, reflected the economic organisation of a society in which outmoded aristocratic ideals of responsibility, magnanimity and service were being supplanted by a cash nexus which eroded distinctions and overrode human ties.

> But a market, they say, does suit the king well,
> Who the Parliament buys and revenues does sell,
> And others to make the similitude hold
> Say his Majesty himself is bought too and sold.[11]

When in the closing scenes of *The Country-Wife*, Margery Pinchwife, rejecting all prudential considerations, seeks to assert the claims of natural feeling ('I don't intend to go to him again; you shall be my Husband now . . . I do love Mr. *Horner* with all my soul, and no body shall say me nay', v.iv.204–5, 330–1), she is forcibly silenced and, in a general conspiracy of cuckolds and dissemblers, 'sent back' into the power of the husband she has learned to despise (v.iv.1).[12] Ultimately, Horner, like the dupes whose values he shares, loves only himself: the libertine pattern is to stamp one's ownership and then pass on, indifferent or actively hostile once the moment of conquest is over. Peter Brooks describes a similar pattern in terms of a psychology of victimisation and control: 'The libertine, who pursues, seduces, then brings a rupture to recommence the process of pursuit and seduction, remains free, while his victims are deprived of freedom by his control of their psychological movements and their reputations.'[13]

Again and again the works to be discussed in this study demonstrate how the ideology of libertinism can justify oppression in the name of freedom, liberating the will to possess and destroy or its masochistic counterpart. *The Country-Wife* brings to the fore the element of aggression and violence within sexuality: 'Write as I bid you, or I will write Whore with this Penknife in your Face' (IV.i.92–3). For rakes and cuckolds alike in this play, the sexual act is a symbolic enactment of mastery, most satisfying (and conversely, most galling) when performed before witnesses, with the cuckold an unwilling, passive voyeur or auditor of his own humiliation. Where Freud interprets the 'need for a debased sexual object' as a projection of male self-loathing, some recent feminist theorists, recoiling from the aggression and misogyny implicit in the libertine ethos, have assimilated all heterosexual relationships to a model of rape and colonisation, presenting the male's 'thrusting into' the female as 'an act of invasion and ownership undertaken in a mode of predation'.[14] A less reductive variant of this argument restates the polarity as tyrant and victim, of either sex, and locates it specifically in a fear-laden 'unfree society' in which, as in the nightmare vision of Sade, the desire to dominate and tyrannise becomes all-embracing, and the ultimate sexual pleasure is murder: 'Sexuality, stripped of the idea of free exchange, is not in any way humane; it is nothing but pure cruelty . . . The act of predation . . . is the assertion of the abyss between master and victim. There is no question of reciprocal sensation; the idea of it is abhorrent to the Sadeian libertine . . . because to share is to be robbed.'[15]

The notorious 'china scene' in *The Country-Wife*, with its string of double entendres, anatomises a society in which sex is a quantifiable commodity both for women and for men, and in which, as in the model of human behaviour proposed by Hobbes, all members of a society are locked in an unceasing struggle for dominance, masked by the polite formulas of decorum:

SQUEAMISH. O Lord, I'le have some China too, Good Mr. Horner, don't you think to give other people China, and me none, Come in with me too.
HORNER. Upon my honour I have none left now.
SQUEAMISH. Nay, nay I have known you deny your China before now, but you shan't put me off so, Come –
HORNER. This Lady had the last there.
LADY FIDGET. Yes indeed Madam, to my certain knowledge he has no more left.
SQUEAMISH. Oh but it may be he may have some you could not find.

LADY FIDGET. What d'y think if he had any left, I would not have had it
  too, for we women of quality never think we have China enough.
  (IV.iii.180–92)

The exchange, in which the two women in coded language fight
over the sexual favours of Horner, reverses conventional expectations in presenting the women as aggressive and the male as post-
coitally passive. Quite explicitly, the passage equates the competitive and sexual drives, unmasking the unbridled, ravenous desire for
dominance and sexual satisfaction which motivates these two female
libertines.[16] One possible reading of the passage is that Lady Fidget
and Mrs Squeamish, a fortiori, stand for all mankind, with their
stratagems for concealing the desires that master them. But it can
also be read as expressing a male hostility and fear directed toward
an alien sex with a sexual capacity imagined as boundless, where
that of the male is a slave to limit.

The treatment of female sexuality in libertine writings of the
Restoration period is highly ambivalent. Even those works by male
authors which consciously subvert stereotypes of male power and
female passivity, treating sexually active women with a degree of
sympathy rather than as monstrous embodiments of unbridled
appetite, frequently present women as servants to the divine phallus,
accessory to the sexual pleasures of the male. Rochester's 'Song of a
Young Lady. To her Ancient Lover' employs a female persona who,
in a poem of considerable wit and charm, embodies the principles of
natural fertility, youth and sexual vigour, a dream of regeneration
associated with the Lucretian Venus, earth goddess and Queen of
Love. Yet it is striking that in this poem, as in a comparable passage
in the sharply satirical 'scepter' lampoon on Charles II, the woman's
formidable energies are wholly directed toward giving her male
partner an erection.

> Thy Nobler part, which but to name
> In our Sex would be counted shame,
> By Ages frozen grasp possest,
> From his Ice shall be releast:
> And, sooth'd by my reviving hand,
> In former warmth and Vigor stand.
> All a Lover's wish can reach,
> For thy Joy my Love shall teach:
> And for thy Pleasure shall improve,

All that Art can add to Love.
Yet still I love thee without Art,
Ancient Person of my Heart.[17]   (15–26)

As this poem illustrates, the representations of women in libertine
works are projections of male desire and male fears. This is no less
true of poems like Rochester's 'A Letter from Artemiza in the Town
to Chloe in the Country' and 'The Imperfect Enjoyment', where, as
in the lines just quoted, the idealised female figures are associated
with an imagined unfallen sexuality, than of his most vitriolic
obscene lampoons. Rochester employs the same conceptual vocabulary of 'naturall freedomes' and 'gen'rous passion' for praise and
dispraise, in giving a prelapsarian dignity and pathos to 'that lost
thing (Love)' in 'Artemiza to Chloe' (38–40) and in attacking the
whorish inclinations of Corinna in 'A Ramble in Saint James's
Parke' (97–8). This quality of ambivalence is especially pronounced
in 'Upon his leaving his Mistriss', with its tone elegantly poised
between admiration and contempt for a female libertine who,
putting the doctrine of sexual equality into practice, dispenses her
bounty like a goddess.

> Favours like *Nature* you dispense,
> With Universal influence.
>
> See the kind Seed-receiving earth,
> To ev'ry Grain affords a *Birth*;
> On her no Show'rs unwelcome fall,
> Her willing *Womb*, retains 'em all,
> And shall my *Celia* be confin'd?
> No, live up to thy mighty *Mind*,
> And be the Mistriss of *Mankind*.   (13–22)

Libertinism thus has its territorial side, and resistance to female
encroachment is a recurrent motif in libertine writings of the Restoration period. As the *OED* notes dispassionately, the term 'libertine'
is 'rarely applied to a woman', making the transgressive, indecorous
assertion by a woman of her 'naturall freedomes', rivalling the men,
all the more a cause for anxiety.

The erotic element so prominent in libertine writing, as Reichler
has pointed out, in certain respects breaks down the customary
barrier between self and Other, exciting the imagination of the
reader and encouraging direct involvement, identification and

imitation. In other ways such works are profoundly alienating, producing sexual excitation and release of a purely physical, mechanical kind. No one in seventeenth-century England or France bought the clandestine *Tullia and Octavia* or *L'Ecole des filles* for the sake of the plot, characters or sentiments, but for a direct, practical end, immediately apparent in male readers by an erect penis; the aim of such pornographic works, in David Foxon's clear definition, is 'principally to arouse sexual desire and encourage erotic fanta- sies'.[18] If pornography entices and seduces, obscenity, with its fore- grounding of the violently aggressive elements in sexuality, com- bines elements of attraction and repulsion. The poems of Rochester are occasionally pornographic and frequently obscene, and in both respects they illustrate, in a particularly striking form, some problematical aspects of the ideology of libertinism in the Restor- ation period.

The obscene poems for which Rochester is notorious set out to embarrass or trap the reader by bringing out into the open what normally is kept discreetly concealed.

> By all *Loves* soft, yet mighty *Pow'rs*,
>   It is a thing unfit,
> That Men should *Fuck* in time of *Flow'rs*,
>   Or when the *Smock's* beshit.
>
> Fair nasty *Nymph*, be clean and kind,
>   And all my joys restore;
> By using Paper still behind,
>   And spunges for before.   ('Song', 1–8)[19]

As often is the case with Rochester, the shock administered by these lines is partly satiric in intent. The advice tendered is severely practical, and the lines contain an objective, factual element, useful to the social historian in providing evidence for the state of feminine hygiene in the later seventeenth century. But aesthetically they gain their effect by deliberately violating the reader's expectations and common standards of propriety, thus causing acute physical pain. The conventionally elevated diction of the opening lines prepares the reader for the standard sentiments of love lyric: the descent from flattering euphemism to menstruation and fecal stains is like a slap in the face. Doctrinally Yeats makes a similar point in more decorous language in 'But Love has pitched his mansion in/The place of excrement',[20] but the emphasis is entirely different. There is no room for love in Rochester's poem, only fucking.

In some ways, these lines are closer to graffiti than to anything we would ordinarily describe as poetry. The emotional energy behind these lines, and others like them, can be described as a desire to deface or destroy, a free-floating aggressiveness of considerable intensity. The impulse to cause pain, to lash out at and, if possible, destroy one's enemies has traditionally been associated with satire and in particular with the writings of Swift: 'Though it must be understood,/I would hang them if I could'.[21] In these lines as in Swift's 'The Lady's Dressing Room', the aggressive energy seems somehow in excess of the circumstances, has not entirely been channelled toward the poem's didactic end. Ultimately the poem defeats any single rational, coherent interpretation. Does Rochester's 'Song' express a healthy Rabelaisian sexuality and acceptance of bodily needs? Or does it express a loathing of the flesh, a disgust at one's own mortality in its reduction of the 'Fair Nymph' to a bag of bones and excrement?

This sense of an overflow of destructive energy, causing uncertainty or instability of tone, is even more pronounced in another satire in lyric stanzas, 'On Mistress Willis', which once again presents menstrual blood ('Flowers') as an emblem of degradation and pollution.

> Against the Charms our *Ballox* have
>   How weak all human skill is
> Since they can make a Man a slave
>   To such a Bitch as *Willis.*
>
> Whom that I may describe throughout
>   Assist me Bawdy Powers
> I'le write upon a double Clowt
>   And dipp my Pen in Flowers . . .
>
> A Prostitute to all the Town
>   And yet with no man Freinds
> She rails and scolds when she lyes down
>   And Curses when she Spends.   (1–8, 13–16)

The opening stanza would suggest that the concerns of the poem are in part general, even philosophical: Rochester is commenting on the slavery the sexual appetite exercises over all men, whatever their grand intentions. Here the contrast between 'high' and 'low' terms, between the poetic resonances of 'Charms', 'slave' and 'human skill' and the blunt deflation of 'Ballox' and 'Bitch' makes Rochester's point with witty economy. In lines 13–16, the penultimate stanza, the poet remains thoroughly in control of his medium, as he uses the characteristic Augustan devices of balance, antithesis and chiasmus ('A Prostitute to all the Town . . . with no man Freinds') to paint a memorable satiric portrait. The lines lack the element of pity for the benighted victim we find in Pope's 'Epistle to a Lady', but, as in passage after passage in that poem, the rhetoric, echo to the sense, builds up a character sketch of a woman divided against herself.[22]

A similar point is implied by the successive oxymora in stanza 3:

> Her looks demurely Impudent
> Ungainly Beautifull
> Her modesty is insolent
> Her witt both pert and dull.   (9–12)

It is possible to read these lines as suggesting that Mrs Willis is a pretender to wit and beauty, whose 'modesty' is a whore's come-on, but the passage is more interesting if we read it not as a catalogue of insults, but as an analysis of gifts misapplied. No empty-headed ninny but 'a Foole of Parts' like the Fine Lady of 'Artemiza to Chloe', her 'Impertinence' and lack of 'discretion', her inability to judge the fitness of an occasion, cause her to become a parody of her own good qualities ('Artemiza to Chloe', 149, 161, 168, 257). Promiscuous, she is at all times alone and, devoted to sex, she robs the sexual act of any pleasure. Yet the tone of the last stanza veers violently away from the witty understatement of 'And Curses when she Spends'.

> Bawdy in thoughts, precise in Words,
> Ill natur'd though a Whore,
> Her Belly is a Bagg of Turds,
> And her Cunt a Common shore.   (17–20)

The last two lines of the poem come across as a cry of rage and pain, an expression of a misogynist recoil from the female genitalia, represented, in language negating any possibility of desire, as loathsome and unclean. As manifestation of the double standard, the poem both violates and erects taboos.[23] The shock of the offensive language, ill prepared for, with no attempt to make the accusation particularly appropriate to the character built up in the previous lines, does not provide an effective satiric climax, but signifies a loss of artistic control.

The same kind of satiric overkill can be found in the second stanza of the 'Mock Song', a parody of a romantic lyric by Sir Carr Scroope.

> I swive as well as others do,
>   I'm young, not yet deform'd,
> My tender Heart, sincere, and true,
>   Deserves not to be scorn'd.
> Why *Phillis* then, why will you swive,
>   With *Forty Lovers* more?
> Can I (said she) with *Nature* strive,
>   Alas I am, alas I am a Whore.
>
> Were all my Body larded o're,
>   With Darts of love, so thick,
> That you might find in ev'ry *Pore*,
>   A well stuck standing *Prick*;
> Whilst yet my *Eyes* alone were free,
>   *My Heart*, wou'd never doubt,
> In Am'rous Rage, and Exstasie,
>   To wish those *Eyes*, to wish those *Eyes* fuckt out.

The first stanza is an effective, controlled rebuttal of the 'tender' sentiments of conventional love poetry, as typified by Scroope's 'I cannot change as others do'.[24] Details of language all serve to reinforce the satiric point, the self-deception of the romantic lover. The reassessment of Phillis's character and motivation in cynically realistic terms is at one with the witty rhyming deflation of 'with *Nature* strive' with 'why will you swive', and the verbal and rhythmic echoes of Scroope ('Will still love on, will still love on, and die') serve a similar function. But in the second stanza, the poem changes direction: once again, the emotion released leaves its ostensible object far behind. The vision of female insatiability, the implicit reduction of man to a fucking machine in a Cartesian or Hobbesian universe spinning madly out of control, the sadistic or masochistic intensity of the grotesque imagery, especially in the final line, are profoundly disturbing. Nothing in the first stanza leads us to speculate on the author's psychological state, to seek for a meaning behind or beyond the words on the page; everything in the last stanza encourages such a reaction. The poem thus can be read as a symptom, as an instance of the deformations of an ideology which stigmatises as a monster a woman who takes a series of lovers, while conferring heroic status on a man who behaves in a similar way. In a fantasy of limitless aggression, the prick, equated implicitly with the poet's pen, becomes a weapon by which the feared female adversary can be disabled.

The wit combats so prominent in Restoration comedy are ritual displays of aggression, in which the victor receives tangible reward or acclaim and the vanquished is held up to public shame. The aim is to increase one's own marketable value, while decreasing that of one's opponent. In Etherege's *The Man of Mode* (1676), wit is inseparable from 'ill nature', the desire to 'jeer' and 'Triumph' over an adversary, inflicting pain.[25] 'Taste' in *The Man of Mode* has an oddly literal sense, as the wits feed off the fools, in order to revitalise a jaded appetite and assure themselves of their own superiority: 'Here's the freshest Fool in Town, and one who has not cloy'd you yet' (III.ii.140–1). The treatment of sexual relations in *The Man of Mode*, as in many of the works to be discussed in the chapters that follow, is no less remorselessly competitive; indeed, similar metaphors of appetite and its inevitable decay are the standard stock-in-trade of Restoration libertinism. Loveit, a failure in the world of the play because she is cast aside, no longer a fresh morsel, is fully aware that Dorimant is using her to provide tangible proofs of his 'ascendancy', in scenes enacted in order 'that the Town may know the power you have over me' (v.i.173–4). She is equally acute in her recognition that for him ('You who have more pleasure in the ruine of a womans reputation than in the indearments of her love'), the sex act itself is an assertion of dominance (v.i.193–4). By his display of mastery over Loveit, a scene put on partly for Bellinda's benefit, he is advertising to Bellinda a sexual potency she can taste for herself later in private. It is Dorimant's unscrupulousness that equips him for success in a world where, as Hobbes puts it, force and fraud are the cardinal virtues.[26]

Rochester's tale of Corinna in 'A Letter from Artemiza to Chloe' depicts a similar predatory society, but one where the stakes in the competition are literally life and death. Wit here is presented as entirely destructive; what Corinna learns from her faithless lover, 'a Man of Witt,/Who found, 'twas dull, to love above a day,/Made his ill-natur'd Jest, and went away' (198–200), is the need to find someone less clever than she whose 'want of Sense' (224) will suit him in turn for the role of victim.

> A Woman's ne're soe ruyn'd, but she can
> Be still reveng'd on her undoer Man.

How lost so e're, shee'l fynde some Lover more
A lewde abandon'd Foole, then shee a whore.
That wretched thinge Corinna, who had run
Through all the severall Wayes of being undone,
Couzen'd att first by Love, and living then
By turning the too-dear-bought trick on Men.   (185–92)

The war of wits and fools is depicted here in much darker terms than
in *The Man of Mode*. Rochester's poem is complex structurally, with
the Fine Lady who speaks these lines, a practiced libertine exemplifying the vices of the town, being held up for disapprobation in Artemiza's narrative and then taking over the role of story-teller and satirist herself, in a 'Discourse' lasting, uninterrupted, for seventy-four
lines. The pattern of descent traced in this passage, from innocence
through victimisation to revenge, is, as we shall see, common in the
literature of the period; we find it, for example, in several of Aphra
Behn's works.[27] Where Artemiza condemns the 'Cheates, and
Tricks' by which a projected ideal of love associated with 'Innocence' and spontaneity (40–3) has been debased, the Fine Lady
argues for their utility in a world where survival is all-important.
The libertinism of the Fine Lady and those like her is, as Artemiza
presents it in quasi-Miltonic terms, a loss of true liberty, as well as a
fall from an imagined perfection:

Our silly Sexe, who borne, like Monarchs, free,
Turn Gipsies for a meaner Liberty,
And hate restraint, though but from infamy.
They call whatever is not Common, nice,
And deafe to Natures rules, or Loves advice,
Forsake the pleasure, to pursue the Vice.
To an exact perfection they have wrought
The Action Love, the Passion is forgott.   (56–63)

But in the overall context of the poem, where the Fine Lady is
allowed to present her side in the debate, the expression of feeling by
male or female combatants leads to surrender of power, humiliation,
defeat. Dorimant's reaction to the first stirrings of love in *The Man of
Mode* is to fear being disarmed or unmanned, like the hero of Rochester's 'The Imperfect Enjoyment'; it is as though he has no vocabulary to express sexual feeling other than the language of domination.

DOR. ASIDE. I love her, and dare not let her know it, I fear sh'as an
    ascendancy over me and may revenge the wrongs I have done her sex.
    (IV.i.151–3)

If the Fine Lady who tells Corinna's story, wrapped in comfort, is able to treat with open contempt the 'kinde easy Foole' (124) who pays her bills, Corinna herself, more needy and desperate, finds that 'to have subdu'd/Some Fopp, or other' (181–2) is not enough, but is led to make possession of his property certain. The chain of exploitation ends in death:

> And when to the height of fondnesse he is growne,
> 'Tis tyme, to poyson him, and all's her owne . . .
> Nature, who never made a thinge in vayne,
> But does each Insect to some ende ordeyne,
> Wisely contriv'd kind-keeping Fooles, noe doubt,
> To patch up Vices, Men of Witt weare out.   (246–55)

In its mixture of pity and moral disapproval, Rochester's satire differs greatly from *The Man of Mode*, despite the thematic resemblances. Yet the society reflected in both works is one in which, in Hobbes's terms, happiness consists 'not in having prospered, but in prospering': the market has no memory and no sentiment.[28]

The equation of sex and power central to the ideology of libertinism entails a fear of failure, damaging to the reputation of the would-be conqueror, who can in a moment be overwhelmed by 'Rage and Shame'. Male dreams of omnipotence, centred in the mighty phallus, are deflated to comic effect in Behn's 'The Disappointment' and Rochester's 'The Imperfect Enjoyment', two poems in the same genre which treat similar materials but differ in their approach. Both poems are characterised by ironic distance, carefully judged shifts in tone, as they portray the embarrassment, comic to the reader but not to the participants, of a sudden, catastrophic failure by the male to perform adequately in a sexual encounter. Behn's language, observing the decorum of pastoral romance, is consistently euphemistic as, in a third-person narrative, she presents the thwarted sexual union of shepherd and shepherdess, 'the Amorous *Lysander*' and 'fair *Cloris*'. The first ten stanzas show the pursuit of the 'yielding' fair from the male participant's point of view ('he seeks . . . he saw . . . he saw'), but in stanzas XI–XIII the perspective changes:

> *Cloris* returning from the Trance
> Which Love and soft Desire had bred,
> Her timerous Hand she gently laid
> (Or guided by Design or Chance)
> Upon that Fabulous *Priapas*,

The Potent God, as Poets feign;
But never did young *Shepherdess*,
Gath'ring of Fern upon the Plain,
More nimbly draw her Fingers back,
Finding beneath the verdant Leaves a snake:

Then *Cloris* her fair Hand withdrew,
Finding that God of her Desires
Disarm'd of all his Awful Fires,
And cold as Flow'rs bath'd in the Morning-Dew.
Who can the *Nymphs's* Confusion guess?[29]

In these lines the 'disappointment' is on the woman's part, as anticipated joys fail to materialise and the 'God of her Desires' falls short of its reputation. The phallic snake shocks her because it is *not* dangerous, as, in a reversal of sexual roles, the ardent lover is feminised in pastoral imagery evoking passive, ephemeral natural beauty.[30] Though the narrative voice is not explicitly feminine and treats the predicament of the male and female figures with the same amused tolerance, the effect of the lines is to direct sympathy toward the woman, who is not to blame and who, the poem suggests, deserves better: 'The *Nymph's* Resentments none but I/Can well Imagine or Condole' (131–2).

Little of this can be found in Behn's source, a French libertine poem which assumes a male point of view throughout, makes virtually no use of pastoral imagery and treats its principal female figure exclusively as a sex object, with several stanzas in praise of her 'bijou' ('Petit thresor de la Nature,/Estroite et charmante prison . . .') and a recurrent tone of knowing complicity between male author and male reader.

Ha! Cloris, quand je m'en souviens
Je m'imagine estre Lisandre,
Et me semble que je vous tiens.[31]

The most striking difference is that in the French poem, 'L'occasion perdue recouverte', as the title indicates, Lysander's failure is presented as no more than a temporary inconvenience, prelude to a triumphant conclusion. As another contemporary translation puts it:

Five or six times these Doves together went,
And full as oft in active Measures Danc 't . . .
All that was sweet in Love in them abounds.

In Behn's poem there is no equivalent recovery ('The Disappointment', 140): as in Rochester's 'The Imperfect Enjoyment', the poem
ends with the discomfiture of the male figure, trapped in the '*Hell* of
Impotence' with no prospect of escape.[32]

Rochester casts his poem in the first person, telling his story
entirely from the perspective of the male participant. But he is no
less merciless than Behn in puncturing pretensions of mastery and
control:

> The nimble *Tongue* (*Love's* lesser Lightning) plaid
> Within my *Mouth,* and to my thoughts conveyd
> Swift Orders, that I shou'd prepare to throw
> The *All-dissolving Thunderbolt* below.   (7–10)

The decorum of these lines, as of the first half of the poem generally,
is mock-heroic, with the magniloquent, expansive language implying its own refutation. Rochester's poem like Behn's presents the
prospective sexual delights as mutual, with the lovers 'equally
inspir'd with eager fire', the woman as well as the man 'flaming with
desire' for consummation (3–4). But Rochester's concerns in 'The
Imperfect Enjoyment', to a far greater extent than in any other
example of the genre, are philosophical: his subject is the disproportion between our desires and their fulfilment. The poem evokes an
ideal of a perfect love, an expression of spiritual union through the
sexual act, betrayed by a body which can never be trusted and by an
imagination which inevitably deceives.

> My flutt'ring *Soul,* sprung with the pointed kiss,
> Hangs hov'ring o're her *Balmy Brinks* of Bliss.
> But whilst her busie hand, wou'd guide that part,
> Which shou'd convey my *Soul* up to her *Heart,*
> In liquid *Raptures,* I dissolve all o're,
> Melt into Sperme, and spend at ev'ry Pore.   (11–16)

In elegant, ironic couplets, with an echo of Donne's 'The Exsta-
sie' in lines 11–12, Rochester anatomises the human condition,
rendered problematical by an uneasy mixture of the flesh and
spirit: if we were angels or goats, the difficulties would not occur.
The lines convey the physical scene graphically, while maintaining the decorum of mock-heroic periphrasis ('liquid *Raptures*',
'clammy joys'). In the first thirty-six lines, Rochester only twice
employs direct, obscene terms, and the effect of the sudden

descent is to deflate the pretensions of the persona, suggesting that the idealisation of mutual love is yet another self-aggrandising fiction:

> Is there then no more?
> She cries. All this to Love, and *Rapture's* due,
> Must we not pay a debt to pleasure too?
> But I the most forlorn, lost *Man* alive,
> To shew my wisht Obedience vainly strive,
> I sigh alas! and Kiss, but cannot Swive.   (22–7)

In the second half of the poem, idealisation is left far behind, as the impulse of shame, powerfully conveyed in evocative language ('Trembling, confus'd, despairing, limber, dry,/A wishing, weak, unmoving lump I ly'), is succeeded by bitter anger directed at the 'Base Recreant' penis (35–6, 61). In personifying the disobedient penis as independent force, following its own priorities and ignoring its nominal master, Rochester here illustrates (and by implication criticises) that divergence of the sensual and affectionate currents which, according to Freud, entails 'a physical debasement of the sexual object': 'Where they love they do not desire and where they desire they cannot love. They seek objects which they do not need to love, in order to keep their sensuality away from the objects they love.'[33] As in a number of libertine poems by Rochester and others, the element of aggression in the closing lines of 'The Imperfect Enjoyment' is intense and disturbing, as the elevated language of mock-heroic poetry is replaced by violent, insulting obscenity. The lines angrily deny any possibility of spiritual transcendence, as they envisage a world of unrelieved, mechanical physicality.

> Worst part of me, and henceforth hated most,
> Through all the *Town*, a common *Fucking Post*;
> On whom each *Whore*, relieves her tingling *Cunt*,
> As *Hogs*, on *Gates*, do rub themselves and grunt.   (61–4)

For all its wit and comic verve, the poem, like others to be discussed in later chapters, reflects a state of impasse. If the physical realities of prick and cunt refute the self-deceiving dream of transcending human limitations, the poem nevertheless suggests that without these illusions, elevating men and women above hogs and blocks of wood, there is little to live for. Self-hatred, lashing out in the urge to mutilate or destroy the feared Other, localised as source of the body's treason, constitutes the darker side of libertinism, expressed here in a vision of the body as riddled by venereal disease and racked by intolerable physical suffering.

> May'st thou to rav'nous *Shankers*, be a *Prey*,
> Or in consuming *Weepings* waste away.
> May *Strangury*, and *Stone*, thy *Days* attend,
> May'st thou ne're Piss, who didst refuse to spend,
> When all my joys, did on false thee depend.   (66–70)

The contradictions of libertinism, as a philosophy of pleasure leading to pain and a philosophy of freedom leading to imprisonment, will be explored further in subsequent chapters of this study.

Chapter 1, 'Hobbes and the libertines', seeks to establish an appropriate historical context for Restoration libertinism, in showing how the philosophical doctrines of Hobbes and of Epicureanism were adapted or reinterpreted by Rochester and other writers associated with the court of Charles II. A consistent theme, in this and later chapters, will be the problems which arise when ideas originally developed in a political context by such authors as Hobbes and Locke are applied to the domestic sphere, and in particular to the conduct of sexual relationships inside and outside the constraints of marriage. In his influential 'The Myth of the Rake in "Restoration Comedy"', Robert Hume has argued that late seventeenth-century comedy is fundamentally conservative in its sexual attitudes and that the plays gave 'little support to libertinism . . . did not endorse libertinism nor were they genuinely hostile to marriage'.[34] In chapter 1 and the following chapters, I argue that the drama of the Restoration period, like the poems of Rochester, took libertine ideas seriously, and that words like 'support' or 'endorse' fail to do justice to the complex ideological position of such works as *The Man of Mode*, *The Way of the World* or *The Provok'd Wife*.

Chapters 2 and 3 explore some of the tensions inherent in the rake's ethos of untrammelled sexual freedom, as they find expression in the writings of Rochester, licensed rebel of the Restoration court. An unresolved ambivalence toward the competing claims of freedom and authority, of rebelliousness and security, of the assertion of power and the need for love finds expression in Rochester's poetry, as well as in his attempts at drama, rarely discussed by critics, which include the obscene farce *Sodom*, his adaptation of

Fletcher's *Valentinian* and the fragmentary 'Conquest of China'. In his own day Rochester was recognised as the archetypal libertine, encapsulating all the painful paradoxes of a life dedicated to transgression and tormented by fear of retribution, the stone statue's revenge:

> Son of A whore God dam you can you tell
> A Peerless Peer the Readyest way to Hell? . . .
> Ive swived more whores more ways than Sodoms walls
> Ere knew or the College of Romes Cardinalls.
> Witness Heroick scars, look here nere go
> Sear cloaths and ulcers from the top to toe.
>
> ('To the Post Boy', 1–2, 5–8)[35]

A God-haunted atheist, pornographer and panegyrist of 'that lost thing (Love)' ('Artemiza to Chloe', 38), misogynist and protofeminist, Rochester's writings are riddled with contradictions, which chapters 2 and 3, 'The tyranny of desire: sex and politics in Rochester' and 'Absent from thee', examine in some detail. These chapters, like the two which follow, place particular emphasis on the implicit political dimension in the sexual ideology of libertinism, which both challenges and pays obeisance to the reigning hierarchy of church, state, and family.

Chapters 4 and 5 raise the question of what happens when women as well as men lay claim to a similar unrestricted sexual freedom as 'an English Woman's natural Right'.

> Wherefore are we
> Born with high Souls, but to assert our selves,
> Shake off this vile Obedience they exact,
> And claim an equal Empire o'er the World?[36]

In both passages quoted, from Otway's *The Atheist* (1684) and Rowe's *The Fair Penitent* (1703), the arguments, put in the mouths of female characters, draw on the recognised vocabulary of contemporary philosophical and political discourse, invoking the Hobbesian idea of competition, a universal desire for domination or 'Empire', as well as the idea of inalienable natural right, as developed by Locke and others.

The challenge posed to male domination by liberated female desire, with its claim of 'equal Empire', is a central concern in chapters 4 and 5. In these chapters, works by Aphra Behn, the most prominent woman writer of the period, are compared with those by her contemporaries, male and female. The works in various genres discussed here in some respects embody and in some respects challenge the ideology of libertinism, as licence for predators.

Chapter 4, 'Playing trick for trick: domestic rebellion and the female libertine', discusses a number of works by woman authors which explore strategies to contest patriarchal domination. The ideological position of the poems of Aphra Behn, Sarah Fyge and Lady Mary Chudleigh, as of the prose writings of Mary Astell, is complex and to some extent self-contradictory. To an appreciable extent, all the works by woman authors discussed in this chapter are dependent on the competitive model characteristic of libertinism. Attempts to give a voice to the powerless in a society where, in Astell's words, 'Men are possess'd of all Places of Power, Trust and Profit', the works discussed here challenge a dominant ideology without being able to present a fully articulated alternative. The paradox of sleeping with the enemy can involve a simultaneous wish to loosen and to maintain emotional and matrimonial ties or an attempt to resolve ambivalence by aggressive retaliation, as with Rochester's Corinna or the heroines of Behn's fiction, Sylvia, Isabella and the 'fair jilt' Miranda, who, tutored by their betrayers, have learned to survive at the expense of others, 'turning the too-dear-bought Trick on Men' ('Artemiza to Chloe', 192).[37]

The final chapter, 'My masculine part: Aphra Behn and the androgynous imagination', examines the literary career of Aphra Behn, with particular attention to the ways in which her writings tend to destabilise conventional gender boundaries. Behn, unlike Rochester, was a professional writer, 'forced to write for Bread and not ashamed to owne it', tailoring her plays for specific performers and at all times aware of the practical difficulties of competing in a market rigged against women.[38] In Behn's writings, resentment at 'the scanted Customes of the Nation' which condemn women to the servitude of a 'State of Ignorance', denying them their heritage of freedom, is seen as a spur to action: as in the polemical writings of Mary Astell, 'a generous Emulation to excel in the best things' is contrasted with passive submission to unjust power.[39] Images of androgyny, frequent in Behn's poetry and fiction, celebrate an amoral transgressive force which defies categorisation in terms of gender. Working with traditional materials, Behn reinterprets and redefines them in ways which implicitly challenge the dominant ideology of her day. In this chapter, variations on the themes of free female desire and androgyny are examined in a number of plays by Behn and her male contemporaries and rivals in the contested terrain of literary tradition: the spirited heroine adopting male dress in an attempt to break out of a proposed or actual confinement, the would-be female libertine, the virago or female warrior, and the unhappy, frustrated wife longing for some form of deliverance. Here as in other works discussed, desire is fuelled by the presence of obstacles, and the lure of freedom is all the greater because it appears unattainable.

CHAPTER I

Hobbes and the libertines

The name of Hobbes is frequently invoked in twentieth-century critical discussions of Restoration comedy and of the poems of Rochester.[1] Certainly, there can be no doubt of the pervasiveness of libertine views in court circles during the Restoration period: a fashionable 'atheism' and scorn for the 'dullness' of conservative belief served as badges of acceptance among the fraternity of wits. The large number of pamphlets directed against libertine principles during the period testified that such views, usually associated with the demonised figure of Hobbes, were widely perceived as dangerous, a widely disseminated 'poyson' for which an antidote must be provided. A similar vocabulary of seduction and contagion – 'Ill *Qualities* ought to have ill *Names*, to prevent their being *Catching*' – characterises Jeremy Collier's attack on Restoration comedy in *A Short View of the Immorality, and Profaneness of the English Stage* (1698) and the dire warnings of Thomas Tenison in *The Creed of Mr. Hobbes Examined* (1670) about how the philosophy of Hobbes, having 'seduc'd and poyson'd [the] Imaginations' of susceptible readers, has 'spread its malignity amongst us' and 'infected some who can and more who cannot read a difficult Author'.[2]

Throughout the period, 'modern atheism' and its Epicurean predecessors tended to be conflated. As Thomas Creech writes in the preface to his translation of Lucretius: 'The admirers of Mr. *Hobbes* may easily discern that his *Politicks* are but *Lucretius* enlarg'd; His state of *Nature* is sung by our *Poet* . . . the beginning of *Societies*; the *Criterions* of *Just* and *Unjust* exactly the same, and natural *Consequents* of the Epicurean Origine of Man.'[3] Hobbes and Lucretius were essentially alike in their appeal. Both were perceived as radical, anti-establishment figures – in Peter Gay's words, each was 'a disturber of the peace whose work was too great to be ignored but whose name was too disreputable to be praised'. It is extraordinary how often translators of Lucretius felt the need to apologise for making available to readers such equivocal and dangerous material: either they carefully dissociate attractive form from pernicious content, or they include detailed hostile commentaries intended to 'expose the principles of *irreligion*' and refute Lucretius's arguments.[4] Those sympathetic to the message of Lucretius – as illustrated in the rapturous praise of 'great Lucretius' in the opening lines of Shadwell's *The Virtuoso* as a 'profound Oracle of Wit and Sence' who 'doest, almost alone, demonstrate that Poetry and Good Sence may go together' – saw him as a great liberator, freeing men from bondage to 'slavish fear' (Rochester and Creech use the same phrase) of their imagined masters in the sky. This aspect of Lucretius is brought out vividly in Creech's translation:

> Long time men lay opprest with slavish fear,
> Religion's Tyranny did domineer,
> Which being plac'd in Heaven look'd *proudly* down,
> And frighted abject spirits with her frown.
> At last a mighty one of *Greece* began
> T'assert the natural liberty of Man,
> By senseless terrors and vain fancy led
> To slavery, *streight the conquer'd Fantoms fled.*[5]

Hobbes's attitude toward religion was less straightforward: he was a sworn enemy of priestcraft, consistently urged the subordination of religion to the commands of the civil power and, in explaining the psychology of religious belief, placed great emphasis on 'perpetual fear' of things unknown, 'anxiety of the time to come' as 'the natural cause of religion'. Though he is careful to distinguish pagan from Christian religion (men create the pagan gods and acknowledge the Christian God) and can be said throughout *Leviathan* to redefine the Christian God in highly restrictive, heterodox terms in accordance with his polemical purposes, rather than flatly denying the existence of God, Hobbes's position remains closely akin to that of Lucretius and the Epicureans (XII, pp. 70–1).[6] Mintz quotes an 'Atheist's Catechism' of 1666 to illustrate the popular libertine interpretation of Hobbes's doctrines:

Q. What is it that men call Religion?
A. A Politick Cheat put upon the World.
Q. Who were the first Contrivers of this Cheat?
A. Some Cunning men that designed to keep the World in subjection and awe.

Q. What was the first Ground of it?
A. Men were frighted with Tales that were told them, about Invisible
   Nothings.

Rochester in his conversations with Gilbert Burnet expresses similar
views: the pretence of 'that business of Inspiration' is a fraud
perpetrated by cynical priests, voracious of the 'power to cheat the
World', who take advantage of men's fearful and credulous natures
to reduce them to slavery:

For Prophecies and Miracles, the World had been always full of strange
Stories; for the boldness and cunning of Contrivers meeting with the
Simplicity and Credulity of the People, things were easily received; and
being once received passed down without contradiction . . .

The believing Mysteries, he said, made way for all the Juglings of Priests,
for they getting the People under them in that Point, set out to them what
they pleased; and giving it a hard Name, and calling it a *Mystery*, The
people were tamed, and easily believed it.[7]

Hobbesian doctrines serve the libertine poets and dramatists as a
way of interpreting human conduct. Libertines like Rochester, a
professed disciple, reinterpreted Hobbes, choosing to emphasise
certain aspects of his philosophical system and ignore others as it
suited them, and in the process – quoting or paraphrasing Hobbes
out of context as unscrupulously as his opponents did – transformed
arguments intended to prove beyond doubt the absolute necessity
for submission to authority into a manifesto of 'the natural liberty of
Man'. Hobbes was both an extreme radical and an extreme
reactionary: Rochester and the other libertines adopted his scepticism, his critical, satirical bent, his ironic questioning of established truths and institutions, while jettisoning his conclusions. The
state of nature, which Hobbes depicts in powerful understated prose
as an intolerable condition from which man, by the iron laws of
self-preservation, must seek at all costs to escape, the libertine poets
and playwrights of the Restoration period present as 'the way of the
world', an empirical description of the life around them. Hobbes to
some extent anticipates them here by treating the state of nature
sometimes as a theoretical construct, an ironic secular equivalent of
the myth of unfallen man, and sometimes as a psychological or
sociological truth verifiable by observation:

Let him therefore consider with himself, when taking a journey, he arms
himself, and seeks to go well accompanied; when going to sleep, he locks his
doors; when even in his house he locks his chests; and this when he knows

there be laws, and public officers, armed, to revenge all injuries shall be done him; what opinion he has of his fellow-subjects, when he rides armed; of his fellow citizens, when he locks his doors; and of his children, and servants, when he locks his chests. Does he not then as much accuse mankind by his actions, as I do by my words? (*Leviathan*, XIII, pp. 82–3)

Libertinism is a young man's philosophy, a rebellion of the sons against the fathers. The conventional, middle-aged virtues – discretion, prudence, responsibility, the patient accumulation of wisdom or of worldly goods – are rejected out of hand as suitable only to those whose senses have been dulled by age or natural incapacity:

> My love is full of noble pride
>   And never will submit
> To let that fop, discretion, ride
>   In triumph over it.
>
> False friends I have, as well as you,
>   Who daily counsel me
> Fame and ambition to pursue,
>   And leave off loving thee.
>
> When I the least belief bestow
>   On what such fools advise,
> May I be dull enough to grow
>   Most miserably wise.[8]

Where Hobbes and Lucretius challenged false, illegitimate authority, the libertines assumed that *all* authority was illegitimate: the state, the church, the family were institutions equally parasitic on man's fear of freedom. The closing stanzas of Rochester's 'The Disabled Debauchee' and 'Upon Nothing' leave little untouched by the author's pervasive irony, as monarch and whore, friendship, obligation and worldly greatness, 'wise' statesman and aging roué, are presented as instances of the universal reign of nothingness:

> Thus *States-man*-like, I'll sawcily impose,
> And safe from Action valiantly advise,
> Shelter'd in impotence, urge you to blows,
> And being good for nothing else, be wise.
>
>> ('The Disabled Debauchee', 45–8)
>
> The Great mans Gratitude to his best freind
> Kings promises, Whors vowes towards thee they bend
> fflow Swiftly into thee, and in thee ever end.
>
>> ('Upon Nothing', 49–51)

Though 'Upon Nothing' parodies the language and form of a philosophical demonstration, there is nothing systematic about Rochester's thought or that of his fellow wits. The sense of inexorability, of a trap closing, in the final line of each poem comes not from its being the last step in a logical proof but from the powerful suggestions unleashed by the imagery and syntax. Since both poems are ironic in method and since 'Upon Nothing', rather than being an exposition of a consistent philosophy of life, is a display of wit, shooting out paradoxes like a Catherine wheel, it is difficult to know how seriously one can take any of the statements they contain. But it is clear that the author of these two poems and *A Satyr against Mankind* is a rebel, a pessimist, a flayer of illusions, a 'poet of unbelief'. Hazlitt's comment on Rochester nicely indicates the weaknesses as well as strengths of this instinctual, unsystematic anarchism: 'his contempt for everything that others respect, almost amounts to sublimity'.[9]

As Underwood has pointed out, libertinism is anti-rational in its assumptions. Such works as the *Satyr against Mankind* contrast sense or instinct with the faculty of discursive reason, presented as unreliable, unduly restrictive and destructive in its effects:

> Your *Reason* hinders, mine helps t'enjoy,
> Renewing Appetites, yours wou'd destroy.
> My Reason is my *Friend*, yours is a *Cheat*,
> Hunger call's out, my Reason bids me eat;
> Perversly yours, your Appetite does mock,
> This asks for Food, that answers what's a Clock?   (104–9)

In Rochester's hedonist ethics, 'lifes happiness' (96) is identified with the removal of artificial fetters, the indulgence of natural appetite. The beauty of nature, the Restoration libertines argue with the partial logic of Comus, is there for the taking. As Rochester says in Burnet's report: 'The restraining a Man from the use of Women, except one in the way of Marriage, and denying the remedy of Divorce, he thought unreasonable Impositions on the Freedom of Mankind.' This is a highly aggressive, if not exploitative, conception of freedom, in which men 'use' women as they consume other natural objects; in another passage Rochester speaks of the 'free use of Wine and Woman'.[10] Shadwell's Don John in *The Libertine* (1676) prefers a rape, with a bit of murder and sacrilege thrown in for spice. Though Shadwell, like Oldham in his 'Satyr against Vertue', tries to blacken his rake figure in order to make the character's 'impassable Iniquity' manifest and detestable, yet, as Underwood shows, their exaggerated portraits call attention to the problems implicit in a philosophy of life which denies all restraint and sees men as ruled entirely by the tyranny of their own desires.

> O Great *Lucretius*, thou shalt be my Guide,
> Like thee I'll live, and by thy Rules abide:
> Measure my *Pleasures* by my *Appetites*,
> And unconfin'd, pursue the *Worlds* Delights.
> For *liberty* makes every action sweet,
> And Relishes our *Joys*, as *Salt* our Meat . . .
> My Native Freedom, therefore I'll employ,
> Chuse what I like, and what I like, Enjoy.[11]

Though this passage is hopelessly inaccurate as a summary of Epicurean doctrines, it effectively catches what the court libertines of the period made of their favourite poet and philosopher, the way they read Lucretius and Hobbes. One need not accept post-structuralist theories of intertextuality to recognise that all literary influence is 'wilful revisionism', what Harold Bloom calls 'misprision'. The history of literature, like the history of philosophy, is a series of creative misunderstandings, in which poets proceed by 'misreading one another, so as to clear imaginative space for themselves'.[12]

What Restoration writers saw as attractively or dangerously radical in Hobbes and the Epicureans was their effective denial of natural law, the traditional Christian deity and any clear sanctions governing human conduct. As Mintz puts it, with admirable precision: 'In Hobbes's hands nominalism and materialism became the instruments of a powerful scepticism about the real or objective existence of absolutes, and in particular about such absolutes as divine providence, good and evil, and an immortal soul.' God was in effect dethroned: the mordant, corrosive materialism of Hobbes was directed not only at 'vain philosophy, and fabulous traditions' – angels, demons, 'abstract essences' existing only in man's overheated imaginations – but at the entire dualistic tradition with its legacy of guilt, shame and moral self-examination (*Leviathan*, XLVI, pp. 435, 440–3), the assumption stated by the *adversarius* in the *Satyr against Mankind* that man is uniquely privileged in the possession of an immortal soul, subject to reward and punishment:

> Best glorious *Man*! to whom alone kind *Heav'n*,
> An everlasting *Soul* has freely giv'n;

> Whom his great *Maker* took such care to make,
> That from himself he did the *Image* take.   (60–3)[13]

Hobbes's position is uncompromising:

The *universe*, that is, the whole mass of things that are, is corporeal, that is to say, body: and hath the dimensions of magnitude, namely length, breadth, and depth: also every part of body, is likewise body, and hath the like dimensions; and consequently every part of the universe, is body, and that which is not body, is no part of the universe; and because the universe is all, that which is no part of it is *nothing*, and consequently *nowhere*. (*Leviathan*, XLVI, p. 440)

Hobbesian psychology, consistent in its materialism, interprets '*conceptions* and *apparitions* as nothing *really*, but *motion* in some internal substance of the *head*' and the passions, defined hedonistically as appetites and aversions, impulses of pleasure or pain, as 'nothing really but motion about the heart'.[14]

Neither Hobbes nor Lucretius was in a strict sense an atheist, but the deity in both the Hobbesian and Lucretian system was stripped of all the traditional moral attributes and denied any influence over human affairs. Though, as we shall see, there were considerable doctrinal distinctions between the determinism of Hobbesian ethics and a classical Epicureanism which emphasised rational choice among alternatives, contemporary anti-Hobbesian polemicists were justified in treating the theological position of the two as essentially similar. The most striking characteristic of the Hobbesian God and of the gods in Lucretius is their fundamental indifference to man: though the Epicureans asserted free will and Hobbes denied it, both divorced morality from any considerations of divine judgement and postulated, at the centre of their imagined universe, deities which were remote, unreachable and in no sense anthropomorphic.

> The *Gods*, by right of Nature, must possess
> An Everlasting *Age*, of perfect Peace:
> Far off, remov'd from us, and our Affairs:
> Neither approached by *Dangers*, or by *Cares*:
> Rich in themselves, to whom we cannot add:
> Not pleas'd by *Good* Deeds; nor provok'd by *Bad*.

The close parallel between these lines from *De Rerum Natura* (II.646–71) as translated by Rochester and Rochester's own 'Speculations about God and Religion' in his conversations with Burnet suggests that the passage can be considered a libertine manifesto.

Imitation here, as elsewhere in Rochester's writing, served an expressive function.

When he came to explain his Notion of the Deity, he said, He looked on it as a vast Power that wrought everything by the necessity of its Nature: And thought that God had none of those Affections of Love and Hatred, which breed perturbation in us, and by consequence he could not see that there was to be either reward or punishment.[15]

Hobbes's God, unlike that of Rochester (in the passages quoted) or the Epicureans, is recognisably the Christian God, but shorn of nearly all the familiar trappings. Hobbes is scornfully dismissive of the man-made attributes with which we clothe God, looking to attract his notice by a claim of kinship: 'Therefore, to attribute *figure* to him is not honour; for all figure is finite: Nor to say we conceive, and imagine, or have an *idea* of him, in our mind: for whatsoever we conceive is finite: . . . Nor to ascribe to him . . . passions that partake of grief; as *repentance, anger, mercy*' (*Leviathan*, XXXI, pp. 237–8). What is missing from the catalogue of 'negative attributes' appropriate to the Hobbesian deity, as the philosopher's opponents pointed out, is goodness: the duty man owes to God, like the duty of obedience which according to Hobbes subjects owe to *any* earthly ruler exercising de facto power, is morally indistinguishable from the traveller's forced submission to the armed robber, the tribute paid by weakness to strength: 'They therefore whose power cannot be resisted, and by consequence God *Almighty* derives his right of sovereignty from the *power* itself . . . Now if God have the right of sovereignty from his power, it is manifest that the *obligation* of yielding him obedience lies on men by reason of their weakness.'[16]

This strikingly amoral conception of the relationship between God and man is consistent with Hobbes's general theological and ethical position: though at times, as a conforming Anglican, he paid lip service to 'the good and evil of the life to come', he denied in passage after passage the existence of any spiritual realm, was highly critical of conventional notions of the afterlife and redefined heaven and hell as psychological states. His opponents attacked him with particular ferocity for these eccentric theological doctrines, accusing him of undermining the fundamental tenets of Christian faith in denying 'the eternal Life, Hell, Salvation, the World to come, and Redemption, which all other Christians do believe'.[17]

Hobbesian ethics departed no less radically from the dominant classical and Christian tradition, denying any authority to private

judgement and removing all external sanctions on behaviour other
than as declared by positive law. A sin was what the monarch called
a sin: theft in one set of circumstances was commendable enterprise
in another, and 'copulation which in one city is matrimony, in
another will be judged adultery'.[18] However hard modern inter-
preters seek to present Hobbes as a traditional moralist, his contemporaries consistently saw him as engaged in a campaign to
overturn the widely accepted doctrine of natural law – that there are
'fixt Principles in Nature', 'certain Propositions of unchangeable
Truth' discoverable by reason, by the aid of which men could direct
their conduct toward a moral end.[19] Hobbes did not abandon the
terminology of natural law, but redefined it in a way which stripped
it of its traditional associations. As Rochester, following his master's
example, in the *Satyr against Mankind* appropriated the term 'right
reason' from his opponents and identified it with instinct, Hobbes
made the natural desire for self-preservation the fundamental law of
nature. Nothing in Hobbes aroused more animosity than his
deconstruction of natural law: 'But neither *right Reason*, or *Right*, are
thus *pliable* to every Man's pleasure. These are as *inflexible* as the
Beam of the Balance is suppos'd to be; for *right Reason* consists in a *rigid
Conformity with Things Themselves*, whose Natures are *Invariable* . . .
and *Right* extends itself no father than *right Reason permits*.'[20]

In his treatment of moral absolutes, Hobbes was a thoroughgoing
nominalist, and his ethical relativism found a sympathetic hearing
among the libertines. Good and evil are for Hobbes psychological
rather than moral terms, determined for the individual not by
rational choice but by physical 'motion' within the body. The
appeal of the Hobbesian conception of human psychology to the
libertines lay not in the naive and literal materialism on which it
depended, but in its practical utility in providing a coherent
account of human motivation which they found congenial. Hobbes's
position was both radical and modish; the defence of moral absolutes, in the hands of opponents who were less skilful polemicists,
without his easy mastery of the telling phrase, could appear old-
fashioned. Rochester makes mincemeat of the 'formal Band, and
Beard' (46) who represents conventional morality in the *Satyr against
Mankind*, but the power of his satiric assault on the '*Nonsense*, and
impossibilities' (89) of his opponent's position cannot entirely disguise the shakiness of his own ethical position, an eclectic mixture of
Epicurus and Hobbes:

Thus, whilst against false reas'ning I inveigh,
I own right *Reason*, which I wou'd obey;
That *Reason* that distinguishes by sense,
And gives us *Rules*, of good and ill from thence:
That bounds desires, with a reforming Will,
To keep 'em more in vigour, not to kill.   (98–103)[21]

The modified Epicureanism of this passage accords with Hobbes in its amoral, non-ascetic treatment of the passions and desires, at variance with the prevalent tradition of Platonic and Pauline dualism. But nowhere does Hobbes differ more sharply from Epicureanism than in his refusal to admit the possibility that 'sense' (the senses, instinct) is capable of generating workable '*Rules*, of good and ill'. Epicurean philosophy sought to reconcile the pursuit of pleasure with the schooling of the mind toward virtue, arguing a position Hobbes fiercely denied: that man was an independent moral agent, able to 'regulate his Actions' and to choose among alternatives, acting in accordance with principles other than immediate competitive advantage in a world of enemies. Though committed like Hobbes to a materialist psychology of appetite and aversion, the Epicureans allowed for the discovery, through experience, of 'Canons, or Rules, for the guidance or regulation of our Affections, or Passions'.[22] In Hobbesian psychology, in sharp contrast, there is no room for the self-regulating mechanism or inner barometer which Rochester presents in the *Satyr* as providing 'bounds' for 'desires', and indeed the relatively optimistic tone of that passage is rare in Rochester's writings, which tend to take a darker view of human nature.

To Hobbes, good and evil are no more than terms indicating preferences:

But whatsoever is the object of man's appetite or desire, that it is which he for his part calleth *good*: and the object of his hate and aversion, *evil*; and of his contempt, *vile* and *inconsiderable*. For these words of good, evil, and contemptible, are ever used with relation to the person that useth them: there being nothing simply and absolutely so; nor any common rule of good and evil, to be taken from the nature of the objects themselves. (*Leviathan*, VI, p. 32)

According to the iron logic of the position argued here, there can be no grounds for privileging any man's judgement over another's; indeed, the process of choosing, to Hobbes, is identical in beasts and humans, a simple matter of alteration of physical impulses, brought inevitably to an end by the swipe of the paw: 'This alternate succession of appetites, aversions, hopes and fears, is no less in other living creatures than in man: and therefore beasts also deliberate . . . In *deliberation*, the last appetite, or aversion, immediately adhering to the action, or to the omission thereof, is that we call the WILL; the act, not the faculty, of willing' (*Leviathan*, vi, pp. 37–8). Though Rochester in *A Satyr against Mankind* inverts the customary hierarchy in exalting the 'wisdom' and contentment of beasts over deluded, fear-ridden man, the force of his satire on human pride depends, as in *Gulliver's Travels*, on the reader's simultaneous recognition of kinship with and alienation from the less complicated animal kingdom. Hobbes, on the other hand, collapses all such distinctions.[23] The radical scepticism of Hobbes's views horrified opponents who viewed moral choice in more traditional terms:

And therefore, though a Wench that had the Green-Sickness, by reason of her depraved Appetite, may fancy Tobacco-pipes, or Charcoal to have an excellent relish, and so be good for her; yet will not her thinking so, make them a wholesome nourishment . . . And therefore it is not true, which Mr H. here lays down, That all Good and Evil is only to be taken in respect of him whom at that time it pleases or displeases: Whereas every rational Man ought first rightly to judge what things are good, and then to desire them, because they are really so.[24]

Aside from their differing attitudes toward moral choice, the fundamental disagreement between the Hobbesian and Epicurean versions of philosophical hedonism lay in their conceptions of earthly felicity. They agreed in their rejection of the transcendental; both saw happiness in material terms as the satisfaction of desire, the discharge of pent-up energy. Rochester's account of paradisal bliss in 'The Fall' typifies Restoration Epicureanism in taking the sexual act as paradigmatic of all pleasure.

> Naked beneath cool Shades they lay,
>   Enjoyment waited on desire,
> Each *Member* did their Wills obey,
>   Nor cou'd a wish set pleasure higher.[25]

The attainment of pleasure – seen here as bodily, instinctual, unclouded by thought – depends on narrowing the gap between desire and fruition. To Rochester as to Hobbes, that gap can never entirely be bridged: both, in their different ways, see frustration and restlessness as defining the human condition. By locating the ideal of perfect sensory fulfilment in a lost Eden, Rochester puts it forever beyond reach, and Hobbes presents human life as an endless cycle of desire. Where classical Epicureanism identifies happiness as a state of rest, contentment of mind, Hobbes attacks such a view of felicity as self-delusion:

Continual success in obtaining those things, which a man from time to time desireth, that is to say, continual prospering, is that men call FELICITY; I mean the felicity of this life. For there is no such thing as perpetual tranquillity of mind, while we live here; because life itself is but motion, and can never be without desire, nor without fear, no more than without sense. (*Leviathan*, VI, p. 39)

When Donne, Herbert, Vaughan or Traherne presents restlessness as the key to human psychology, it is always 'a holy thirsty dropsy' leading man ultimately to God. 'There is a Countrie/Far beyond the stars' where human longings are finally stilled:

> Yet let him keep the rest,
> But keep them with repining restlesnesse:
> Let him be rich and wearie, that at least,
> If goodnesse leade him not, yet wearinesse
> May tosse him to my breast.[26]

The Hobbesian system, in contrast, does not allow any dimension beyond 'this life', any possibility of eventual forgiveness and repose. Epicureanism, equally atheist and materialist in its basic assumptions, is nevertheless consolatory and ethically normative, concerned with ways of freeing man from the pangs of desire, in order to achieve on earth the kind of inner peace frequently associated with transcendent beatitude. In the Epicurean tradition, pleasure is defined as the absence of pain, and as a serenity of mind which can triumph over circumstances.[27] Hobbes explicitly disavows the Epicurean 'perpetual tranquillity of mind' as an attainable or even a suitable end: desire is not something to be escaped from or triumphed over, but the essence of human life on earth. 'For there is no such *finis ultimum*, ultimate aim, nor *summum bonum*, greatest good, as is spoken of in the books of the old moral philosophers. Nor can a man any more live, whose desires are at an end, then he, whose senses and imaginations are at a stand' (*Leviathan*, XI, p. 63).

Hobbes's axiom that 'life itself is but motion', as adapted in such works as Rochester's *Satyr against Mankind* and Etherege's *The Man of Mode*, is primarily psychological, with implications for the conduct of everyday relations within society: 'Felicity is a continual progress of the desire, from one object to another; the attaining of the former, being still but the way to the latter. The cause whereof is, that the object of man's desire, is not to enjoy once only, and for one instant of time; but to assure for ever, the way of his future desires' (*Leviathan*, xi, p. 63). The hidden premise on which this argument is based is the absence of an afterlife, with the Christian scheme of salvation. Animal appetite, unlike human desire, is finite, and can be satiated in 'one instant of time': humans imagine tomorrow's hunger or remember yesterday's, impairing their enjoyment of today's steak. Man to Hobbes, as to Rochester, is a material being who rebels against his imprisonment by material circumstances, a prey to his desires which can never be satisfied, since the ultimate object of desire is illusory and any mediate object may be snatched away, as in the myth of Tantalus: 'So that in the first place, I put for a general inclination of all mankind, a perpetual and restless desire of power after power, that ceaseth only in death' (*Leviathan*, xi, p. 64). The Hobbesian view of man is thus potentially tragic, as well as providing the opportunity for ironic comedy of thwarted aspirations, restless intrigue and mutual deception.

The human predicament comes in the clash of each man's infinite needs with the equally pressing, unstillable desires of the clamouring rivals who hem him in on all sides. By the principles of egoist psychology, all men (and women) are by nature deadly enemies, competing for possession of a single object. Scholars who identify Hobbesian man with 'bourgeois man', the 'possessive individualism' of a nascent seventeenth-century capitalism, are probably accurate, since Hobbes's psychology is that of a market, with permanent conditions of scarcity. As Hobbes presents them, armed invasion, sexual rivalry, commercial rivalry and wit combats are interchangeable: all embody the desire to establish ownership, to exclude rival claimants, to dominate in a '*race* we must suppose to have no other *goal*, nor other *garland*, but being foremost'.[28] The accounts of human motivation in *De Cive*, *Leviathan* and *Human Nature*, as in Rochester's *Satyr against Mankind*, place particular emphasis on envy, emulation and the fear of defeat or dispossession – in Freudian terms, the assertion of phallic power in an attempt to overcome castration-anxiety. But any psychoanalytic or Marxist gloss can only underline the central fact that for Hobbes it is the existence of other people that makes human life intolerable:

From this equality of ability, ariseth equality of hope in the attaining of our ends. And therefore if any two men desire the same thing, which nevertheless they cannot both enjoy, they become enemies; and in the way to their end, which is principally their own conservation, and sometimes their delectation only, endeavour to destroy, or subdue one another. (*Leviathan*, XIII, p. 81)

This is precisely the world depicted in many Restoration comedies. Fainall and Mirabell in *The Way of the World* are enemies not because of any qualities of character in either man, but because each wants the same thing, in a world in which the desire for possession is infinite and the rewards limited. The differences in character and outlook of the two men become more and more evident as the play progresses, but in their situation they are exactly alike. They begin the race at the same point, as do Mrs Marwood and Mrs Fainall, similarly presented as rivals not by choice but by the nature of the society they live in:

> To see one out-gone whom we would not, is *pity*.
> To see one out-go whom we would not, is *indignation*.
> To hold fast by another, is *love* . . .
> Continually to be out-gone, is *misery*.
> Continually to out-go the next before, is *felicity*.
> And to forsake the course, is to *die*.[29]

To Hobbes, the inevitable rivalry of all men is conditional on their intrinsic equality, defined as an equal ability to kill or maim one another:

Nature hath made men so equal, in the faculties of the body, and mind; as that though there be found one man sometimes manifestly stronger in body, or of quicker mind than another; yet when all is reckoned together, the difference between man, and man, is not so considerable, as that one man can thereupon claim to himself any benefit, to which another may not pretend, as well as he. For as to the strength of the body, the weakest has strength enough to kill the strongest, either by secret machination, or by confederacy with others, that are in the same danger with himself. (*Leviathan*, XIII, p. 80)

The careful patterning of the opening scenes of *The Way of the World* establishes just such an equality among the contending characters in the competition for spoils, as well as their mutual distrust. The rituals of society are covert expressions of a state of war: Fainall and Mirabell exchange barbed epigrams at cards ('Yet you speak with an Indifference which seems to be affected'), and Mrs

Marwood and Mrs Fainall, probing one another's defences like boxers, conduct a hostile dialogue under a thin veneer of civility, in which each word or involuntary physical reflex is scrutinised for signs of weakness ('You change Colour . . . By the Reason you give for your Aversion, one would think it dissembl'd'). These scenes establish the prevailing values of the 'world' in which the dramatic action takes place: as Fainall says to Mrs Marwood, 'hide your Face, your Tears. You have a Mask; wear it a Moment.'[30] The rule for survival is to trust no one. Just as professions of friendship are likely to be dissembled, sexual relationships are compromised by fears of betrayal, exploitation, the pressures of social conformity. The open expression of passionate feelings can make one vulnerable to attack; love, though not precluded in such a world, may weaken one in the struggle for success, since pausing 'to carry him on that so holdeth',[31] voluntarily assuming the burden of another, will slow one down, giving less scrupulous rivals an advantage.

One of the most disturbing passages in *The Way of the World* is an exchange between Mirabell and Mrs Fainall:

MIR. You should have just as much disgust for your Husband as may be
      sufficient to make you relish your lover.
MRS. FAIN. You have been the cause that I have lov'd without Bounds,
      and wou'd you set Limits to that Aversion of which you have been the
      occasion? Why did you make me marry this Man?
MIR. Why do we daily commit disagreeable and dangerous Actions? To
      save that Idol Reputation. If the familiarities of our Loves had
      produc'd that Consequence of which you were apprehensive, where
      could you have fix'd a Father's Name with Credit, but on a Husband?
      I knew *Fainall* to be a Man lavish of his Morals, an interested and
      professing Friend, a false and a designing lover; yet one whose wit and
      outward fair Behaviour have gain'd a Reputation with the Town
      enough to make that Woman stand excus'd who has suffer'd herself to
      be won by his Addresses. A better Man ought not to have been
      sacrific'd to the Occasion; a worse had not answer'd to the purpose.
      When you are weary of him, you know your Remedy. (ii.i.284–304)

At this point there is little to choose between hero and villain. The symmetry of the parallel scenes points up the resemblances: we watch two adulterous couples carrying on private conversations under the guise of a promenade through the park, a visual emblem of the risks and pleasures of dissembling. Both men are manipulative, both urge prudence and control, where both women give vent to their emotions. The elegance and formal beauty of Mirabell's language, like the ready wit of Dorimant in *The Man of Mode* as he fends off Mrs Loveit's entirely justifiable accusations ('Think on your Oaths, your Vows and Protestations, Perjur'd Man!', II.ii.211–12), may predispose a viewer to admire him for playing the game so exquisitely.[32] And yet the directness, honesty and baffled pain of Mrs Fainall's outburst make Mirabell's well-turned euphemisms ring hollow. For all Mirabell's professed independence of mind, he shows himself a slave to 'that Idol Reputation', justifying behaviour he knows not only to be 'disagreeable' but injurious to others. He knows that Fainall's 'outward fair Behaviour' is false, and with open eyes he deliberately chooses to 'sacrifice' two people in the interest of expediency. The passage is unsettling, formally as well as morally, because a character who has been presented as the hero of the play is behaving in an apparently reprehensible way, and the audience is denied the usual comforting categorisation into right and wrong. We appear to be in a world of Hobbesian relativism, in which there is no 'common rule of good and evil, to be taken from the nature of the objects themselves' (*Leviathan*, VI, p. 32).

And yet there is a major difference between *The Way of the World* and such Rochester poems as *A Satyr against Mankind* or 'A Ramble in Saint James's Parke', as well as *The Man of Mode*. In these works by Rochester and Etherege we are encouraged to view man from a Hobbesian or libertine perspective, because there is no viable alternative offered; even where the narrator or protagonist makes statements which may not command our assent, we cannot be sure of the presence of irony, or disentangle the authorial voice from that of the speaker. Both the *Satyr against Mankind* and *The Man of Mode* depend throughout on a Hobbesian view of human motivation which, explicitly or implicitly, forms the basis of the author's attack on human folly or dispassionate observation of human behaviour:

> Look to the bottom, of his vast design,
> Wherein *Mans* Wisdom, Pow'r, and Glory joyn:
> The good he acts, the ill he does endure,
> 'Tis all from fear, to make himself secure.
>
> (*Satyr against Mankind*, 153–6)[33]

'A Ramble in Saint James's Parke', like some of Rochester's other obscene poems, presents a view of human nature which is unrelievedly base: though there are no explicit echoes of Hobbes, the poem can be seen as a Hobbesian nightmare, chapter XIII of the *Leviathan* brought to life. The assumptions of the narrator and the governing principles of the world he describes are a reductive parody of Hobbesian doctrine: a dogmatic materialism, an insistent emphasis on competition, desire, 'Appetite' (135) as the motivating forces of man in society and a denial that human psychology differs in any way from animal instinct.

> So a prowd Bitch does lead about
> Of humble Currs the Amourous Rout
> Who most obsequiously doe hunt
> The savory scent of salt swoln Cunt. (83–6)[34]

This version of the evening promenade, so different from that in Act II of *The Way of the World*, presents men and women as wholly ruled by their sexual impulses, not so much machines – 'for what is the *heart*, but a *spring*' (*Leviathan*, Introduction, p. 5) – as walking genitalia. It is possible, reading the poem as a dramatic monologue, to argue that the social world described is purely a projection of the protagonist's rage and pain, with no objective existence. But whatever irony we can find in the poem is destabilising, rather than providing grounds for judging the protagonist, a set of moral values around which the poem is organised – a parallel in Browning would be 'Childe Rolande to the Dark Tower Came', rather than 'My Last Duchess' or 'Porphyria's Lover'. There seems to be no solid ground beneath our feet.[35]

Yet if we look again at Mirabell's speech, we find that it is packed with normative terms, carefully designed to reflect unfavourably on the speaker. One striking example of this is the sentence characterising Fainall, in which virtually every phrase can be applied to Mirabell himself, as he appears at the moment; a further, more complex irony resides in his assumption that he is superior to the value of 'the Town', when the very words he is speaking demonstrate the opposite; and there is more than a hint of disapproval aimed at his use of eloquent language to make the worse cause seem the better. Mirabell's charm is no less the object of ironic scrutiny here than that of Henry Crawford or Frank Churchill, and indeed his moral weakness, as demonstrated in his behaviour to Mrs Fainall in this scene, is akin to theirs. 'When you are weary of him, you know your Remedy' is a bit of authorial obfuscation, planting a clue which points toward the denouement while at the same time misleading the audience: the immediate context suggests sexual consolation with Mirabell or another willing lover, and there is no reason to think of black boxes or deed of conveyance. In retrospect, the words, as addressed to Mrs Fainall, come to have another meaning, and suggest aspects of Mirabell's character more apparent at the end of the play. When, in the final scene, Mrs Fainall can say 'Thank Mr *Mirabell*, a cautious Friend, to whose Advice all is owing' (v.i.628–9), we have been brought to see both caution and friendship in a different light. Congreve's management of plot forces us to revalue the character of Mirabell, as he demonstrates that it is possible to behave morally and responsibly, aware of the dangers of 'the World' and its values but not succumbing to them. Indeed, the behaviour not simply of Mirabell, but of Millamant, Mrs Fainall and Sir Wilfull in this scene can serve to refute Hobbesian egoism:

MIR. Sir *Wilfull* is my Friend: he has had Compassion upon lovers, and generously engag'd a Volunteer in the Action, for our Service. (v.i.636–9)

By the ingenious twists and turns of the plot, we have been led through a world of moral uncertainties, where all appearances deceive and no one is to be trusted, to one in which both love and friendship are possible.

The Way of the World, like Congreve's other comedies, contains and transcends the Hobbesian vision. What is celebrated at the end, in the triumph of Mirabell and his allies over Fainall and Mrs Marwood, is not amoral success, but cleverness turned to the service of morality. Mirabell is no less aware than Fainall that life is a struggle for power, but he exercises that power for different ends, protecting the freedom of Mrs Fainall and agreeing to a mutual bond of affection with Millamant in the proviso scene, where Fainall wants to imprison both women and take everything for himself. What Congreve has done here as in *The Double Dealer* is to split the morally ambivalent libertine figure in two (more subtly here than in the earlier play, where Mellefont is naive, good-hearted and trusting, and all the intellectual agility lies with the dissembling Maskwell), to allow for a reassuring didactic conclusion in which virtue triumphs. The action of the play tests both Mirabell and Fainall, brings out a potential for generosity in one case, and savage vindictiveness in the other, which ordinary social intercourse might not have revealed: 'You thing that was a Wife shall smart for this. I will not leave thee wherewithal to hide thy Shame: Your Body shall be naked as your Reputation' (v.i.544–7). In showing Fainall's

gradual transformation from elegant rake to snarling, impotent
villain, drawing his sword (like Iago) on his wife, Congreve employs
a method akin to the reductio ad absurdum of satire: the libertine
interpretation of Hobbesian principles, in which life is seen as
unlimited, deadly competition, is shown to be self-defeating and
inimical to civilised life.[36]

The witty exchanges of Mirabell and Millamant, no less than
the sexual intrigues of Dorimant, Horner or Nathaniel Lee's
'Town Bull', Nemours, see sexual freedom as power, and men and
women as natural rivals: 'Wine gives you liberty, Love takes it
away', as Horner says (*The Country-Wife*, I.i.206). 'Love', as presented here, means the loss of autonomy, and though in some
poems and plays of the period this may reflect a male fear of
female sexuality, of the female spider lying in wait for the male fly
– 'they are having you take a Lease for life, and you are for being
Tenants at will'[37] – it is striking how often these works present
men and women as equals, motivated by the same desire to assert
and retain a power over the circumstances that threaten to hem
them in. Millamant's psychologically astute remark recognises the
imperatives of a market society, where the choice is dominion or
slavery: 'One's Cruelty is one's Power, and when one parts with
one's Cruelty, one parts with one's Power: and when one has
parted with that, I fancy one's Old and Ugly' (*The Way of the
World*, II.i.426–9). The many jokes in Restoration comedy at the
expense of the middle-aged and elderly reflect the predominant
social values of an intensely competitive society in which 'a
Woman's past her prime at 20, decay'd at four and 20 and
unsufferable at 30' (*The Man of Mode*, IV.i.38–9). Etherege's title
She wou'd if she cou'd, like the names Cockwood, Wishfort and
Loveit, may at first glance suggest a crudely cynical, reductive
view of woman as lustful by nature, but the psychology of the
characters in Etherege's play is more complicated than that, and
more authentically Hobbesian. Lady Cockwood is motivated by
physical frustration, unsatisfied desire: all she wants is for her
husband to stay home at night and when he flees from her
embraces she searches ineffectually for substitutes. Her absurdity is
an index of her powerlessness, and her inability to control events is
manifested in her transparently inappropriate and insincere language, which deceives no one. The same is true of her husband,
Sir Oliver, another victim of biology, middle-aged in a society

which places a premium on youth. When he comes roaring on stage pretending to be a rake ('Now I am as rampant as a Lyon, Ned, and I could love as vigorously as a Sea-man that is newly landed after an East-India voyage'), we recognise immediately that it is fraudulent, and ineptly so: all he is capable of doing is getting drunk and falling asleep (III.iii.261–3). What is at issue between the Cockwoods is 'dominion' (III.iii.361); each tries to exercise it over the other, since they are both defeated in the game of life. When in the opening scene the bored Freeman describes his social milieu as a stagnant market with trade in decay (I.i.17–23), his witty metaphor is more accurate than he realises: the society depicted in the play is one where all the characters, old and young, are prey to dissatisfaction and frustration, where rewards are limited, freedom largely illusory and failure punished severely.

Play after play during the period reflects the view, ultimately derivable from Hobbes, that man is a power-seeking animal and that life in society is defined by ruthless, unending competition. The assertion of freedom in libertine thought is predicated on a defiant materialism, a scepticism directed at conventional structures of authority and an egoist psychology which is potentially anarchic. The problem, as with the political notion of absolute liberty, is what happens if two bodies wish to occupy the same space, if appropriation or invasion is resisted and two rival claimants demand their sovereign rights? If the psychology and ethics of *Leviathan*, Book I, are accepted, but the proposed political remedy for the inconveniences of the state of nature – the unconditional surrender of individual rights in return for a guarantee of public order – is rejected, then the Hobbesian nightmare vision must be taken as an accurate account of human behaviour in society. The choice faced by Restoration authors who selectively reinterpret Hobbes in libertine terms is to show that it is possible to live after all in a state of universal war or to look for a means of escape other than the one Hobbes suggests.

It is not uncommon for both of these attitudes, Hobbesian and anti-Hobbesian, to be expressed side by side in the same work. Here, for example, are several excerpts from a single play, John Crowne's *The Countrey Wit* (1675), spoken by or about the same character, Ramble, the play's principal male figure, 'a wild young Gentleman of the Town'. The first passage is a straightforward paraphrase of standard Hobbesian doctrine:

Come, to the business in hand; however 'tis in other affairs, I am for reducing Love to the state of Nature: I am for no propriety, but every man get what he can: however Invasion in this case I am sure is lawfull; when a pretty young woman lies in the possession of an old Fellow, like a fair fertile Province under the Dominion of the Turk, uncultivated and unenjoy'd, no good Christian but ought to make War upon him.[38]

Ramble does not change appreciably during the course of the play, retaining the same 'Ayrieness and Gayetie of . . . temper' throughout (Act I, p. 7), cheerfully admitting his fickleness in the midst of proclaiming his ardent love for the fair Christina:

'Tis not for want of love to her, for the enjoyment of other women, give me not so much delight as a smile from her: and yet, I gad, the enjoyment of her would not keep me from the chase of other women . . . You cannot blame a poor thirsty Traveller, if he takes a sip here and there by the way. (Act III, p. 33)

Yet at the end of the play, Ramble, without in any sense abandoning his libertine professions, is shown as behaving in accordance with an ideology wholly at variance with that expressed in the first passage.

SIR THOMAS. How on thy Knees, Mr. *Ramble*? I swear we rather ought to kneel to thee. Rise, rise, man, were I not to forfeit a thousand pound Bond, thou shouldst have my Daughter before any man.

RAMBLE. Say you so, Sir, Dirt shall never be laid in the Scale of Beauty, I will pay the forfeiture.

ISABELLA. This is brave, I swear, now Madam, you are bound in Honour and Gratitude to forgive him.

SIR THOMAS. Mr. *Ramble*, this is so generous a Proposition, that I will pay the forfeiture of the Bond, give thee my Daughter, and a Thousand pound more, with her, than ever I design'd for her Portion with any Man – take her – she's thine. (Act V, p. 87)

This competition in generosity, which concludes the play, with Ramble, Sir Thomas, the pert servant Isabella and the steadfast Christina falling all over themselves to see which of them can behave more nobly, is as incompatible with the Hobbesian view of man expressed elsewhere in *The Countrey Wit* as its ethical vocabulary of 'Honour', 'Gratitude' and absolute value beyond measure.

Within the libertine tradition in the Restoration period, we find, along with the pessimistic view of human nature discussed in the first part of this chapter, a far more optimistic view, which can be described as Epicurean rather than Hobbesian. It is not generally recognised that there are two quite different kinds of libertine heroes in Restoration comedy, rakes and rovers, one aggressive and exploitative and the other happy-go-lucky, accepting whatever pleasures the moment may bring. There is no element of malice or even of calculation in such characters as Ramble in *The Countrey Wit*, Townly in Edward Ravenscroft's *The London Cuckolds* (1682) or Willmore in Aphra Behn's *The Rover* (1677).[39] Where Dorimant's or Horner's wit is tempered by 'ill nature' (*The Man of Mode*, II.ii.290), a hard, ruthless drive toward mastery, these characters are good-humoured, equable, content in amorous intrigues as in all else to 'take women . . . when they come in thy way by accident', convinced that 'Love like riches comes more by fortune than industry'. Willmore and Sir Harry Wildair of Farquhar's *The Constant Couple* (1700), both great favourites with contemporary audiences, are likeable blunderers, each of whom can be described as 'never ruffled by misfortune . . . entertaining to others and easy to himself, Turning all Passion into Gaiety of Humour'.[40] It is entirely characteristic of each to mistake a virtuous woman for a whore, since to them all women are alike and no opportunity should be neglected. As a 'Rover of Fortune', Willmore accepts the buffets and windfalls chance may bring: when a discarded mistress threatens him with a pistol, asking 'hast thou no Horrour at this Sight?' Willmore replies: 'Faith, no Child, my Blood keeps its old Ebbs and Flows still, and that usual Heat too, that could oblige thee with a Kindness, had I but opportunity.'[41]

The themes of fortune and opportunity are especially prominent in Behn's *The Lucky Chance* (as the title indicates) and in *The London Cuckolds* which, with considerable comic inventiveness, contrasts the amorous adventures of Townly, 'a Gentleman of the times, careless of Women, but fortunate', and his friend Ramble, 'a great Designer on Ladies, but unsuccessful in his Intrigues'. The distinction between the two men is not simply that one is lucky and the other unlucky, but that one has the improvisatory wit and boldness to grasp the offered opportunity. In *The Lucky Chance*, the action similarly turns on the need to 'Receive what Love and fortune present you with', grasping a 'dear Opportunity' which may never come again.[42] 'I laugh at your faint heart', the witty and lascivious Arabella tells Ramble in *The London Cuckolds*, losing interest in him as a prospective sexual partner when he is discomposed by an unexpected turn of events. Ramble is the recipient of the most extensive, and funniest, physical chastisement of any of the fools and pretenders in Restoration comedy, as he finds himself stuck in a window, knocked on the head, laughed at by his friend and the woman he has been attempting to seduce, a chamberpot emptied on him, robbed of his sword and periwig, covered with soot and, a crowning humiliation, farted at by a passing chimney-sweep. Ramble's response to this 'unfortunate adventure', couched in language ludicrously inappropriate to his circumstances, shows an inability to learn from experience: 'Sir, I am a Gentleman, and one that scorns such base actions – I'll tell in short, Sir, how I came to be fastened in your window.'[43] The ideology of the 'critical minute' in these plays, as in a number of erotic poems of the period, is Epicurean, drawing a carpe diem moral from the unpredictability of fortune's wheel: take advantage of whatever 'blind bargain' chance may bring your way, including sexual pleasures, in Willmore's words 'neither design'd nor premeditated . . . pure Accident on both sides' (*The Rover*, iii.iii, p. 54), since there are no second chances.[44]

In the gradual shift of emphasis in Restoration plays from hero to heroine, from courtship to marriage and its consequences, and, within the heroes, from sharpness of wit to generosity of spirit, we can trace a movement away from the psychology, ethics and politics of Hobbes to a rival view associated with Locke and with such influential Latitudinarian divines as Isaac Barrow and John Tillotson.[45] In plays written after the publication of *Two Treatises of Government* in 1689, the Lockean influence may be direct, but more generally the change in emphasis can be attributed to the efflorescence of anti-authoritarian political theory during the Exclusion Bill crisis and the Revolution of 1688. Locke, as modern scholarship has shown, is one of several authors in the period who develop similar arguments, accepting some of the premises of Hobbes and other opponents while disputing others, and, as Hobbes himself had done, appropriating large chunks of his opponents' terminology, while redefining the terms.[46] The Latitudinarian influence on the plays, like that of Locke, is probably indirect rather than direct, and indeed the same arguments recur in political tracts and sermons, so that the two lines of influence are not entirely separate. Where these plays of the 1690s and later differ most sharply from Hobbes and from the plays and poems within the Hobbesian orbit is in their identification with victim more than aggressor, their consistent emphasis on rights and on the need for contractual protection and their rejection of self-interest as the primary human motive.

When, in the climactic scene of Congreve's *Love for Love* (1695), Valentine, spontaneously triumphing over his own instincts of self-preservation, rips into shreds the paper that would give him financial security, we could not find a neater juxtaposition of two competing ideologies than the reaction of his friend Scandal and his mistress Angelica. Scandal, a loyal friend but in his dealings with men and especially women a cynic with his eye to the main chance, adheres to the code of the Restoration rake, which assumes the universality of self-interest as a law governing conduct: ''Sdeath, you are not mad, indeed, to ruin yourself?' (v.i.589–90). Angelica, who up to that point had been justifiably suspicious of her improvident and possibly inconstant lover and has never let either Valentine or the audience know how she feels towards him, responds with a spontaneous outburst to match Valentine's own: 'Generous *Valentine!*' (v.i.598). We are in the world of Tom Jones and Sophia Western.

As in *The Way of the World*, the ingenious manipulations of the plot, which involve teasing and partly misleading the audience, withholding necessary information until the denouement, reinforce the moral design. Valentine, who, as Congreve explicitly tells us, is presented as a fallible hero, 'a mix'd Character', whose 'Faults are fewer than his good Qualities', can be thought of as midway between Aphra Behn's Willmore and Charles Surface: characterised by his good nature, his high spirits, his openness of feeling, his spontaneity, but by no means free of mercenary motives or calculation and in no way destined for success.[47] The test which Angelica imposes is thus a complex one, which can turn out either way, and it is cleverly designed as a double test, exposing and punishing Sir Sampson as it reveals the true worth of his son:

ANG. Well, Sir *Sampson*, since I have played you a Trick, I'll advise you how you may avoid such another. Learn to be a good Father, or you'll never get a second Wife. I always lov'd your Son, and hated your unforgiving Nature. I was resolv'd to try him to the utmost; I have try'd you too, and know you both. You have not more Faults than he has Virtues; and 'tis hardly more Pleasure to me, that I can make him and myself happy, than that I can punish you. (v.i.618–27)

This is the first time that Angelica has admitted her true feelings, even in aside or soliloquy, and up to this point she may not fully know them herself: she too is being tested, and only now does this play exclude the possibility of a bitterly ironic ending (akin to that in *The Country-Wife*, where truth is silenced and vice rewarded), in which the nasty old man walks off with the girl and leaves the hero stranded.

Angelica fully recognises that life is a competition for power and freedom and that appearances are not to be trusted: 'Uncertainty and Expectation are the Joys of Life. Security is an insipid thing, and the overtaking and possessing of a Wish discovers the Folly of the Chase. Never let us know one another better, for the Pleasure of a Masquerade is done when we come to show Faces' (IV.i.847–52). The pleasure she so evidently takes in the exercise of mastery in her exchanges with Valentine and his father show Angelica to be in some respects a practical disciple of Hobbes, and the vision of infinitely extended desire in this passage simultaneously recalls Hobbes and, in its wit and undertone of regret, the lyrics of Rochester. The world of the play is one of mutual distrust, where brothers, sisters, parent and child, are natural rivals – 'We are the Twin Stars and cannot shine in one Sphere: when he Rises I must set' (III.i.238–9) – and the characters spout Hobbist aphorisms as they plot to undo one another:

SCANDAL. Yes, faith, I believe some Women are Virtuous too; but 'tis as I believe some Men are Valiant, thro' fear. For why shou'd a Man court Danger, or a Woman shun Pleasure? (III.i.722–5)[48]

Angelica's wit is not untinged with malice – 'if I don't play Trick for Trick, may I never taste the Pleasure of Revenge' (IV.i.72–3) – and, up to the very end, she gives no evidence that she does not adhere to the same principles of conduct which guide Mrs Frail, Mrs Foresight, Tattle and Scandal in their behaviour: the pursuit of one's own advantage, even if it means injury to another.

ANGELICA. 'Tis true, you have a great while pretended Love to me; nay, what if you were sincere? Still, you must pardon me, if I think my own Inclinations have a better Right to dispose of my Person, than yours. (VI.i.578–82)

The selfish and generous instincts are thus shown as delicately balanced throughout the play, and it is significant that Valentine acts not on motives of generalised benevolence, but by a sudden, uncalculating rush of feeling. Valentine's behaviour in the final scene is entirely in accordance with the loosely Epicurean principles he has followed throughout, treating 'Pleasure' as the sovereign good, and with the code of a gentleman, instinctively recoiling from mercenary considerations as unworthy. The qualities of character which manifest themselves in the opening scenes as prodigality (begetting bastards, squandering his inheritance) now appear as liberality, the 'bountifull *Disposition*' which contemporary conduct books saw as particularly appropriate to a gentleman.[49]

VALENTINE. I have been disappointed of my only Hope; and he that loses hope may part with anything. I never valu'd fortune but as it was subservient to my Pleasure; and my only pleasure was to please this lady. I have made many vain Attempts, and find at last that nothing but my Ruin can effect it: which, for that Reason, I will sign to – give me the Paper. (v.i.592–7)

His 'reform' is thus not an arbitrary plot device, imposed by fiat of the author, a magical transformation from rake to paragon, but carefully motivated: in fact, what he is rewarded for in the end, as Angelica, finally letting down her guard, awards love for love, is his consistency of character, and the final scene celebrates the victory of love's prodigal madness over the sanity of 'suspicion' and self-interest.[50]

ANGELICA. I have done dissembling now, *Valentine*; and if that Coldness which I have always worn before you should turn to an extreme Fondness, you must not suspect it.
VALENTINE. I'll prevent that suspicion – for I intend to doat on at that immoderate rate that your Fondness shall never distinguish itself enough to be taken notice of. If ever you seem to love too much, it must be only when I can't love enough. (v.i.658–66)

The rival ideologies of egoism and natural feeling are contrasted early in the play in the scene of confrontation between father and son (II.i.289–437). Echoes of Locke are present elsewhere in the play – at one point, Valentine, feigning madness, says of Angelica, 'You are all white, a sheet of lovely spotless Paper, when you first are Born, but you are to be scrawl'd and blotted by every Goose's Quill' (IV.i.683–6) – but here the echoes are structural rather than decorative, as Sir Sampson behaves like an absolute monarch, stepping out of the pages of *Patriarcha* or *Leviathan*:

Why, Sirrah, mayn't I do what I please? Are you not my Slave? Did I not beget you? And might not I have chosen whether I would have begot you or no? Ouns, who are you? Whence came you? What brought you into the

World? How came you here, Sir? Here, to stand here, upon those two legs, and look erect with that audacious face, hah? Answer me that! Did you come a Volunteer into the World? Or did I beat up for you with the lawful Authority of a Parent, and press you to service? (II.i.348–58)[51]

Ideologically this passage is interesting because it assumes that the audience, schooled by at least ten years of political controversy, culminating in the deposition of James II, will disapprove of the absolutist sentiments expressed, where in *The Man of Mode* Hobbesian ideas are presented more sympathetically. As with Hobbes and Lucretius on religion, the differing versions of absolutist theory propounded by Hobbes and Sir Robert Filmer are not distinguished: Sir Sampson sees himself as patriarchal tyrant, denying any rights to his subjects while claiming absolute liberty for his own will, and he interprets the relations of father and son as entirely contractual, admitting no obligation beyond what is written down 'under Black and White' (II.i.189). Deaf to Valentine's appeals to 'Fatherly fondness' (312) and protests against his 'Barbarity and Unnatural Usage' (346–7), he sees his parental role merely as the exercise of power: 'What, I warrant my Son thought nothing belong'd to a Father but Forgiveness and Affection; no Authority, no Correction, no Arbitrary Power; nothing to be done but for him to offend and me to pardon' (II.i.183–6). The total identification of paternal and regal authority in Sir Sampson's speeches recalls the theories of Filmer, who denied any reciprocal obligations of the ruler to the ruled, and there may be a direct echo of Locke's refutation of Filmer in the *First Treatise*:

... a Divine unalterable Right of Sovereignty, whereby a Father or a Prince hath an Absolute, Arbitrary, Unlimited, and Unlimitable Power, over the Lives, Liberties, and Estate of his Children and Subjects; so that he may take or alienate their Estates, sell, castrate, or use the Persons as he pleases, they being all his Slaves, and he Lord or Proprietor of every Thing, and his unbounded Will their Law.[52]

If Sir Sampson's words are Filmerian, Congreve makes it plain that his underlying motivation, in libertine and Hobbesian terms, is sexual jealousy directed at a more vigorous younger generation, fear of impotence expressing itself in empty blustering: as Ben says, 'I fear his Fire's a little better than Tinder, mayhap it will only serve to light up a Match for somebody else' (v.i.449–51). When not acting the tyrant, Sir Sampson affects libertine sentiments; like Rochester's disabled debauchee he has learned nothing from experience, and can serve as illustration of the futility of the rake's ethos of power and appetite in one whom time's ravages have made 'good for nothing else' (*The Disabled Debauchee*, 48): 'Pox o'th'time! There's no time but the time present, there's no more to be said of what's past, and all that is to come will happen. If the Sun shine by Day and the Stars by Night, why we shall know one another's Faces without the help of a Candle, and that's all the Stars are good for' (II.i.206–11).

Where in *The Way of the World* Mirabell uses the protection of a legal contract to secure the rights of Mrs Fainall against a husband who would tyrannise over her, seizing every shred of her property, in *Love for Love* no such reconciliation of legal form and individual emotion is proposed. In both works, the ideology is fundamentally Lockean, rejecting the authoritarian doctrine of Hobbes and Filmer that all property belonged of right to the sovereign and that the rights of individual subjects extended no further than the all-powerful state, or its analogue the all-powerful parent, permitted:

The constitution of *mine*, and *thine*, and *his*; that is to say in one word *propriety* . . . belongeth in all kinds of commonwealth to the sovereign power.

Now the magistrate is lord of all his subjects, by the constitution of government . . . Thy *dominion* therefore, and *propriety*, is just so much as he will, and shall last so long as he pleases; even as in a family, each son hath such *proper* goods, and so long lasting, as seems good to the father.[53]

But in *Love for Love* contracts and covenants are entirely associated with the false values Valentine comes to disavow at the end. Contracts, as Congreve presents them here, are ways of reducing human relations to the cash nexus: Sir Sampson revels in the economic power he can exert over his son, clutching the physical paper in his hand or dangling it tantalisingly before Valentine's eyes. The treatment of the legal bond is thus similar to that in *The Merchant of Venice*, as the rigid and implacable insistence on the letter of the law – 'look you perform Covenants' (II.i.435) – is contrasted with the impulse of charity. Fainall too insists on enforcing the utmost letter of his claim: 'I come to make demands. – I'll hear no objections . . . That shall not urge me to relinquish or abate one tittle of my Terms' (*The Way of the World*, v.i.316–17, 524–5). But the difference of the two denouements is that in *The Way of the World* Mirabell beats

Fainall at his own game, as it were substituting a Lockean for a Hobbesian contract, on the principle that '*the end of law* is not to abolish or restrain, but *to preserve and enlarge Freedom*'.[54] Angelica resolves the conflict differently: she tears the paper up, releasing Valentine from his bonds.

This contrast between incompatible values, one of which is seen as transcending the other, is anticipated in the scene of confrontation of father and son in Act II. Valentine, in disputing his father's claim of unrestricted power over the son he begot – 'mayn't I do what I please?' – does not seek to debate with him, as Locke does with Filmer:

The Argument, I have heard others make use of, to prove that Fathers by begetting them, come by an Absolute Power over their Children, is this; that *Fathers have a Power over the Lives of their Children, because they give them Life and Being*, which is the only proof it is capable of, since there can be no reason, why naturally one Man should have any claim or pretence of Right over that in another, which was never his, which he bestowed not, but was received from the bounty of another. 1° I answer, That every one who gives another, anything, has not always thereby a Right to take it away again. But, 2° They who say the *Father* gives Life to his Children, are so dazled with the thoughts of Monarchy, that they do not, as they ought, remember God, who is the *Author and Giver of Life: 'Tis in him alone we live, move, and have our Being*.[55]

Instead, he indicates his allegiance to a series of imperatives which his father's narrowly materialist and egoist principles do not admit, and in so doing defines the word 'appetite' in a way that consciously departs from Hobbes. Congreve may portray a world where it is assumed that 'all well-bred Persons lie' (II.i.662–3), where rule by 'mercenary Ends and sordid Interest' (IV.i.780–1) is considered the norm, but his moral stance toward that world, unlike that of Etherege or Rochester, is secure and unambiguous. The view of natural law and of man implicit in *Love for Love* is far closer to the traditionalism of Hobbes's opponents than to the radical questioning of Hobbes. When his father tells him he must 'go naked out of the World as you came into't', impervious like Fainall to any claims of natural ties of blood or affection, Valentine answers: 'My clothes are soon put off; but you must also divest me of Reason, Thought, Passions, Inclinations, Affections, Appetites, Senses, and the huge Train of Attendants that you begot along with me' (II.i.364–70). His servant Jeremy remarks a moment later, 'I find I was born with

those same Whoreson Appetites too, that my Master speaks of'
(391–3). It is this conception of a man as capable through his
'Inclinations, Affections, Appetites' of behaving generously and
sympathetically, ruled by some principle other than the desire 'to
destroy, or subdue one another', that differentiates the world of
Congreve from the world of Hobbes.

CHAPTER 2

The tyranny of desire: sex and politics in Rochester

Any discussion of sexual ideology in the writings of Rochester is hampered by the lack of a reliable biography. Vivian de Sola Pinto's *Enthusiast in Wit* and Graham Greene's *Lord Rochester's Monkey*, both nearly fifty years old, are studded with inaccuracies and credulous in their handling of evidence, though Greene's book is worth reading for its psychological insight, with the truth of fiction rather than fact.[1] The two principal biographical sources, essential for an understanding of Rochester's poetry, are his letters, edited by Jeremy Treglown,[2] and Gilbert Burnet's *Some Passages of the Life and Death of . . . John Earl of Rochester* (1680). Burnet's book is not a formal biography, but a narration of 'some passages', an account of a sinner's repentance explicitly homiletic in intent, with the avowed 'design' of 'doing what I can toward the reforming a loose and lewd Age'. Though Burnet proclaimed his care to speak 'nothing but Truth' in reporting his conversations with Rochester during the poet's last illness, modern critics have often been suspicious of the veracity of his account, seeing it as 'determinedly cosmetic' (*Letters*, p. 37), an exemplary fiction.[3] There is no doubt that Burnet makes himself the hero of his own narrative, presenting Rochester's heretical views in order to refute them. Indeed, if the exhausted poet on his sick-bed had to listen to Burnet's interminable lectures on morality and revealed religion (the proportion of Burnet to Rochester in the related conversation, as Greene points out, is over five to one, 1,671 lines as against 302 lines), it may well have made the release of death more welcome. Nevertheless, though it is possible that Burnet's own contributions to the dialogue were embellished afterwards, there is no reason to distrust in its essentials his account of Rochester's death-bed conversion, or impugn the accuracy of his reporting of Rochester's beliefs and opinions, as expressed during their conversations, especially where these accord with statements in

Rochester's poems and letters. 'He would conceal none of his Principles from me, but lay his thoughts open without any Disguise; nor would he do it to maintain Debate, or shew his Wit, but plainly tell me what stuck with him.'[4]

Virtually all commentators of Rochester have seen his life as an exemplary rake's progress, since that is the way he saw his own life. He was spectacularly self-destructive, seemingly lacking in the elementary instincts of self-preservation his favourite philosopher saw as natural to man. Burnet writes:

There were two Principles in his natural temper that being heighten'd by that heat carried him to great excesses: a violent love of Pleasure, and a disposition to extravagant Mirth. The one involved him in great sensuality: the other led him to many odd Adventures and Frollicks, in which he was oft in hazard of his life. The one being the same irregular appetite in his Mind, that the other was in his Body, which made him think nothing diverting that was not extravagant.

Burnet's vocabulary here is essentially mechanistic, a mixture of Renaissance humours psychology ('natural temper') and the atomistic determinism of Hobbes or Descartes: Rochester's mind is seen as an adjunct of his body, a battlefield over which conflicting forces sweep, carrying all before them, with primal heat and cold contending for supremacy. Rochester, in this view, did not choose to behave extravagantly, or even incline toward extravagance, but was propelled headlong toward it by his natural constitution. The moralist in Burnet suggests that the libertine poet ought to have exerted rational mastery over himself and resisted these impulses of the blood, while the practical psychologist notes the great difficulty he might have had in putting such 'Heroick resolutions' (*Letters*, p. 75) into practice, given his physical makeup. Rochester's remark to Burnet that he was 'continually Drunk' for five years may reflect a certain amount of poetic licence, as well as some ignorance of physiology, but its insight into the psychology of addiction is profound. The impulse toward self-destruction is accompanied by a desire to deny any volition, shifting the blame onto an impersonal force outside human control. Like several of his lyric poems and letters, Rochester's account of his behaviour as reported by Burnet betrays a weak will and a guilty conscience, a gnawing awareness of the gap between ideal and reality:

As he told me, for five years together he was continually Drunk: not all the while under the visible effect of it, but his blood was so inflamed, that he was not in all that time cool enough to be perfectly Master of himself. This led him to say and do many wild and unaccountable things: By this, he said, he had broke the firm constitution of his Health, that seemed so strong, that nothing was too hard for it.[5]

Rochester employs the same vocabulary of heat and cold to describe human motivation in a letter to his wife, and once again the dualistic framework can be interpreted either as minimising the element of choice (men act as their predominant humours direct) or as suggesting that, for a creature half angel and half beast, moral choice is imperative. The predominant mood in the passage is one of wry comic realism, the awareness that the grand pretensions of the 'head' are likely to be subverted by the ignoble yet irresistible demands of the 'taile'. In the poems, such a contrast is likely to be sharply satiric, a violent attack on false idealising using obscenity as a bludgeon: 'Permitt me your fair hand to kiss;/When at her Mouth her Cunt cries yes' ('A Ramble in Saint James's Parke', 77–8). In this letter, as in such lyrics as 'Absent from thee', the Christian terminology of 'originall sin' and 'grace' has quite another effect, suggesting, at the very least, an ambivalence toward the traditional morality of 'formal Band and Beard' he attacks elsewhere (*Satyr against Mankind*, 46). Treglown has made the shrewd point that 'religious structures of myth and language' were for Rochester associated with a lost world of childhood innocence (*Letters*, pp. 14–15).[6] We need not be surprised at the religious elements in Rochester's poetry, the pervasive imagery of flesh and spirit at war, or at his death-bed conversion, when we realise that *Paradise Lost*, *Paradise Regained*, Traherne's *Centuries of Meditation* and *The Pilgrim's Progress* are all Restoration works. In the passage that follows, the ironic wit as one of its functions allows the satirist to disappear behind his material, defusing the potential seriousness of the content, especially as it might reflect on the poet's own behaviour rather than that of the court ladies he dismisses with jocular offhand contempt:

. . . considering how men & woemen are compounded, that as heate and cold, soe greatness and meaness are necessary ingredients that enter both into the making up of every one that is borne, now when heate is pre-dominant we are termed hott, when cold is wee are call'd cold; though in the mixture both take theire places, els our warmeth would bee a burning, & our cold an excessive freezing, soe greatness or virtue that sparke of primitive grace is in every one alive, & likewise meaness or vice

that seede of originall sin is (in a measure) alsoe; for if either of them were
totally absent, men & woemen must bee perfect angells, or absolute divills,
now from the preheminence of either of these quallityes in us we are termed
good or bad; but yett as contrarietyes though they both reside in one body,
must they ever bee opposite in place, thence I inferr that as heate in the
feete makes cold in the head, soe may it bee wth probabilyty expected too,
that greateness & meaness should bee as oppositely seated, & then a
Heroick head is liker to bee ballanc't wth an humble taile, besides reason,
Experience has furnish'd mee with many Examples of this kind, my lady
Morton nell Villers, & twenty others, whose honour was ever soe exessive
in theire heads that they suffered a want of it in every other part. (*Letters*,
p. 75)

It is sometimes difficult to disentangle the historical Rochester
from the legendary Rochester, the age's archetypal rake-hero, who
figures in countless apocryphal anecdotes. Art and life, here as
elsewhere, are intertwined: Rochester, conscious of living up to his
role, helped create his own legend, relishing his reputation as
Wicked Lord, virtuoso of sin:

His sins were like his parts, (for from them corrupted they sprang) all of
them high and extraordinary. He seem'd to affect something singular and
paradoxical in his Impieties, as well as in his Writings, above the reach and
thought of other men . . . Nay so confirm'd was he in sin, that he lived, and
oftentimes almost died, a Martyr for it.[7]

The imagery here in Parsons's funeral sermon, derived essentially
from the persona projected in Rochester's poems and public actions,
is that of the 'great Sinner', whose 'excellent abilities' are, by a wilful
perverseness, directed toward false and dangerous ends: 'by his own
corrupt stomach, or some ill juices after, . . . turned into poison to
himself and others'. This view of Rochester is expressed with memorable force in the epigram 'To the Post Boy', which Vieth and Anne
Barton consider to be a satiric self-portrait, though in my view it is
more likely to be a satire on Rochester by an unknown contemporary. Again the image which emerges is that of a deliberate,
conscious sinner, using his utmost ingenuity to find 'the Readyest
way to Hell' (2), striving to outperform all earthly rivals in debauchery ('Ive out swilld Baccus . . . Ive swived more whores more
ways that Sodoms walls/Ere knew', 5–6) and bring about his own
damnation.[8] The inevitable comparison is to Satan – not the traditional father of lies so much as Milton's fallen angel, victim of his
own perverse nature. Dryden's Achitophel, Etherege's Dorimant

('Oh, he has a Tongue, they say, would tempt the Angels to a second fall', *The Man of Mode*, iii.iii.123–4), and the legendary Rochester, product of a partly self-created myth, all follow the same pattern of great talents 'turned into poison', seeking proselytes in sin: 'And truly none but one so great in parts could be so: as the chiefest of the Angels for knowledge and power became most degenerate.'[9]

There was something of the same ambivalence in Rochester's relationship with Charles II. In the Restoration court, he was constantly in trouble because of his rebelliousness and his violations of propriety: the claim in the *Memoirs of Grammont* that he was banished in disgrace 'at least once in the year' is exaggerated, but he seems to have popped in and out of favour with remarkable speed and frequency.[10] In 1669, for example, he struck the dramatist Thomas Killigrew in the King's presence, an act of *lèse-majesté*, and so outraged some of the more conservative courtiers in doing so that the King, who initially condoned the offence, felt it necessary to exile him to France for several months. His role in the court, as Graham Greene comments, was in part that of licensed jester, and he often exceeded the limits: take heed, sirrah, the whip.[11] Most of his offences, in act or in writing, were direct challenges to royal authority. Of the two epigrams Rochester is supposed to have spoken as impromptus in the King's presence and at his request, one ('Here's Monmouth the witty') is relatively mild in its reflections on royalty, while the other, though severe in its implications, mingles praise with its censure in appealing to Charles as a fellow wit:

> God bless our good and gracious King
> 	Whose promise none relyes on
> Who never said A foolish thing
> 	Nor ever did A wise one.[12]

His notorious 'scepter' lampoon was a less pardonable offence. The story that Rochester 'fled from Court' after 'delivering (by mistake) into the King's hands a terrible lampoon of his own making against the King, instead of another the King had asked him for' – another version of the story is that the King pulled the poem out of the poet's pocket – may well be a picturesque invention, but the incident is a classic Freudian slip, a sword cutting its victim and its wielder at once.[13] There are certain things one does not say to a reigning monarch, or allow to circulate in a closed court circle where the King is likely at some point to see a copy. The poem is characteristic of Rochester both in its shockingly indecorous language and in the scorn it directs at the institution of monarchy.

It differs from most of Rochester's other satires against King and court in being explicitly political as well as personal. Rochester's sympathies seem to have been more or less Whiggish, but (unlike his friend the Duke of Buckingham, a leader of the opposition after 1673) he rarely attended Parliament, and his satiric comments on the royal mistresses tended to emphasise sexual insatiability rather than the greed and political ambition which are recurrent accusations in Country Party lampoons. Nell Gwyn was a friend, and in his poems and letters is generally treated with sympathy and amused affection. A number of strong Whig satires on Charles II, some of them explicitly republican in their sentiments, were attributed to Rochester in early editions (these include 'The History of Insipids', 'Portsmouth's Looking-Glass' and 'The Royal Angler'), but all can be shown to be inauthentic.[14] Rochester's main obligations to the Crown were financial, rather than the more tenuous bonds of friendship. He was in receipt of two separate annuities from the Crown (dating from 1661 and 1666), held court office continuously for thirteen years and received further patronage in generous grants of land and sinecures – Keeper of the King's Game, Master of the King's Hawks and Keeper of Woodstock Park, which became his chief residence. Charles's treatment of Rochester was remarkably indulgent, since he continued and even increased his patronage after the poet's temporary banishment for the 'scepter' lampoon, and payments on the two annuities continued after drunken brawls had resulted not only in the wanton destruction of crown property, but in a death for which Rochester was threatened with indictment for murder.[15]

For all Rochester's ties to the crown and court, the 'scepter' lampoon contains passages which are as hostile to the monarchy as anything in the more explicitly partisan satires circulated during the 1670s by the radical opposition. In versions of the poem printed in Vieth's and Walker's editions, it ends with the couplet 'All monarchs I hate, and the thrones they sit on,/From the hector of France to the cully of Britain' (32–3).[16] The reference to 'the hector of France' is no mere afterthought: throughout, Louis XIV and Charles II are seen as the patterns of strong and weak king, one driven by 'ambition' and the desire for 'renown' (5) to fruitless military adventures ('Like the French fool, that wanders up and down/Starving his people, hazarding his crown', 6–7) and the other passive, weak, a man of 'peace' (8) disinclined to any effort, content to be ruled by his mistresses and whores. Both exemplify the folly of earthly greatness and the vanity of desire, and equally deserve to be treated with a mixture of pity and contempt – and indeed the terms by which both monarchs are characterised ('wanders', 'restless') anticipate the author's later, more philosophical satires. Other contemporary satires on the power of the royal mistresses lack this universal dimension, but they make many of the same charges against Charles II: 'Was ever prince's soul so meanly poor,/To be enslav'd to ev'ry little whore?' Charles in these accounts is a *'Royal Cully'*, the unmanly slave to his own lusts ('Go practice Heliogabalus's sin: /Forget to be a man and learn to spin'), while the true rulers of England are the royal whores and the intriguing courtiers whose interests they promote. Such poems as John Lacy's 'Satire', and 'The Royal Angler' even include variants on the 'scepter' lampoon's central image: in one, the scepter-penis becomes a fishing-rod, by which the would-be angler is caught, in the other a magnetic needle led 'to ev'ry craving hole'.[17] All the poems depend on similar paradoxes, the ruler ruled, the King the slave of his own desires, the bestial appetites overthrowing the rational faculty.

Rochester's poem differs from the others in two main respects. Though the grounds of the attack on Charles II here and in the other poems largely agree, there is not a shadow of a suggestion of possible action. As in the conclusion of 'Tunbridge Wells', the poem ends not in a recommendation of possible reform, but in an explosion of 'hate' for incorrigible man, washing one's hands of such a ridiculous, benighted creature. In contrast, John Lacy's 'Satire' warns the king that he needs to 'amend' to avoid a justified rebellion of his subjects; 'The Royal Angler' and 'Portsmouth's Looking-Glass' suggest he throw off the influence of his corrupt counsellors 'ere it be too late'; and 'The History of Insipids' ends with a bold republican call to arms.

> Of kings curs'd be the power and name,
>   Let all the earth henceforth abhor 'em:
> Monsters which knaves sacred proclaim
>   And then like slaves fall down before 'em.
> What can there be in kings divine?
> The most are wolves, goats, sheep, or swine.
>
> Then farewell, sacred Majesty.
>   Let's pull all brutish tyrants down!

> Where men are born and still live free,
>   There ev'ry head doth wear a crown.
> Mankind, like miserable frogs,
> Is wretched, king'd by storks or logs.[18]

The other difference is aesthetic: none of its companion poems can match Rochester's 'Satyr on Charles II' in the artistic control with which it develops its central conceit. The wit not only makes the satire more palatable (as Dryden says of his lines on Zimri), but intensifies the force of the attack, while presenting its primary satiric target more as passive victim than as conscious malefactor. Ultimately, the ethical position underlying Rochester's poem is not the republican claim to equality of opportunity, with every man a king, but the mordant recognition that all men are equally slaves:

> Nor are his high desires above his strength:
> His scepter and his prick are of a length;
> And she may sway the one who plays with th'other,
> And make him little wiser than his brother.
> Poor prince! thy prick, like thy buffoons at Court,
> Will govern thee because it makes thee sport.   (10–15)

The devaluation of human desires and ambition to the physical penis is characteristic of Rochester: the shock effect of the obscene language serves not only to demystify 'sacred Majesty', but to suggest that human fantasies of power, wisdom and dignity are self-delusion. What makes the conceit so effective is the literalness with which the idea is rendered: the poet uses the techniques of metaphysical verse to subvert any expectations of spiritual transcendence, denying the existence of any dimension beyond the corporeal. The comic concreteness of the image of masturbation in line 12 makes its point more sharply and economically than solemn accusations of the impropriety of petticoat government ('Almighty Pow'r of Women! . . . you will ever reign') or direct, naive railing ('Look back and see the people mad with rage/To see the bitch in so high equipage').[19] The penis is given a life of its own, and yet is shown as wholly subservient to those who, pretending to flatter its demands, 'govern' its owner. King and buffoon are interchangeable: a life devoted entirely to the pursuit of pleasure, the lines suggest, can produce only frustration and unexpected reversals.

> 'Tis sure the sauciest prick that e'er did swive,
> The proudest, peremptoriest prick alive.
> Though safety, law, religion, life lay on't,

> 'Twould break through all to make its way to cunt.
> Restless he rolls about from whore to whore,
> A merry monarch, scandalous and poor.   (16–21)

Here, by a surprising transformation, Charles becomes Louis, as the 'easy', indolent, unambitious king by the influence of his penis's absolutist demands becomes a tyrant. The lines are a powerful indictment of monarchy as an institution which, because of its concentration of unchecked power, inevitably corrupts its possessor. The blind battering ram of the penis, ruled by the animal instinct of self-gratification, is equivalent to the insatiable demands of royal power, claiming sovereign sway over private property, freedom of conscience, law, public safety, even life itself. What should restrain this mindless, voracious power – rationality, tradition, law, the public interest – has failed to do so. A similar image, without the political implications, occurs in 'The Imperfect Enjoyment': 'Stiffly resolv'd, 'twou'd carelessly invade/*Woman* or *Man*, nor ought its fury staid,/Where e're it pierc'd, a *Cunt* it found or made' (41–3). The obscenity here is more ambivalent in its effect: is the libertine poet defiantly flaunting his bisexuality and sexual buccaneering in scorn of conventional ideas of restraint, or is the persona satirised for his selfish pursuit of sexual pleasure devoid of feeling? In either case, the mock-heroic language ironically comments on the equivalence of warrior and rake, each in his own way a devotee of mindless violence, indifferent to the consequences of his acts.

A similar equation of authoritarianism and the tyrannous rule of sexual desire underlies the satire of *Sodom*, too often stigmatised as mere pornography, and informs Rochester's play *Valentinian*, with its sharp criticism of Charles II and his court.[20] The opening speech by the tyrant Bolloximian in *Sodom*, with its parody of the first lines of Dryden's *The Conquest of Granada*, is another variant on the central conceit of the 'scepter' lampoon, identifying sexual conquest and arbitrary political power:

> Thus in the zenith of my Lust I reigne
> I eat to swive, and swive to eat againe . . .
> my Pintle only shall my Scepter be
> my Laws shall act more pleasure then Coṁand
> and with my Prick I'le governe all the Land.[21]

The flattering, complaisant courtiers are shown as willing to act not only as instruments of the King's 'boundless . . . will' in the political sphere, but as pimps and catamites: ''Tis all I wish that Pockanello's

Arse/May still find favor from yor Royall Tarse'. Though the element of fantasy prevents one from reading *Sodom* as a *roman-à-clef*, the charges of tyranny, political corruption and sexual licence resemble those directed at the court of Charles II in such contemporary satires as Marvell's 'The Kings Vowes'.[22] *Valentinian* presents many of the same criticisms of the Restoration court. In Rochester's adaptation of Fletcher's play, the Emperor is characterised as abandoned voluptuary, ignoring imperial responsibilities for sexual dalliance: 'Empire and Life I ever have despis'd,/The vanity of Pride, of Hope and Fear,/In Love alone my Soul found real Joys'.[23] Yet for all his scorn of 'the servile Pride of Government', Valentinian acts as a tyrant, surrounds himself with corrupt and servile courtiers and brooks no restraint on his unchecked will, like a Hobbesian absolute monarch: 'Can you believe your Husband's Right to you/Other than what from me he does derive?/Who justly may recall my own at pleasure./Am I not Emperor? This World my own?' (1.i, p. 7).[24]

Though the poet here as in 'A Satyr on Charles II' rejects the Hobbesian politics of authoritarianism, the vision of man common to all these works can be called Hobbesian in its psychology. Its central tenet, defining human motivation as a 'perpetual and restless desire for power after power, that ceaseth only in death' (*Leviathan*, xi, p. 64), leads to a radical ontological insecurity and an ethic of ruthless egoism, seen both as necessary for survival in the jungle of the world and as emotionally intolerable. The monarch-penis, in 'A Satyr on Charles II' and 'The Imperfect Enjoyment', as in *Sodom*, finds his dreams of glory deflated by the weakness and unreliability of the flesh. 'Restless' and unsatisfied, the 'merry monarch' ('A Satyr on Charles II', 20–21) consumes his own substance and drains the public purse, making himself a laughing stock and endangering the survival of the commonwealth. The lines that follow, in which the king is described, in his 'declining years' (23), as unable to maintain an erection, continue the emphasis on the vanity of desire, the body's treason. As in 'The Imperfect Enjoyment' and *Sodom*, impotence and detumescence provide irrefutable proof that illusions of omnipotence, sexual or political, testify only to the persistence of human folly.

The ambivalence of Rochester toward Charles II had profound psychological roots. His philosophy of life and his satirist's stance precluded any respect for venerable institutions, the 'holy Cheats, and formal Lyes' of received religion and morality, any pretensions either of the dignity of man or of the natural superiority of those occupying positions of power. All attempts to mystify human power are fraudulent, contemptible expedients by those who seek 'over their fellow *Slaves* to tyrannize' (*Satyr against Mankind*, 177–8). Yet, as Basil Greenslade points out, from an early age Rochester scarcely knew any world but the Court. His father, a companion of Charles II in exile, had died in 1658, when the poet was ten, and the unusual forbearance which the King showed in pardoning his repeated offences may have come from the older man's assuming, from the time of the poet's adolescence, an avuncular role, even that of a surrogate father: 'Returning to England in time of Christmas 1664 at the age of seventeen, he went straight to the court at Whitehall. It was the obvious place to go. True, he had a home with his mother in Oxfordshire, but the court was to be a second home, with the King a kind of second father at its head.'[25] Certainly, the early loss of a father – and the father's prolonged exile meant that, aside from a visit to Paris when John was six, he is unlikely to have seen his father more than once or twice during his childhood – contributed to the poet's sense of insecurity, his search for a haven associated with 'Love and Peace and Truth', the domestic virtues. The duality of court and country, attractive urban hell and placid rural heaven, so central in Rochester's life and writings, seems to have had its roots in the experience of exile and instability the poet shared with his generation, children of the interregnum. Indeed, though there is no evidence that his relations with his mother showed any of the pervasive sense of guilt evident in his correspondence with Elizabeth Barry and his wife, as in his poems, it is probable that the origins of the recurrent psychological pattern of anger, self-hatred and repentance lay in a childhood and early adolescence in which the dominant figure was this strong-willed, manipulative countrywoman, whose chief interests appear to have been religion and the management of her estate.[26]

Burnet says that though Rochester was the King's drinking companion, a source of constant 'diversion' by his wit and conviviality, there was little personal affection in the relationship: 'The king loved his company for the diversion it afforded, better than his person: and there was no love lost between them.'[27] This may well be so, and Burnet catches well a certain guardedness in the relationship: neither kings nor satirists are ever to be trusted to behave with generous spontaneity, and as Rochester comments to his closest

friend Henry Savile, nothing is more destructive to love or friendship than the network of obligation and rivalry so characteristic of a
court: 'The meane Pollicy of Court prudence . . . makes us lye to one
another all day, for feare of being betray'd by each other att night'
(*Letters*, p. 67). Yet there is something of Falstaff and Hal (with the
ages reversed, or rather with the role of prince and tempter in the
same man) in the relationship of Rochester and the King, seventeen
years his senior. The primary bond remains the pull of pleasure, the
attractions to both King and aristocrat of 'playing holiday', dressing
up in the borrowed robes of misrule – with the added *frisson* that the
boon companion, whether snarling satirist or monarch seeking
diversion, is at any time capable of turning round and mauling one,
like a pet lion cub. Yet, whatever Charles's feelings (and Halifax
suggests that the King's affability and air of easy familiarity reflected
a certain coldness and indifference), to the young Rochester the
King represented both parental authority and rebellion, a fount of
preferment and a tutor in sin, the central figure in a world he loved
and despised.

> They who would be great in our little government seem as ridiculous to me
> as schoolboys who with much endeavour and some danger climb a crab-
> tree, venturing their necks for fruit which solid pigs would disdain if they
> were not starving. (*Letters*, p. 119)[28]

His letters to Savile constantly proclaim the need to remain
independent of the values of the court, yet they are, without exception, letters of one courtier to another, full of references to mutual
friends, shared experience and court gossip. His letters to his wife
frequently express a similar impatience with life at court ('I doe
seriously wth all my heart wish my selfe wth you, & am endeavouring
every day to get away from this place which I am soe weary of, that I
may be said rather to languish than live in it', *Letters*, p. 52), but he
was never able to break the bonds that tied him to a world 'to which
from his greenest Youth both his Birth and Choice had accustom'd
him' and in which he had a reputation to live up to.[29] The author of
the memoir prefixed to the 1707 and 1709 *Works* (a piece of hack
work generally not to be trusted) makes the shrewd point that 'as a
Beauty owes her Ruin to her own Charms, so did my Lord':[30] for all
the power inherent in the aggressive male roles of rake and satirist, it
is striking how often, in poems and letters, Rochester presents
himself as trapped, powerless, a passive victim:

If there bee a reall good upon Earth, 'tis in the Name of freind, without wch all others are meerly fantastical, how few of us are fitt stuff to make that thing, wee have dayly the melancholy experience . . . This thought has soe intirely possest mee since I came into the Country (where only one can think, for you att Court thinke not att all or att least as if you were shutt up in a Drumme, you can thinke of nothing but the noise is made about you). (*Letters*, p. 93)

Of his three principal correspondents, Henry Savile, Elizabeth Barry and his wife, the only one with whom his relationship was stable and consistently affectionate was Savile. As with many of the rakes of Restoration comedy, the bottle was a more agreeable and less threatening companion than any woman.

> Farewel *Woman*, I intend,
>   Henceforth, ev'ry *Night* to sit
> With my lewd well-natur'd *Friend*,
>   Drinking, to engender *Wit*.
>
> ('Song': 'Love a woman', 9–12)

A substantial number of Rochester's poems and letters express conventional denigratory attitudes toward women as 'the idlest part of Gods Creation' (4), a source only of vexation and distress: 'But I thank God I can distinguish, I can see very woman in you, and from yourself am convinced I have never been in the wrong in my opinion of women' (*Letters*, p. 181). The world of the 'Rivall Bottle' ('To A Lady, in A Letter', 7), of male friendship, is presented as excluding women, except as objects to be used when the need arises. Among the references to shared pleasures in his letters to Savile is the recommendation of a catamite ('The greatest and gravest of this Court of both sexes have tasted his beauties, and I'll assure you Rome gains upon us here in this point mainly', *Letters*, p. 230), and the 'Song' quoted above ends with a quatrain in praise of sodomy as providing a simple, straightforward outlet for sexual tensions, without any emotional investment.[31]

> Then give me *Health, Wealth, Mirth,* and *Wine,*
>   And if busie *Love* intrenches,
> There's a sweet soft *Page,* of mine,
>   Does the trick worth *Forty Wenches.*   (13–16)

The blunt devaluation of 'love' to a physical reflex to be satisfied by the readiest available means can be paralleled in a number of libertine poems of the period by Rochester and others – the comparison 'as men with Close-stools, to ease Nature', in one poem once

attributed to Rochester, is even more contemptuously dismissive of
'so vile a Creature' as woman, and even more reductive in its
implicit view of humanity. Heterosexual love is seen, with aristocratic scorn, as the province of 'the Rabble', as exhausting and unpro-
ductive drudgery (cf. 'A Satire against Marriage', another supposi-
tious poem: 'Drudge on till Fifty at thine own Expense . . ./Repeat
thy loath'd embraces ev'ry Night,/Prompted to act by Duty, not
Delight'), and as the product of a timorous, prudential outlook
unworthy of a gentleman:

> Let the *Porter*, and the *Groome*,
>   Things design'd for dirty *Slaves*,
> Drudge in fair *Aurelias Womb*,
>   To get supplies for Age, and Graves.
>
> ('Song': 'Love a woman', 5–8)[32]

Something of the same impatience shows itself in Rochester's
letters to Elizabeth Barry – Rochester is always conscious of
imagined slights, demanding the special privileges due him by his
rank and his wit – but here the spiritual, transcendent dimension,
derided as sham elsewhere in his writings, is omnipresent.

All time between that and the next visit is no part of my life, or at least like
a long fit of the falling sickness wherein I am dead to all joy and happiness
. . . But in the evening I will see you and be happy, in spite of all the fools in
the world.

You may be sure I cannot choose but love you above the world, whatever
becomes of the King, Court, or mankind and all their impertinent business.

The little joy I take in everything wherein you are not concerned, the
pleasing perplexity of endless thought which I fall into wherever you are
brought to my remembrance; and lastly, the continual disquiet I am in
during your absence, convince me sufficiently that I do you justice in
loving you so as woman was never loved before.

Your favours to me are the greatest bliss this world, or womankind – which
I think Heaven – can bestow, but the hopes of it. (*Letters*, pp. 99, 102, 103,
118)

The letters read like first drafts of love poems, and their characteristic paradoxes recall Donne's *Songs and Sonets* as well as Rochester's
own lyrics. Rochester's divided nature is apparent not so much in
seeing women at one time as emblems of hell, at others of heaven,
but in the identification of the lover's pleasing pain with absence,
imagination, memory, anticipation, 'the pleasing perplexity of

endless thought', all incompatible with the dogmatic, reductive materialism he professes elsewhere.

Rochester cannot have been an easy man to live with: his behaviour was consistently extravagant, generally self-destructive and frequently cruel. His relationship with Elizabeth Barry began with protestations of undying love and ended, three years later, with violent jealousy, 'anger, spleen, revenge and shame' (*Letters*, p. 180); his last letter to her informs her that he has removed their child from her care on the grounds that she was an unfit mother. His early letters to his wife are full of impetuosity and good humour ('I'le hould you six to fower I love you wth all my heart', *Letters*, p. 50), but within a short time, their correspondence is full of mutual recriminations, accusations on her side and apologies and counter-attacks on his. 'God knows when you will find in your hart to leave the place you are in', she writes plaintively in 1676:

Pray consider with your selfe wheather this be a reasonable way of proceeding . . . Pray lay your commands on me what I am to doe and though it be to forgett my children and the long hopes I have lived in of seeing you, yett I will endeavour to obey you or in the memory only torment my selfe with out giving you the trouble of puting you in the mind thear lives such a creature. (*Letters*, p. 129)

Plainly the Countess had learned her husband's characteristic vocabulary of torments and fading memory, and his fundamental pessimism.

The arrangement Rochester arrived at early in his marriage was to spend half the year in London, leading a riotous life of debauchery, and half the year living quietly on his family estate, reading, writing and begetting lawful heirs. Unlike Byron and the young Donne, who were able to write in the morning and drink in the evening, Rochester seems to have found it necessary to separate his active and contemplative selves physically, throwing himself into the life of pleasure with total abandon, relishing the loss of control and coming as close as possible to oblivion. John Aubrey writes, 'he was wont to say that when he came to Brentford the Devill entered into him and never left him till he came into the Country again'.[33] The 'sad Intervals and severe Reflections' which he had during his sober moments provided the perspective necessary for writing, but never enabled him to break off a course of life which he knew was killing him. He ruined his health before he was thirty – as his letters show, during the last three years of his life his recurrent illnesses

were so severe that he was virtually incapable of writing, and he was
convinced that he would die soon: 'My most neglected Wife, till you
are a most respected Widdow, I find you will scarce bee a contented
woman, and to say noe more than the plaine truth, I doe endeavour
soe fairly to doe you that last good service, that none but the most
impatient would refuse to rest satisfy'd' (*Letters*, pp. 170–1).[34] He
succeeded in dying at the age of thirty-three, as the result of syphilis
and its complications, possibly compounded by cirrhosis of the liver:
a rake's progress indeed.

The drive toward the abyss in Rochester stemmed less from a
'violent love of Pleasure' (Burnet's explanation) than from a conviction that nothing was real beyond the momentary impulse, the
violent electrical charge of pleasure or pain.

> Fantastick Fancies fondly move;
>   And in frail Joys believe:
> Taking false Pleasure for true Love;
>   But pain can ne're deceive. ('The Mistress', 29–32)

Classical hedonist theory posits the pursuit of pleasure and avoid-
ance of pain as fundamental human motivations, defining 'good'
and 'evil' essentially in psychological rather than moral terms.
Rochester, starting from the same materialist and relativist
premises, suggests a hedonist calculus of a somewhat different kind.
With a scepticism learned from Hobbes, he rules out as possible
guides for behaviour both the traditional reliance on absolute,
transcendent principles and the Epicurean tenet that man should
seek to attain a state of passionless content or *ataraxia*, immunity
from the disturbance of pain.[35] To Hobbes, as we have seen, 'felicity
is a continual progress of the desire, from one object to another'
(*Leviathan*, XI, p. 63). Rochester goes one step further in narrowing
the scope of possible 'felicity': though in other poems, especially *A
Satyr against Mankind*, he equates instinctual gratification with 'lifes
happiness' (96), here he presents the pursuit of pleasure as no less
delusory than the hope of attaining serenity. Sexual pleasure, taken
here as the norm for all pleasures, is 'false' because it does not last
and because it is based on lies, the delusion of fidelity and stability.
With characteristic sexual realism, Rochester in several poems fixes
on the orgasm as illustrative of the problems inherent in the hedonist
ethic to which he was committed. The intense momentary pleasure

of sexual fulfilment, he suggests in 'A Ramble in Saint James's Parke', is a lie because it lulls the critical faculty to sleep:

> When leaneing on your faithless breast
> Wrapt in security and rest
> Soft kindness all my powers did move
> And Reason lay dissolv'd in Love.   (129–32)

Pain, on the other hand, is true because it does not misrepresent or disguise the nature of reality. 'Jealous Doubts, tormenting Fears,/ And Anxious Cares' ('The Mistress', 33–4), far from being shunned as instances of avoidable pain, should therefore be cherished, since they are *real* in a world where most things are evanescent and deceptive.

'The Mistress', like a number of Rochester's other poems, both asserts and denies materialism. Its implied ethic is not only hedonist, but, as in Hobbes, egoist, in that it gives a uniquely privileged status to a world circumscribed by the lover's senses and emotions, effectively denying any validity to the conventional values and blunt, 'profoundly dull' (19) sensibilities of the ostensibly 'Wiser men' (13) who dominate society. Even the mistress herself is largely seen as object and occasion of the narrator's flood of emotions, rather than as having any independent existence. Though the paradoxes of the opening stanzas are of course themselves conventional in Renaissance love poetry (see for example, 'The Canonization' or 'The Sunne Rising'), the emphasis throughout the poem on intensity and complexity of feeling as a touchstone, on the pleasure in pain and the pain in pleasure, is characteristic of Rochester's writings, and reflects an unresolved contradiction in his thought. There are two possible readings of the final stanza. One, more conservative in its psychology and epistemology, is that the 'perplexity' and 'disquiet' associated with love (*Letters*, p. 102) unite pleasure and pain in giving us the hope of a happiness beyond our immediate grasp. We recognise their value retrospectively, though while under their temporary sway we may register them as pain:

> Kind Jealous Doubts, tormenting Fears,
>   And Anxious Cares, when past;
> Prove our Hearts Treasure fixt and dear,
>   And make us blest at last.   (33–6)

But another reading of the lines, placing less emphasis on the words 'when past' (or seeing these words as partly ironic in effect), would see the experience of the moment as an end in itself, rather than as logical proof of the existence of a 'blest' state of reciprocal love where the element of doubt, the restlessness by which both Hobbes and Rochester define the human condition, no longer needs to exist. Nothing in the rest of the poem leads us to believe that such a state of secure certainty is attainable, other than in an imagined ideal realm beyond reach. The poem as a whole is not written from the safe harbour of fulfilled love, but adrift in the sea of contradictory emotions, where love is tested and refined by uncertainty and pain.

The apparent contradiction in the two final stanzas of 'The Mistress' – with the last stanza asserting in quasi-religious language what the penultimate stanza, together with many other passages in Rochester, has denied, the existence of a transcendent dimension 'beyond material sense' (*Satyr against Mankind*, 67), where the heart's treasure does not rust – reflects the same impasse evident in his conversations with Burnet. The polarities recur again and again: the clash of a religious sensibility and materialist convictions, a longing for certitude as against a sceptical, critical temperament. Until the final stanza, the emotions attributed to the lover are predominantly painful: when he is with her he anticipates separation and when apart from her he undergoes the pangs of death.

> An Age in her Embraces past,
>   Would seem a Winters day;
> When Life and Light, with envious hast,
>   Are torn and snatch'd away.
>
> But, oh, how slowly Minutes rowl,
>   When absent from her Eyes
> That feed my Love, which is my Soul,
>   It languishes and dyes.   (1–8)

The lover projected as persona here is a connoisseur of suffering: where an ordinary man might take some pleasure in his mistress's embraces, he feels, with an acute physical wrench, forebodings of mortality. The poem as a whole seeks to justify the lover's sufferings not as prelude to some ultimate state of timeless bliss but as indexes of a finer sensibility. Through his imagination, an inner world stigmatised as 'mad' (20) by conventional standards, he has access to what, the poet hints, may be the only spiritual dimension available to man. The shift in tone in the middle stanzas, from emotion-charged hyperbole ('envious hast', 'languishes', 'mournfully' (10), 'living Tomb' (12)) to a slightly embarrassed man-of-the-world briskness – 'on Shades of Souls, and Heaven knows what' (15) – suggests an inability to break free of the worldly values that constrain and threaten love. Indeed, the outward signs of the lovers' relationship indicate disharmony and imperfection: they 'sigh and lament, Complain and grieve' (23), exhibiting spleen more than tenderness. Jealousy is 'Sacred' (25) not because it in any way ennobles their existence, but because it educates them in the ways of pain, provides the incontrovertible 'Proof' (27) of the aching senses that they are awake and not dreaming. Hell and heaven, as 'The Mistress' suggests, are to Rochester as to Hobbes not literal physical locations but psychological states.[36]

As his letters, his conversations with Burnet and (insofar as we can read them as drawn from and commenting on his own experience) a number of his poems suggest, Rochester was very much aware that he was wasting his life and his talents. One thing that makes him interesting as a poet, and distinguishes him from most of his fellow courtiers, is that he saw clearly what was wrong with his life, just as he saw through the hollowness and frivolity of the court, and yet he was unable to change or to suggest in his poems a satisfactory, attainable alternative. Rochester's poems focus on the difference between seeing something and being able to act on it, between what one knows and what one is able to do – there is, he says in a letter to his wife, 'soe great a disproportion 'twixt our desires and what it has ordained to content them' (*Letters*, pp. 241–2).

If there is any hope, it lies in art, not life: perhaps the ability to see clearly is in its way enough after all. This is illustrated strikingly by a poem not included in the Vieth edition and printed by Walker among 'poems possibly by Rochester', though in all probability it is authentic. The poem is frankly and brutally obscene, but its indecorous, shocking language is necessary to the aesthetic effect, by no means gratuitous. Vieth, on the flimsiest of evidence, takes the poem to be an extemporised lampoon on Rochester, spoken in Rochester's presence by his friend the Earl of Dorset. But the ascription to Dorset is merely a matter of gossip, and the variant cited by Vieth, with 'you' substituted for 'I', has no textual authority and, indeed, robs the poems of the ironic force the use of the first person gives it.[37] 'I rise at eleven' is neither a *jeu d'esprit* nor an autobiographical effusion. Though the poem has never been recognised as such because of its unwarranted exclusion from the canon, 'I rise at eleven' is a highly effective, carefully constructed satire, using a persona to depict the life of a typical courtier and rake.

> I Rise at Eleven, I Dine about *Two*,
> I get Drunk before Seven, and the next thing I do,
> I send for a *Whore*, when for fear of a *Clap*,
> I Spend in her Hand, and I Spew in her Lap;
> There we Quarrel and Scold till I fall asleep,
> When the Bitch growing bold, to my Pocket do's creep.
> Then slily she leaves me, and to revenge the Affront,
> At once she bereaves me of Money and *Cunt*.
> If by chance then I wake, hot-headed and drunk,
> What a Coil do I make for the loss of my Punk?
> I storm, and I roar, and I fall in a rage,
> And missing my Whore, I Bugger my Page.
> Then Crop sick all Morning, I rail at my Men
> And in Bed I lie yawning till Eleven agen.[38]

The character portrayed in the poem leads a life similar to what we know of Rochester's own life, and indeed that of many of his friends and contemporaries: the materials of which the portrait is made up – whoring, drinking, rising late, killing time – are thus familiar and described from firsthand knowledge. But if to some degree he can be said to be writing about himself, he does so with absolute, cold objectivity. If the poem were not cast in the first person, it would lose half its effectiveness. The use of the first person, as with many satires which employ a persona, helps to involve the reader in the poem, while at the same time, it narrows the perspective. However unsatisfactory the life depicted is, the poem doesn't present an alternative. The circular form suggests that for the character tomorrow will be exactly like today – entirely empty, pointless and sterile. 'I Spend in her Hand, and I Spew in her Lap': sex could hardly seem less enjoyable and more mechanical. All human relationships, all emotions, are degraded. Ejaculation and vomiting become virtual equivalents, and both sex and drinking are robbed of their expected favourable associations. The mistress here is reduced to an even lower state than that of 'A passive pott for Fools to spend in' ('A Ramble in Saint James's Parke', 102) – not only a mere receptacle, but the wrong one. Later on, lust becomes indistinguishable from rage, aggressiveness a sign of impotent frustration, injured reputation, loss of power ('*the power of a man*, to take it universally, is his present means, to obtain some future apparent good'; *Leviathan*, x, p. 56). Psychologically, physically and morally, the anal rape of the page – a dependent servant, unable to resist even if he wanted to – is the equivalent of a kick, the relief of pent-up energies on the nearest available object. This, then, is a life of pleasure which in fact produces no pleasure at all. The poem is a vision of hell on earth – 'Compar'd to our unhappy *Fate*;/We need not fear another *Hell*' ('The Fall', 3–4) – with no way off the treadmill.[39] This is not to say that there are no standards by which the protagonist is judged: his equation of 'Money and *Cunt*', for example, betrays his crass materialism, in both senses of the word, as well as his tendency to regard others as instruments for his convenience. But the poem makes it clear, in its cyclical structure and control of a limited point of view, that the narrator – seen throughout as representative of his society and its values – is unable even to conceive of an alternative to a life which is plainly intolerable.

The relentless obscenity which is the most striking feature of many of Rochester's poems serves several functions, both expressive and satiric: the amoral desire to shock the reader, flaunting the author's credentials as devotee of wickedness and scourge of the conventional, the more philosophically serious desire to remind the reader of man's inescapable animal nature, the impulse of hatred and self-hatred stemming from frustrated idealism. It is striking how often the element of sexual disgust, fear of the female genitalia as all-devouring mouth, finds expression even in such relatively light-hearted, uncomplicated poems as 'Signior Dildo'.[40] This can be seen in moral rather than psychological terms as a disapproval of the subordination of the head to the tail, yet poem after poem sees woman as insatiable, man as her helpless, half-reluctant victim:

> Our dainty fine Dutchesse's have got a Trick
> To Doat on a Fool, for the sake of his Prick,
> The Fopps were undone, did their Graces but know
> The Discretion and vigor of Signior Dildo.
>
> That Pattern of Virtue, her Grace of Cleaveland,
> Has swallowed more Pricks, then the Ocean has Sand,
> But by Rubbing and Scrubbing, so large it do's grow,
> It is fit for just nothing but Signior Dildo.
>
> ('Signior Dildo', 33–40)

In the first quatrain, the reader can feel comfortably superior to the fops (whose heads are empty, Rochester says in 'To A Lady, in A Letter', though their 'Codds' are 'full', 22–4) and the society ladies. The satiric stance here is secure, and opposing values are sketched in deftly: each of the objects of satire is exposed and discomfited, the ladies, as in *The Country-Wife*, by the revelation of the secret springs of their behaviour ('though Cunt be not Coy, reputation is Nice', he remarks in 'Quoth the Duchess of Cleavland to Councillor Knight', 4), the fops by the warning that even in the one respect where they excel they can be outperformed by a mechanical object and will be discarded in their turn.[41] But in the second quatrain, what is attacked is not false standards of judgement but irremediable human nature. The Duchess of Cleveland, rather than being presented as unnatural in her ravenous, indiscriminate lust, is the female principle incarnate: the guiding doctrine of the poem is that *all* women 'Worship Signior Dildo' as priapic deity (16), desire a prick at all times. References to the size and capacity of female genitalia are common enough in pornography, but the lines quoted above are characteristically Rochesterian in their emphasis on 'disproportion' – that between desire and fulfilment, common to both sexes and that between men, seen (accurately, according to Masters and Johnson and other studies) as subject to physiological limits in their sexual performance, and women, whose unbridled appetites and capacity for multiple orgasms are treated here with a degree of fear and envy.

Most pornographic writings are pornutopias, with heroes of unlimited potency, before whom an infinite series of largely indistinguishable women fall like ninepins. This is never the case with Rochester, even in *Sodom*, which because of its announced aim of sexual arousal can be classified as pornography (though it has satiric elements as well). The prologue to *Sodom* imagines both author and audience in a state of continual sexual excitement: the play, we are told, will 'make all P—ks to stand and Cunts to gape', while 'the authors Prick was so unruly growne/Whilst writing this he could not keep him downe'.[42] Yet in the play itself, as in 'The Imperfect Enjoyment' and 'A Ramble in Saint James's Parke', sex becomes far more troubling and problematical. Aside from one delightful stage direction, a dance of six naked men and six naked women who 'do obeysance to' one another's sexual organs 'and so fall to Copulation after which the women Sigh and the men look Simply and so sneak off' (Act II, p. 129) – a rival to 'exit, pursued by a bear' in testing a producer's ingenuity – there is scarcely an act of successful sexual coupling presented or described. The women howl with unfulfilled desire, while the men on two separate occasions ejaculate prematurely, spilling their seed on the ground: as the young prince complains, 'You have let out all the Spiritts of my blood/Yo've ruin'd me and done yo' selfe no good' (III, p. 133). Not only is the sexual apparatus consistently portrayed as unreliable, but homosexuality, presented in some other poems by Rochester as an alternative means of sexual expression no better or worse than any other, is here seen as a symptom of a diseased commonwealth. The court physician, acting as authorial spokesman, speaks these lines near the end of the play, shortly before fire and brimstone consume the kingdom of Sodom:

> Buggery . . . do's that destroy
> which nature gave with pleasure to enjoy
> Please her and She'll be kind if you displease
> Shee turns into Corruption and disease.   (v.ii, pp. 143–4)

Frustration and dissatisfaction characterise the heterosexual encounters in the play. The barren queen longs for the king's embraces and then is rejected by her would-be lover, who is drained by her insatiable demands:

> Yo' Menstrous blood do's all yo' reines supply
> with unexhausted lechery whilst I
> Like a decrepid lecher must retire
> with Prick to weak to act what I desire.   (IV, p. 135)

It is curious how often female sexuality in Rochester is associated with 'Menstruous blood', as though the menses were both the cause of woman's desire and a badge of shame, a sign of the body's impurity, associating sexuality with dirt, stains, bad smells. The fear thus expressed is identified by Freud as castration anxiety, but it can equally well be associated with fear of losing control, fear of being held up to ridicule, of being rendered helpless by the body's involuntary betrayal: to the psychologist Freud and the satirist Rochester, sexual performance and social performance are closely connected.[43]

Women, as Rochester presents them, are more at ease with their bodies, and with an uncomplicated hedonist ethic, than men are. To the men in *Sodom*, 'the Toyles of Cunt are more than Toyles of warr', where to the women sexual 'Ease and pleasure' are 'all that wee can deare or happy call' (Act II, p. 135). In 'A Ramble in Saint James's Parke', woman's sexual freedom is treated with considerable ambivalence:

Had she pickt out to rub her Arse on
Some stiff prickt Clown or well hung Parson
Each jobb of whose spermatique sluce
Had fill'd her Cunt with wholesome Juice
I the proceeding should have praisd
In hope she had quench'd a fire I rais'd.
Such naturall freedomes are but Just
There's something Genrous in meer lust.
But to turn damn'd abandon'd Jade
When neither Head nor Taile perswade
To be a Whore in understanding
A passive pott for Fools to spend in. (91–102)

What the persona – and though he may be in part an object of satire, in this respect his values seem identical with Rochester's own – condemns Corinna for is not sexual promiscuity, which is true to nature, honest and socially acceptable, but giving her self sexually to a fool. Her failure is one of 'understanding', allowing the confusions of the head to interfere with the messages of the tail. Some irony is directed at the protagonist here, a thoroughly unreliable narrator whose passions distort his judgement. The praise of a 'stiff prickt Clown' as a more suitable sexual partner, like Othello's jealous imaginings, betrays the speaker's underlying insecurity and self-contempt, and the misogynistic bitterness of the passage may well reflect a belief that women are naturally inferior to man in their endowment of reason – a doctrine at variance with the poem's ostensible praise of natural instinct. Is the ambivalence the author's or the character's? It is hard to tell, since the two are not distinguished as clearly as in 'I rise at eleven'. But Rochester is consistent in presenting women's sexual capacities as greater than those of men and in treating sexual slavery as in part a function of sexual inadequacy, the inability to act what one desires. To characterise women as able to take on several men at once, as Rochester does in several poems, allows him to express both contempt and envy, to degrade women in one sense while exalting them in another:

Here is a Mine, an Ocean full of treasure
Tis wee alone enjoy the Cheifest pleasure
While men doe toyle and Moyle and spend their Strength
The pleasure doth redound to us at length
Men when they're Spent are like some peice of wood
Or an insipid thing tho flesh and blood
Whilst wee are still desirous of more

> And Valiantly dare challenge halfe a score
> Nay Canthes like wee'll swive with forty men
> Then home to our husbands and there swive againe.[44]

For all the sexual realism of 'A Ramble in Saint James's Parke', the poem is oddly ascetic in its attitudes: a disgust with the human body pervades the poem, and the vituperation is as much directed at the narrator himself as at the ostensible object of his rage, the faithless Corinna. Several passages serve almost as exorcism, an attempt to root out a love for an unworthy object – and indeed, Freud points out that many men are emotionally drawn only to sexual partners they despise, seeing women as unattainable angels, surrogates for the mother, or as whores, pits of iniquity.[45] If the poem is ultimately unsuccessful, it is because the verbal and emotional energies which are unleashed are not sufficiently kept under control. The power of these images of hate, fear and physical aversion is unmistakable, but the narrator is not treated with enough distance, so that one is tempted to read the lines as evidence of emotional pathology:

> Did ever I refuse to bear
> The meanest part your Lust could spare[?]
> When your lewd Cunt came spewing home
> Drench't with the seed of halfe the Town
> My dram of sperm was sup't up after
> For the digestive surfeit water.
> Full gorged at another time
> With a vast meal of nasty slime
> Which your devouring Cunt had drawn
> From Porters Backs and Footmens brawn
> I was content to serve you up
> My Ballock full for your Grace cupp.   (111–22)

The contrast between the 'dram' or cup and the 'vast meal' on which she is 'gorged' night after night – wittily presented here as his contribution to aid her digestion – again presents women's sexual appetites as boundless, men's as finite. Though on one level the lines serve to justify her promiscuity (since no single man could satisfy lust of such monumental proportions), the terms by which Corinna is described consistently carry strong negative connotations. The emotional weight of the passage finds concentrated expression in a series of highly charged verbs and participles, which evoke visual and kinetic image of an unsettling kind: 'spewing', 'Drench't', 'gorged', 'devouring', all suggesting not only moral disapproval but physical aversion. Corinna is described as a sexual glutton, eating to repletion, making herself physically disgusting by her inability to stop. As in 'I rise at eleven', sexual climax and vomiting are equated, and as in the 'scepter' lampoon, the object of satire, and by implication all humanity, are reduced to bodily functions, denied reason or volition as they are turned into grotesque perambulating sexual organs. The difference between these poems and 'A Ramble' is that there the destructive impulses are turned outward, with the cleansing, cathartic effect of satire: 'there were some people that could not be kept in Order, or admonished but in this way'.[46] Here on the other hand, the impulse of hatred is turned inward, and self-abasement, impotent rage, a vision of a universe befouled become indexes of a disappointed idealism.

In the closing lines, the gap between narrator and author narrows, but Rochester's control over his rhetoric permits the passage to be read as a satiric peroration and a final triumph over the feared rival: 'Daddy, daddy, you bastard, I'm through'. The lines, which take the form of a solemn curse or anathema, serve as a farewell to love, a demonstration of the terrible powers of the satirist to kill or maim, and an affirmation of the ability of art to endure when the emotions of the moment have passed. As parallel passages in Wyatt, Donne and Plath show, the curse, or the exorcism of the troubling demon, is enacted in the poem, as narrator and poet merge.[47] The words, both uttered and inscribed on the page, are able to serve an expressive function, while gaining the autonomy of art:

> In that most lamentable state
> I'le make her feel my scorn and hate
> Pelt her with scandalls, Truth or lies
> And her poor Curr with Jealousies
> Till I have torn him from her Breech
> While she whines like a Dogg-drawn Bitch
> Loath'd, and despis'd, Kick't out of Town
> Into some dirty Hole alone
> To chew the Cudd of Misery
> And know she owes it all to Mee.
>   And may no Woman better thrive
> That dares prophane the Cunt I swive. (155–66)

Though the final couplet to some extent withdraws sympathy from the protagonist, showing his 'Revenge' (153) to be the product of hurt pride, in general the concluding curse serves to objectify and provide some resolution to the conflicting emotions in the poem. Even the image of the dog pulled bodily away from a bitch in heat, shocking in its physicality and its devaluation of human sexuality, is less a frontal assault on Corinna's 'prowd disdain' (36) and the reader's comforting illusions than it is a metaphor for human incompleteness, the afflictions that all flesh is heir to. The tone is akin to that in Wyatt's 'My lute awake' ('Perchance thee lie, wither'd and old . . .'): to speak of compassion would underestimate the predominant aggressiveness, but we are led to see Corinna's final state, 'Loath'd', 'despis'd', cast out, as pathetic and frightening, however much she may deserve punishment. If the closing lines are a triumph of hate, the passage and the poem as a whole makes us feel what a sterile, unsatisfactory emotion hate is.

If all pleasure is illusory – as this poem, no less than 'I rise at eleven' and 'The Imperfect Enjoyment', shows – then pain, inflicted or felt on the pulses, is the only thing that distinguishes the living from the dead. Rochester's pursuit of vain pleasure, knowing it to be vain, thus serves the purpose of self-flagellation, and at the same time seeks to test the limits of sensory experience. It is a challenge directed at a universe devoid of apparent meaning: without God, everything is possible.

> Absent from thee I languish still,
> Then aske me not, when I return?
> The straying Fool 'twill plainly kill,
> To wish all Day, all Night to Mourn.
>
> ('Absent from thee', 1–4)

As a justification of inconstancy, a poetic message to the recipient (along the lines of several letters quoted earlier in the chapter) that the poet loves her after all, in spite of spending all these nights away, the opening stanza of 'Absent from thee' is odd indeed. First he says he hasn't been enjoying himself all that much, so that if she's unhappy, he's more unhappy: though he may appear to have been dissolved in ecstacy in the arms of one or another rival, what he's *really* been doing in these strange beds is weeping. At no point does he deny his sexual infidelity to her (note the reference to 'some base heart' in the final stanza); instead, he treats it as producing pain, not pleasure. 'Ask me not when I return' means 'I can't tell you when I'll return, because my actions are not within my power', with the further implication that all human desires are doomed to unfulfilment. Suffering thus becomes a test, through which, however unworthy he has been so far, his impurities may be scourged away; or, more likely, suffering can provide him with a series of increasing tortures, ending in the death which, because of his transgressions, he deserves. The primary emotion in this powerful, beautiful poem would appear to be a displacement of religious sentiment, with the estranged mistress (in this case, Rochester's wife, ensconced in Adderbury) filling the place of an absent God, withholding approval and confirming his sense of abandonment, his conviction that he is unable to change. Though the emotion expressed in his celebrated drunken assault on the glass sundial at Whitehall is far cruder, the incident serves a similar existential function as an attempt, however ludicrous, to overcome feelings of ontological insecurity, passivity, helplessness: 'Dost thou stand here to fuck Time?'[48] Here the destructive impulses are turned outward, as a rival, equipped with a permanent erection beyond the dreams of men, is rendered powerless. The act is a direct challenge to authority and respectability: immediately, to the King, surrogate father and embodiment of order in the family and the state, and another, more philosophical level, to time, to mortality, to the implacable gods who rule the hostile universe. Overtly, the act is an assertion of the poet's masculine side and a denial of the feminine passivity evident in 'Absent from thee': rather than defending time against her ravisher, he is displaying his own superior masculinity, attempting to master time with his penis. In the last act of 'Sodom', parodying the characteristic rhetoric of heroic drama, the deluded tyrant Bolloximian declaims in comic hybris:

> I'le heaven invade and bugger all the Gods
> And drein the spring of their Imortal Codds
> I'le make em rubb till Prick and ballocks Cry
> You've frightn'd us out of imortality.   (v.ii, pp. 142–3)

Here, as in the sundial incident, the exaggerated claims of human power, by their comic inappropriateness, become confessions of weakness, testimony to the futility of desire.

CHAPTER 3

Absent from thee

In his uneasy dualism, Rochester is entirely at one with his age. In both France and England, libertinism was the product of a highly centralised, competitive court society whose most articulate members were conscious of the increasing marginality and power-lessness of the social class to which they belonged and with which they identified. Sir Carr Scroope's contemptuous taunt, 'thy Pen, is full as harmlesse as thy Sword', applied not only to Rochester but to a hereditary nobility more and more stripped of real power and reduced to displays of ritual.[1] Though politically France and England differed greatly – one a smoothly functioning absolute monarchy, the other a bitterly divided, inefficient state obsessed with the memory of Civil War and regicide – the intellectual climate in which the court libertines of France and England moved was strikingly similar.

Art is by no means a mere precipitate of social and economic forces: as Barbara Everett has said in her essay on Rochester, 'a work of art is recognized by its incapacity to be absorbed wholly by the society which produces it, and which it represents so admirably'.[2] Sartre has defined the artist in existentialist terms as free in his awareness of his situation, able to give expression to a common predicament. Lucien Goldmann argues a similar position with regard to the writers of seventeenth-century France, whose works like those of Rochester presuppose a close identification between artist and audience. In Sartre's words: 'In trying to become clear about his own personal situation, he clarifies theirs for them. He mediates, names, and shows them the life they lead from day to day in its immediacy, the life they suffer without finding words to formulate their sufferings.'[3] And yet, as Sartre points out, innocence is lost in the act of writing and in the act of reading: self-conscious-ness implies guilt, and the more an artist sees himself as implicated in a society and its compromises, the greater will be his hostility toward his readers and paymasters.

If society sees itself and, in particular, sees itself as *seen*, there is, by virtue of this very fact, a contesting of the established values of the régime. The writer presents it with its image; he calls upon it to assume it or to change itself . . . Thus, the writer gives society a *guilty conscience*; he is thereby in a state of perpetual antagonism toward the conservative forces which are maintaining the balance he tends to upset . . . Functionally, he moves in opposition to the interests of those who keep him alive.[4]

The artist is thus a representative of his class and a traitor to it. Rochester's ambivalence toward authority is characteristic of his overall dualism: lyrics and satires alike are acts of rebellion against a condition of dependency, perceived simultaneously as intolerable and unalterable.

The contradiction at the heart of libertinism is that it asserts and denies human freedom. Libertinism is based on a perceived absence: in all the varied uses of the term in the seventeenth century – antinomian, religious sceptic, voluptuary, cocksman – the libertine is one who is free from moral law, either because he considers himself exempt or (more commonly) because in his view ethical norms are nonexistent or delusory.[5] To Rochester, as to the French seventeenth-century writers with whom Goldmann is concerned in *The Hidden God*, such freedom is not welcomed, but perceived with dread. The situation is a classic double-bind: what the mind perceives as true, the heart feels as an aching void. 'I rise at eleven', 'A Ramble in Saint James's Parke' and *A Satyr against Mankind* in their different ways all assert a freedom that mocks and entraps in its denial of value 'beyond material sense' (*Satyr against Mankind*, 67). The delicate balance of belief and unbelief, the yearning for a transcendence for which the analytical intellect, trained in habits of scepticism, can find no rational grounds, marks Rochester as the child of his time. 'That God should be always absent and always present', Goldmann argues, is for both Pascal and Racine the 'centre of the tragic vision'.[6]

In his *Pensées*, Pascal engages in a dialogue with contemporary French libertinism, addressing his arguments to those who 'want to be cured of unbelief'. His implicit audience is courtly, educated, committed (as Pascal himself was) to the ideal of the *honnête homme*, aware of and sympathetic to the advanced scientific thought of the time.[7] But though his arguments are tailored to the capacities and interests of his audience of worldly sceptics, he is uncompromising in his attitude toward their cherished values. The world's ways and God's ways are incompatible, and reason, efficient enough in its own sphere, is wholly impotent when faced with areas of experience beyond its province: 'Nous connaissons la verité non seulement par la raison mais encore par la coeur.' Pascal shares with the Rochester of the *Satyr* a concern to 'humble reason', but to an entirely different end, and indeed the equation of man with beast in the writings of some of Rochester's French libertine predecessors is one of the fallacies Pascal most strongly attacks. Where Rochester in the *Satyr* exalts 'certain instinct' (10) above the phantoms of reason, Pascal sees both instinct and reason as fallible guides to a higher truth toward which we may aspire.[8]

Pascal distinguishes two kinds of libertine atheists: those who are indifferent, uncaring, occupied only with the round of momentary diversions, 'without a thought for the final end of life', and the guilt-ridden, unhappy, questing atheists, in search of a conviction they cannot find. It is 'the atheists who seek',[9] trapped by allegiance to metaphysical and moral principles they feel to be hollow, but unable to make the leap into faith, who provide the other side of the dialogue in the *Pensées*. If the voice we hear in the *Pensées* at times strikingly resembles that in Rochester's poems, it is because both see the dialogue between faith and doubt as an internal debate, a quarrel with oneself, and see human bondage to an illusory freedom as meriting compassion as well as scorn.

'Doubt and anxiety', as Pascal sees them, are the potential breeding grounds for faith, though they may equally lead to despair and a sense of abandonment. It is no mere coincidence that the libertine poet Des Barreaux, cited by Pascal as one who would 'renounce reason and become a brute beast', like Rochester, ended his career of blasphemy and defiance with a spectacular religious conversion: 'Si je ne puis vivement croire,/Ayde à mon incredulité'.[10] As we have seen with Rochester, the radicalism of the questioning of authority in libertine thought was itself productive of anxiety: the category of blasphemy ceases to be meaningful outside a framework of generally accepted faith, and Don Giovanni's invitation to the statue is simultaneously a gesture of defiance and a request for chastisement. From the first notes of Mozart's overture, with its ominous 'statue' motif, we know Don Giovanni's cry of *viva la libertá* will ring hollow. When Donna Anna, Donna Elvira and Don

Ottavio echo the same words, they have an entirely different meaning in mind, and their harmony ironically prefigures Don Giovanni's ultimate defeat. The libertine assertion of self, as Pascal points out, denies the existence of any principle of order beyond the self: 'En un mot le moi a deux qualités. Il est injuste en soi en ce qu'il se fait centre de tout. Il est incommode aux autres en ce qu'il les veux asservir, car chaque moi est l'ennemi et voudrait être le tyran de tous les autres.' Where Pascal differs from Hobbes and the libertines, whose analysis of human motivation is otherwise strikingly similar, is in his insistent use of evaluative terms: 'injuste', or earlier in this paragraph, 'le moi est haïssable'. If 'la pente vers soi est le commencement de tout désordre', then to Pascal a countervailing principle is necessary to restore the balance. But if, as with Rochester, the desire to escape from the desert of self is accompanied by an inability to find any stable values, or grounds to believe in them, the results must be a sense of impasse and a longing for deliverance: 'C'est donc une manifeste injustice où nous sommes nés, dont nous ne pouvons nous défaire et dont il faut nous défaire.'[11]

The particular affliction to which Pascal applies the traditional term 'despair' involves deep feelings of unworthiness, focused on a sense of exclusion from the company of the blest. Standard psychoanalytical theory, both Freudian and Kleinian, would associate such feelings with the half-remembered pain of parental rejection at an early age.[12] Yet 'the despair of the atheists', as Pascal presents it, differs from Faustus's conviction that he is irrevocably damned, in itself a form of pride, a competitive assertiveness in sin. Rather, it suggests that the libertines know half of a truth, which partially liberates and partially enchains: 'Il est également dangereux à l'homme de connaître Dieu sans connaître sa misère, et de connaître sa misère sans connaître le Rédempteur qui l'en peut guérir.'

The capacity for thought, the gift of reason, is for Pascal the source of the atheist's dilemma, but also provides a way of finally resolving it. Self-consciousness is a curse and a blessing, the origin of guilt, pain, the sense of alienation and wretchedness: 'Le grandeur de l'homme est grande en ce qu'il se connait misérable; un arbre ne se connait pas misérable.'[13] Here he parts company from Rochester and the philosophical libertines. In the *Satyr against Mankind*, Rochester like Des Barreaux argues that reason is an affliction and only that: the desire to 'know' and not simply, like the beasts, to 'enjoy', is the cause of unhappiness which Rochester presents as foolish and unnecessary: 'His wisdom did his happiness destroy,/ Aiming to know that *World* he shou'd enjoy' (33-3).[14] Yet, as I shall argue later in this chapter, the libertine assertion of the joys of thoughtlessness in itself embodies a paradox, which contains the seeds of its own overthrow. Like Pascal, Rochester employs reason to rebuke reason: the *Satyr* is carefully argued, using the structure of a deliberative oration or formal academic dispute, with the arguments of an opposing debater presented and refuted.[15] In similar fashion, the poem uses wit (puns, metaphors, antitheses, neatly turned couplets) to prove that wit is no more than a 'vain frivolous pretence' (35), which inevitably turns against its possessor. The *'Paradox'* (221) on which the poem's arguments are based is not simply, as Walker maintains,[16] a challenge thrown at the accepted orthodoxy of the age, by inverting the customary elevation of man above beast. Beasts cannot argue or write poems: the very existence of the *Satyr against Mankind* thus serves as an instance of 'wantonness' rather than 'necessity' (138), demonstrating in every witty analogy or closely reasoned definition the very alienation from the natural kingdom it purports to rectify.

It is entirely consistent, therefore, that Rochester should conclude the first section with a firm 'I'le nere recant' (113), and yet end the poem, stating specific conditions: 'I'le here recant my *Paradox* to them' (221). The textual status of the recantation or coda which concludes the poem (lines 174–225 in the Walker edition) is uncertain. The two versions of the poem, with and without the 'Apology' or 'Addition', are equally well represented in contemporary manuscript miscellanies and early printed editions. The first published edition (1679) contains the shorter version, as do *Poems, &c. on Several Occasions* (1691) and ten MSS, where *Poems on Several Occasions* (1680) and eleven MSS include the longer version. One edition (*Miscellaneous Works of Rochester and Roscommon*, 1707) and two MSS include the coda only. In all probability, the original poem ended with line 173, and the concluding section is an afterthought, commenting on and qualifying what has gone before. The opening lines of the 'Apology' are retrospective, not only in their change of tense ('All this with indignation have I hurl'd', 174) but in their explicit stance of commenting on an already established text, to which the final lines may add an explanatory gloss. The first version can conjecturally be dated 1674, and the additional lines after 24 February 1675, when Edward Stillingfleet attacked '*Saty-*

rical Invectives against *Reason*' embodying a 'wish, to have been Beasts rather than men' in a sermon preached before the King.[17] The recantation largely consists of satire directed at courtiers and churchmen, with a specific dig at Stillingfleet in lines 195–7. Its argument can be paraphrased: if there are just and pious men, my paradox is refuted; but there are no such men; therefore the paradox still stands. And yet though the burden of the satire suggests that it is empirically unlikely that there can be a single 'just Man' (180) among the corrupt courtiers, a single '*Church-Man* who on *God* relyes' (191) among the bloated worldly prelates, the existence of one exception would destroy the entire edifice of argument Rochester had built up, since he is purporting to prove universal truths applicable to 'all Men' (158) – or, as Stillingfleet puts it, 'to represent all the World as alike bad altho' not alike cunning'.[18]

There is no doubt that the coda is a retreat from the radical implications of the earlier position, adopting a far more conventional moral stance. The concluding couplet, though no less indebted to traditions of libertine scepticism, abandons the boldness of the first part of the poem for a series of tame concessions to an opponent, scorned earlier, who suddenly appear to have the best of the argument:

> If such there are, yet grant me this at least,
> *Man* differs more from *Man*, than *Man* from *Beast*.   (224–5)[19]

The added lines, carefully designed (But if . . . If . . . Is there . . . But . . .) to lead up to this highly qualified conclusion, are social satire of a kind familiar in the period, an attack on specific abuses in church and state, with clearly stated standards of judgement. Positive terms are balanced against negative: if some politicians accept bribes, others, at least in theory, may be 'upright' and 'unbyass'd' (185–6), and worldly clergymen are found wanting in the conservative terms of the theology they profess, as Rochester explicitly works in the names of six of the Seven Deadly Sins.[20] The suggestion in these lines, entirely at variance with the Hobbesian naturalism of the rest of the poem, is that moral standards are unchanging, valid whether or not at any given moment there are individuals who put them into practice. Where the first 173 lines dismiss all human pretences at virtue as folly and hypocrisy, arguing from Hobbesian materialist premises that men must inevitably turn '*Knaves* . . . in their own defence' (160), the 'Apology' negotiates terms of surren-

der with the orthodoxy the rest of the poem attacks. Indeed, the
closing lines exemplify a striving after spirituality which the earlier
part of the poem castigates as arrant folly. The lines are precisely
balanced between a suppliant's humility and a satirist's arrogance,
between belief and unbelief:

> But a meek humble Man, of honest sense,
> Who Preaching peace, does practice continence;
> Whose pious life's a proof he does believe,
> Misterious truths, which no *Man* can conceive.
> If upon *Earth* there dwell such *God-like Men*,
> I'le here recant my *Paradox* to them,
> Adore those *Shrines* of *Virtue*, *Homage* pay,
> And with the *Rabble World*, their *Laws* obey.   (216–23)

Consistency with the earlier philosophical satire, materialist in its
assumptions and pessimistic in its tone, would require the lines to be
read with some ironic reservations: men must be either godlike or
the 'basest' (128) of all creatures, with no possibility of an intermedi-
ate state. Yet the prevalent religious imagery here reflects the sense
of guilt we have seen elsewhere in Rochester, and the yearning for
deliverance from the prison of the flesh which Pascal sees as the
hallmarks of the God-haunted atheist.

The dilemma of the seventeenth-century libertine rests in his
inability to emancipate himself from traditional dualistic thinking,
which provides the very terms by which he perceives experience.
Though the epilogue may be an afterthought, calling into question
all that has gone before, it only makes explicit a conflict adumbrated
earlier in the poem. To Pascal as to Rochester, the divine and the
human are incommensurable: man is condemned to live in darkness
and misery, on a desert island from which there appears to be no
means of escape.[21] The unbridgeable gap between the human '*Myte*'
and 'the Infinite', the painful discrepancy between man's distorted
image of himself and what that flattering delusion seeks to hide, are
to both authors an object of compassion as well as scorn:

> This supernatural gift, that makes a *Myte* –,
> Think he's the Image of the Infinite:
> Comparing his short life, void of all rest,
> To the *Eternal*, and the ever blest . . .   (76–9)

Rochester in these lines may be rebuking spiritual pretensions,
where Pascal seeks to show that spiritual reality is ultimately all that
matters, yet the two writers present the human condition in essen-

tially the same terms. Though the Rochesterian deity here has Epicurean characteristics (existing, remote from human striving, in 'an Everlasting Age, of perfect Peace'), the emotional weight of the passage suggests a longing for a recovered wholeness, a desire to achieve the transcendence the lines stigmatise as '*Nonsense*' (189).[22]

Pascal no less than Hobbes and Rochester sees the human condition as 'void of all rest': 'Et ainsi le présent ne nous satisfaisant jamais, l'experience nous pipe, et de malheur en malheur nous mène jusqu'à la mort qui en est un comble éternel.' Yet though all three writers see men as driven by an endless search for diversion, preferring the hunt to the capture,[23] and fruitlessly pursuing a satisfaction they can never find, the lesson which Pascal draws from the ubiquity of human craving is diametrically opposed to the position argued in the first 173 lines of the *Satyr against Mankind*. If the absence of God from human affairs is the unspoken premise on which both the epilogue and the rest of the poem is based, only the epilogue, in recanting the defiant materialist assertions of the first part, accepts Pascal's conclusions. The first part of the poem argues that man must learn to live without God; the epilogue, that man must seek God.

The argument of the epilogue suggests a means of filling the infinite void, by finding a worthy object of 'Homage' and adoration. In this passage the imagery is implicitly Platonic rather than Epicurean, since it assumes that proximate objects of desire can lead one toward attaining oneness with the transcendent Form.[24] A similar assumption, equally inconsistent with the earlier part of the *Satyr*, underlies a number of Rochester's love poems. In 'The Mistress', rather than positing an irremediable separation between earthbound humanity and the 'blest' deity (*Satyr against Mankind*, 79), the poet claims that the painful emotions of anxiety, doubt and fear have a beneficial effect in that they 'Prove our Hearts Treasure fixt and dear,/And make us blest at last' ('The Mistress', 35–6). Restoration libertinism is full of such contradictions, since the assertion of self is always a cry for deliverance from self: there is no God, and may God strike me dead if I am wrong. On the materialist premises of the first part of the *Satyr against Mankind*, anyone who is fool enough to 'believe' in 'Misterious truths, which no *Man* can conceive' (218–19) must be self-deluded. Such belief in a world inaccessible to sense is subjected to a relentless barrage of deflating comparisons showing it to be chimerical: it is an '*Ignis fatuus*', a

'*Vapour*', a '*Cheat*', a recourse to 'Bladders' which seek to keep the desperate swimmer afloat in a 'boundless Sea' or, most dismissive and cutting of all: 'So charming Oyntments, make an Old Witch flie,/And bear a Crippled Carcass through the Skie' (12, 23, 106, 19–21, 86–7). Yet in none of these passages is the anger unmixed with pity for the victims of charlatanry and illusion: a 'Crippled Carcass' can never be an object of mere contempt, especially if it is one's own. What is despised (75) – and this is true of the entire poem, including the epilogue – is the self and its weaknesses and fears.

The recantation is a recurrent feature in a libertinism which inevitably defines itself in terms of opposition to an established order. All the libertine can say in the end is 'no'. In the epilogue to *Don Giovanni* – yet another partial recantation, frequently criticised as a sop to the orthodox and sometimes omitted in performance as anticlimactic – comic harmony succeeds tragic dissonance, as the remaining characters pair off, seek new employment and go about their business of rational compromise.[25] The morality in the words they sing is as impeccable as the music to which the words are set is conventional and efficient. It is the victory of the corporate spirit over the individual: one passage is even set fugally, with Donna Elvira and then Zerlina, no longer willing victims of the clever seducer, introducing the melodic line which the others take up in turn. In the previous scene (an extended Mozartian finale which concludes the opera's main action), the Commendatore represents all those forces Don Giovanni has defied – the family, the church, the honour traditionally due to age and rank, the demand of reparation under a strict and exacting moral code, the iron bands of nemesis by which men pay for their past misdeeds. Neither the music nor the dramatic action leaves any doubt who will win the final confrontation. And yet Don Giovanni remains defiant to the last, even amid the swirling fires of hell. Though we know – and Don Giovanni knows – the Commendatore's 'si' is as unanswerable as his ice-cold grip, the libertine hero's consistent response, repeated six times with increasing intensity, is 'no'. Elvira runs away and Leporello cowers at the sight of the stone visitor, but Don Giovanni, ever the aristocrat, welcomes the apparition courteously, retaining his courage, his integrity and his habit of defiance to the end. The tragic force of the scene comes from the clash of two incompatible imperatives, explicitly presented here as flesh and spirit, the glory in the moment and the sober truth of eternal judgement. Neither effaces the other, so that the libertine's inevitable defeat embodies a kind of triumph. Who has ever watched the opera and wanted to be Don Ottavio? Who has ever watched the opera and not wanted to be Don Giovanni?

Of all libertine lyrics of seduction, perhaps the most subversive is *La ci darem*. Morality, respectability, caution, the stability of marriage – all are helpless before the insinuating melody of desire, the naturalist arguments of the body's 'si'. We are seduced together with Zerlina: 'Vorrei e non vorrei/Mi trema un poco il cor.' When Zerlina echoes Don Giovanni's melodic phrases, we know she has already half-accepted his arguments and will eventually obey his 'andiam'. The stages of the seduction are enacted in the music of the duet, in which Don Giovanni's bold, ringing call to trust the impulse of the moment, leaving all hesitation and delay behind, is met with weaker and weaker resistance: 'presto non son più forte, non son più forte, non son più forte'. When the two voices unite, the words they sing confirm the mutuality of desire: there is no irony in the phrase 'un innocente amor', as the exultation of the music overrides any possible moral or practical objections. Kierkegaard, in his brilliant essay, sees Don Giovanni as life-affirming, as he releases the erotic potential in those on whom he fixes his attention:

But what is this force, then, by which Don Juan seduces? It is desire, the energy of sensuous desire. He desires in every woman the whole of womanhood, and therein lies the sensuously idealizing power with which he at once embellishes and overcomes his prey. The reaction to this gigantic passion beautifies and develops the one desired, who flushes in enhanced beauty by its reflection.[26]

Yet, as Kierkegaard points out, the libertine hero is inevitably a product of the very dualism of flesh and spirit he seeks momentarily to transcend. Don Giovanni must always confront the Commendatore, each reminding the other of what he lacks. My argument in this chapter is that the libertine assertion of freedom contains both a 'si' and a 'no' – on the one hand, a celebration of the instincts of the moment; on the other, a dogged, even Quixotic resistance against those forces it knows it can never defeat, which will be satisfied with nothing less than a recantation.

As we have seen, Rochester was strongly affected by the philosophy of Hobbes, with its unflattering view of man, its doctrinaire materialism and its ethical relativism. As a practical atheist in the Hobbesian manner (not, as he told Burnet, 'an entire Atheist, who fully believed there was no God', but one whose 'Notion of this Being . . . amounted to no more than a vast Power, that had none of the Attributes of Goodness or Justice, we ascribe to the Deity'), Rochester could find no natural or supernatural sanctions to govern human behaviour. Rejecting any element of transcendent spirituality as delusory or unproved, considering conventional religion and morality to be mere sham, he advanced arguments for a hedonist ethic in his conversations with Burnet similar in many ways to those in the 'reforming will' passage of the *Satyr against Mankind*:

> Upon this he told me the two *Maxims* of his *Morality* then were, that he should do nothing to the hurt of any other, or that might prejudice his own health: And he thought that all Pleasure, when it did not interfere with these, was to be indulged as the gratification of our natural Appetites. It seemed unreasonable to imagine these were put into a man only to be restrained, or curbed to such a narrowness.[27]

It is clear from Burnet's account that the two participants in the friendly debate were arguing from incompatible premises. The notion that there might be a 'higher principle' beyond the calculation of advantages or the prompting of impulse was, according to the libertine creed, simply inadmissible. The material is seen as real, solid, evidential, where the existence of any spiritual dimension is at best speculative. What one man might interpret as the inward stirrings of spiritual regeneration, 'he said must be the effect of a heat in Nature . . . he did not doubt but if one could turn to a *Problem* in *Euclid* . . . it would have the same effect'.[28] In passages like this, Rochester is not so much presenting arguments for materialism as appealing to materialist assumptions, taken as self-evident, in order to deflate what he considers cant or self-deception.

A similar polemical strategy informs the poem 'Fair *Cloris* in a Piggsty lay', though here as in the *Satyr against Mankind*, Rochester uses his control over the poetic medium to win the reader's assent to the devaluation of the spiritual or ideal as contrary to 'Nature':

> Fair *Cloris* in a Piggsty lay
>   Her tender herd lay by her
> She slept; in murmring Gruntlings they
> Complayneing of the scorching Day
>   Her slumbers thus inspire . . .

> Frighted she wakes and wakeing Friggs
>   Nature thus kindly eas'd
> In dreams rais'd by her murmring Piggs
> And her own Thumb between her leggs
>   She's Innocent and pleas'd.   (1–5, 36–40)

The effortless evocation of pastoral conventions in the diction of the opening stanza – 'Fair *Cloris*,' 'tender', 'murmring', 'Complayneing', even the 'scorching Day', as in Marvell's 'Damon the Mower' – reassures the reader by the familiarity of the poetic landscape, and this effect is reinforced by the Latinate syntax of lines 3–5, with its suspended period. But the presence of the unaccommodating pigs from the outset of the poem renders the familiar treacherous: the dream of love is exposed as a masturbatory fantasy, stirred up by the physical propinquity of Cloris's fellow animals. The blunt physicality of the language and action in the final stanza suggests that Rochester's object of attack, here as elsewhere, is not only the illusion of female 'Honor' (27) – a familiar enough target in the anti-Platonic, naturalist tradition in which he is writing – but any attempts to *'dignifie'* human *'Nature*, above *Beast'* (*Satyr against Mankind*, 65).[29] Technically Cloris remains 'Innocent' because she manages to eat her cake and have it too, preserving her virginity while pleasing herself manually. But the clear implication of the two final stanzas is that *all* sexual gratification is innocent – if the defloration of the penultimate stanza ('Now pierced is her virgin Zoan', 31) had been real, as it first appears, rather than an embodiment of Cloris's as yet unfulfilled desires, it would remain an act of natural instinct, not subject to moral condemnation. In contrast, Burnet in his conversations with Rochester consistently treats 'Nature' as fallen and sinful. His position, conservative and orthodox, is that a standard of judgement beyond 'Appetite', the fulfilment of bodily needs, was essential to avoid moral chaos:

There is not strength enough in that Principle to subdue Nature, and Appetite . . . And that could not be effected, except a mans Nature were internally regenerated, and changed by a higher Principle: Till that came about, corrupt Nature would be strong, and *Philosophy* but feeble: especially when it struggled with such Appetites or Passions as were much kindled, or deeply rooted in the Constitution of ones Body. This, he said, sounded to him like *Enthusiasme*, or *Canting*: He had no notion of it, and so could not understand it: He comprehended the Dictates of *Reason* and *Philosophy*, in which as the Mind became more conversant, there would soon follow as he believed, a greater easiness in obeying its Precepts.[30]

The optimism of these last remarks, in which the mind is presented as gradually becoming habituated to reason's dictates and thus able to slide easily into virtue, is relatively rare in Rochester. A similar complacency can be detected in the 'two *Maxims* of his *Morality*' cited by Burnet: though doctrine cannot entirely be judged by practice, neither Rochester's vocation as a satirist nor his compulsive self-destructiveness inspires confidence in the solidity of these principles of natural restraint. There are passages in the *Satyr against Mankind*, more carefully argued, which are compatible with the conservative morality of the poem's distant source, Boileau's Satire VIII, or even of Bacon or Milton:

> But thoughts, are giv'n, for Actions government,
> Where Action ceases, thoughts impertinent:
> Our *Sphere* of Action, is lifes happiness,
> And he who thinks Beyond, thinks like an *Ass*.   (95–8)

Here the object of Rochester's attack, as in Raphael's mild rebuke to the inquisitive Adam, is the abuse of reason when it concerns itself with 'things remote/From use, obscure and subtle' rather than 'what concerns thee and thy being'. The passage assumes there is a proper as well as an improper use of reason.[31] Boileau's satire attacks the pride and folly which lead man to behave as though he had neither reason nor sense – the ass, he says, is wiser than man, because he does not, with his bizarre voice, challenge the birds to a singing contest – but his contrast of sensible beast and foolish man does not denigrate the gift of reason itself, as Rochester does in many passages.

> L'Ambition, l'Amour, l'Avarice, ou la Haine,
> Tiennent comme un forçat son esprit à la chaine . . .
> L'Homme seul, l'Homme seul en sa fureur extrême
> Met un brutal honneur à s'égorger soi-même.

Rochester like Boileau draws on the tradition of theriophily (the inversion of the customary hierarchy of beast and man) in his satire, but in a way which is more philosophically serious and more pessimistic.[32]

In both the *Satyr against Mankind* and Boileau's Satire VIII, 'lifes happiness' is defined in essentially hedonistic terms. At the outset of his poem, Boileau sets forth an Epicurean definition of 'Sagesse', never challenged by the 'docteur de Sorbonne' who serves as interlocutor, which applies equally to beasts and men:

Qu'est-ce que la Sagesse? Une égalité d'ame,
Que rien ne peut troubler, qu'aucun desir n'enflâme.

In contrast, Rochester allows no possibility of serenity either in the animal kingdom or among humans. Where Boileau's animals, all seemingly herbivorous, respect one another's territory, obeying their guides, nature and instinct, 'sans murmure', Rochester's world of nature is a Hobbesian jungle, where 'Savage *Man*' outdoes the beasts in bestiality:

> *Birds*, feed on *Birds*, *Beasts*, on each other prey,
> But Savage *Man* alone, does *Man*, betray:
> Prest by necessity, they Kill for Food,
> *Man*, undoes *Man*, to do himself no good.   (129–32)[33]

The closest equivalent in the *Satyr* to Boileau's definition of 'Sagesse' occurs about halfway through Rochester's poem, and it is characteristically Hobbesian rather than Epicurean in its assumptions: wisdom is an efficient matching of ends to means, exemplified by a quick kill.

> Those *Creatures*, are the wisest who attain,
> By surest means, the ends at which they aim.
> If therefore *Jowler*, finds, and Kills his *Hares*,
> Better than *Meres*, supplyes Committee Chairs;
> Though one's a *States-man*, th'other but a *Hound*,
> *Jowler*, in Justice, wou'd be wiser found.   (117–22)

The comparison here, as so often in Rochester, is meant to shock, rather than to appeal to accepted truths held in common by author and reader as *honnêtes hommes*. Rather than presenting idealised beasts as moral exemplars, Rochester is reducing man's empty pretensions of 'Wisdom, Pow'r, and Glory' (154) to a material base, exposing moral abstractions as fraudulent.[34]

The opening lines of the *Satyr*, as Ken Robinson has remarked, simultaneously assert and deny materialism, as they present man as alienated from the untroubled existence of the natural creation by the burden of self-consciousness. 'Two apparently irreconcilable ways of regarding human experience' are manifest even in the convoluted syntax, expressing a condition disclaimed in advance as unattainable:

> Were I (who to my cost already am
> One of those strange prodigious Creatures *Man*)
> A Spirit free, to choose for my own share,

> What Case of Flesh, and Blood, I pleas'd to weare,
> I'd be a *Dog*, a *Monkey*, or a *Bear*,
> Or any thing but that vain *Animal*,
> Who is so proud of being rational. $(1-7)^{35}$

The equivalent passage in Boileau's Satire VIII is much cooler and more Olympian, with none of the element of self-reflexive regret. Rochester's use of the first person not only works effectively as a rhetorical device to ensnare the reader, but introduces elements of guilt and pain entirely foreign to Boileau's satire:

> De tous les Animaux qui s'élevent dans l'air,
> Qui marchent sur la terre, ou nagent dans la mer,
> De Paris ou Perou, du Japon jusqu'à Rome,
> Le plus sot animal, à mon avis, c'est l'homme.[36]

What limits man's freedom, Rochester's lines imply, is not so much his inability to choose his destiny as his ability to imagine an alternative destiny. By being wholly determined, paradoxically, beasts are free, where man, trapped in a dualism of flesh and spirit, is unable to achieve a 'happiness' (33) which for the beasts is wholly unproblematic. Curiously, the classical fragment which probably provides a source for the initial conceit is unencumbered by the dualistic vocabulary in which 'Flesh, and Blood' serve as a 'Case' for 'Spirit', and its tone has none of the baffled anger of Rochester's first three lines. Instead, it offers a comic myth of metempsychosis in which wishes can be granted at once: 'If one of the gods should say to me, "Crato, when you die, you shall immediately be reborn and you shall be whatever you wish, a dog, a sheep, a goat, a man, a horse . . . Choose whatever you wish." "Anything," I think I should immediately say, "make me anything rather than a man."'[37]

The fundamental inconsistency in the poem, encapsulated in lines 6–7, is that Rochester's object of attack is at times the correctable fault of pride (as with Boileau in Satire VIII and Pope in *An Essay on Man*), at times the capacity of reason itself.[38] His redefinition of 'right Reason' in libertine terms as the '*Friend*', not opponent, of appetite defiantly proclaims a Hobbesian materialism by which ethical choice is reduced to immediate response to physical stimuli:

> Your *Reason* hinders, mine helps t'enjoy,
> Renewing Appetites, yours wou'd destroy.
> My Reason is my *Friend*, yours is a *Cheat*,
> Hunger call's out, my Reason bids me eat;

Perversely yours, your Appetite does mock,
This asks for Food, that answers what's a Clock?   (104–9)

If this seems unsatisfactory as a guide to conduct or as a positive norm
providing the satire's ethical centre, one cause may be that the lines
are too evidently manipulative in posing a false dichotomy. In their
clever sophistry, they illustrate the capacity they purport to deny.

A similar unresolved dilemma underlies the extended conceit
which immediately follows the initial statement of the polarity of
'certain instinct' and erring reason (10–11). But here the author
recognises and exploits the ambiguity which the doctrinaire materialism of the later passage slides over. The boundary lines between
the illusory and real are less clear-cut, as the passage pays tribute to
the power of the imagination to conjure up phantoms which become
palpable. In this allegorical episode, '*Reason*' is presented not as
empty speculation, or as perverse denial of solid fact, but as the
intuition of a realm of experience inaccessible to sense, and as such it
is an infinitely more formidable force than the feeble, caricatured
antagonist of the other passage.

These powerful lines embody the central paradox of the poem, in
the wrenching incompatibility between their emotional effect and
their ostensible ideological burden. What from one perspective is
avoidable folly is, from an alternative perspective, irremediable,
since the split between '*Mind*' (12) and body, illustrated in detail
after detail in the passage, erects an impassable barrier between man
and the happy beasts Rochester sets up as models. Gulliver,
embarked on his own hopeless quest, is in the course of Book IV of
Gulliver's Travels trapped within a similar dilemma, and here too
comic folly shades imperceptibly into tragic blindness.

> *Reason*, an *Ignis fatuus*, in the *Mind*,
> Which leaving light of *Nature*, sense behind;
> Pathless and dang'rous wandring ways it takes,
> Through errors Fenny-*Boggs*, and Thorny *Brakes*;
> Whilst the misguided follower, climbs with pain,
> *Mountains* of Whimseys, heap'd in his own *Brain*:
> Stumbling from thought to thought, falls headlong down,
> Into doubts boundless Sea, where like to drown,
> Books bear him up awhile, and make him try
> To swim with Bladders of *Philosophy*.   (12–21)

Thus far, the tone of the passage is delicately balanced. Strong
kinaesthetic words like 'Stumbling', 'headlong', 'heap'd', 'climbs

with pain' are charged with emotion, but their primary effect is not
so much to evoke sympathy for the misguided pilgrim as to promote
the reader's active participation in the laborious journey. The
dazzling brilliance of the conceit, with its periodic syntax extended
like a bridge over a chasm, deflects attention from subject to author
and thus serves as distancing device. Though evaluative terms like
'misguided', 'Whimseys', 'dang'rous', 'errors' provide grounds for
moral judgement, all these terms function metaphorically in an
allegorical narrative which, as in Spenser, Coleridge and Tolkien,
encourages suspension of judgement. By thus making abstractions
vividly concrete, in the manner of metaphysical wit or of Bunyanes-
que narrative – like the *Patricks Pilgrim* he treats with such scorn
later in the poem – Rochester effectively refutes his own materialist
premises.

The relationship of this passage to the tradition of the Christian
psychomachia is complex. On one level, the lines conduct a sustained polemic against accepted Christian belief in the dignity of
man, made in the image of God and graced with the unique gift of
reason. Rochester's method is a form of parody, as he adapts the
familiar materials of Christian apologetics to demonstrate that the
belief that man is enabled, through analytical and intuitive reason,
to 'search Heav'n and Hell, find out what's acted there,/And give
the World true grounds of hope and fear' (70–1), is vanity and
delusion. This allegorical episode is thus a *Pilgrim's Progress* in which
the pilgrim is tempted and besieged not by the enemies of faith,
internal and external, but by the myth that there is a transcendent
spiritual truth. Spenser's truth (*The Faerie Queene* I.i) is Rochester's
error, productive only of doubt and endless wandering in pathless
woods. A similar inversion characterises the poet's use of his immediate source for the '*Ignis fatuus*' image, a religious poem by Francis
Quarles, where the 'faire', 'deceitfull' tempter is lust. Rochester
exploits the traditional associations of the 'wandering fire' (*PL*, IX,
634) with the enchantment of sin and error, but places the temptation both inside and outside the mind, as a projection of a desire to
escape from unpalatable truths.[39] Some of the emotional complexity
of the passage comes from its compassionate treatment of man's need
to deceive himself: the 'pain' is real for the sufferer, the 'boundless
Sea' terrifying, even if they are in part self-created. The phantasma-
goric landscape of this episode, with its sudden, inexplicable transformations, is recognisably that of allegory – Griffin points out a

parallel with Vaughan's 'Regeneration' as well as Bunyan – and the emotional appeal of the passage is partly dependent on the traditional values and deeply-rooted fears thus conjured up.[40]

As the passage continues, the tone modulates toward the tragic, as the victims, if not the perpetrators, of illusion are treated with more pity than contempt. By returning to the physical image of the light dancing beyond the wanderer's reach, Rochester externalises the delusion, absolving the traveller from blame: it is like the concluding paragraph of *The Great Gatsby*, where the hero's quest is universalised as part of a tragic pattern over which individual actors have no control.

> In hopes still t'oretake th'escaping light,
> The *Vapour* dances in his dazzling sight,
> Till spent, it leaves him to eternal Night.
> Then Old Age, and experience, hand in hand,
> Lead him to death, and make him understand,
> After a search so painful, and so long,
> That all his Life he has been in the wrong;
> Hudled in dirt, the reas'ning *Engine* lyes,
> Who was so proud, so witty, and so wise.   (22–30)

The crushing finality of this epitaph to a wasted life is a product of the author's mastery of the rhetoric and form of the heroic couplet. After the triplet brings both the narrative of the arduous journey and the long periodic sentence to an end at their unexpected destination – the echoing phrase 'eternal Night' – three sombre epigrammatic couplets point the moral. These are virtually the first end-stopped and syntactically complete lines in the passage, and the first which make appreciable use of the caesura: it is as though the author, in keeping with the decorum of his subject matter, moves from a style which, except for the use of rhyme, resembles the 'sense variously drawn out' of Milton to one which anticipates the Pope of the *Moral Essays*. The grotesque deflating comedy of the splendidly physical 'Bladders of *Philosophy*' gives way to the quiet domesticity of 'hand in hand' and the slow stately movement of the procession to the tomb. Though there may be an ironic echo of the closing lines of *Paradise Lost*, Griffin is surely right in relating this passage to the 'Summons of Death' in the tradition of the medieval morality play and to the allegorical method of Rochester's contemporary Bunyan.[41] The entire episode, indeed, may be seen as a refutation of *The Pilgrim's Progress*, with the destined end to the journey sharply

contrasting with the one Bunyan supposes. Rochester's concern, like
Bunyan's, is with the moral education of reader and pilgrim. Yet
what Rochester seeks to 'make him understand' is that the promises
of religion have all been lies, that nothing exists beyond the grave,
that man must ultimately return to the dirt from which he was
constituted. The beauty and power of these lines are in part a
function of their profound ambivalence toward the *memento mori*
tradition on which they draw for their imagery, vocabulary and
emotional colouring, while at the same time challenging many of the
basic moral and intellectual assumptions held in common by writers
in that tradition. The lines are self-evidently the work of a religious
poet, who presents man's life, here and in other poems, as an endless
yearning after a satisfaction he can never find.

The uncompromising atheism of this passage links it with the most
celebrated of Rochester's translations from the Latin, his version of a
chorus in Seneca's *Troades*. It is curious that Rochester's friend, the
deist and religious controversialist Charles Blount, to whom Rochester sent a copy of his version of Seneca in 1680, cites it as evidence for
the existence of the 'immortal . . . Spirit' which both Rochester and
the Senecan original seek to refute as an imposition on credulous
man:

I cannot but esteem the Translation to be, in some measure, a confutation
of the Original; since what less than a divine and immortal Mind could
have produced what you have there written? Indeed, the Hand that wrote
it may become *Lumber*, but, sure, the Spirit that dictated it, can never be
so.[42]

Though Blount's flattering language, directed at a potential aristocratic patron, must be treated with some suspicion, this letter has
considerable interest as one of three addressed to Rochester on
philosophical subjects included in Blount's *The Oracles of Reason*. His
choice of Rochester as recipient for a disquisition 'Concerning the
Immortality of the Soul' suggests a continuing dialogue in which the
translation of Seneca (treated by Blount as one of many classical
writers speculating about metaphysical questions) plays a prominent part – only here the debate is not, as with Burnet, between
believer and unbeliever, but between two fellow sceptics, disciples of
Hobbes and seekers after an elusive truth.[43]

Rochester's lines from Seneca are, like the *Satyr against Mankind*, a
libertine manifesto and a challenge to orthodoxy. In the very
vehemence of their negation, they express a metaphysical anguish

differing markedly in tone from the Stoic certainty of the Senecan original:

> After Death, nothing is, and nothing Death,
> The utmost Limit of a gaspe of Breath;
> Let the Ambitious Zealot, lay aside
> His Hopes of Heav'n, (whose faith is but his Pride)
> Let Slavish Soules lay by their feare;
> Nor be concern'd which way, nor where,
> After this Life they shall be hurl'd;
> Dead, wee become the Lumber of the World,
> And to that Masse of matter shall be swept,
> Where things destroy'd, with things unborne, are kept.
> Devouring tyme, swallows us whole
> Impartiall Death, confounds Body, and Soule.
> For Hell, and the foule Fiend that Rules
> God everlasting fiery Jayles
> (Devis'd by Rogues, dreaded by Fooles)
> With his grim griezly Dogg, that keepes the Doore,
> Are senselesse Stories, idle Tales
> Dreames, Whimseys, and noe more.

Rochester's first line is a close translation (post mortem nihil est ipsaque mors nihil) and the second line, though it departs from Seneca in evoking the moment of death itself in sharply physical terms, nevertheless remains fairly close to the original. After that, Rochester expands three and a half Senecan lines to ten, turning the poem into a polemic against the accepted tenets of Christian belief, similar in its tone and its materials to passages in the *Satyr*.[44] Seneca contrasts hopes and fears and introduces the powerful image (transposed by Rochester to line 11) of time the devourer: 'spem ponant avidi, solliciti metum;/tempus nos avidum devorat et chaos'. But the association of faith with pride, the attacks on zealotry and ambition, all reminiscent of the first part of the *Satyr* and its epilogue, add elements foreign to Seneca's poem. The characteristic tone of Rochesterian satire, anger tinged with pity, is particularly apparent in lines 8–10, where, taking the merest hint from Seneca's two final lines, he unleashes the powerful, disturbing metaphorical associations of 'Lumber' and 'swept' to refute the comforting illusions of human dignity. This reduction of man to logs and sawdust in its implications goes well beyond Seneca, who argues for the mortality of the soul but not, as here, for the Lucretian or Hobbesian position that nothing exists in the universe but a 'Masse of matter'.[45] The second half of the poem sticks more closely to the Senecan text, except that the underworld becomes Christian as well as classical. Rochester's main addition here is the parenthetical aside in line 15, a libertine attack on priestcraft which treats the myth of the afterlife as a product of conscious fraud in a world where rogues and fools are symbiotically bound together by their mutual need to deceive and be deceived. The note of bleak finality in 'noe more' recalls Rochester's pilgrim's discovery at the end of his journey, as well as the animating paradox of the earlier 'Upon Nothing', though there the idea of the void at the centre of all things is developed in terms that are more comic than tragic.[46]

In his conversations with Burnet, the poet argues a position in many ways similar to that in the Senecan imitation. The most striking difference is that the tone here is more tentative, more troubled; rather than mounting a ferocious assault upon belief as a sham, he expresses dissent in terms which, in doctrine and vocabulary, are closer to such lyrics as 'Absent from thee', 'The Mistress' and 'The Fall' than to his satires:

He was neither perswaded that there was a special Providence about Humane Affairs; Nor that Prayers were of much use, since that was to look on God as a weak Being, that would be overcome with Importunities . . . He doubted much of Rewards or Punishments: The one he thought too high for us to attain, by our slight Services; and the other was too extream to be inflicted for Sin.[47]

This can be read as a confession of unworthiness, a conviction, born of despair, that one is mired in sin and cut off irredeemably from God's grace. Psychologically, the statement that no men are worthy of salvation can be seen either as an extrapolation from one's own fears or a defence mechanism to make such fears more tolerable (I'm no worse off than anyone else). The unforgiving parent – male here, female in 'Absent from thee' – is a projection of self-contempt, enshrined in the distant skies or across an impassable barrier. It is possible to read 'After Death, nothing is' in similar terms as expressing a desire for oblivion as release from pain, affirming the absent God through blasphemy as the only language the sinner knows. Certainly the passage just quoted from Burnet displays the classic marks of the first stage of conversion: the language and tone are that of a sick soul calling out for wholeness. Despite the obvious differences in social class and intellectual allegiances, one can recognise a fundamental kinship with the Bunyan of *Grace Abounding*.[48]

When, in his dialogue with Burnet, Rochester uses the familiar comparison of man and beast, he has restored man to his traditional place in the hierarchy. Beset by depression and weakened by a continued 'low state of health', he shows himself a step further on the road to conversion. The 'Beast' has become a symbol not of natural freedom but of corrupted nature, infected with sin – or, more literally, with the later stages of syphilis:

[He] was very much ashamed of his former Practices, rather because he had made himself a Beast, and had brought pain and sickness on his Body, and had suffered much in his Reputation, than from any deep sense of a Supream Being, or another State: But so far this went with him, that he resolved firmly to change the Course of his Life; which he thought he should effect by the study of *Philosophy*, and had not a few no less solid than pleasant Notions concerning the folly and madness of Vice: but he confessed he had no remorse for his past Actions, as Offences against God, but only as Injuries to himself and to Mankind.[49]

Though, as elsewhere, we need to be aware of Burnet's polemical intentions (to him, the 'deep sense of a Supream Being' and the need to repent 'Offences against God' are self-evident truths), Rochester's own arguments here prefigure his ultimate submission to Christian orthodoxy, and by their relative feebleness can be said to demonstrate the inadequacy of the '*Philosophy*' of hedonist calculation as medicine for the wounded mind. At this point in his troubled career, Rochester has lost his materialist convictions – 'These things he said made him inclined to believe, the Soul was a substance distinct from matter: and this often returned into his thoughts'[50] – though he still employs the Hobbesian vocabulary of pleasure, pain, injury and reputation. In a late letter to his wife which complains of the 'disproportion' made inevitable by desires never to be satisfied, he once more rewrites the opening lines of the *Satyr against Mankind*, and there too the difference reflects the poet's own doubts about the materialism he professed: 'Were that mans soule plac't in a body fitt for it, he were a dogg, that could count any thing a benifitt obtain'd wth flattery, feare, & service' (*Letters*, pp. 241–2). Here the 'dogg' is not freed from crippling illusions of rationality, but reduced to a crass animality that leaves no room for moral discrimination. 'Feare', which in the *Satyr* is the universal human motivation, the key to the mystery of man's behaviour, is now the property of those who reject their higher selves (in theological terms, the unregenerate). The beast has become Descartes's 'engine', where man as an

ethical being is free. In justifying his own dissatisfaction by identifying it with the ability to imagine a 'prospect of felicity', he has
moved from Hobbes's position to one closer to Pascal or Traherne:
'Theire are those soe intirely satisfyed wth theire shares in this world,
that theire wishes nor theire thoughts have not a farther prospect of
felicity & glory' (*Letters*, p. 242).[51]

Rochester then was an unbeliever who desperately wanted to
believe – if not in God, in something. In his poems, he conceives of
the human predicament as his own predicament writ large – a
battle, never to be resolved, between the spiritual and the carnal,
doubt and faith. The anguished theological speculations of
Maximus in *Valentinian* cannot of course be interpreted in literal
autobiographical terms: a dramatic character in Rochester's play,
shocked at his sudden education into the reality of evil and injustice
by the rape and suicide of his beloved wife, is giving vent to his
overwhelming feelings of helpless grief. But though the passage is
entirely appropriate to its dramatic context, its assault on orthodoxy, in a tone poised uneasily between blasphemy and suppli-
cation, is congruent with the religious questionings of the *Satyr* and
the conversations with Burnet. We hear in the lines the voice of a
poet who 'loved to talk and write of Speculative Matters',[52] calling
on the gods to prove him wrong:

> Gods! would you be ador'd for being good,
> Or only fear'd for proving mischievous?
> How would you have your Mercy understood?
> Who could create a Wretch like *Maximus*,
> Ordain'd tho' guiltless to be infamous?
> Supream first Causes! you, whence all things flow,
> Whose infiniteness does each little fill,
> You, who decree each seeming Chance below,
> (So great in Power) were you as good in Will,
> How could you ever have produc'd such ill?
>
> (*Valentinian*, iv.iii, p. 56)[53]

These speculations on the problem of evil remind us yet again that
Rochester and Milton were contemporaries: what is at issue is the
evident anomaly of a deity who gratuitously inflicts suffering on his
'guiltless' creatures, and the proposed answer to the conundrum is a
divorce, in God and man, of power and will. God thus becomes a
projection of human impotence, or is defined as blind power, ruling
like the Hobbesian monarch and Machiavellian prince by fear

rather than love. The temptation of despair, resisted by Milton's Samson and Adam, as by the Bunyan of *Grace Abounding*, is voluptuously embraced by Maximus, who advances arguments, similar to those stated elsewhere by Rochester, for a deity of 'vast Power' but monumental indifference:

> Had your eternal minds been bent to good[,]
> Could humane happiness have prov'd so lame,
> Rapine, Revenge, Injustice, thirst of Blood,
> Grief, Anguish, Horror, Want, Despair and Shame,
> Had never found a Being nor a Name.
> 'Tis therefore less impiety to say,
> Evil with you has Coeternity,
> Than blindly taking it the other way,
> That merciful and of election free,
> You did create the mischiefs you forsee.   (IV.iii, pp. 56–7)[54]

As with 'After death, nothing is', the deity under challenge in these lines is patently Christian, despite the Roman setting. The references to foreknowledge and free choice in the last lines may recall *Paradise Lost*, III, 103–19: the twelve-book version of Milton's epic poem was published in 1674, and *Valentinian* was announced for performance the following year.[55] Though Satan's great soliloquy in Book IV ends with his expressed claim to hold 'divided empire with heaven's king' (III.iii), the Manicheanism suggested by Maximus was a heresy Milton explicitly rejected. Such a doctrine precisely fits the psychology of the would-be penitent, overwhelmingly conscious of his own guilt and unable to make the leap into faith. Feeling himself befouled with sin, he projects his own self-division into a cosmic vision excluding grace, where evil reigns unchecked.

It is therefore wrong to see Rochester's death-bed religious conversion as an aberration: his entire rake's progress had led up to this inevitable conclusion, and his poems obsessively juxtapose the need to hope with the conviction that all hopes were vain. The impasse he shows himself to have reached in his conversations with Burnet is that anatomised by Pascal and powerfully evoked by Bunyan in *Grace Abounding* – the despair of those who have reached the stage of knowing their own misery without knowing a Redeemer: 'I saw as if they were set on the Sunny side of some high Mountain, there refreshing themselves with the pleasant beams of the Sun, while I was shivering and shrinking in the cold, afflicted with frost, snow, and dark clouds.' The world is sharply divided into the innocent and the tainted, the pure of heart, confident of their own salvation, and the paralysed victims of their own 'inward pollution',[56] unable to escape by an act of the will a conviction that they are damned: 'He said, They were happy that believed; for it was not in every mans power . . . He said, If a Man says he can not believe, what help is there? for he was not master of his own Belief, and believing was at highest but a probable Opinion.'[57] Rochester's very vocabulary here reflects his divided allegiances, as he laments and justifies his lack of faith in the conventional language of contemporary philosophical speculation. Happiness, radically redefined from the straightforward egoist hedonism argued in the *Satyr against Mankind*, is projected as the exclusive property of a community of the blest from which he sees himself as excluded, trapped within the prison of self. The passage is simultaneously a cry for help and a despairing assertion that no help will be forthcoming. In similar fashion, when he adapts the Erastian arguments of Hobbes and Blount that religion in the state is useful primarily insofar as it is conducive to civil peace, he transforms these worldly counsels into a prayer for deliverance:

He often confessed, that whether the Business of Religion was true or not, he thought those who had the perswasions of it, and lived so that they had quiet in their Consciences, and believed God governed the World, and acquiesced in his Providence, and had the hope of an endless Blessedness in another state, the happiest men in the World: And said, He would give all that he was Master of, to be under those Perswasions, and to have the Supports and Joys that must needs flow from them.[58]

The sense of 'divided empire' comes across strongly in many of Rochester's lyrics and in his correspondence, though the tone there is rarely so sombre. With a characteristic mixture of aristocratic arrogance and contrition, he revels in his status as a sinner, finding some consolation in the reflection that 'ther's noe mid way (it seemes) twix't heav'n and hell'. It is possible to find elements of ascetic self-loathing in the fragment 'Sab: Lost', though this enigmatic poem can also be read as an exercise in witty blasphemy or as a mock-heroic retelling of the Fall in terms of earthly seduction:

> Shee yeilds, she yeilds, Pale Envy said Amen
> The first of woemen to the Last of men.
> Just soe those frailer beings Angells fell
> Ther's noe mid way (it seemes) twix't heav'n and hell.   (1–4)[59]

'The Last of men' would appear to refer to the speaker's rival, treated as contemptible ('this Heavy thing/Artless and witless, noe way meritting', 11–12 – the fragment ends here), who has succeeded where he has failed. A similar situation is presented in the Ovidian elegy 'Could I but make my wishes insolent', but that poem directs its scorn both at the 'hard hearted' mistress and the 'blockhead' she has rewarded with her favours: 'Tis some reliefe in my extreame distress/My rivall is Below your power to Bless' (9, 17, 25–6). 'Sab: Lost' illustrates a pattern, common in Rochester's poems, in which religious imagery, as applied to sexual love, expresses an emotional impasse where no 'relief' is possible: the wish for a bodiless heaven confirms the reality of a genital hell.

In another poem, a satire on fashionable whores, Rochester deliberately exploits the clash between sexual and spiritual in a delicious irreverent conceit. There is no touch of idealisation here:

> O! Yee mercifull powers, who of Mortalls take Care,
> Make the Woman more modest, more sound, or less fayre.
> Is it just, that with death cruell Love should conspire,
> And our Tarses be burnt by our hearts taking fire?
> There's an end of Communion, if humble Beleavers
> Must be damn'd in the Cup, like unworthy Receavers.
>
> ('Lampoone' [To longe the Wise Commons have been
> in debate'], 13–18)

Neither the association of sexual pleasure with punishment nor the grim joke about unrepentant sinners courting damnation need be taken entirely seriously. But the association of the sexual act and the Eucharist, cunt and chalice, is genuinely shocking, and serves as reminder that in Rochester's writings, for all their sexual explicitness, there is a recurrent fear and distrust of sexuality as inherently sinful.

What most of these poems have in common is a sense of helplessness before an overwhelming force, treated in most cases as a principle of corruption against which all defences are vain. Lucina's account of her terrifying dream in *Valentinian*, like the fragment 'Sab: Lost', equates the onset of sexual experience, a male intrusion on a privileged female domain, with a second fall:

> In what Fantastique new World have I been?
> What Horrors past? What threatning Visions seen?
> Wrapt as I lay in my amazing Trance,
> The Host of Heav'n and Hell did round me Dance . . .
> Mishapen Monsters round in Measures went

> Horrid in Form with Gestures insolent;
> Grinning throu' Goatish Beards with half clos'd Eyes,
> They look'd me in the face frighted to rise!
> In vain did I attempt, methought no Ground
> Was to support my sinking Footsteps sound.
> In clammy Fogs like one half choak'd I lay,
> Crying for help my Voyce was snatch'd away.
>   And when I would have fled,
>   My Limbs benumm'd, or dead
> Could not my Will with Terror wing'd obey.   (III.iii, pp. 31–2)[60]

Lucina's plight, in which she is reduced to being a helpless voyeur of her own destruction, is parallel to that of her 'absent Lord' Maximus in his address to the gods (III.ii, p. 32). The paralysis of the will afflicting her, evoked in the physical detail of the nightmare, reflects the impotence of the forces of good which should 'protect' her but decline to act (III.iii, p. 32). The demons, alarmingly phallic, may be seen as projections of her own sexual fears or as objective embodiments of the forces ranged against her, enacted moments before as an anti-masque of Satyrs dancing round her recumbent form. In either case, the scene makes clear, in language echoing the last two stanzas of 'Absent from Thee', that the 'Peace and Rest' which Lucina, 'half dead throu' Absence', seeks fruitlessly in the remembered unfallen world of nature are brutally denied her (III.ii, p. 32). Pursued even into the citadel of innocence, the 'dear solitary Groves' she loves (III.ii, p. 27), she sees round her a universe compromised by aggressive sexuality and complaisance with the debaucheries of a corrupt and tyrannous court.[61]

Rochester's ambivalence toward the court world he depicts in *Valentinian* is evident in the situation of Maximus, torn between his moral instincts and the loyalty and self-interest which bind him to his 'lawful Prince' (IV.iii, p. 56).[62] A further instance of that ambivalence, even more striking, is the poet's use in *Valentinian* of a love lyric originally addressed to Lady Rochester in a scene of erotic dalliance between the tyrannous voluptuary Valentinian and his catamite Lycius, immediately before Æcius bursts in to avenge the crime against the innocent, martyred Lucina:

> Beauty does the Heart invade,
> Kindnesse only can perswade;
> It guilds the Lovers Servile Chaine
> And make the Slave grow pleas'd and vaine.
>   ('Song: Give me leave to raile at you', 13–16)[63]

These lines are, in a version extant in MS and printed in Walker's edition, part of an exchange between lover and mistress, in which the mistress justifies her 'Scorne, and cold disdaine' as the most effective means of stimulating renewed affection in an inconstant lover – rather like the advice Cleopatra offers Charmian in *Antony and Cleopatra*, 1.iii.2–10. If the lines acquire ironic resonance in the dramatic context of *Valentinian*, they are no less problematical in their other version, as part of an extended dialogue.

Both Vieth and Walker assume that the lines headed 'The Answer' are in fact by Lady Rochester, and the manuscript evidence seems to support this view, though the exchange can also be read as an exercise in which the poet assumes two voices, male and female, in parallel statement and response.[64] In a sense it hardly matters whether the neatly turned characterisation of 'Thirsis' is the work of Rochester imagining what his wife might say about him or of Lady Rochester herself, playing the game of antiphonal answer-poem: as with 'I rise at eleven' and 'To the Post Boy', two other poems of disputed authorship, the satiric portrait of the libertine 'Rebell' is based on the paradox of estrangement of the self from the desires by which it seeks absolution and release.

> Thinke not Thirsis I will e're
> By my Love, my Empire loose,
> You grow Constant through despair,
> Love return'd, you would abuse.
>
> ('The Answer', 24, 9–12)

The assumptions behind these lines are no less Hobbesian than in the cynical libertine statement that sexual intercourse can gild the lover's chain, affording him a momentary pleasure that might allow him briefly to forget the ignominy of his servitude. In her 'Answer', the mistress recognises the dangers of losing her ascendancy over her lover by exposing her feelings. Like Millamant, she would 'be solicited to the very last, nay, and afterwards' (*The Way of the World*, IV.i.180–1), knowing from experience that any 'Kindnesse' she has expressed towards him – the word means both the granting of sexual favours and unselfish affection – has simply enabled him to 'insult' over her, confident in his unchecked 'Pow'r' ('The Answer', 4–8).[65] Rochester uses similar language in a letter to his wife, commenting on the recurrent pattern of their relationship and his own self-divided nature, capable of turning wholesome food to poison and rejecting what it most desires:

'Tis not an easy thing to bee intirely happy, But to bee kind is very easy and that is the greatest measure of happiness; I say not this to putt you in mind of being kind to mee, you have practis'd that soe long that I have a joyfull confidence you will never forget it, but to show that I myself have a sence of what the methods of my Life seeme soe utterly to contradict. (*Letters*, p. 278)

It is not certain whether the third stanza of 'The Answer' (the fifth in the exchange) is meant to be spoken by the mistress or lover: the metaphors of 'Empire' and 'Chain' were initially used to describe her rule over him, but the female speaker could be turning his own language back on him. The 'Conquests' could be the property of either lover: they fit better with the historical Rochester than Lady Rochester, who cannot have had many opportunities at home in Adderbury, though the first stanza of 'Give me leave to raile at you' portrays the mistress as conventionally 'false' in the man's eyes. On the other hand, the 'Pow'rfull Charms' of the loved one tilt the balance somewhat towards a male speaker. But again, in some ways it makes relatively little difference which one is speaking, since the lines present an ideal of mutuality meant to transcend the view, common to both speakers in stanzas I–IV, of love as combat in a world where all relationships are infected with distrust. Whether the author is Rochester or Lady Rochester, the final stanza of the exchange seeks explicitly to provide an alternative to the libertine ideology. Though its imagery, unlike that in 'Absent from thee', is entirely secular, it complements that poem in presenting, in its closing lines, an ideal of all-encompassing love, sexual and spiritual, through which the riven soul can find wholeness:

> You that cou'd my Heart subdue;
> To new Conquests, ne're pretend,
> Let your Example make me true
> And of a Conquer'd Foe, a Friend.
> Then if e're I shou'd complaine,
> Of your Empire, or my Chain,
> Summon all your Pow'rfull Charms,
> And fell the Rebell in your Armes.
>
> ('The Answer', 17–24)[66]

This exchange, whether it is finally to be regarded as an exercise in impersonation by Rochester or a genuine dialogue between 'fugitive' lover[67] and distrustful mistress, suggests the dual nature of sexual love in Rochester's poems and in the libertine ethos: a field of war or a possible pathway to peace, a temporary anodyne or a means of transcendence. One part of Rochester was convinced that nothing existed beyond the self, seen in Hobbesian terms as essentially appetitive, ruled by desires and aversions, the apprehended reality of pleasure and pain. Other poems by Rochester express the contrary side in an internal debate, suggesting that life in a mechanical universe stripped of all hope is intolerable. 'Absent from thee' agrees with the *Satyr against Mankind* in its Hobbesian definition of the human condition as characterised by a restlessness unappeased in the mortal state. In both poems, man's 'short life, void of all rest' (*Satyr*, 78) brings pain which, in his self-division, he wantonly courts; in both poems, the unhappy, driven wanderer, trapped within a repetitive pattern of self-inflicted suffering, is contrasted with other beings whose undivided state is presented as enviable but somehow out of reach. Both poems draw on contemporary Epicureanism in associating this desirable state with 'Everlasting rest' ('Absent from thee', 16; *Satyr*, 78–9). But one major difference, evident in the Christian overtones of the final, resonant words of 'Absent from thee', is that the lyric allows for the possibility of intercession, forgiveness, purgation from sin, where the deity of the *Satyr against Mankind* is a cruel joker, who treats his creatures with an indifference bordering on contempt.

One recurrent strain in Rochester, especially prominent in his satires, is a pessimism which sees all human effort as futile and misdirected:

> But Turncote-time assists the foe in vayne
> And brib'd by Thee destroyes their short-liv'd Reign
> And to thy hungry wombe drives back thy slaves again.
>
> ('Upon Nothing', 19–21)

In the ironic creation-myth of 'Upon Nothing', the primal force from which all things take their origins and find their ends is nothingness: a mother who devours her children, the universal void stands astride all creation, abetted by the power of time, to reveal a truth akin to that learned, to his own cost, by the pilgrim of the *Satyr against Mankind* at his journey's end.[68] The lines on wit in the *Satyr* use a disturbing sexual analogy to suggest that a similar principle of entropy afflicts self-divided man in his efforts to turn his talents to advantage. Gifts become afflictions, as immediate pleasure is converted to lingering syphilitic pains, or as the 'sudden glory' (*Levia-*

than, VI, p. 36) the wit can extract from a circle of listeners marks him for eventual destruction at the hands of those whose 'hate' and 'fear' he has aroused (45):

> And *Wit*, was his vain frivolous pretence,
> Of pleasing others, at his own expence.
> For *Witts* are treated just like common *Whores*,
> First they're enjoy'd, and then kickt out of *Doores*:
> The pleasure past, a threatening doubt remains,
> That frights th'enjoyer, with succeeding pains.   (35–40)

If social or sexual relations are an uninterrupted state of war, then, these lines suggest, no eventual outcome is possible but defeat. To forswear wit as merely vain and frivolous is to go unarmed, or to endorse the position of the pompous, self-satisfied *adversarius* – no one can knowingly choose to be a fool – and the self-evident wit in the lines effectively rules out this possibility. The speaker in the *Satyr*, like the praiser of Nothing whose every line materially reduces the empire whose ultimate victory he prophesies, is caught within a dilemma which cannot, under the materialist premises of these two poems, be resolved.[69]

When in 'Upon Nothing' Rochester uses the image of a desired haven of rest, it is with ironic intent. The emotion of yearning is seen, here as elsewhere in his writings, as natural to man, and indeed it underlies the structure of the poem, with its long, largely unpunctuated sweep towards an inevitable end, both feared and desired. But in this poem, as in the *Satyr against Mankind*, the dissatisfaction the poem arouses and anatomises – man is 'afraid' of 'ending' (3), whether it is a poem or a life – is presented as the most persistent and damaging of illusions, a disease for which the poem seeks to provide radical surgery:

> Is or is not, the two great ends of ffate
> And true and false the Subject of debate
> That perfect or destroy the vast designes of State –
>
> When they have wrackt the Politicians Brest
> Within thy Bosome most Securely rest
> And when reduc't to thee are least unsafe and best.
> ('Upon Nothing', 31–6)

The anti-intellectualism evident here is akin to that in the *Satyr*, and the praise of the 'least unsafe', warning against the potentially subversive nature of intellectual inquiry, is Hobbesian. Hobbes provides a precedent for the odd logic which links metaphysical speculation and political intrigue:

It is to this purpose, that men may no longer suffer themselves to be abused, by them, that by this doctrine of *separated essences*, built on the vain philosophy of Aristotle, would fright them from obeying the laws of their country, with empty names; as men fright birds from the corn with an empty doublet, a hat, and a crooked stick. (*Leviathan*, XLVI, p. 442)

But Hobbes does not attribute the politician's ambition to an unassuageable inward pain; his aim, to stress 'what is necessary to the doctrine of government and obedience' (*ibid.*), is far more straightforward than Rochester's, and he does not treat man's hunger for certainty with an equivalent tragic irony.

The materialism and scepticism which, with varying degrees of ambivalence, Rochester argues in the *Satyr*, 'Upon Nothing' and 'After Death, nothing is' are explicitly rejected in 'Absent from thee'. A comparison with 'To A Lady, in A Letter', another lyric which superficially resembles 'Absent from thee' in its initial dramatic situation, may indicate how far 'Absent from thee' departs from the libertine ethos, to which the other poem adheres in a particularly uncompromising fashion. Proposing to his mistress a bargain by which each condones any lapses by the other, the libertine speaker of 'To A Lady, in A Letter' argues for a heightening of pleasure by ruling out all considerations beyond the moment. If 'restless Jealiousy' brings 'torment', then the 'Enjoyments' of love can be 'perfect' only if they are 'free': if a male rake has found a female rake who is his 'Match' in the single-minded pursuit of pleasure, then neither should demand a phantom constancy, imposing unrealistic standards of conduct on the other:

> Let us (since Witt instructs us how)
> Raise pleasure to the topp,
> If Rivall Bottle you'll allow,
> I'll suffer Rivall Fopp.[70]

In a stanza eventually discarded, the parallel with 'Absent from thee' is clear: 'Then ask me not, when I return' matches 'Upbraide mee not that I designe' syntactically and rhythmically, suggesting the element of dialogue in each poem through the intimacy of direct address. Though the emotion of 'longing' is associated with both lovers in 'Absent from thee' and only the mistress in the other poem, this stanza complicates the overall tone by adding the element of guilt:

> Upbraide mee not that I designe
> Tricks to delude your charmes
> When running after mirth and wine
> I leave your Longing Armes.   (Version b, 25–8)

In 'Absent from thee', the outstretched arms of the woman and the headlong flight of the man are both given a significance beyond the physical, suggesting a possibility of transcendence which 'To A Lady, in A Letter', no less than the *Satyr against Mankind*, rules out as delusory. By presenting 'Love' as wholly a physical, mechanical act, in which the empty heads of Cloris's foppish 'Admirers' provide no impediment if 'their Codds be full', Rochester projects a victory which is virtually indistinguishable from defeat. The reduction of 'Passion' to its barest essentials, the presentation of a relationship 'perfect' in its equal distribution of vacancy, thus end the poem on an equivocal note, praising a state which is not so much mutual tolerance as the anaesthesia of feeling:

> While I, my Passion to pursue
> Am whole Nights takeing in
> The lusty Juice of Grapes, take you
> The lusty Juice of Men.[71]

Psychoanalytically these lines could be interpreted in terms of the author's bisexuality, as he, with minimal displacement, expresses a desire to assume the passive female role and be penetrated. It is possible, of course, that the homosexual overtones, like the paradoxical praise of a whore for mindless promiscuity, are intended primarily to shock; in terms of polemical strategy, accusations of unfaithfulness can be parried easily by the *ad hominem* argument that the accuser is no better than a whore.

In 'Absent from thee', the relationship presented is again one in which the male is essentially passive, and the strong element of masochism might indicate a half-recognised desire to transgress the conventional boundaries of gender definitions. But here there is no element of aggression toward the woman addressed. Instead, the speaker, rather than attempting to defend himself against her charges, eagerly accepts them, adding new accusations of his own to the reproaches suggested in lines 2 and 5. All the aggression is turned inward:

Dear; from thine Arms then let me flie,
  That my Fantastick mind may prove,
The Torments it deserves to try,
  That tears my fixt Heart from my Love.   (5–8)

What is most striking here is the extraordinary power the speaker attributes to the woman. 'Let me flie' implies volition on the part of the male protagonist, who like Adam errs of his own free choice. But it also suggests that she had somehow permitted his 'wandring' (13), sits in judgement over him and through the agency of conscience has directed punishments, severe but just, appropriate to a sin against love. In the discarded stanza of the poem to Cloris and in the references to 'lingering pain' and 'care' in Lady Rochester's poems, the abandoned mistress is described as suffering; here all the pain is displaced onto the male.[72] Psychologically this could serve as a simple defence-mechanism or an appeal for sympathy (you aren't really suffering, because I'm suffering much more), but in terms of the religious imagery which dominates the poem, the suggestion that the sufferings of the protagonist may subserve an educative pattern not immediately apparent provides a possible way out of the impasse the first two stanzas so powerfully present.

Each of the verbs in the first two stanzas carries a charge of emotion, predicated in each case on links between an intolerable present and an uncertain future. Even in the choice of tense, the lines deny the libertine doctrine that 'the present Moment's all my Lott' ('Love and Life', 8): the only two verbs in the present indicative are 'languish', which describes a continuing, recurrent state, a wasting disease or an imprisonment without foreseeable release, and 'tears', where the wrenching kinaesthetic impact of the verb comes partly from the paradoxical juxtaposition of 'fixt' – unalterable yet, against its nature, forced to alter – so that the single agonising moment is extended indefinitely, like the eagle gnawing at Prometheus's liver. These torments, inflicted by the sovereign mind on the subject body (8) or proliferating endlessly within the mind itself (6), provide compelling subjective arguments against materialism. The 'Fantastick' mind, capricious, impulsive, able to call up more devils than vast hell can hold, is shown in these lines to have great powers and yet to be utterly unreliable. In some ways, this stanza is compatible with the *Satyr against Mankind*, since it presents the instincts of the 'Heart' as sound, the 'mind' as the source of alienation and error. The difference is that 'Absent from thee', instead of severing the link between spiritual and material, proposes a way of reintegrating the two.

The tone of the poem changes measurably after the second stanza, and this is partly due to a relaxation of the syntax. In stanza two, the grammatical progress of the sentence is as tortured as the thought, and the obsessive dwelling on self is reflected in the insistent presence of first-person pronouns. Stanza three, in contrast, is hymn-like in its simplicity of language and syntax.

> When wearied with a world of Woe,
>> To thy safe Bosom I retire
> Where Love and Peace and Truth does flow,
>> May I contented there expire.　　　　　(9–12)

In religious terms, the penitent, having been brought to a conscious-ness of his own odious sinfulness, moves from the self-scourging of stanza two, where all experience appears to be compounded of pain, to the contemplation of divine grace and the possibility of release from suffering. The diction, rhythm and syntax reflect the harmony of the blessed, presented here through imagery emphasising the maternal. Though 'expire' has sexual connotations (brought out more explicitly in the final stanza), referring both to death and orgasm, the mistress in this stanza seems remarkably chaste, in keeping with her role as guarantor of salvation. Indeed, this stanza like the next can be read as a prayer for deliverance from the bonds of the flesh, actively embracing death as a source of contentment, in the manner of several religious poems of the century: 'Dead to my selfe, I live in Thee'.[73] As such, it represents a step further on the road to conversion than the passages in Burnet which show Roches-ter unable to cross over the line separating doubt from faith.

The religious imagery in the last two stanzas, in which human love is seen as a type of divine love, thus represents a psychological strategy for survival, while at the same time, it functions as a conscious artistic device, as in Donne, Vaughan or Crashaw. In the final stanza, the choice faced by the wanderer is uncompromisingly posed as a restless sexual freedom which excludes salvation and a peace attainable only when the demands of the flesh are finally stilled. Life on earth, as the final stanza presents it, consists of ceaseless motion, but there is no Hobbesian determinism here. Man, the lines suggest (I generalise from the particular instance the poem presents), impelled by sexual desire and a longing for forbidden fruit, wilfully chooses the path which leads to damnation, alienating himself from God's offered grace:

> Lest once more wandring from that Heav'n
> I fall on some base heart unblest;
> Faithless to thee, False, unforgiv'n,
> And lose my Everlasting rest.   (13–16)

Rochester's affinities with Donne, the last stanza of whose 'Valediction forbidding Mourning' is distantly echoed in these lines, are evident in the way he universalises the particular, presenting himself as a representative instance. In theological terms, what the last stanza expresses is a fear of backsliding: the repentant sinner, having been vouchsafed a glimpse of the light of grace, is unable to persevere, but in his weakness succumbs to the temptations of the flesh and falls into a state of reprobacy. 'Fall on some base heart unblest' must be taken literally: the speaker fears that he will be struck dead in the midst of fornication (one of the fates Hamlet predicts for Claudius in the prayer scene) and will thus instantly and irrevocably be damned. In his illness, Rochester expressed a similar wish to Burnet, fearing that his restless inclinations would lead him back again to the familiar life of sin:

And though it was a foolish thing for a Man to pretend to chuse, whether he would die or live yet he wished rather to die. He knew he could never be so well, that life should be comfortable to him. He was confident he should be happy if he died, but feared if he lived he might Relapse. And then said he to mee, *In what a condition shall I be, if I Relapse after all this?*[74]

What the last stanza conveys with memorable force is the hell of guilt, the fear of being cast into eternal darkness, separated by one's own unworthiness from what is most desired. Hell is not a future state, but an indefinite prolongation of present misery in an endlessly repetitive cycle. Where Donne's 'Valediction' ends with the assurance of reunion on earth or in heaven, 'Absent from thee' ends in anguish, as the vision of a secular heaven in the first line of the stanza intensifies the pain of the relentless self-condemnation in the final lines. This lyric, in which hope and fear are so finely balanced, illustrates how for Rochester poetry could serve both as self-expression and an attempt to escape from the prison of self, by objectifying the personal.

CHAPTER 4

Playing trick for trick: domestic rebellion and the female libertine

As Rochester's poems illustrate, the attitude of male authors toward female sexuality during this period is ambivalent and self-contradictory, with a marked aggressiveness one of its constituent elements. A particularly striking instance of such unresolved ambivalence is Thomas Otway's *The Orphan* (1680), which, like many of the works I have been discussing, simultaneously expresses and interrogates libertine ideology. To an appreciable extent, Otway is expressing his own hostility to the unattainable yet sexually promiscuous Elizabeth Barry (to whom at roughly the same time he was writing love-letters full of self-contempt and frustrated longing) in the speeches of Castalio violently abusing the blameless Monimia in *The Orphan*. He has the pleasure of killing her off at the end of Act v, while at the same time presenting the play to the actress as a love-offering.[1]

The dark side of libertinism, *The Orphan* suggests, is exploitation. If sexual relations, inside and outside marriage, are based entirely on power, then the doting lover can easily turn into the merciless oppressor, as Castalio does in Otway's play.

CAST. Sure now sh'has bound me fast, and means to Lord it,
To rein me hard, and ride me at her will,
Till by degrees she shape me into Fool
For all her future uses. (III.547–50)

The imagery here, as elsewhere in the play, combines the sexual and political: though the basic metaphor is taming a horse, 'will' and 'uses' express fear of women's sexual capacity, seen in terms of a lust for domination even in the sex act. Though Castalio prides himself on his heritage of freedom (anachronically citing Magna Carta), he is the slave of convention in his attitude toward women: men should ride and women be ridden, men should be the monarchs and women their dutiful subjects.

CAST. No more, *Monimia*, of your Sexes Arts,
They are useless all: I'm not that pliant Tool,
That necessary Utensil you'd make me,
I know my Charter better – I am Man,
Obstinate Man; and will not be enslav'd.
MON. You shal not fear't: Indeed my Nature's easie;
I'll ever live your most obedient Wife,
Nor ever any privilege pretend
Beyond your will: for that shall be my Law;
Indeed I will not.
CAST. Nay, you shall not, Madam,
By yon bright Heav'n, you shall not; all the day
I'll play the Tyrant, and at Night forsake thee;
Till by afflictions and continued Cares,
I've worn thee to a homely household Drudge;
Nay, if I've any too, thou shalt be made
Subservient to all my looser pleasures,
For thou hast wrong'd *Castalio* (IV.119–34)

Monimia's very submissiveness increases Castalio's rage and suggests to him ways of pressing his advantage home. The psychology underlying the scene is that of Rochester's *Satyr against Mankind*: 'Wretched *Man*, is still in Arms for fear' (140). It is the fear of being unmanned which drives Castalio to humiliate his yoke-fellow and adversary, denying any natural bond of feeling. In this degradation of the once-praised mistress to a household drudge or common whore, this deliberate inflicting of pain in order to prove one's superiority, Castalio unmasks the libertine ideology in which love is a form of conquest. In this passage, Otway is not so much attacking hypocrisy as revealing the inner contradictions which under less testing circumstances might never have come to the surface: a desire to destroy and enslave, which calls itself love, and at other times may call itself virtue, patriotism or the love of liberty.

No doubt the frequency of paired heroines in Restoration tragedy, passionate villainess and 'Ravish'd Virgin', sexually experienced, restless intriguer and passive victim, reflects Restoration theatrical practice in providing parts for specific actresses (in particular, Elizabeth Barry and Anne Bracegirdle).[2] But the bifurcation of Dark Lady and female saint, differentiated by the indelible stain of sexual knowledge, has deep psychological roots. As Freud points out, the very sharpness of the contrast between idealised and debased love-object disguises a perceived or feared identity: 'what, in the conscious, is found split into a pair of opposites, often occurs in the unconscious as a unity'.[3] Thus, the idealised image of women is in many writers during this period presented as false, born of man's susceptibility to temptation and capacity for self-delusion – Milton's Dalila, 'that specious monster, my accomplished snare'. The debased, foul image (the stripped Duessa) is, in contrast, presented as the inner layer of truth which remains when the momentary enchantment has been dispelled.[4]

The Restoration period saw a flourishing sub-genre of satires against women, violently abusive in tone. Such poems of 'Juvenalian' railing as Robert Gould's *Love Given O're: or, A Satyr against the Pride, Lust and Inconstancy, & c. of Woman* frequently employ the convention of love turned to hate, treating the sexual allure of female beauty as a sign of corruption and disease, a 'gilt close-stool' enclosing 'a nasty Soul'. These works, bitterly ascetic, present woman as intrinsically sinful, 'the Original of Mischief', Satan's natural allies, to be avoided like 'the pains of Hell' itself.[5] Such a view denies the possibility of virtue or chastity in woman, as well as excluding all sympathy: angels on the outside, 'frightful *Fiend* within', women, irrevocably damned themselves, remorselessly seek partners in damnation.

> O *Lucifer*, thy Regions had been thin,
> Wer't not for Womans propagating Sin:
> 'Tis they alone that all true Vices know;
> And send such Throngs down to thy Courts below.

In this version of the Eden story, Eve is not the victim of temptation, but the tempter, her beauty an apple hiding rottenness within:

> So were those Apples too,
> Which in the midst of the first Garden grew;
> But when they were examin'd, all within,
> Wrapt in a specious and alluring skin,
> Lay the rank baits of never-dying Sin.[6]

Sarah Fyge's *The Female Advocate* (1686) and the anonymous *Sylvia's Complaint* (1692), in attacking the basic assumptions of such fiercely misogynist poems, reject the view of woman as embodiment of evil. Though there is an element of game-playing in any such literary exchange – indeed at least one author contributed poems to both sides of the debate – *The Female Advocate* is wholly serious in challenging on theological grounds the 'notorious Principle' that 'all

Men are good, and fitting for Heaven because they are Men; and Women irreversibly damn'd, because they are Women'.[7] To make woman 'the Scape-goat' to 'bear sins of all the land', Fyge argues, is to disclaim moral responsibility for one's own actions. Her own theological position is closely akin to that argued in *Paradise Lost* and *Areopagitica*: man and woman alike are fallible, with freedom to err a condition of their creation.

> Tho' I confess there's some that merit blame:
> But yet their faults only thus much infer,
> That we're not made so perfect but may err;
> Which adds much lustre to a virtuous mind,
> And 'tis her prudence makes her soul confin'd
> Within the bounds of Goodness, for if she
> Was all perfection, unto that degree
> That 'twas impossible to do amiss,
> Why heaven not she must have the praise of this.
> But she's in such a state as she may fall,
> And without care her freedom may enthrall.[8]

The element of compassion for those who 'go astray', lacking the 'power to make defence/Against those many tempting pleasures' which assail them, is even more marked in *Sylvia's Complaint*, which has little of the moral sternness of *The Female Advocate*. Here the tone is one of worldly tolerance: it is natural for woman to succumb to the '*Arts of fine Dissembling*', but they are not to blame. The myth of the Fall is reinterpreted to present woman not as sexual aggressor but as destined victim whose nature – 'like Tinder, apt to fire' – makes her an easy prey:

> Like our great *Grandame Eve*, we all suppose,
> No treachry under fair Pretences grows,
> Her Longing too in us has taken root,
> We ne're should else Disire forbidden Fruit.[9]

In some ways, *Sylvia's Complaint* is no less dismissive of women than the poems it seeks to refute. Though the poem employs a female persona in all but the opening and closing lines, we are always aware that the forsaken 'Sylvia', glimpsed in elegant *déshabillé* in the initial narrative frame, is woman as seen by, as well as controlled by man. Though the poem is consistently sympathetic to woman's plight, it allows woman no role other than victim, a physical being whose desires betray her whether they are fulfilled or unfulfilled:

> Alike you all with *flattery* begin,
> To tempt and draw us to the Pleasing Sin;
> Alike ye all forsake us when ye find
> We Love you, and without Reserve, are kind.   (p. 9)

The assumptions of this passage are those of contemporary libertinism, as are those in a later passage where 'Sylvia', rather than including herself in the common fate, narrates in the third person a Progress of Marriage. Enjoyment rapidly brings about satiety in the male, where in women, according to the poem, the sexual act begets longing ('And still the more enjoy'd, the more she loves'). Love, it is implied, is inherently unstable in that *all* partners are incompatible: the birth of love is the death of love.

> By frequent use grown weary of her Charms,
> He comes with *dull Indifference* to her Arms . . .
> In solitary Sheets she pines and grieves,
> Whilst like a *Rake-hell Libertine* he lives.   (p. 15)[10]

The element of pathos here, intensified by an authorial command over the rhetoric of the heroic couplet largely absent from *The Female Advocate* and most other poems in the debate, enables this passage to break free of the patronising tone which characterises much of *Sylvia's Complaint*.

An emphasis on 'pity' as appropriate emotion for author and reader becomes increasingly pronounced in the latter part of the poem. Even the whore, painted in such lurid colours by most contemporary satirists, is presented sympathetically in *Sylvia's Complaint* as yet another instance of the inability of women to exercise any control over the conditions of their lives.

> I pity from my Soul th'*unhappy Maid*,
> By *Arts of Men*, and her own *Wants* betray'd;
> To act a *Crime* she never knew before,
> And has the choice to *Starve* or be a *Whore:*
> O *Poverty*! thou undermining Ill,
> Whose fatal Damp too oft does *Vertue* kill.   (p. 13)

This passage, like the brothel scenes in Behn's *Town-Fopp*, anticipates Defoe ('Give me not Poverty lest I steal') as well as such nineteenth-century writers as Dickens and Mayhew, in treating the causes of prostitution as economic rather than moral. In *Sylvia's Complaint*, as in the plays of Behn to be discussed in the next chapter, prostitution and marriage alike are presented as slavery.[11]

In his treatment of marriage, the unknown author to some extent inverts the arguments of his opponents who, presenting the miseries of the married state entirely from the male point of view, depict it as the greatest plague which can befall a once-free man. But *Sylvia's Complaint*, together with a number of works written in the 1690s, sees a woman's lot in political terms derived from the revolution of 1688 and the earlier Exclusion Bill controversy, as illustrating the dangers of arbitrary power. The attempts of 'freeborn' women to resist domestic tyrants, demanding liberty as 'an English Woman's natural Right', are treated no less sympathetically by the Tories Otway and Behn than by the Whig Shadwell, whose heroine Gertrude in *Bury-Fair* (1689) declares in ringing tones, 'I am a free Heiress of *England*, where Arbitrary Power is at an end, and I am resolv'd to choose for my self'.[12] In many plays written at this time, the assumptions of Locke and his allies replace those of Hobbes. Liberty, in *The Provok'd Wife*, *The Wives Excuse* and *The Way of the World*, as in the extended passage on 'the *Matrimonial Noose*' in *Sylvia's Complaint*, is identified with the protection of rights against tyrannous demands, and shown to be incompatible with unlimited desire. Anticipating by several years the feminist arguments of Mary Astell and others, *Sylvia's Complaint* protests against the patriarchal system enshrined by law, under which woman on her marriage is delivered into a state of legal and economic bondage, surrendering all rights over property, inherited or acquired, to her husband:

> What Yoaks and Fetters does the *Female* choose,
> Who enters in the *Matrimonial Noose?*
> To be the Partner of anothers Flame,
> Gives up her self, her Fortune, and her Name,
> Her Hours of soft Repose and Liberty,
> Nay her own will then cease to be free;
> For what Commands may not a *Husband* lay,
> When the Wifes part, *is only to Obey?*
> And we the blest Effects may see each hour,
> Of such unbounded *Arbitrary Power*. (p. 14)[13]

Characteristically, the poem offers no alternative to a state it presents as intolerable.

Lady Mary Chudleigh's *The Ladies Defence* (1701) mounts a spirited attack on accepted patriarchal assumptions in similar terms but again has little to offer as remedy:

> Must Man command, and we alone obey,
> As if design'd for Arbitrary Sway;
> Born petty Monarchs, and, like Homer's Gods,
> See all subjected to their haughty Nods? . . .
> Why are not Husbands taught as well as we;
> Must they from all Restraints, all Laws be free?
> Passive Obedience you've to us transferr'd,
> And we must drudge in Paths where you have err'd.[14]

Yet 'Passive Obedience', Christian resignation in the face of injustice by those in authority, is all that Chudleigh, hesitant to countenance rebellion in the domestic sphere, can suggest as practical advice to abused or neglected wives.[15]

> But if our soft Submissions are in vain,
> We'll bear our Fate, and never once complain.   (p. 22)

And if it is their hard Fortune to be marry'd to Men of brutish unsociable Tempers, to Monsters in Humane Shape, to Persons who are at open defiance with their Reason, and fond of nothing but their Folly, and under no other Government but that of their irregular Passions, I would perswade them to struggle with their Afflictions, and never leave contending, 'till they have gain'd an absolute Victory over every repining Thought, every uneasie Reflection: And tho' 'tis extremely difficult, yet I wou'd advise 'em to pay 'em as much Respect, and to obey their Commands with as much readiness, as if they were the best and most indearing Husbands in the World. (Epistle Dedicatory)

Chudleigh's writings in verse and prose, like those of her friend Astell, paradoxically combine strong criticism of the abuse of power in the domestic sphere with a fear of disorder; since, according to the doctrine of 'Passive Obedience', even the worst of tyrants must be obeyed, the abused wife must look for her reward in the 'Prospect of Heaven' or within the citadel of the mind (p. 22). 'With want of Duty none shall us upbraid', Chudleigh writes, counselling her female readers 'that the greater the Difficulties are with which they encounter, the greater will be the Glory of the Conquest; and that when Death has put an end to their Conflicts, Vertue will remain victorious, and the Rewards of a Future-state abundantly compensate for all the Miseries of this'.[16] As Astell says in *Reflections upon Marriage* (1706):

She who elects a Monarch for Life, who gives him an Authority she cannot recall however he misapply it, who puts her Fortune and Person entirely in his Power . . . had need to be very sure that she does not make a Fool her

Head, nor a Vicious Man her Guide and Pattern, she had best stay till she can meet with one who has the Government of his own Passions, and has duly regulated his own Desires, since he is to have such an absolute Power over hers . . . 'Tho the Order of the World requires an *Outward* Respect and Obedience from some to others, yet the Mind is free, nothing but Reason can oblige it, 'tis out of the Reach of the most Absolute Tyrant.[17]

Chudleigh's 'To the Ladies', like Astell's *Serious Proposal to the Ladies* (Part I, 1694; Part II, 1697), proposes another possible solution: do not marry. The single state, Astell suggests, is in all significant respects preferable to being 'inveigled and impos'd upon . . . bought or sold' and delivered over to the 'continual Martyrdom' of marriage: 'for this Reason 'tis less to be wonder'd at that Women marry off in hast, for perhaps if they took time to consider and reflect upon it, they seldom wou'd marry'. In her educational tract, Astell therefore proposes as an alternative to marriage a Utopian community of women providing for temporary or permanent residents a 'Happy Retreat which will be introducing you into such a Paradise as your Mother *Eve* forfeited', an 'Amicable Society' excluding men, with 'no Serpents to deceive you', in the form of 'those Follies, which in the time of your ignorance pass'd with you under the name of love'.[18] Once a woman enters the trap of marriage, both Astell and Chudleigh suggest, there is no escape. The 'fatal Knot' cannot be dissolved, the arbitrary rule of petty tyrants cannot be challenged because such institutionalised brutality is embodied in and enforced by 'Law'. Once again, the clear conviction that certain accepted practices are unjust, that 'freedom' is the natural birthright of all rational creatures, male and female, is set against a conservative distaste for open rebellion:

> Wife and Servant are the same,
> But only differ in the Name:
> For when that fatal Knot is tied,
> Which nothing, nothing can divide:
> When she the word *Obey* has said,
> And Man by Law supreme has made,
> Then all that's kind is laid aside,
> And nothing left but State and Pride:
> Fierce as an eastern Prince he grows,
> And all his innate Rigor shows . . .
> Then shun, oh shun that wretched State,
> And all the fawning Flatt'rers hate:
> Value your selves, and Men despise,
> You must be proud, if you'll be wise.[19]

Vanbrugh's Lady Brute invokes similar political principles in 1696, but to a different end as, drawing on the contract theory widely cited to justify the recent deposition of James II, she finds scope for the exercise of freedom within marriage, as she debates with herself whether adultery is permissible as a form of revenge.

What opposes? My matrimonial vow? Why, what did I vow? I think I promised to be true to my husband. Well; and he promised to be kind to me. But he han't kept his word. Why then I'm absolved from mine. Ay, that seems clear to me. The argument's good between the king and the people, why not between the husband and the wife?

The 'argument' advanced here is standard Whig constitutional theory after 1688, as set forth (for example) in Defoe's *The True-Born Englishman* (1701), with its witty allusion to Rochester's *Satyr against Mankind*:

> *That Kings, when they descend to Tyranny,*
> *Dissolve the Bond, and leave the Subject free . . ,*
> A Chaos free to choose for their own share,
> What Case of Government they please to wear.[20]

The Whig Vanbrugh and the Tory Astell apply the same analogy to domestic life, but in *Reflections upon Marriage* Astell's attitude toward the rebel in the home is characteristically ambivalent; what may be regrettable, even unjustified, in theory, proves irresistible 'in *Fact*'. Though reluctant 'to stir up Sedition of any sort', Astell still seeks 'to retrieve, if possible, the Native Liberty, the Rights and Privileges of the Subject' in the domestic sphere.[21] Tyranny will be resisted; indeed, as many of the works to be discussed in this chapter and the next illustrate, the attempt to impose arbitrary rule on free-born subjects in itself provokes resistance. For all her respect for duly constituted authority in the state, Astell's ultimate appeal is to the right of revolution, by which tyrannous abuse will be revenged, 'Injury for Injury':

To conclude, perhaps I've said more than most Men will thank me for, I cannot help it, for how much soever I may be their Friend and humble Servant, I am more a Friend to Truth . . . If they have Usurpt, I love Justice too much to wish Success and continuance to Usurpations, which tho' submitted to out of Prudence, and for Quietness sake, yet leave every Body free to regain their lawful Right whenever they have Power and Opportunity. I don't say that Tyranny *ought*, but we find in *Fact*, that it provokes the Oppress'd to throw off even a Lawful Yoke that sits too heavy.

And if he who is freely Elected, after all his fair Promises and the fine Hopes he rais'd, proves a Tyrant, the consideration that he was one's own Choice, will not render more Submissive and Patient, but I fear more Refractory. For tho' it is very unreasonable, yet we see 'tis the course of the World, not only to return Injury for Injury, but Crime for Crime; both Parties indeed are Guilty, but the Aggressors have a double Guilt, they have not only their own, but their Neighbours ruin to answer for.[22]

Many of these works address the same problem: the perpetuation of a state of affairs, enforced by all the power of 'law and custom', in which the pleasures of freedom are open to one sex and denied to the other. The disconsolate 'Sylvia' in *Sylvia's Complaint*, in words steeped in the ideology of libertinism, can only lament fruitlessly what she (and quite possibly, her male author) perceives as unalterable.

> *Oh! could I change my Sex*, but tis in vain,
> To wish my self, or think to be a Man,
> Like that *wild Creature*, I would madly Rove,
> Through all the Fields of *Galantry* and *Love*;
> Heighten the Pleasures of the Day and Night,
> Dissolve in Joys and Surfeit with Delight,
> Not tamely like a *Woman*, wish and pray,
> And sigh my pretious Minutes all away,
> *Woman* a Creature one may justly call,
> Natures and Mans, and Fortunes *Tennis-Ball*.   (p. 18)[23]

In contrast, Astell, addressing both male and female readers, envisages a future in which women, freed by education from the chains they tamely accept, come to know their own strength and men, who 'are possess'd of all Places of Power, Trust and Profit . . . make Laws and exercise the Magistracy', recognise the injustice of the tyranny they exercise over a fellow rational creature.[24]

Though *Reflections upon Marriage* treats the theme of resistance against domestic tyranny with great caution, and is full of caveats against blowing 'the Trumpet of Rebellion' and prompting women 'to Resist, or to Abdicate the Perjur'd Spouse', Astell, far more than any of the other writers we have been discussing, denies the validity of the ideological assumptions underlying patriarchy, directing withering irony at the 'Tame, Submissive and Depending Temper' of 'those Women who find themselves born for Slavery'. In *Reflections upon Marriage*, she delivers a direct assault on the doctrine of 'absolute Sovereignty' in the family, appealing to the consciences of her readers, with the explicit aim of bringing about significant changes in attitudes and practices sanctioned by custom:

That the Custom of the world has put Women, generally speaking, into a State of Subjection, is not deny'd; but the Right can no more be prov'd from the Fact, than the Predominancy of Vice can justifie it . . . Is it not then partial in Men to the last degree, to contend for, and practise that Arbitrary Dominion in their Families which they abhor and exclaim against in the State? . . . If *all Men are born free*, how is it that all Women are born Slaves?[25]

The rebellious witty heroines of Restoration comedy – Hellena in Behn's *The Rover*, Millamant in *The Way of the World*, Ariana and Gatty in Etherege's *She wou'd if she cou'd* – frequently question 'those priviledges which custom has allowed' (*She wou'd if she cou'd*, I.ii.152–3) men and not women, rejecting passive imprisonment in their expected sexual roles or, as with Vanbrugh's Lady Brute, in the established institutions of courtship and marriage. Freedom, in these plays and in the society on which they comment, is defined as control over the property rights in one's self, and the scope for freedom in those who 'have been married already, that is, sold', was limited.[26] Marriage meant imprisonment: as *feme covert*, a woman at marriage relinquished control over her property, as well as most legal rights, during the lifetime of her husband. As Astell observes in *Reflections upon Marriage*, in any domestic struggle for domination, male and female contestants must start off from positions of marked inequality.

Because she puts her self entirely into her Husband's Power, and if the Matrimonial Yoke be grievous, neither Law nor Custom afford her that redress which a Man obtains. He who has Sovereign Power does not value the Provocations of a Rebellious Subject, but knows how to subdue him with ease, and will make himself obey'd; but Patience and Submission are the only Comforts that are left to a poor People, who groan under Tyranny, unless they are Strong enough to break the Yoke, to Depose and Abdicate, which I doubt wou'd not be allow'd of here. For whatever might be said against Passive-Obedience in another case, I suppose there's no Man but likes it very well in this.[27]

Yet the ideology of order and obedience did not prevent the deposition of two British monarchs within forty years, and, as I shall show in the rest of this chapter and in the next, women writers of this period display in their poetry, plays and fiction a considerable range of insurrectionary strategies.

Rebellion, successful or unsuccessful, against patriarchal hegemony is a recurrent theme in the works of Aphra Behn, and is virtually the only theme in the poems of Sarah Fyge, author of *The Female Advocate*. Though their writings, like Astell's *Reflections upon Marriage*, show an awareness of how difficult it is to 'break the Yoke' which the authority of family, church and state uphold, Behn and Fyge again and again challenge a double standard which simultaneously enslaves women and enfranchises men. Unlike the conservative moralists Astell and Chudleigh, neither of these writers has much use for the conventional ideas of chastity and fidelity: sexual freedom, they suggest, is no less desirable (if problematical) for women than for men. In their writings, protests against confinement and involuntary servitude to 'insulting Tyranny' are accompanied by warnings that repeated provocation will bring about retaliation.[28] The limits and effectiveness of domestic rebellion of this kind, in a world where patriarchal authority remained massively in place, will be a central concern in the rest of this chapter.

The poet Sarah Fyge, who throughout her embattled career sought to assert her own independence and the rights of women in defiance of 'Tyrant Custom' ('The Emulation', p. 108) and the established institutions of society, provides an object lesson of how difficult it was in this period for women to exercise control over their own lives. After publishing *The Female Advocate* in 1686 at the age of sixteen, she was punished for her boldness by her father by being exiled from London to a 'lonely Village' and married off against her will ('On my leaving London', p. 24).

> But ah! my Poetry, did fatal prove,
> And robb'd me of a tender Father's Love;
> (I thought that only Men, who writ for Fame,
> Or sung lewd Stories, of unlawful Flame,
> Were punish'd for, their proud or wanton Crime,
> But Children too, must suffer if they'll Rhyme).
> ('To the Lady Cambell, with a Female Advocate', p. 22)[29]

After the death of her first husband she had a 'short Parenthesis' of joy in a love affair with Henry Pierce ('On my leaving London', p. 23) to whom, under the name of 'Alexis', she addressed a number of poems and 120 letters 'expressive of the most violent and outrageous love', and then in 1700 married a second time, to the Rev. Thomas Egerton, a much older man. Her relations with Egerton were stormy: satirised in Delariviere Manley's *New Atalantis* as an archetypal termagant ('her Tongue is at perpetual War; her Discourse one continu'd Reproach'), she ran away to London with Pierce, and in 1703, the year in which her *Poems on Several Occasions* were published, she and Egerton filed suit against one another, she for divorce on the grounds of cruelty and he for the estate left her by her first husband.[30] The powerful 'On my wedding Day' (evidently, from the reference to widow's weeds, written before her second marriage) extrapolates from her experience to attack the custom of arranged marriages, presenting the 'trembling', 'reluctant' bride as sacrificial victim of a rigid patriarchal society.

> If my first Offering had been Free-Will,
> I then perhaps might have enjoy'd thee still:
> But now thou'rt kept like the first mystick Day,
> When my reluctant Soul did Fate obey,
> And trembling Tongue with the sad Rites comply'd,
> With timerous Hand th'amazing Knot I ty'd,
> While Vows and Duty check'd the doubting Bride.
> At length my reconcil'd and conquer'd Heart,
> When 'twas almost too late own'd thy Desert.   (p.71)

Both the biographical accounts and the poems suggest that Fyge actively resisted domination, using the weapon of her wit. The transgression which her father and Egerton found most unforgivable was her writing, through which, declining to act as a piece of disposable property, she exposed in print what they considered their shame.

She's a *Wit* . . tho' I understood never a Word of what she *writes*, or *says*: Deliver me from a poetical Wife, and all honest Men for my sake!

Sir, I suppose you must needs be privy to my madam's secrets, being that lovely youth, the dear undoer of her soul, and charmer of her nicer fancy; and therefore desire you to acquaint me, what settlement she made upon her estate.[31]

The 'Slavery' entailed upon women by 'Law' and by the 'impositions' of custom, she argues in 'The Emulation', is the result of fear on the part of those who hold power. Where most of the poems in the volume employ the first person singular, with any generalisations, as in 'On my wedding Day', arising from the individual instance, here Fyge speaks throughout in collective terms, of 'Womankind . . . in every State'. In 'The Emulation' Fyge proposes a competitive model, loosely Hobbesian, for relations in marriage and for human behaviour in general:

> They're Wise to keep us Slaves, for well they know,
> If we were loose, we soon should make them, so.
> We yield like vanquish'd Kings whom Fetters bind,
> When chance of War is to Usurpers kind;
> Submit in Form; but they'd our Thoughts controul,
> And lay restraints on the impassive Soul.   (pp. 108–9)

In her use of the political metaphor of slavery and tyranny, Fyge allows, far more than either Chudleigh or the author of *Sylvia's Complaint*, for the practical possibility of resistance to arbitrary power. Yet in her poems, freedom is defined as unattainable, as that which is desired yet ever beyond reach. Chudleigh and Astell ultimately appeal to a shared ideal of rationality, projecting a harmonious limited monarchy within the household in which male sovereign treats female subject with respect and understanding:

And Lastly, I would have them look upon them as Friends, as Persons fit to be confided in, and trusted with their Designs, as such whose Interest is inseparably united with theirs: by such Methods as these, they would not only win their Love, but preserve it, and engage 'em to a reciprocal Esteem; and when once they have secur'd their Affection, they need not doubt of their Obedience; the desire to please will render the most difficult Commands easie.[32]

Fyge, in contrast, presents in her poems a state of universal domestic war, where the only alternatives envisaged are unwilling, resentful submission to superior force or an imagined reversal in which the slave, magically freed of her bonds, can become tyrant in turn.

'The Emulation' begins with a series of statements, bitter and angry, which severely limit the hope of independent action for women, ruling out the hope of 'escape' from institutionalised servitude except within the citadel of the mind.

> From the first dawn of Life, unto the Grave,
> Poor Womankind's in every State, a Slave,
> The Nurse, the Mistress, Parent and the Swain,
> For Love she must, there's none escape that Pain;
> Then comes the last, the fatal Slavery,
> The Husband with insulting Tyranny
> Can have ill Manners justify'd by Law;
> For Men all join to keep the Wife in awe.   (p. 108)

For Fyge, the lover and the husband, though ostensibly representing rival interests, are allied in a male conspiracy to keep women in their place. All the men, real or fictional, who appear under pastoral pseudonyms in Fyge's poems, are selfish and unreliable, the 'wealthy *Strephon*' ('The Fate', p. 50) and the 'perjur'd' Philaster, deceiving another 'poor cousen'd Fool' with his 'worn-out Sighs' ('To Philaster', p. 34) no less than the 'base, designing' Alcander, looking for an easy sexual conquest.

> Why should I suffer, for your lawless Flame?
> For oft 'tis known, through Vanity and Pride,
> Men boast those Favours which they are deny'd:
> Or others Malice, which can soon discern;
> Perhaps may see in you some kind Concern.
> So scatter false Suggestions of their own.
>
> ('The Repulse to Alcander', pp. 25–7)

Betrayal is thus the norm and sexual love, explicitly defined in several of Fyge's poems as adulterous, an attempt to break out of the confinement of marriage, becomes yet another form of imprisonment. In these poems, with their cold, designing men and fiery women ('Love glows in every Atom of my Frame', 'The Invocation', p. 58), the erotic impulse is defined as 'inherent Pain' ('To One who said I must not Love', pp. 42–3) intensified by the sense of guilt, 'a dangerous Liberty' ('The Fatality', p. 73) simultaneously feared and desired.

> But now these soft Allays are so like Sin,
> I'm forc'd to keep the mighty Anguish in . . .
> Distorted Nature shakes at the Controul,
> With strong Convulsions rends my strugling Soul;
> Each vital String cracks with th' unequal Strife,
> Departing Love racks like departing Life.
>
> ('To One who said . . .')[33]

Marriage thus brings imprisonment in the fetters of convention and 'insulting Tyranny', where love brings the pangs of guilt ('The Emulation', p. 108). The struggles of the 'conquer'd Heart' are depicted by Fyge in 'On my wedding Day' and 'The Gratitude' (pp. 68–70) with their promises, accompanied by tidal waves of emotion, to mourn a husband she did not love. In 'The Gratitude', one of many poems in which she presents her life as a chain of calamities, Fyge writes about her inability to overcome feelings of resentment toward her first husband, castigating herself for being 'negligent' while he was alive. In 'To One who said I must not Love', commenting on her second marriage with undisguised contempt, she treats marital vows and love, adulterous and therefore 'Criminal', as two kinds of slavery:

> Weary'd at last, curst *Hymen's* Aid I chose;
> But find the fetter'd Soul has no Repose.
> Now I'm a double Slave to Love and Vows:
> As if my former Sufferings were too small,
> I've made the guiltless Torture Criminal. (p. 42)[34]

The search for freedom, as Fyge presents it in poem after poem, is thus delusory: the hope for 'change' only brings new varieties of pain.

> Like a distracted Man that will not bear,
> Those Fetters which Discretion makes him wear,
> But frets and raves, and breaks the friendly Chain,
> Which did from greater Injuries restrain . . .
> Thus I from one Misfortune force my Way,
> By Means that does to greater still betray;
> One Sorrow seldom attends long on me,
> I have a torturing Variety,
> I change and change, yet still 'tis Misery. ('The Fatality', p. 73)

A limited scope for freedom, under the competitive model of relationships between the sexes, is suggested in 'The Emulation' which, like an anonymous earlier poem under the same title in the miscellany volume *Triumphs of Female Wit* (1683), proposes 'Learning's World' as a suitable field for female endeavour. The attempt by males, jealously guarding their unjust privileges, to monopolise 'the Sciences and Arts', is presented by Fyge as contrary to natural right and to the Protestant principle of the equality of individual souls before God.

> They fear we should excel their sluggish Parts,
> Should we attempt the Sciences and Arts.
> Pretend they were design'd for them alone,
> So keep us Fools to raise their own Renown;
> Thus Priests of old their Grandeur to maintain,
> Cry'd vulgar Eyes would sacred Laws Prophane . . .
> But in this blessed Age, such Freedom's given,
> That every Man explains the Will of Heaven.
> ('The Emulation', p. 109)[35]

In similar terms, the anonymous author of the 1683 'Emulation' attributes imposed ignorance, the forced captivity of the 'rational, unbounded Mind', to a male desire to dominate, and insists that men and women are equals:

> Shall they be blest with intellectual Light,
> Whilst we drudge on in Ignorances Night?
>   We've Souls as noble, and as fine a Clay,
> And Parts as well compos'd to Please as they.
>   Men think perhaps we best obey,
>   And best their servile Business do,
>   When nothing else we know
> But what concerns a Kitchin or a Field.[36]

The rhetoric is explicitly political in Fyge's call to arms: 'Wit's Empire' is not, as in Astell's *Serious Proposal*, praised for its own sake, but as a suitable arena for competition, providing an opportunity to 'reverse' the master/slave relationship: 'No, we'll be Wits, and then Men must be Fools'. 'Excursions in Philosophy' thus become another instance of playing trick for trick, a compensatory dream by which the powerless turn the tables on their oppressors:

> And shall we Women now sit tamely by,
> Make no excursions in Philosophy,
> Or grace our Thoughts in tuneful Poetry?
> We will our Rights in Learning's World maintain,
> Wit's Empire, now, shall know a Female Reign.   (p. 109)

By focusing on intellectual endeavours, arguing a case for increased opportunities in women's education as enabling the enfranchisement of 'the noble Females Soul from the slavery of an entailed Ignorance unto the freedom and more agreeable pursuit of Learning and Wisdom', Fyge's 'The Emulation', like its anonymous predecessor, concedes the case for a monopoly of power by men in the family and in the state. Fyge's tone is more consistently combative: both the 1683 'Emulation' and *The Ladies Defence* tend to be apologetic and placatory, backing away from any challenge they offer:

> We've now no *Amazonian* Hearts,
> They need not therefore guard their *Magazine* of *Arts*.
>   We will not on their treasure seise,
> A part of it sufficiently will please:
>   We'll only so much Knowledge have
>   As may assist us to enslave

> Those Passions which we find
> Too potent for the Mind.
> 'Tis o're them only we desire to reign,
> And we no nobler, braver, Conquest wish to gain.[37]

Yet Fyge in 'The Emulation', no less than these writers, even while questioning the 'impositions' of 'tyrant Custom', draws short of confronting patriarchal power directly, limiting rebellion to the sphere of 'Thoughts' (pp. 108–9), the imagination which the strictest prison cannot confine. As Chudleigh puts it in *The Ladies Defence*:

> The Tyrant Man may still possess the Throne;
> 'Tis in our Minds that we wou'd Rule alone:
> Those unseen Empires give us leave to sway,
> And to our Reason private Homage pay.   (p. 18)[38]

In Fyge's lively poem 'The Liberty' the grounds for rebellion are again 'private' and domestic. The stance Fyge assumes in this poem is bold, openly challenging the 'Fetters' and 'Manacles' imposed on women by the 'dull fulsome Rules' of social conformity. As in 'The Emulation', she attacks 'the Idol Custom' and the fear of 'the Devil Censure' as contemptible, causing women to behave like 'timerous Infants' and 'obsequious Fools'.

> My daring Pen, will bolder Sallies make,
> And like my self, an uncheck'd freedom take;
> Not chain'd to the nice Order of my Sex,
> And with restraints my wishing Soul perplex:
> I'll blush at Sin, and not what some call Shame.   (pp. 19–21)

Yet the poem confines its 'uncheck'd freedom' to the minutiae of behaviour, in a strictly regulated world of 'visits' and gossip, applauding such minor triumphs as staying out in company after eight at night, telling a mildly indecorous joke or, behind closed doors, reading a forbidden book:

> My Sex forbids, I should my Silence break,
> I lose my Jest, cause Women must not speak.
> Mysteries must not be, with my search Prophan'd,
> My Closet not with Books, but Sweat-meats cram'd.
>
>   (pp. 19–20)

'The Liberty' is an expression of anger and frustration at powerlessness, the protest of a 'wishing Soul' desiring to be free, but hemmed in on all sides. Indeed, Fyge's whole career shows how powerful the fear of 'Shame' was during this period in regulating the lives of women: as counterbalance against the heavy weight of officially sanctioned disapproval and ostracism which threatened all open rebels – adulteresses, shrews, women with an immodest thirst for learning and interests beyond 'useful Houswifery' – she could only cite, petulantly, 'my own Humour'. The closing lines, in their claim that women 'keep those Rules, which privately we Curse', revealingly emphasise not strategies of contesting power, but sullen obedience, forced submission: 'With what reluctance they indure restraints' (pp. 20–1).

On the face of it, the literary career of Aphra Behn, a professional writer who competed on equal terms with male colleagues, publishing over fifty volumes of plays, translations, poems and prose fiction in twenty-odd years, was far more successful than that of Sarah Fyge, and far less subject to the 'restraints' Fyge found so galling.[39] Yet from the outset of her career, Behn's writings were subject to attacks of extraordinary virulence, which equate female authorship with prostitution and raging, indiscriminate sexual appetite. To the misogynist satirist Robert Gould, writing in 1691, the transgression of authorship by a woman, breaking a silence prescribed by custom, was exactly equivalent to sexual transgression: 'the scribling Itch' was an immediate consequence of the loss of virginity.

> What has this Age produc'd from Female Pens,
> But a wide Boldness that outstrides the Mens? . . .
>
> *Ephelia*, poor *Ephelia*, Ragged Jilt,
> And *Sapho*, Famous for her Gout and Guilt,
> Either of these, through both Debaucht and Vile,
> Had answer'd me in a more Decent Style:
> Yet *Hackney Writers*, when their Verse did fail
> To get 'em Brandy, Bread and Cheese, and Ale,
> Their Wants by Prostitution were supply'd,
> Shew but a Tester, you might up and Ride;
> For *Punk* and *Poetess* agree so pat,
> You cannot well be *this*, and not be *that*.[40]

Rochester, ventriloquising through his female persona Artemiza, puts a similar comparison in more favourable terms, associating the composition of poetry with the inversion of normal expected patterns of female behaviour and with the assertion of a sexuality perceived by a male-dominated society as threatening.

Chloe, in Verse by your commande I write;
Shortly you'l bid me ride astride, and fight.
These Talents better with our sexe agree,
Than lofty flights of dang'rous poetry . . .
Whore is scarce a more reproachfull name,
Than Poetess.   ('Artemiza to Chloe', 1–4, 25–6)

The popular image of Behn in her lifetime, among admirers as
well as detractors, was as a woman 'proficient both in the theory and
practice' of sexual passion, openly scandalous in being 'bawdy in her
works, unchaste in her life'.[41] Scurrilous attacks on her as a second
Messalina, descending to the 'common Stews' in pursuit of new
sexual partners, and praise of her ability to arouse 'amorous Ecsta-
sies' in the male reader through 'the resistless Charms' of her
seductive verse, share the assumption that sexual knowledge was the
necessary condition of her art. The praise is no less demeaning than
the overt misogyny of the satires ('And so you might have often seen
her swiv'd') in its relegation of woman to a state of sub-rational
passivity, a slave where man is naturally free.

Thus *Afra*, thus despairing *Sappho* mourn'd,
Sure both their Souls are to your Breast return'd.
By the same Tyrant-Passion all enslav'd,
Like you they wrote, like you they lov'd and rav'd.[42]

Poetry thus becomes a product of the genitals – the 'black Ace' in
one account of 'the Poetesse Afra', which treats as equivalent
achievements 'the Plays she had writ, and the Conquests she had
won'.[43] Later critics, even when they write as Behn's champions,
again and again treat her writings as thinly disguised autobiography. Here as elsewhere, critics seem disinclined to believe that
a woman could invent anything or exercise the discipline of a
conscious artist. Three biographies of Behn published in recent
years, all avowedly feminist in approach, seek to rehabilitate her
reputation, presenting her as a writer with a 'radical', 'revolutionary' view of 'sexual freedom, for women as well as men', a resolute
critic of the dominant patriarchal assumptions of her society.[44] Yet
all three biographers, when they consider Behn's exploration of
female sexuality, automatically turn each poem into an autobiographical confession, at times in an embarrassingly bathetic way,
using a critical vocabulary which is pure Mills and Boon. On the
poem 'To Lysander at the Musick Meeting', which employs a

wholly conventional 'fair singer' motif, wittily adapted to male singer and female panegyrist: 'She was now in her late thirties and for the first time she felt real physical desire.' On a pindaric ode 'On Desire', again highly traditional in its materials and form: 'In her poem "On Desire", Aphra associated her newly discovered sexual feelings with a young man whose identity she hid.' The lyric 'Amyntas led me to a grove', used in the play *The Dutch Lover* and recycled with a change of sex in the speaker in *Covent Garden Drolery* (1672) as 'I led my Silvia to a grove', before reappearing, again with a female speaker, in *Poems* (1684), becomes 'a direct acknowledgment of her own desire'. Even the premature ejaculation of 'The Disappointment' is charged to the personal failings of John Hoyle, Behn's reluctant lover.[45]

'The Golden Age', to which Behn gives particular prominence as the first poem in her 1684 collection, is highly interesting to the student of sexual ideology during the period, not least as the acknowledged work of a woman author. Yet once again, where it has been noticed at all, it has either been presented as autobiography or quoted very selectively to illustrate a simple doctrinal point. To see the 'diatribes against honour' in the poem as 'expressions of personal resentment' is both patronising and naive, and a critic who, recognising the poem's gestures at universality, ignores its traditional elements, is no less misleading.[46] As an imitation of one of the most celebrated Renaissance poems, Tasso's 'O bella età de l'oro', Behn's carefully wrought poem is radical in some ways, conventional in others, partly reflecting and partly interrogating the fashionable libertinism of the day.

The first three stanzas of Behn's poem follow, in an expanded form, the general outlines of Tasso's original, presenting a *locus amoenus* of a highly traditional kind: 'Eternal Spring' (5), 'unwearied' singing of birds (29), serpents without venom, fields producing plenty without the aid of 'the stubborn Plough' (31). There are two striking additions in the early stanzas: in stanzas I–III the landscape is eroticised far more than in Tasso (with 'willing Branches' exchanging 'thousand Kisses' and birds intermixing 'Love and Musick' in their amorous play, 12, 30), and in stanzas IV–V a political dimension absent from Tasso's poem is introduced.

> Monarchs were uncreated then,
> Those Arbitrary Rulers over men;
> Kings that made Laws, first broke 'em, and the Gods

By teaching us Religion first, first set the World at Odds . . .
Right and Property were words since made,
    When Power taught Mankind to invade:
When Pride and Avarice became a Trade;
    Carri'd on by discord, noise and wars,
    For which they barter'd wounds and scarrs;
And to Inhaunce the Merchandize, miscall'd it Fame,
    And Rapes, Invasions, Tyrannies,
    Was gaining of a Glorious Name:
Stiling their salvage slaughters, Victories.   (IV, 51–4, V, 65–73)[47]

As Goreau has suggested, Behn in these lines is using the myth of a primitive unfallen natural domain to mount a sharp attack on 'the "masculine" principles of aggression and acquisition', as deformations imposed on man by an ideology in which 'Power' over others has become the supreme value.[48] In singling out the restless desire for power as a motivating force and in treating religion, with a satirist's scorn, as an instrument of social control created by man, Behn is indebted to the tradition of Hobbesian libertinism, as she is elsewhere in the poem. But, taking issue both with Hobbes and with liberal contract theorists, Behn explicitly excludes the concepts of 'Right' and 'Property' from her state of nature: private property, as she presents it here, is allied to tyranny, and not a bulwark against it.[49]

In its hedonist ethics, its appeal to a natural unfettered liberty in men and in women expressing itself in sexual terms, its attack on 'Tyrant Honour' and on the belief that desires are shameful, needing restraint, 'The Golden Age' follows Tasso's original closely:

    Then it was glory to pursue delight,
And that was lawful all, that Pleasure did invite,
    Then 'twas the Amorous world injoy'd its Reign;
And Tyrant Honour strove t'usurp in Vain . . .
Oh cursed Honour! thou who first didst damn,
    A Woman to the Sin of shame.   (V, 80–3, VIII, 117–18)[50]

The reference to 'the Sin of shame', added by Behn, may suggest a particular sympathy for women as victims of a hypocritical ideology. But the extensive additions in stanzas VI and VII interpret sexual freedom from an essentially male point of view, in a manner familiar in Restoration libertinism.

> The Nymphs were free, no nice, no coy disdain,
> Deny'd their Joyes, or gave the Lover pain;
> The yielding Maid but kind Resistance makes;
> Trembling and blushing are not marks of shame,
>   But the Effect of kindling Flame:
> Which from the sighing burning Swain she takes,
> While she with tears all soft, and down-cast eyes,
> Permits the Charming Conqueror to win the prize. (vi, 97–104)

The last line suggests a residue at least of the Hobbesian competitive model within Behn's ideal state of sensuous enjoyment. 'Free' in the first line means 'freely available' as much as 'expressing a natural liberty'; 'kind' and 'yielding', in the standard vocabulary of Restoration libertinism, similarly privilege male desire as sovereign, implying not reciprocity but surrender. Though men and women are both depicted as feeling bodily desire (expressed, with no intervention of the conscious will, as 'Trembling and blushing'), some sexual partners are more equal than others.

The stanza which follows, again added by Behn, treats male and female desire as equivalent, with no implicit hierarchy, but again situates itself firmly in the tradition of Hobbesian libertinism, in its treatment of religion and the 'Politick Curbs' by which those occupying positions of power in church and state seek to maintain control. Like Rochester, Behn in 'The Golden Age' reinterprets Hobbes to support arguments for natural freedom, rather than order. The vocabulary of the final lines of the stanza is that of the liberal, constitutionalist tradition, and, as we have seen, that of contemporary feminist attacks on 'arbitrary Sway' in the domestic sphere as contrary to natural right: man and woman are 'freeborn' and restraints on their liberty have no rational foundation.[51]

> The Lovers thus, thus uncontroul'd did meet,
> Thus all their Joyes and Vows of Love repeat:
>   Joyes which were everlasting, ever new
>   And every Vow inviolably true:
> Nor kept in fear of Gods, no fond Religious cause,
>   Nor in Obedience to the duller Laws.
> Those Fopperies of the Gown were then not known,
> Those vain those Politick Curbs to keep man in,
> Who by a fond Mistake Created that a Sin;
> Which freeborn we, by right of Nature claim our own.
>   Who but the Learned and dull moral Fool
> Could gravely have forseen, man ought to live by Rule?
>
> (vii, 105–16)

There are some writings of Behn which, like the poems of Fyge, have an avowedly autobiographical, expressive element. The 1696 collection *Histories and Novels Of the Late Ingenious Mrs Behn*, edited by Charles Gildon, includes a series of love letters by Behn to John Hoyle. This sequence of eight letters, documenting a historically verifiable relationship, occupies the disputed territory between fact and fiction. All evidence suggests that these are private letters, not intended for publication, and though some letters printed in miscellany volumes attributed to well-known writers (including other 'Behn' letters published elsewhere) are fabrications, these letters are evidently genuine.[52] Yet what is most striking about these letters is how literary they are: in expressing and analysing her feelings at being rejected by Hoyle, Behn accommodates herself to the decorum of the epistolary novel and the rejected heroines of fiction and drama. At roughly the same time in which she herself was writing such an epistolary novel in *Love-Letters between a Nobleman and his Sister* (1684–7) and shortly after the influential *Portuguese Letters*, a French novel masquerading as a collection of found letters, was translated into English, Behn, as it were, models herself on one of these fictional seduced and abandoned women in writing to Hoyle.[53]

Possibly you will wonder what compels me to write, what moves me to send where I find so little Welcome; nay, where I meet with such Returns, it may be I wonder too . . . My Soul is ready to burst with Pride and Indignation; and at the same time, Love, with all his Softness assails me, and will make me write; so that, between one and the other, I can express neither as I ought. (*Histories and Novels*, pp. 405, 412)[54]

Like Clarissa, the Mariana of the *Portuguese Letters*, and other heroines of epistolary novels, Behn uses 'write' to mean 'express oneself', 'establish communication', break out of the trap of enclosure. The letters to Hoyle, like the fictional letters of Mariana, are an attempt to create the illusion of dialogue out of absence. They use the epistolary form to 'speak with' (p. 403) someone infuriatingly silent and unresponsive, with an implicit appeal to an imagined wider, disinterested audience less deaf to the claims of passion and justice.

In similar fashion, Hoyle is presented in these letters as a familiar literary character, the cold and manipulative libertine. Love, as anatomised here, feeds on neglect and disdain, increases in proportion to the obstacles set up by the unaccommodating lover.

I burst to speak with you, to know a Thousand Things; but particularly, how you came to be so barbarous, as to carry away all that cou'd make my

Satisfaction . . . 'Twas with that Design you came; for I saw all Night with
what reluctancy you spoke, how coldly you entertain'd me, and with what
pain and uneasiness you gave me the only Conversation I value in the
World . . . I am undone, and will be free; I will tell you, you did not use me
well: I am ruin'd, and will rail at you. (Letter II, *Histories and Novels*,
pp. 403–4)

The speaker's language here echoes that of the impulsive, ardent
Mariana, as the author skilfully uses the epistolary form to characterise the sharply contrasting letter-writer and recipient.[55] In
accusing Hoyle of 'reluctancy', indifference, even an aversion to her,
Behn casts herself in the role of abandoned maiden, 'undone' and
'ruin'd', atypically, by a man's refusal to play the game of seduction.
Throughout the sequence of letters, passionate avowals of the intensity of her love jostle against a realistic awareness that the object of
her affections is a man whose capacity for emotion is limited indeed.

The deliberate construction of Hoyle's character, in which he is
presented, with a degree of irony, as fulfilling a recognisable pattern
of libertine behaviour, is even clearer in an earlier work which resists
categorisation as fact or fiction. A playful poem called 'Our Cabal',
in which several of Behn's circle of friends (eleven in all) are given
pastoral pseudonyms, with their real names or initials printed as
headings to each verse paragraph, includes a character sketch of
Hoyle. Like many of the poems of Katherine Philips, 'Our Cabal' in
its published form resembles a private transaction made public, with
the cryptic 'Mr. Je. B', 'Mr. J. H.', 'My dear *Amoret*, Mris. B.' both
concealing and revealing privileged information.[56] The poem predates the period of her intense involvement with Hoyle, and its tone
is one of amused detachment, but the character emerges as very
similar: a man who holds all women equally in low esteem, and
whose success as a libertine is directly the result of his refusal to love.
In Don Juanesque fashion, once a woman surrenders, he loses all
interest in her:

> His Tongue no Amorous Parley makes,
> But with his Looks alone he speaks . . .
> Nor will but Love enough impart,
> To gain and to secure a heart:
> Of which no sooner he is sure,
> And that its Wounds are past all Cure,
> But for New Victories he prepares,
> And leaves the Old to its Despairs:
> Success his Boldness does renew,

And Boldness helps him Conquer too.
He having gain'd more hearts then all,
Th'rest of the Pastoral Cabal.   (165–80)

The lines would appear to provide ample warning (which, in her subsequent relationship with Hoyle, she did not follow), and another passage in 'Our Cabal' delicately touches on a further reason for Hoyle's coldness toward women, his homosexual preferences, 'too Amorous for a Swain to a Swain' (188), which eventually resulted in prosecution for the capital offence of buggery: as an unreconstructed partisan of the Good Old Cause, one contemporary satirist put it, 'he always loved the Rump'.[57] In the letters, Hoyle is consistently presented as remote, disapproving, gratuitously cruel in his behaviour, a 'Miser' in the expression of affection but, in his 'severe Prudence and Discretion', free with his censure. In addressing the unresponsive Hoyle, the letters anticipate, even court rejection, assuming that any overtures will be rebuffed (*Histories and Novels*, p. 406).

In one letter where, as in the poem 'To Lysander, on some Verses', Behn develops an extended financial conceit – in this case drawn from gambling, running up a debt, fulfilling a contract – she explicitly attacks the double standard in which a man, 'Greedy', 'Ungenerous' and indifferent to fairness, expects unquestioning adoration and fidelity from a woman, while behaving in an entirely different fashion himself. As we shall see, this is a central concern in Behn's poems, as in her plays. But in contrast to those poems which wittily warn a male addressee that his conduct risks retaliation in kind by an aggrieved mistress, here the clever deployment of prudential arguments only intensifies the sense of impasse.

This, I say, may be the Danger; I may come off unhurt, but cannot be a *Winner*: Why then shou'd I throw an uncertain cast, where I hazard all, and you nothing? Your staunch Prudence is Proof against Love, and all the Bank's on my side: You are so unreasonable, you wou'd have me pay where I have contracted no Debt: you wou'd have me give, and you, like a Miser, wou'd distribute nothing. (Letter IV, *Histories and Novels*, p. 406)

The poems of Behn are firmly embedded in a social context, as well as being full of literary echoes, frequently commenting on previous texts. In many cases they take the form of answer-poems, with such titles as 'To Lysander, who made some Verses on a Discourse of Loves Fire', 'To Lysander, on some Verses he writ, and asking more for his Heart than 'twas worth', 'To Alexis, in Answer of his Poem against Fruition'. In each of these poems, a hypothesised emotional relationship between a man and a woman finds expression in an exchange of manuscripts, embodying a debate between two representative intellectual positions.[58] The vocabulary and assumptions of these poems, as with 'The Golden Age', are frequently those of Restoration libertinism, but in taking the woman's part, acting as female advocate, they place particular emphasis on male strategies of domination.

> Take back that Heart, you with such Caution give,
>   Take the fond valu'd Trifle back;
> I hate Love-Merchants that a Trade would drive;
>   And meanly cunning Bargains make.
>
>   ('To Lysander, on some Verses', 1–4)

Each of these poems is in its own way an attack on the double standard. Behn does not include in her miscellany volume the poem by 'Lysander' she is answering, but she does not need to do so, since his position is a familiar one: the man in any relationship should have licence to roam widely, while the woman must wait patiently for his return, nursing her sorrow. The first four stanzas of 'To Lysander, on some Verses', with caustic wit, develop an extended mercantile conceit, contrasting the 'Heart Unfeign'd and True' appropriate to love with the selfish desire to 'Monopolize' the 'free Trade' of the affections (9–12). Where the letters to Hoyle use similar imagery to analyse the predicament of being trapped in a sterile, obsessive relationship, here from the opening lines the poet suggests an alternative to the 'hopeless Pain' of frustrated desire, to which the poem gives poignant expression in several stanzas:

> And every Hour still more unjust you grow,
>   Those Freedoms you my life deny,
> You to *Adraste* are oblig'd to show,
>   And give her all my Rifled Joy.
>
> Without Controul she gazes on that Face,
>   And all the happy Envyed Night,
> In the pleas'd Circle of your fond imbrace:
>   She takes away the Lovers Right . . .
>
> Whilst like a Glimering Taper still I burn,
>   And waste my self in my own flame,
> *Adraste* takes the welcome rich Return,
>   And leaves me all the hopeless Pain.   (21–8, 41–4)

Like a number of the works discussed in this chapter, 'To Lysander, on some Verses' applies the terminology of contemporary political debate to sexual relations, condemning as 'unjust' a conception of 'Freedom' which enslaves and tyrannises over others.

In the poem, as in several others by Behn, the principal female figure refuses to accept the role of passive victim. Instead, in the closing stanzas, the poem, no less explicitly than Astell's *Reflections upon Marriage* a few years later, appeals to principles frequently invoked in the political controversies of the 1680s and applied, by many of the writers we have been discussing, to private rather than public conduct: natural freedom and equality, the right of revolution.

> Be just, my lovely *Swain*, and do not take
>   Freedoms you'll not to me allow;
> Or give *Amynta* so much Freedom back:
>   That she may Rove as well as you.
>
> Let us then love upon the honest Square,
>   Since Interest neither have design'd,
> For the sly Gamester, who ne're plays me fair,
>   Must Trick for Trick expect to find.   (45–52)

As the echo of the title of her best-known play suggests, the heroines of Behn's plays and novels claim the same right as their male counterparts to 'Rove' and if necessary to play 'Trick for Trick'. Here as elsewhere in works in this tradition, the impulse toward domination and the desire for freedom are closely intertwined. Neither 'To Lysander, on some Verses' nor Behn's other writings in various genres on similar themes, dramatising struggles for power and freedom within sexual relationships, assume any benevolence in those in positions of authority, who are unlikely to heed warnings to 'be just'. Instead, these works suggest that injuries received will, after continued provocation, be revenged, that pent-up desire will erupt, with consequences no one can predict.

In 'To Lysander, who made some Verses on a Discourse of Loves Fire', the attack on the double standard is equally strong, but the poem is more equivocal in treating the possibility of aggressive retaliation. Here Lysander, like the convention-ridden 'Wiser men' of Rochester's 'The Mistress' (13), is represented as objecting to the 'Marks of Passion' evinced by 'Jealousie' – in this case, the reproaches of a lover made uncomfortable by his casual infidelities

('To Lysander, on Loves Fire', 1–4). The poem, like Behn's 'On Desire', accepts the libertine position that sexual desire is not by its nature confined, and presents the sexual instincts in essentially mechanistic terms:

> 'Tis true, when Cities are on fire,
> Men never wait for Christal Springs;
> But to the Neighb'ring Pools retire;
> Which nearest, best Assistance brings;
> And serve as well to quench the raging Flame,
> As if from God-delighting Streams it came. (13–18)

'To Lysander, on Loves Fire' concedes that, in unromantic fact, 'that Fire/I kindle, may another warm': the sexual itch may be allayed by any convenient, available object, with the aid of the transformative powers of 'Fancy' (7–8, 19). Yet Behn in this poem argues the case for self-denial, less on moral than on prudential grounds. Naturalist arguments, here as in the pindaric ode 'On Desire', support promiscuity for both sexes, in whom the operations of sexual desire are alike.[59]

> Tell me, yee fair ones, that exchange desire,
> How 'tis you hid the kindling fire.
> Oh! wou'd you but confess the truth,
> It is not real virtue makes you nice:
> But when you do resist the pressing youth,
> 'Tis want of dear desire, to thaw the Virgin Ice . . .
> Oh tell me, how do you remain discreet?
> How you suppress the rising sighs,
> And the soft yeilding soul that wishes in your Eyes?
> ('On Desire', 89–94, 98–100)

In 'On Desire', virtue is, in the standard vocabulary of Hobbesian libertinism, 'but a cheat/And Honour but a false disguise' (103–4). In 'To Lysander, on Loves Fire', on the other hand, 'Honour' (25) is presented as a form of enlightened self-interest rather than as a self-deceiving ideology of artificial restraint. Infidelity, however much it may correspond to a natural 'Wish' (25) for untrammelled liberty, destroys the trust on which a relationship is built, breeding either a reciprocal infidelity or sexual rejection.

> Take in no Partners to your Fire,
> For who well Loves, that Loves one more?
> And if such Rivals in your Heart I find,
> Tis in My Power to die, but not be kind. (33–6)

Yet in 'To Lysander, on Loves Fire', unlike its companion poem 'To Lysander, on some Verses', the 'Power' rests almost wholly with the male, who is free to rove where the woman is constrained: 'What Lover wou'd pursue a single Game,/That cou'd amongst the Fair deal out his flame?' (29–30). The poem's conclusion is remarkably weak and equivocal: it appeals to a self-restraint which it admits is unlikely to govern male sexual pursuit, holding out to the female object and victim of desire only the power to decline to 'be kind', denying sexual favours the indifferent male may no longer want.

In the exchange with 'Alexis' concerning 'Fruition' (sexual intercourse), Behn even more explicitly takes the role of female advocate, arguing that in a sexual relationship the interests of men and women are frequently incompatible. Though Behn is working within a well-worn tradition of witty poetic debate, most seventeenth-century poems on the topic present sexual pleasure exclusively from a male perspective, in which women serve exclusively as catalysts for male desire. In poems against fruition by Suckling and Cowley, postponing 'enjoyment' becomes a kind of masturbatory device, to increase the quantum of pleasure.

> Women enjoy'd (what se're before th'ave been)
> Are like Romances read, or sights once seen.

> That monster Expectation feeds too high
> For any Woman e're to satisfie.

> *Love*, like a greedy *Hawk*, if we give way,
> Doth over-gorge himself, with his own *Prey*.

The contempt for women which underlies the hedonism of these poems is made overt in a phrase by Suckling, with its self-fulfilling prophecy: 'She's but an honest whore that yields'.[60] When Rochester in 'The Platonick Lady' undertakes a poem in this genre, he adopts a female persona and, like Behn, presents women as able to feel as well as arouse desire. Yet Rochester's poem shares many of the assumptions of others in the tradition, embodying a male fantasy of endless female availability, imagining woman as a neutral field on which male desire can 'toye' and 'play'. 'Freedom' for a woman is once again limited to the liberty to serve man:

> I love a youth, will give mee leave
>   His Body in my arms to wreath;
> To presse him Gently and to kisse,
>   To sigh and looke with Eyes that wish.

> For what if I could once Obtaine,
> I would neglect with flatt disdaine.
>
> I'de give him Liberty to toye,
> And play with mee and count it Joye,
> Our freedom should be full compleate,
> And nothing wanting but the feate:
> Let's practice then, and we shall prove,
> These are the only sweets of Love –   (13–24)[61]

The poem by 'Alexis', which Behn includes in her miscellany volume, takes a more philosophically serious stance, partly influenced by Montaigne and partly by Rochester's *Satyr against Mankind*. Rather than arguing the advantages of extended foreplay or celebrating the unlimited energies of the imagination, Alexis's 'Poem against Fruition' laments the 'wretched' condition of mankind, endlessly searching for an unattainable happiness. In its psychology, the poem is indebted to Hobbes and, in its characteristic rhetoric, to Rochester:

> Hurried by our fantastick wild desire
> We loath the present, absent things admire . . .
> Our boundless vast desires can know no rest,
> But travel forward still and labour to be blest.
> Philosophers and Poets strove in vain
> The restless anxious Progress to restrain,
> And to their loss soon found their Good supreme
> An Airy notion and a pleasing Dream. . .
> Left to our reason, and by that betray'd,
> We lose a present bliss to catch a shade.[62]

In her answer poem, Behn accepts a number of these premises: the joys so eagerly sought after are transitory and deceptive, 'like lightning flash and are no more' ('To Alexis', 2), and so are the valued attributes of body and mind. But inconstancy and restlessness in Behn's poems are not so much universal principles, the sad lot of mankind, as they are excuses men use to justify their calculating exploitation of women. The brevity of the sex act is made a symbol not of the inability of reality to match expectations, but of male betrayal:

> While all our joys are stinted to the space
> Of one betraying enterview,
> With one surrender to the eager will
> We're short-liv'd nothing, or a real ill.   ('To Alexis', 11–14)

Throughout the poem, Behn uses the pronoun 'we' in a very different manner from Alexis, expressing solidarity with other women, to whom she offers counsel. All men, she warns, are 'like *Alexis*', losing interest as soon as the 'wisht Possession' has been secured: 'Then heedless nymph, be rul'd by me/If e're your Swain the bliss desire' (34–7).

Behn's answer poem is no less libertine in its assumptions than the poems which take the other side of the debate: nothing lasts, love is a fraud, self-interest should rule. The advice she is offering, half-seriously, is not simply to say 'no', resisting the blandishments of the tempter, or (as with Pope's advice to Belinda) to modify the false values women have learned from society. Elaine Hobby reads a straightforward feminist moral into the final stanza: the author, in this reading, is 'calling on her sisters to reject the whole set-up', to opt out of the game altogether: another version of the advice offered by Chudleigh in 'To the Ladies' to 'shun the wretched State' of marriage offered by the tempter man.[63] And yet the force of the rhetoric of 'To Alexis', with its exhaustive list of possible alternatives, antithetically balanced, leaves no real possibility of opting out. The identification of speaker with audience as a member of the class to which the bleak generalisations apply adds to the feeling of inevitability in these witty, poignant lines. All women, however they may choose to behave, end up as 'Trophies' of 'conquest' (31), to be casually discarded when they have served their purpose for the predatory males:

> Since Man with that inconstancy was born,
> To love the absent, and the present scorn.
>   Why do we deck, why do we dress
>   For such a short-liv'd happiness?
>   Why do we put Attraction on,
> Since either way 'tis we must be undon?
>
>   They fly if Honour take our part,
> Our Virtue drives 'em o're the field,
>   We lose 'em by too much desert,
>   And oh! they fly us if we yield.
>
> ('To Alexis', 15–24)

Like many poems by Behn, 'To Alexis' raises questions to which there are no easy answers. As we shall see, this is equally the case with works by Behn in other genres which, like her poems, dramatise the problematical aspects of freedom in domestic relations.

Female libertines, single-mindedly intent on the pursuit of sexual pleasure, are relatively rare in Restoration literature. Mirtilla in Behn's comedy *The Younger Brother* (1696), a 'Jilt' unencumbered by feelings of conscience or loyalty, openly expresses a rake's ethos, glorying in 'Dissimulation' and in the exercise of will: 'A new desire of humouring my wish, sways all my Interest, and controuls all my Honour. Why should I lose a Pleasure for a Promise, since Time, that gives our Youth so short a Date, may well excuse our needful Perjury.'[64] Like Miranda, the heroine of Behn's novel *The Fair Jilt* (1688), Mirtilla presents herself as having been instructed by men in selfishness and deceit: in a world where merciless competition is the accepted norm, one must use the weapons at one's disposal, without compunctions, as Mirtilla remarks to a discarded lover who accuses her of fickleness:

Hast thou took care wisely to teach me all the Arts of Life, and dost thou now upbraid my Industry? Look round the World, and thou shalt see, *Lejere*, Ambition still supplies the Place of Love. The worn-out Lady, that can serve your Interest, you swear has Beauties that outcharms Fifteen; and for the Vanity of Quality, you feign and languish, lye, protest, and flatter – all Things in Nature Cheat, or else are Cheated. (IV.i, p. 35)

In *The Younger Brother*, Behn follows the conventional pattern, by which the 'jilt' is exposed to public shame (as with Olivia, Manly's deceitful fiancee in *The Plain-Dealer*) or led to see the error of her ways and to repent. The dramatic situation encourages the audience to sympathise with the female rake's victims.

Female libertines in Restoration drama tend to be presented as motivated by the assertion of power through revenge. Thomas Durfey's *Madam Fickle*, for example, has as its central figure a jilt who has sworn vengeance on the male sex, using her 'quick designing Wit' to ensnare a series of victims, while remaining unscathed herself:

My Panthers breath shall draw 'em to the Snare: my Tongue shall Charm; my Smiles kindle Loves Fire on their amorous Souls, till they're scorched severely; then forsake 'em . . . The more difficulty lies in the matter, the better 'tis often performed: hard shifts, and dangerous plots suit Womens Wits better than dull adventures; and whilst in tedious search dull men run on, arm'd by one minutes thought, the thing is done.

Like Lady Lurewell in Farquhar's *The Constant Couple* (1700), Madam Fickle repents in the end, once the lover who in her early youth had forsaken and 'betrayed' her unexpectedly returns: 'My dear *Friendlove*! Can this be true? Am I then once more blest with thy Caresses?'[65]

No such happy endings are provided in Thomas Southerne's bitter and entirely unsentimental *The Maid's Last Prayer* (1693). Here the libertines, male and female, pursue pleasure as Hobbesians, viewing sexual intrigue either as a struggle for power or as a straightforward cash transaction. As an aging bawd recommends, pleasure in the sex act is greater 'where we have no Concern': 'Madam, Madam, every Woman wants a Thousand Pound: And for your Inclinations, if you allow them to get the better of you, you are undone. There are a great many pretty Gentlemen to be had: but what will you get by any of 'em in the End?'[66] Nothing in Southerne's play can be said to contradict the bawd's prudential advice. Lady Trickitt, a female libertine expressing attitudes normally associated with her male counterparts, angrily asserts her independence from a possessive lover. Pleasures, it is suggested, are self-seeking and aggressive, with no reciprocity possible: sexual equality here is an equality of competition, in a fight to the death.

Sir, I won't be suspected, I won't be enquir'd into: a Husband can do no more; and I have enough of one Husband and his ill Humours at home, I thank you, ever to allow a Husband abroad to torment me. Perhaps you think I can't break with you; I wou'd have you to know, Sir, I can, and will break with you and fifty more, rather than break one hours Rest for any of you. I'll change as often as I shift my Cloaths, but I'll light upon a Man that has Sense enough to value his own pleasure, without invading mine. If I depended on you indeed, and there were no body else to be had, you might tye me to your own terms, but, make us thankful, there's roving room enough in this dear Town: I can provide my self, I warrant you. (IV.iv.159–69)[67]

The ideology of libertinism, with its emphasis on 'change', self-interest, 'roving room', is central to Behn's *The History of the Nun* and *The Fair Jilt*, two novellas with fallible, inflammatory heroines impatient of restraint. In the first of these the wayward nun Isabella, who begins as a model of beauty and piety, 'a saint in the chapel, and an angel at the Grate', ends up, spectacularly, as 'the murderess of two husbands (both belov'd) in one night'.[68] Critics have often been uneasy with the 'lack of moral placing' in Behn's fiction, accusing Behn of moral and aesthetic 'incoherence' in fiction in which wrongdoers do not meet their expected end and crime 'seems to pay'. Other critics, notably Elaine Hobby, applaud the seeming amorality of *The History of the Nun* and *The Fair Jilt*, treating their blood-spattered heroines as feminist role models, whose crimes of adultery, bigamy and attempted or successful murder are explained away as 'the assertive expression of desire'.[69] The grim comedy of the concluding pages of *The History of the Nun*, with bodies tumbling into the stream, tends to foreclose sympathy for any of the characters, rather than, as Hobby suggests, directing sympathy toward Isabella as victim of an unjust society. Yet though Isabella and her two lovers Henault and Villenoys are reminded repeatedly of the claims of the forces of order – at the time of the initial elopement, for example, as 'criminals, first, that had transgress'd the law: and next, as disobedient persons, who had done contrary to the will and desire of their parents' (p. 185) – what is strikingly absent from *The History of the Nun* is the sense that these social imperatives have any binding force or any intrinsic validity. The ironies of *The History of the Nun* and *The Fair Jilt* in no way serve a didactic end.[70]

Isabella's first marriage is the result of an overmastering passion, but after, schooled by adversity, she has learned the market value of 'her charming face and mien', she marries a second time 'for interest' (pp. 192–3). When her first husband, supposedly killed in the wars, returns after eight years absence, Isabella is faced with a moral dilemma, which she resolves by a series of practical arguments, dominated by considerations of self-interest. At no point does she give a moment's thought to the possible feelings of either husband, but only of the danger of public humiliation, a precipitate and irreversible decline in reputation from 'glory' to 'the scorn of the town, who will look on her as an adulteress' (p. 197). At this juncture in the narrative, Behn inserts a passage drawing a general conclusion from Isabella's experience, expatiating, in terms familiar in the libertine tradition, on the transience of love. The appeal to what, in a similar passage in her novel *Love-Letters Between a Nobleman and His Sister*, Behn calls 'a most certain truth' applicable to all lovers makes the heroine's behaviour seem less culpable, less a matter of conscious volition:

Besides, she could not recall her love, for love, like reputation, once fled, never returns more. 'Tis impossible to love, and cease to love (and love another), and yet return again to the first passion, tho the person have all the charms, or a thousand times more than it had, when it first conquer'd.

This mistery in love, it may be, is not generally known, but nothing is more certain. One may a while suffer the flame to languish, but there may be a reviving spark in the ashes, rak'd up, that may burn anew; but when 'tis quite extinguish'd, it never returns or rekindles. (p. 197)[71]

In the opening paragraphs of *The History of the Nun*, Behn introduces Isabella's career of destructiveness by situating it in terms of a prevalent libertine ideology, in which men serve as tutors of the women they betray.

What man does not boast of the numbers he has thus ruin'd, and, who does not glory in the shameful triumph? Nay, what woman, almost, has not pleasure in deceiving, taught, perhaps, at first, by some dear false one, who had fatally instructed her youth in an art she ever after practis'd, in revenge on all those she could be too hard for, and conquer at their own weapon? . . . The women are taught, by the lives of the men, to live up to all their vices, and are almost as inconstant; and 'tis but modesty that makes the difference, and hardly inclination. (pp. 152–3)

The pattern of conduct traced here is what Astell in *Reflections upon Marriage* describes as returning 'Injury for Injury . . . Crime for Crime' (p. 91), and what Rochester in 'Artemiza to Chloe' calls 'turning the too-dear-bought trick on Men' (192): the 'fond believing wretch' learns by bitter experience that it is preferable to be the exploiter rather than the exploited (*History of the Nun*, p. 152).

In both *The History of the Nun* and *The Fair Jilt*, the heroine begins her career as a nun. Nuns as they appear in literary tradition (as Hamlet's celebrated pun would suggest) are sexually ambivalent figures, at once emblems of chastity and provocative, enigmatic objects of desire. Nuns have always featured prominently in pornography, much of which combines anti-clerical satire with a desire to titillate the reader with the lure of the forbidden.[72] Such works are often profoundly misogynist, depicting women as sexually available and burning with lust despite their pious pretences. Yet if the conventional libertinism of pornography shows the nun, under her demure garb, as secretly admitting 'no Bounds' to her lustful desires,[73] the opening paragraphs of *The History of the Nun* treat the plight of the 'young nuns enclos'd' in a far more sympathetic manner.

Nevertheless, I could wish, for the prevention of abundance of mischiefs and miseries, that nunneries and marriages were not to be enter'd into, till the maid, so destin'd, were of a mature age to make her own choice; and

that parents would not make use of their justly assum'd authority to compel
their children, neither to one or the other; but since I cannot alter custom,
nor shall ever be allow'd to make new laws, or rectify the old ones, I must
leave the young nuns enclos'd to their best endeavours, of making a vertue
of necessity; and the young wives, to make the best of a bad market.
(p. 154)

Much of the critical commentary on this passage has treated it as
autobiographical, speculating on whether the young Aphra Behn
really was 'design'd a humble votary in the house of devotion'
(p. 153).[74] But what is most interesting, and most characteristic of
the author, is the emphasis on the role of patriarchal authority in
stocking 'nunneries and marriages' with young women barely out of
childhood (like 'the little Isabella'), turned into objects of exchange,
with no power to choose for themselves (p. 155). Despite the conservative disclaimers Behn carefully inserts ('justly assumed authority', 'I cannot alter custom'), the opening pages of *The History of
the Nun* comprise a feminist protest against the patriarchal organisation of society, with its ritualised traffic in women.[75]

    Miranda in *The Fair Jilt* is less a victim, and more a conscious
agent, manipulative and self-willed. She is introduced not as a
helpless child but an accomplished young woman, 'bred with the
nicest care', and 'practis'd' in all the 'female arts' (pp. 105–6).
Much courted for her beauty and wealth, she is determined to retain
control, aware that her market value may diminish later. The
pleasure she takes in the role of jilt, giver rather than receiver of
pain, is established at the outset:

She was vain enough to glory in her conquest, and make it her business to
wound. She lov'd nothing so much as to behold sighing slaves at her feet, of
the greatest quality; and treated 'em all with an affability that gave 'em
hope . . . Miranda accepted their presents, heard their vows with pleasure,
and willingly admitted all their soft addresses; but would not yield her
heart, or give away that lovely person to the possession of one, who could
please it self with so many. (pp. 106–7)

The Fair Jilt begins with an extended tribute, highly ambiguous
and in part ironic, to the 'wondrous power of love': 'I'll prove to you
the strong effects of love in some unguarded and ungovern'd hearts;
where it rages beyond the inspirations of a god all soft and gentle,
and reigns more like a fury from hell' (p. 104). The conversion of
love into rage is a literary commonplace, as is the identification of

the 'tormenting flames' of unrequited love (p. 197) with the infernal fires: the tragic heroines Medea and Phaedra provide illustrations and, in Restoration comedy, Angelica Bianca in *The Rover* or Loveit in *The Man of Mode*. But the fury of these passionate abandoned heroines and cast-off mistresses, whether treated with tragic intensity or ironic detachment, is always motivated, either by the callous behaviour of men or by guilt and despair. Miranda's behaviour is gratuitous: she is not motivated by revenge in which she turns her betrayer's weapons against him, but by an innate tendency towards inconstancy and an allegiance to the tenets of libertinism.

She was naturally amorous, but extremely inconstant: she lov'd one for his wit, another for his face, another for his mien; but above all, she admir'd quality . . . Wherever she found that, she lov'd, or at least acted the lover with such art, that (deceiving well) she fail'd not to compleat her conquest . . . She knew the strength of her own heart, and that it could not suffer it self to be confin'd to one man, and wisely avoided those inquietudes, and that uneasiness of life she was sure to find in that married life, which would, against her nature, oblige her to the embraces of one, whose humour was, to love all the young and gay. (p. 107)

In actively pursuing her desires, ignoring the conventional restraints of morality, Miranda acts in accordance with a rake's ethos, no less consistently than Dorimant, Horner or the inconstant, manipulative male figures in Behn's poems. As Hobby remarks, she behaves in ways traditionally associated with males, single-mindedly and aggressively intent on sexual conquest, demanding consummation from a passive, unwilling partner whose own feelings she disregards.[76] In a passage of comic eroticism which, in a manner characteristic of Behn's writings, subverts conventional gender boundaries, the young Father Henrick, object of Miranda's illicit desires, is as it were feminised, as in her imagination Miranda undresses 'the charming friar', stripping off his 'coarse, grey, ill-made habit':

She frames an idea of him all gay and splendid, and looks on his present habit as some disguise proper for the stealths of love . . . The robe laid by, she has the lover in his proper beauty, the same he would have been, if any other habit (though never so rich) were put off: in the bed, the silent, gloomy night, and the soft embraces of her arms, he loses all the friar, and assumes all the Prince. (pp. 114–15)[77]

When persuasion, 'soft words' have no effect on the chaste passivity of Henrick, Miranda resorts to force. First, sacrilegiously, she violates the sacraments, and seeks to seduce her confessor before the very altar, using her own beauty as bait. When her attempts to awaken his dormant passions are rebuffed, she reveals her libertine principles more openly, contemptuously dismissing religion as a cheat and all moral constraints as 'dull dissimulation', while extolling sexual fulfilment as constituting 'the greatest blessings of life'. In threatening physical violence – indeed, the female rake here comes as close as possible to being a female rapist – Miranda nakedly exposes the hatred and aggression which underlie the transgressive power of eros. Her 'raging fire' requires satisfaction, and when all else fails this can be provided by the violent destruction of the unresponsive object of her desires (pp. 118, 121).[78]

What is strikingly absent from both *The Fair Jilt* and *The History of the Nun* is any psychological dimension in the presentation of the 'fatal beauty' and her string of victims. Miranda, like Isabella, goes on from crime to crime, and yet there is never any suggestion of the workings of conscience under the deceptively 'fair' exterior: unlike Defoe's Roxana or Beatrice in *The Changeling*, neither of Behn's heroines admits she is the deed's creature. Both works end with public executions, extended theatrical spectacles in which the heroine is metamorphosed into a glittering object to attract the eyes and enthrall the 'hearts' of gazers, a manifestation of the hypnotic, amoral power of transgressive eros, here explicitly allied to death:

All the windows were taken down, and filled with spectators, and the tops of houses; when at the hour appointed, the fatal beauty appear'd. She was dress'd in a black velvet gown, with a rich row of diamonds all down the forepart of her breast, and a great knot of diamonds at the peak behind; and a petticoat of flower'd gold, very rich, and laced. (*The Fair Jilt*, p. 135)

When the day of execution came, she appear'd on the scaffold all in mourning, but with a mien so very majestick and charming, and a face so surprizing fair, where no languishment or fear appear'd, but all chearful as a bride, that she set all hearts a flaming, even in that mortifying minute of preparation for death . . . Without any thing over her face, she kneel'd down, and the executioner, at one blow, sever'd her beautiful head from her delicate body, being then in her seven and twentieth year. (*The History of the Nun*, p. 207)

Despite the somewhat ramshackle episodic construction of both *The Fair Jilt* and *The History of the Nun*, a thematic unity is discernible in both works, as fictional treatment of an overwhelming subversive force which recognises no limits and resists all attempts at moral categorisation.

The sadistic component inherent in this protean libidinal force is emphasised repeatedly in Behn's fiction, which, like her poetry, challenges certain aspects of the ideology of libertinism, while accepting the paradigm of unrelenting, remorseless competition in domestic as well as political life. In the Hobbesian world of human relationships, no less implicit in *The Fair Jilt* and *The History of the Nun* than in such poems as 'To Lysander, on some Verses', the only options open are victory or defeat. Behn's fiction, like her poems, shows how sexual freedom for one partner may mean slavery for another, but at the same time holds out the possibility of a rebellion of the powerless.

I end this chapter by quoting two passages of extraordinary violence, both of which compel a degree of fascinated complicity in the reader, even a vicarious, amoral participation in the brutal scene.[79] One comes from Behn's *Oroonoko*, the other from 'The Wife's Resentment', a novella published in 1720 by Behn's disciple Delariviere Manley in a collection entitled *The Power of Love*.

Look ye, ye faithless crew, said he, 'tis not life I seek, nor am I afraid of dying, (and at this word, cut a piece of flesh from his own throat, and threw it at 'em) . . . At that, he rip'd up his own belly, and took his bowels and pull'd 'em out, with what strength he could; while some, on their knees imploring, besought him to hold his hand.

Violenta . . . raising herself in the Bed, and transported with Wrath, struck the Poinard into his Throat: *Ianthe* hearing him groan, leap'd briskly upon the Bed, and getting upon him with her Knees and Hands kept him down: He struggled, but *Violenta*, like another *Medea*, mad with Rage and Fury redoubled her Stroke, and thrust the Point of the Dagger with such Force into his Throat, that she pierced it through on the other side.[80]

The instinctive force depicted in each of these passages, whether it can be characterised as libidinal energy, a desire to punish and be punished, or naked will, is no less amoral than that depicted in *The History of the Nun* or *The Fair Jilt*. In *Oroonoko*, an anti-slavery tract, the insistent violence to some extent serves a polemical purpose, in arousing sympathy and indignation on behalf of the courageous victim of a cruel and irrational institution. Yet Oroonoko's suffering is initially self-inflicted, the product of grief and remorse for his ritual 'sacrifice' (in a passage charged with erotic imagery and parallel in several details with the scaffold scene in *The History of the Nun*) of his 'lovely, young and ador'd victim', his wife Imoinda (p. 94).[81] His mutilation – a symbolic castration followed by the real thing – enacts common aggressive phantasies, with the murderous impulses turned inward. Masochism, Freud says, is 'a transformation of sadism . . . turned round upon the subject's own self, which thus . . . takes the place of the sexual object'.[82] Oroonoko welcomes the executioner's 'ill-favour'd knife' (p. 98), since it enacts his own desires, in completing the lovers' suicide pact as a final tribute to the power of love.

In the murder scene which provides the climax of Manley's 'The Wife's Resentment', the identity of love and hate is brought out graphically in the passage quoted, which exploits the erotic appeal of violence, making the murder a grotesque parody of the sex act. Sexuality is presented here as the weapon of the dispossessed, as the once-loved seducer, the tables spectacularly turned, is impaled on the phallic source of his power. As in the transformations of Miranda and Isabella, the impersonal force entering Violenta 'like a Torrent' – and the comparisons to Medea and 'a raging *Bacchanal*' explicitly identify that force as libidinal – breaks down all customary barriers, revealing a potential for destructive energy previously buried within (p. 206). Like Brecht's 'Ballad of Pirate Jenny', the scene can be read as the dream of the powerless and unfree (in this case, Violenta and her willing accomplice, the servant Ianthe) for a long-deferred revenge upon their oppressors.

Violenta, like Oroonoko, is the leader of a slave's revolt, doomed to failure, which challenges the moral basis of the master's power, though unable to bring about effective change. The African slave and the neglected wife both earn the praise of onlookers by demonstrating unexpected qualities of 'Courage and Magnanimity' ('The Wife's Resentment', p. 227), overturning usual assumptions of race, class and gender, but neither achieves anything beyond the momentary emotional release afforded by violence. But Oroonoko, unlike Violenta, expresses a coherent ideology which transcends the immediate circumstances of the failed revolt, and this, despite the author's firm Tory allegiances, is a set of principles we find expressed or implied again and again in her writings: liberal contract theory, grounding a right of revolution on principles of equality under natural law. Oroonoko stirs up his reluctant troops with just such arguments: freedom is the inalienable heritage of every human being, and slavery, however much custom and fear may sanctify it, is an ignominy not to be endured by rational creatures.

They suffer'd not like men, who might find a glory and fortitude in oppression; but like dogs, that lov'd the whip and bell, and fawn'd the more they were beaten; that they had lost the divine quality of men, and were become insensible asses, fit only to bear . . . Be esteem'd as his fellow-sufferers, and men that had the courage and the bravery to attempt, at least, for liberty; and if they dy'd in the attempt, it would be more brave, than to live in perpetual slavery. (pp. 83, 85)

Oroonoko's address to his fellow slaves, like Mary Astell's scornful remarks on those women 'Wise enough to Love their Chains' who 'think as humbly of themselves as their Masters can wish', assumes that the responsibility of freedom is a burden not everyone will be willing to bear: 'And therefore as to those Women who find themselves born for Slavery, and are so sensible of their own Meanness as to conclude it impossible to attain to any thing excellent . . . She's a Fool who wou'd attempt their Deliverance and Improvement. No, let them enjoy the great Honor and Felicity of their Tame, Submissive and Depending Temper!'[83] As well as criticising those who, fearing freedom, preferred 'perpetual slavery' to arduous struggle, Behn and Astell in commenting on the political conflicts of the seventeenth century attack the 'Unbounded Licentiousness' of those who, cloaking their ambition in liberty's guise, sought 'the Arbitrary Priv'lege to enslave' ('Of Plants', Bk VI, 70), in an attempt to gain 'such exorbitant Power as may enable them to *Tyrannize* over their Fellow Subjects'.[84] Neither Behn nor Astell approved of the Revolution of 1688. Both were ardent Tory loyalists, who gave only qualified, reluctant allegiance to William III after the deposition of James II. Yet it is wholly characteristic of Behn, with her prickly independence, that in her 'Pindaric Poem' to Gilbert Burnet declining to write a poem in celebration of the new monarch, she presents herself as motivated by conscience, a solitary 'Forsaken' woman resisting unjust male power:

> My Muse that would endeavour fain to glide
> With the fair prosperous Gale, and the full driving Tide
> But Loyalty Commands with Pious Force,
> That stops me in the thriving Course.

> The Brieze that wafts the Crowding Nations o're,
> Leaves me unpity'd far behind
> On the Forsaken Barren Shore,
> To Sigh with Echo, and the Murmuring Wind.[85]

In these witty lines, which exploit and parody the conventional rhetoric of panegyric, Behn, while never breaking the decorum of apparent praise, suggests that Burnet and others like him are time-servers, ruled entirely by self-interest. William's accession, here and in other poems of Behn, is presented as straightforward conquest, a *coup d'état*, with no element of consent. The ability of Burnet and other apologists for power to 'Change every Notion, every Principle/ To any Form, its Great Dictator please', is, Behn implies, an abuse of reason, deploying the 'Commanding Force' of rhetoric to make the worse cause seem better (15, 72–3).[86]

Along with the language of panegyric, Behn in this poem as so often in her writings makes use of the language of Ovidian elegy, ironised by context to call into question the assumptions of a libertinism which casually exploits and discards women. Echoing her own Ovidian imitation 'A Paraphrase on Oenone to Paris', Behn in the lines quoted above plays the role of seduced and abandoned maiden, 'half dead on the forsaken Strand' (174), left 'Useless and Forlorn' to lament ('Pindaric Poem', 87), as 'the Rocks and Hills [her] dire complaints resound' (218).[87] In an earlier stanza, Behn with delicate irony eroticises the relationship between the 'Pow'rful' Burnet (16), using 'soft prevailing Force' (68) to urge submission to the conqueror, and a reluctant female audience, whose 'weak Defence' (18) is in danger of being overwhelmed. Here as in the later passage, seeming praise on closer scrutiny turns into sharp criticism, as the seductions of rhetoric are literalised:

> A thousand ways my Soul you can Invade,
> And spight of my Opinions weak Defence,
> Against my Will, you Conquer and Perswade.
> Your Language soft as Love, betrays the Heart,
> And at each Period fixes a Resistless Dart,
> While the fond Listner, like a Maid undone,
> Inspir'd with Tenderness she fears to own;
> In vain essays her freedom to Regain.   (17–24)

The resistance of the 'stubborn Muse' (48) is presented in the 'Pindaric Poem' as the exercise of rational freedom – not in this case rebelling against tyranny, but refusing to submit to unjust power, declining to 'share the Triumph' (65) of those who would, in domestic as in public life, reduce all human relationships to conquest and submission.

CHAPTER 5

My masculine part: Aphra Behn and the androgynous imagination

Though Aphra Behn in a number of poems presents herself as a disciple of 'the Great, the God-like *Rochester*', citing 'fam'd *Strephon*' as inspiration and model for her own literary career, the two authors could hardly be more different in their social background and their characteristic literary stance.[1] Where Rochester was an aristocrat, son of a distinguished father, writing lyric poems and satires designed for manuscript circulation in the court circle to which he belonged, Behn, whose parentage is unknown (as is the identity or ultimate fate of her shadowy husband), was 'forced to write for Bread and not ashamed to owne it'. Existing precariously on the margins of society, imprisoned at one point for debt, complaining in one letter of 'extreme want' and in another bargaining with her publisher Tonson for an increase of £5 in her fee for a commissioned book, Behn was forced to be practical, to put a price on her talents.[2]

Complaints of 'want of money, having pawned her very rings', of being unable 'to buy so much as a shoe to travel in', dire warnings that she was on the verge of being 'ruined and disgraced in a strange place', forced to 'beg or starve', echo through Behn's letters of 1666–8. She had been sent to the Netherlands on a mission of espionage during the Anglo-Dutch war, reporting on republican exiles, and ended up in a British prison, when her employer, Lord Arlington, refused to acknowledge her services and pay a debt of £150:

I must go to prison to-morrow if I have not the money to-night; they say I am dallied with, and will not allow a few days more. I would break through all, get to the King, and never rise till he had paid the money, but am too sick and weak. I will send my mother to the King with a petition, and not perish in a prison, whence he [Edward Butler, her creditor] swears I shall not stir till I have paid the uttermost farthing. If I have not the money to-night you must send me something to keep me in prison, for I will not starve.[3]

Fifteen years later, in writing to Tonson about the publication of *Poems upon Several Occasions* (1684), she is in a stronger bargaining position, but continues to protest that she 'wants extremely' and therefore must concern herself with 'low gettings', the practical necessities of providing a secure income for herself. The letter is fascinating in its hard-headed professionalism: where Rochester and Katherine Philips express the aristocratic amateur's disdain for those who allow their writings to be 'expos'd to the world . . . to entertain all the rabble', Behn, in contrast, discusses in detail with her publisher the order of poems in the volume, remarks that she will send the printer material as fast as he can print it and drives a hard bargain over the price.

As for ye verses of mine, I shou'd really have thought 'em worth thirty pound; and I hope you will find it worth 25 £; not that I shou'd dispute at any other time for 5 pounds where I am so obleg'd; but you can not think what a pretty thing ye Island will be, and w^t a deale of labour I shall have yet with it . . . But pray speak to your broth^r to advance the price to one 5^{lb} more . . . I vow I wou'd not aske it if I did not really believe it worth more. Alas I would not loose my time in such low gettings, but only since I am about it I am resolv'd to go throw wth it . . . I pray go about it as soon as you please, for I shall finish as fast as you can go on. Methinks the Voyage shou'd come last, as being the largest volume. You know Mr. Cowly's David is last, because a large poem, and Mrs. Philips her plays for ye same reason . . . I wish I had more time, I wou'd ad something to ye verses that I have a mind too, but, good deare Mr. Tonson, let it be 5^{lb} more, for I may safly swere I have lost the getting of 50^{lb} by it . . . I have been without getting so long y^t I am just on the point of breaking, especiall since a body has no creditt at ye playhouse for money as we usd to have, fifty or 60 deepe, or more; I want extremely or I wou'd not urge this.[4]

Behn's conduct of her career as a writer over a period of nearly twenty years shows the same professionalism throughout. In twelve years beginning 1670 she wrote at least thirteen plays for the Duke's Company headed by Thomas Betterton, most of them with parts tailored specifically for the leading actors of the company: Betterton, William Smith, Elizabeth Barry, Betty Currer, Mary Lee and the comic actors James Nokes, Cave Underhill and Anthony Leigh. No other dramatist had more plays produced and published during this period: Dryden, her only rival in this respect, wrote all his plays for the rival King's Company and it is clear from the cast lists in *The London Stage* that Behn and Thomas Otway were the mainstays of Betterton's company. In her first ten years with the company, Barry, the greatest actress of the period, played speaking roles in seven plays by Behn and nine by Otway, all fashioned to suit her particular talents.[5] Some indication of the care Behn took in casting and rehearsing her plays can be found in the dedication to *The Widdow Ranter* (1690), published posthumously:

The play had not that Success which it deserv'd, and was expected by her Friends. The main fault ought to lye on those who had the management of it. Had our Authour been alive she would have committed it to the Flames rather than suffer'd it to have been acted with such Omissions as was made . . . And lastly, many of the Parts being false Cast, and given to those whose Tallants and Genius's suited not our Authors Intention.[6]

Behn's steady income from the playhouse ceased for four years in 1682, when she and one of the actresses in the Duke's company were imprisoned for slandering the Duke of Monmouth in an epilogue spoken on stage. For the next four years, no plays by Behn were performed, and though her next plays to be acted, *The Lucky Chance* (performed 1686, published 1687) and *The Emperor in the Moon* (1687) were great successes, she needed to find another source of income during a period when she was allowed 'no creditt at ye playhouse for money', as in previous years. She found it in Tonson and other publishers, for whom she provided a steady stream of novels, prose and verse translations, and volumes of poetry between 1684 and her death in 1689, including the three volumes of *Love-Letters Between a Nobleman and his Sister* (1684–7), thirteen shorter novels, three collections of poems and eight lengthy translations in prose and verse.[7]

The violent, obscene attacks on Behn, like those on her friend and colleague Elizabeth Barry, equate the public status of professional writer or actress with prostitution:

And as more Public, are more Mens Desire . . .
Now Men enjoy your Parts for Half a Crown,
Which, for a Hundred Pounds, they scarce had done . . .
Since lately you Lay-In, (but as they say,)
Because, you had been Clap'd another Way.[8]

Defamatory statements of this kind have far too often been cited as evidence that Behn or Barry really was 'notorious as a whore', 'a mere harlot', 'mercenary' and pox-ridden, living by selling her sexual services to men. But as Elizabeth Howe has argued, such attempts to blacken the reputation of a figure made vulnerable by her very prominence can be interpreted as 'resentment of a woman who achieved popularity, power and, above all, material success in a public career', akin to the charges that one or another male associate – Hoyle, Otway, Edward Ravenscroft – was the real author of Behn's plays.[9] Indeed, Behn comments in her preface to *The Lucky Chance* that 'there is a sort of Self-Interest' in the 'Malice' of rival authors, 'Railing at every thing they find with pain successful . . . And nothing makes them so through-stitcht an Enemy as a full Third Day' (Sig. A3^v).

In prefaces to several plays, Behn objects strongly to a double standard, as manifested in a fear of female sexuality which would stigmatise as 'unnaturall' and improper in a woman author what is accepted without question in a man. The tyranny of custom and the hypocrisy of those who find their pleasure in seeking out 'Indecencys' come under fierce satiric attack in the prefaces to *Sir Patient Fancy* (1678) and *The Lucky Chance* (1687).

That it was Baudy, the least and most Excusable fault in the Men writers, to whose Plays they all crowd, as if they came to no other end then to hear what they condemn in this: *but from a Woman it was unnaturall* . . . The Play had no other Misfortune but that of coming out for a Womans: had it been owned by a Man, though the most Dull Unthinking Rascally Scribler in Town, it had been a most admirable Play. (Sig. A1–A1^v)

Had the Plays I have writ come forth under any Mans Name, and never known to have been mine; I appeal to all unbyast Judges of Sense, if they had not said that Person had made as many good Comedies, as any one Man that has writ in our Age; but a Devil on't the Woman damns the Poet. (Sig. A4^v)[10]

The competitive model of 'emulation' (defined by *OED* as 'the endeavour to equal and surpass others in any achievements') is apparent in the appeal to literary tradition in the preface to *The Lucky Chance*, a combative 'Vindication' of the play from the 'peevish Cavills' of 'obstinate Criticks' (Sig. A3^v). As in Sarah Fyge's 'The Emulation', discussed in the previous chapter, the intense desire to 'excel' and triumph over one's enemies is fuelled by a keen sense of disenfranchisement or exclusion. The preface to *The Lucky Chance* (written, like so many of Behn's works, under pressure: 'the Play, being all printed off and the Press waiting', Sig. A4^v) grounds its argument on the premises, taken as self-evident, that 'Freedom' is the birthright of both men and women and that, conversely, usurpation is by definition unjust:

All I ask, is the Priviledge for my Masculine Part the Poet in me, (if any such you will allow me) to tread in those successful Paths my Predecessors have so long thriv'd in, to take those Measures that both the Ancient and Modern Writers have set me, and by which they have pleas'd the World so well. If I must not, because of my Sex, have this Freedom, but that you will usurp all to your selves; I lay down my Quill, and you shall hear no more of me, no not so much as to make Comparisons, because I will be kinder to my Brothers of the Pen, than they have been to a defenceless Woman. (Sig. a1)

The partly ironic reference to 'a defenceless Woman' suggests that Behn is not averse to playing the game of flirtation with her audience and exploiting or parodying characteristic 'feminine' roles in badinage with her 'Brothers of the Pen'. Prologues and epilogues in Restoration plays generally alternate in flattering and abusing their audience, and Behn's prologue to her early play *The Forc'd Marriage* (1671), spoken by one of the actors (probably Betterton), seeks to establish a complicity between male speaker and male audience. Here the imagery of amorous warfare is entirely conventional, unthreatening, and implicitly dismissive of 'the vain Sex':

> Women, those charming victors, in whose eyes,
> Lay all their Arts, and their Artilleries;
>   Not being contented with the wounds they made,
> Would by new stratagems our Light invade . . .
> They'le joyn the Force of Wit to Beauty now,
> And so maintain the right they have in you.[11]

Disclaiming any 'design to Conquer' other than in the lists of love, Behn ends the prologue with a passage spoken by one of the actresses coyly asserting that 'all our Aim' is 'to pleasure you' (Sig. A3–A3ᵛ) in what Rochester in one of his poems calls 'loves Theatre the Bed'.[12]

A second passage using the conceit of the female warrior, more defiant in its treatment of the male audience and its values, appears in Behn's epilogue to *Sir Patient Fancy*. Here she develops at some length the image of the Amazon as model of female achievement, in protesting against the presumptions of men who treat 'Sense and Sacred Poetrie' as their exclusive possession.

> We once were fam'd in Story, and cou'd write
> Equall to men; cou'd Govern, nay cou'd Fight.
> We still have passive Valour, and can show
> Wou'd Custom give us leave the Active too,
> Since we no provocations want from you.   (p. 92)[13]

The Amazonian motif is taken up in defences of the 'Parts and . . . natural Capacity' of women by several writers of the period, male and female. In the Duchess of Newcastle's *Bell in Campo* and Rochester's fragmentary *The Conquest of China*, two unstageable heroic dramas, the heroines provide positive role-models by leading armies into battle, and in both works, as in the anonymous 'The Emulation' (1683), such transgressive actions are shown as arousing jealousy and fear in male rivals.

> For they know Women heretofore
> Gain'd Victories, and envied Lawrels wore:
> And now they'll fear we'll once again
> Ambitious be to reign
> And to invade the Dominions of the Brain.[14]

Behn's lines in the epilogue to *Sir Patient Fancy*, spoken by the actress Anne Quin to a male audience, contain a marked element of sexual innuendo absent from these works. 'Passive Valour', with the double entendre common to such passages in Restoration prologues and epilogues, can hint at sexual availability as well as the willingness to 'bear' or 'endure' provocations without taking revenge. The bold claims in the epilogue that women are 'Equall to men' are considerably undercut by the suggestion, a few lines later, that female wit is best or most characteristically demonstrated in sexual encounters: in bed or on stage, women find their fulfilment in giving men pleasure.

> That we have Nobler Souls then you, we prove,
> By how much more we're sensible of Love;
> Quickest in finding all the subtlest waies
> To make your Joys; why not to make you plays? (p. 92)

Catherine Gallagher has argued that Behn in passages like this turns the symbolic equation of female playwright, actress and prostitute to her own advantage, deploying 'the overlapping discourses of commercial, sexual, and linguistic exchange' in order to 'create the effect of an inaccessible authenticity out of the very image of prostitution'.[15] But it is equally possible to find in the lines an unresolvable ambivalence toward the libertine values of an audience on whom, as professional dramatist, Behn is dependent, not only for a 'Third day', but for a more lasting prize, 'Fame', which, in another variation of the Amazon conceit, she claims in the preface to *The Lucky Chance* to 'value . . . as much as if I had been born a Hero' (Sig. a1).

The preface to *The Dutch Lover* (1673) once again appeals to the audience as ultimate judge, in arguing the case for the competitive equality of male and female authors in the market-place. Opposing the view, widely held at the time, that plays are written with the 'design' of 'amending of mens Morals', Behn disclaims any didactic intent in her comedy, stating her allegiance to nature and the 'passions', rather than 'rules'.

For Playes were certainly intended for the exercising of mens passions, not their understandings . . . as I take it Comedie was never meant, either for a converting or conforming Ordinance: In short, I think a Play the best divertisement that wise men have; but I also think them nothing so, who do discourse as formallie about the rules of it, as if 'twere the grand affair of humane life. This being my Opinion of Plays, I studied only to make this as entertaining as I could, which whether I have been successful in, my gentle Reader, you may for your shilling judge.[16]

Much of the preface is taken up with complaints against the inadequacy of women's education, and in particular the 'want of letters' (ignorance of Latin) because of which she and her fellow women have been placed at a disadvantage, cut off from the male preserve of 'Learning'. Paradoxically, Behn argues, this exclusion not only increases competitive desire in women, but equips them better for success in reaching the 'greatest hights' in a field of endeavour where useless knowledge serves only as impediment. In this preface Behn takes the familiar comparison of Shakespeare and Jonson as exemplars of natural abundance and 'learning' (found for example in Dryden's *Essay of Dramatic Poesy*) and applies it to her own writings and to women as a group hitherto denied free expression of their talents.

For waving the examination, why women having equal education with men, were not as capable of knowledge, of whatever sort as well as they: I'l only say . . . that Plays have no great room for that which is mens great advantage over women, that is Learning; We all well know that the Immortal Shakespeares Playes (who was not guilty of much more of this then often falls to womens share) have better pleas'd the World than *Johnsons* works . . . For our Modern ones . . . I dare to say I know of none that write at such a formidable rate, that a woman may not well hope to reach their greatest hights. (Sig. A2ᵛ, a1)

In treating the theme of women's education in her commendatory poem on Thomas Creech's Lucretius, Behn's tone is no less combative, and here she sees no compensating advantages in the prohibitions imposed on women by 'scanted Customes'. As with

George Eliot's Maggie Tulliver, the exclusion presented as especially galling is the enforced 'State of Ignorance' in which the classical languages are interdicted to women, who 'are forbid' to approach the arcane, magical sources of male power. The lines, like Sarah Fyge's 'The Emulation', suggest a virtual conspiracy by men, fearing an assault by women on the citadels of knowledge, to keep women in a state of bondage.

> But I unlearn'd in Schools . . .
> Till now, I curst my Birth, my Education,
> And more the scanted Customes of the Nation:
> Permitting not the Female Sex to tread,
> The Mighty Paths of Learned Heroes dead.
> The God-like *Virgil*, and great *Homers* Verse,
> Like Divine Mysteries are conceal'd from us.
>   We are forbid all grateful Theams,
>   No ravishing thoughts approach our Ear,
>   The Fulsom Gingle of the times,
> Is all we are allow'd to understand or hear.[17]

The libertine defiance of 'dull Religion' as well as secular authority later in this poem is further evidence of Behn's rebelliousness, her refusal to conform with expected models for 'the Female Sex'. Inverting the customary hierarchy of faith and reason, as Rochester does in *Satyr against Mankind*, Behn directs her scorn at priestcraft and its rule by fear, praising Lucretius as a great liberator. Interestingly enough, Creech seems to have been alarmed at the radical sentiments expressed in the lines extolling Lucretius, and he revised the passage when it was published in his edition of Lucretius, to make it seem more orthodox, changing 'Beyond poor Feeble Faith's dull Oracles' to 'As strong as Faiths resistless Oracles'. The passage, in its original form, describes the power of reason in surprisingly erotic terms:

> And Reason over all Unfetter'd plays,
> Wanton and undisturb'd as Summers Breeze . . .
>   It Pierces, Conquers and Compels,
> Beyond poor Feeble Faith's dull Oracles.
>   Faith the despairing Souls content,
> Faith the last Shift of Routed Argument . . .
>   To Gods for fear, Devotion was design'd,
>   And Safety made us bow to Majesty;
>   Poets by Nature Aw and Charm the Mind,
>   And born not made by dull Religion or Necessity.

(pp. 53–4)[18]

In certain respects, Behn's 'To Mr. *Creech*' gives off contradictory signals, beginning with the initial contrast between the 'strong manly Verse' the author says she would prefer to write and the 'Wommanish Tenderness' she presents as a weakness (p. 51). Though one need not take either the modesty *topos* or the conventional hyperbole of commendatory poems literally, the poem's opening lines, in developing an extended metaphor based on Lucretian cosmology, come uncomfortably close to suggesting a hierarchical view by which women fall short of a masculine ideal of perfection:

> But I of Feebler Seeds design'd,
> Whilst the slow moving Atomes strove,
> With careless heed to form my Mind:
> Compos'd it all of Softer Love.
> In gentle Numbers all my Songs are Drest,
>   And when I would thy Glories sing,
> What in strong manly Verse I would express
> Turns all to Womannish Tenderness within.   (p. 51)

Throughout the poem, Creech is presented as a kind of mentor, with the 'humble' Behn as student or disciple, motivated by an unsatisfied 'Appetite' for knowledge, a 'Fire' which his teaching has kindled. Rather than pugnaciously striving to outdo male rivals, here Behn states a more modest goal of enablement, of reaching a level at which competition will become possible:

> For more I owe, since thou hast taught me more,
> Then all the mighty Bards that went before.
> Others long since have Pal'd that vast Delight
> In duller *Greek* and *Latin* satisfy'd the Appetite . . .
> So thou by this Translation dost advance
> Our Knowledge from the State of Ignorance;
> And equals us to Man: Ah how can we,
> Enough Adore, or Sacrifice enough to Thee!   (pp. 51, 52)

Later passages in the poem alternate between addressing her fellow male poets as friends, colleagues, and equals (as Behn does in another poem to Creech, the Hudibrastic 'A Letter to Mr. *Creech* at *Oxford*, Written in the last great Frost') and abasing herself voluptuously before them. The terms of praise for both Creech and Rochester emphasise the erotic, presenting 'Young *Daphnis*' and the 'Charming Hero' Strephon as models of physical beauty and seductiveness in verse. '*Strephon* the Great', here as in Behn's prologue to

Rochester's *Valentinian*, is praised as one 'who Writ, and Lov'd, & Lookt like any God' – a rather one-sided, sanitised view of the scourge of the Restoration court:

> Listen ye Virgins to his charming Song,
> Eternal Musick dwelt upon his Tongue.
> The Gods of Love and Wit inspir'd his Pen,
> And Love and Beauty was his glorious Theam.[19]

Creech, who at this time had published nothing other than translations, is presented in Behn's commendatory poem as Rochester's poetic successor, no less 'Soft' and 'Lovely' in his verse, with its 'Beauty so surprizing', than his predecessor (pp. 55–6). The feminising description of her male colleagues may well express an androgynous ideal, giving an extra erotic charge to the familiar motif of poetic discipleship; or it can be read as an attempt to show that 'Wommanish Tenderness' can be effective in panegyric after all. In all these readings, poetic inspiration is seen as an erotic force, potentially liberating and therefore dangerous.

The image of 'Lineal Descents' among poets, as Dryden develops it in the Preface to the *Fables*, 'To the Memory of Mr. Oldham' and 'To my Dear Friend Mr. Congreve', normally involves a recognition of spiritual brotherhood among two 'Souls . . . near ally'd' and the transmission of a poetic legacy from father to son, 'lineal to the Throne'.[20] When the senior figure, source of inspiration, is male and the acolyte female, as in several poems by Behn, a sexual dimension comes into the relationship, as well as a greater element of uncertainty. In poems commemorating the deaths of the elderly Waller and 'the Young, the Charming' Rochester, the poet depicts herself as virtually paralysed by sorrow and the 'Toils of Sickness', 'uninspir'd' and unable to write, until revivified by direct inspiration from her mentor.

> How, to thy Sacred Memory, shall I bring
> (Worthy thy Fame) a grateful Offering?
> I, who by Toils of Sickness, am become
> Almost as near as thou art to a Tomb?
> While every soft, and every tender Strain
> Is ruffl'd, and ill-natur'd grown with Pain.
> But, at thy Name, my languisht *Muse* revives,
> And a new *Spark* in the dull *Ashes* strives.
>
> ('On the Death of E. Waller, Esq.', 1–8)[21]

Like Creech in the poem just discussed, Waller is presented as 'great *Instructor*', who taught the benighted world 'how to *Love*, and how to *Write*', and by his example served as tutor to the 'Infant *Muse*' of Behn (23, 45, 47). The lines in which she recalls her apprenticeship as a poet stress the inequality of male instructor and female student, eroticising the onset of poetic inspiration as an encounter between Olympian and mortal.

> With thy soft *Food* of *Love* I first began,
> Then fed on nobler *Panegyrick* Strain . . .
> Where e're I *Read*, new *Raptures* seiz'd my Blood;
> Methought I heard the Language of a God.   (27–8, 31–2)

The erotic element is even more pronounced in the poems in praise of Rochester, whose amorous conquests are presented as inseparable from his poetic gifts. Behn uses the same adjectives (soft, charming, lovely, gay) to describe his physical attributes of 'Voice' and 'Meen' and the qualities of his verse: the winning of laurels is virtually a by-product of the winning of mistresses, scattering his maker's image through the land.[22]

> He was but lent this duller World t'improve
> In all the charms of Poetry, and Love;
> Both were his gift, which freely he bestow'd,
> And like a God, dealt to the wond'ring Crowd.
> ('On the Death of the late Earl of Rochester', 7–10)

In a second poem about Rochester, addressed to his niece Anne Wharton, Behn develops themes of lineal descent and poetic inspiration in a curiously androgynous way, once again charged with erotic implications. Here, using the occasion of an exchange of poems indicated in the title – 'To Mrs. W. On her Excellent Verses (Writ in Praise of some I had made on the Earl of *Rochester*)' – Behn presents the younger woman poet as the reincarnation of Rochester, her identity revealed in a dream vision:

> I saw the Lovely *Phantom*, no Disguise,
> Veil'd the blest vision from my Eyes,
> 'Twas all o're *Rochester* that pleas'd and did surprize.   (13–15)

As in the poem to Waller, Behn begins with despondency, depicting herself, 'sad as the Grave', as weighed down by 'Melancholy' and the 'sullen influence' of malignant stars (3, 6, 16). The dream vision, when it appears, is both muse and lover: in setting the scene, Behn eroticises the state of mourning, comparing the 'Whispering' breeze to soft 'Amorous Tales' and equating her own initial situation to that of 'absent Lovers left alone', the 'poor Dove' bereft of its mate (18–23).

> So dull I was, scarce Thought a Subject found,
> Dull as the Light that gloom'd around;
>   When lo the Mighty Spirit appear'd,
>   All Gay, all Charming to my sight;
>   My Drooping Soul it Rais'd and Cheer'd,
>   And cast about a Dazling Light.
>   In every part there did appear,
>   The Great, the God-like *Rochester*,
> His Softness all, his Sweetness everywhere.   (24–32)

What these lines refer to, stripped of the disguise of metaphor, is the receipt of a poem by Anne Wharton, which Behn, in the fashion of commendatory poems, praises beyond its apparent merits. Behn's lines, going beyond the convention, do not simply present Wharton as like Rochester or as a worthy heir to her kinsman, but as 'very very he' (43), as Rochester brought back to life. The figure in the dream vision is, to all appearances, male, the lover returned from the dead to console his mistress, as 'Gay' and 'Charming' as in life (rather like the film *Truly, Madly, Deeply*). If we take the passage as a variation on the trope of lineal descent, the poet's relation to the 'successful Paths' laid down by 'Predecessors', then both Behn and Wharton are depicted as poetic heirs of Rochester – by conscious discipleship in one case and by a transformative inspiration in the other.[23] The 'Mighty Spirit', initially presented as male, is revealed as able to take on male and female form, at once the dead Rochester and the living Wharton. In the passage that follows, Behn is careful in her pronouns to distinguish the '*Phantom*' (it), addressing the narrator in a dream, and the dead poet (himself, he), whose earlier relationship with the narrator is re-enacted symbolically. That relationship, as Behn presents it in these lines, is once again that of tutor and student, possessor of the secret of 'Harmony' and aspirant, desirous of correcting her 'Faults' in the hopes of reaching a state of perfection. Wharton, in the allegory, is shown as inheriting not only the poetic mantle of Rochester but his role as Behn's mentor, and the consolation the poem presents is not so much the endurance of love as the continuity of poetic tradition:

It did advance, and with a Generous Look,
To me Addrest, to worthless me it spoke:
With the same wonted Grace my Muse it prais'd,
With the same Goodness did my Faults Correct:
And Careful of the Fame himself first rais'd,
Obligingly it School'd my loose Neglect.
The soft, the moving Accents soon I knew
The gentle Voice made up of Harmony;
Through the Known Paths of my glad Soul it flew;
I knew it straight, it could no others be,
'Twas not Alied but very very he.   (33–43)[24]

Images of androgyny are frequent in Behn's writings. Several poems, highly traditional in their materials, simply substitute a male for the female figure so common in Renaissance love poetry as the idealised object of beauty and embodiment of erotic desire. 'An Ode to Love', with a female speaker praising a beautiful youth, is in some respects closer to the poems in the Greek Anthology it imitates than many other Renaissance variations on this well-worn theme, since so much Greek love poetry was written by men to men, reflecting a society in which the ideal of beauty was perceived as male rather than female.

Dull Love no more thy Senceless Arrows prize,
Damn thy Gay Quiver, break thy Bow;
'Tis only young *Lysander's* Eyes,
That all the Arts of Wounding know . . .

The Sweetness from thy Eyes he took,
The Charming Dimples from thy Mouth,
That wonderous Softness when you spoke,
And all thy Everlasting Youth.   (1–4, 19–22)[25]

In 'An Ode to Love' the speaker is depicted as a connoisseur of male beauty, rather than as emotionally involved with 'young Lysander', as in three other poems using this name, all placed in close proximity to this 'Ode' in Behn's *Poems upon Several Occasions*. In 'To Lysander at the Musick-Meeting', on the other hand, the narrator is presented as directly susceptible to the beautiful youth's 'Arts of Wounding'. Here again the poet takes a standard motif of Renaissance love poetry, familiar in such a poem as Marvell's 'The Fair Singer', and inverts the sexes of lover and beloved, conqueror and conquered.

It was too much, ye Gods, to see and hear;
Receiving wounds both from the Eye and Ear:
One Charme might have secur'd a Victory.
Both, rais'd the Pleasure even to Extasie.   (1–4)[26]

Though the poem ostensibly is in praise of music, its imagery is predominantly visual, with a strong voyeuristic appeal, in which the reader is encouraged, with 'greedy Eyes' (7), to join in the pleasures of the text. An androgynous ideal of beauty, transgressing conventional expectations of gender, informs the catalogue that follows, which, far more than 'An Ode to Love', sets out to seduce its readers, male or female.

I saw the Softness that compos'd your Face,
While your Attention heightned every Grace:
Your Mouth all full of Sweetness and Content,
And your fine killing Eyes of Languishment:
Your Bosom now and then a sigh wou'd move,
(For *Musick* has the same effects with Love.)   (15–20)

Though the object of desire is male, the details of the description evoke the traditional Circean enchantress – passive, indolent, lying in wait for her prey rather than, as in 'An Ode to Love', active in pursuit of 'the next Fair and Yielding She' (26). As the term 'Attention' implies, Lysander, using the art that conceals art, is conscious of the impression he creates. Yet the suggestion that these beauties are for sale, displayed as advertisement to the potential purchaser – like the picture of the courtesan Angelica Bianca in *The Rover*, 'the fair Sign to the Inn, where a Man may lodge that's Fool enough to give her Price' – makes a commodity of the body itemised and offered to the view. The implications of the lines that follow, characterised by Margaret Anne Doody as an exercise in 'the comic baroque',[27] are not entirely favourable to the beautiful Lysander, likened here to a whore:

Your Body easey and all tempting lay,
Inspiring wishes which the Eyes betray,
In all that have the fate to glance that way:
A carless and a lovely Negligence,
Did a new Charm to every Limb dispence.   (21–5)

In the traditional Renaissance blazon, as Patricia Parker has pointed out, the female body is subjected to an inventory demonstrating 'mastery and ownership' in a 'homosocial discourse or male exchange' between author and reader 'in which the woman herself, traditionally absent, does not speak'.[28] Behn disrupts such expectations, appropriating the device for her own uses – first, by proposing, like Shakespeare in sonnet 20, an ideal of beauty which crosses the boundaries of gender, and second, by asserting female agency, demonstrating the ability of a woman poet to revivify tradition.

'In Imitation of Horace', a free adaptation of *Odes*, i.v, again transforms pre-existing materials, in part by reversing the sexes of speaker and addressee. Dorothy Mermin, in her account of the poem, has emphasised its 'revisionary' aspects, which she sees as allowing the poet 'to redefine woman's position in poetry: to become the subject who desires and speaks'.[29] The opening stanza follows the Horatian original in detail, and Behn is in fact closer to Horace than is Cowley's imitation (1656), in having the fickle, seductive youth 'Braid' rather than 'unbind' his luxuriant hair:

> What mean those Amorous Curles of Jet?
>   For what heart-Ravisht Maid
> Dost thou thy Hair in order set,
>   Thy Wanton Tresses braid?
> And thy vast Store of Beauties open lay,
> That the deluded Fancy leads astray.   (1–6)[30]

Behn like Horace asks a series of questions in the opening lines, but they are different questions: in Horace's poem, much more is made of the 'deluded Fancy' of Pyrrha's current victim, who foolishly thinks the delights of sexual enjoyment will last. Horace's ode is a farewell to love, a warning against the poisoned joys Pyrrha and those like her can offer: 'miseri, quibus/intemptata nites', or in Milton's literal paraphrase, 'Hapless they/To whom thou untry'd seem'st fair'.[31] Behn after the first stanza goes off in a different direction, with three stanzas of direct address to the 'Charming Youth', paying tribute to the power of beauty to overcome resistance, rather than pointing up the folly of succumbing to pleasures which will not endure. The moment of sexual fruition, deferred to enhance pleasure in Behn's poem, is in the Horatian original the source of delusion for the youth 'who now enjoys thee credulous, all Gold' (qui nunc te fruitur credulus aurea).

> For pitty hide thy Starry eyes,
>   Whose Languishments destroy
> And look not on the Slave that dyes

With an Excess of Joy.
Defend thy Coral Lips, thy Amber Breath;
To taste these Sweets lets in a Certain Death.

Forbear, fond Charming Youth, forbear,
  Thy words of Melting Love:
Thy Eyes thy Language well may spare,
  One Dart enough can move.
And she that hears thy voice and sees thy Eyes
With too much Pleasure, too much Softness dies.   (71–8)

Despite all the imperative verbs, the basic decorum in these lines is
one of praise rather than admonition: the lines are not really telling
the youth to 'Forbear', to go away and leave the speaker alone, but
to continue as a source of pleasurable pain to those under his spell.
Behn, like Horace, introduces the first person pronoun, absent until
then, into the closing lines, but in doing so suggests a greater
involvement by the speaker and as the editors of *Kissing the Rod*
suggest, a greater 'vulnerability', where Horace firmly rejects the
enticements of the flesh.[32] Behn's poem moves from the bombard-
ment of the senses to direct physical contact, and from the generic
'the Slave' or 'she' to the more immediately implicated 'me' and
'my'.

Cease, Cease, with Sighs to warm my Soul,
  Or press me with thy Hand:
Who can the kindling fire controul,
  The tender force withstand?
Thy Sighs and Touches like wing'd Lightning fly,
And are the Gods of Loves Artillery.   (19–24)

Another poem addressed to a beautiful youth, once again celebrating the amoral transgressive force of eros, is 'To Amintas, Upon
reading the Lives of some of the Romans'. The poem is a witty
retelling of some of the celebrated stories from Roman history, giving
them a different ending, in which an overwhelming physical beauty
which 'neither sex' can resist is shown as overcoming the barriers of
custom and 'publick shame'. In Behn's revisionist versions of the
deaths of Sophonisba, Cleopatra and Pompey, the most daring is the
retelling of the suicide of that model of virtuous chastity, Lucretia.

Had daring *Sextus* had thy lovely shape,
The fairest Woman living had not dy'd.
But blest the darkness that secur'd the Rape,
Suffering her Pleasure to have debauch't her Pride.

> Nor had he stoln to *Rome* to have quencht his fire,
> If thee resistless in his Camp he'd seen,
> Thy Eyes had kept his virtue all intire,
> And *Rome* a happy monarchy had been.   (21–8)

Elaine Hobby strongly attacks these lines as an instance of the oppressive patriarchal 'myth that a woman could enjoy being raped', but I would read the passage as arguing a version of libertine doctrine, advanced also in Behn's 'On Desire' and 'The Golden Age', which presents the operations of desire as identical in men and women. Pretended honour and virtue are 'a false disguise', 'a cheat', and sexual desire is an imperative which, if given the opportunity, will break through the flimsy defences erected by 'pride'.[33] 'To Amintas' uses its examples from the pantheon of male and female heroism to argue, cynically, that the erotic appeal of a 'charming face' will win a 'victory' over abstract principle:

> Had mighty *Scipio* had thy charming face,
> Great *Sophonisbe* had refus'd to dye,
> Her passion o're the sense of her disgrace
> Had gain'd the more obliging victory.   (9–12)

A similar axiom is stated at the beginning of *The History of the Nun*, in partial explanation of Isabella's apparent descent from virtue to crime: 'The resolution, we promise, and believe we shall maintain, is not in our power, and nothing is so deceitful as human hearts' (p. 153). The beautiful Amintas is presented in the poem as universal object of desire, 'belov'd by both Sexes',[34] and, in alternative rewritings of the history of Rome, would have exercised an irresistible appeal over both Lucretia and a Tarquin deflected from his initial goal by encountering someone more beautiful and more accommodating. Violence and its resistance, in Behn's revisionist version of the familiar tale, are replaced by consummated mutual desire.

Passages of cross-dressing in Behn's writings similarly present an androgynous ideal of beauty, often tantalisingly difficult to pin down as male or female. Sylvia, the heroine of *Love-Letters Between a Nobleman and His Sister*, is able to pursue a number of amorous adventures in male dress, something which, as she realises, adds to her sexual appeal. The first of her conquests in this guise, Octavio, though 'he had a secret hope she was not what she seemed' by the clothes she wore, nevertheless finds 'this new affair of his heart' one which he is 'resolved to pursue, be the fair object of what sex soever'. Sylvia and her unreliable lover Philander both take pleasure in the aesthetic spectacle of her male dress as well as in the freedom it gives her from conventional constraints: art obligingly supplies what nature has neglected to provide.

She, pleased with the cavalier in herself, begged she might live under that disguise, which indeed gave her a thousand charms to those which nature had already bestowed on her sex; and *Philander* was well enough pleased she should continue in that agreeable dress, which did not only add to her beauty, but gave her a thousand little privileges, which otherwise would have been denied to women.[35]

Later in the narrative, after Philander has tired of Sylvia, he dresses his new flame Calista in men's clothing, and his raptures, in a letter to Octavio, once again suggest that the transgressive force of eros ignores the boundaries of gender. Mistaken identities bound in a complicated comic plot, full of suggestions of homoerotic or narcissistic attraction, in which Philander is unaware that his friend Octavio is both his rival and Calista's brother. Shortly afterwards, in a sudden darkening of tone, the 'fair *virago*' Calista is forced to live up to her disguise and use a pistol, hitherto decorative, to shoot her jealous husband when he tries to prevent her escape.

Going into an arbour, by the aid of a dark-lanthorn I carried, she dressed her in a laced shirt of mine, and this suit I had brought her, of blue velvet, trimmed with rich loops and buttons of gold . . . And I must confess to you, my dear *Octavio*, that never any thing appeared so ravishing . . . I never saw any thing more resembling my dear *Octavio*, than the lovely *Calista*. Your very feature, your very smile and air; so that, if possible, that increased my adoration and esteem for her: thus completed, I armed her, and buckled on her sword, and she would needs have one of my pistols too, that stuck in my belt; and now she appeared all lovely man. (III, pp. 317–18)

Of all Behn's celebrations of male beauty, or of beauty which transcends conventional categorisation, the most extraordinary is the passage in volume III of *Love-Letters*, describing the ceremony in which Octavio, renouncing the world and its deceptions, enters a monastery. One can hardly imagine anything less ascetic: as in 'To Lysander at the Musick-Meeting', the ceremony, 'adorned . . . with whatever can charm the eyes; and music, and voices, to ravish the ear', is a feast of the senses, a Rubens ceiling painted in words (III, p. 397).[36] Explicit authorial interventions ('I never saw any thing

more rich in dress . . . For my part, I swear I never was so affected in
my life with any thing, as I was at this ceremony'), rare in *Love-
Letters* except in this passage, encourage the reader's vicarious participation. Octavio's elaborately described ritual of investiture is
presented as love's triumph or apotheosis, as the beautiful youth,
metamorphosed into a deity embodying desire, enters a realm of
unending delight:

> He looked methought, as if the gods of love had met in council to dress him
> up that day for everlasting conquest; for to his usual beauties he seemed to
> have the addition of a thousand more; he bore new lustre in his face and
> eyes, smiles on his cheeks, and dimples on his lips: he moved, he trod with
> nobler motions, as if some supernatural influence had took a particular
> care of him: ten thousand sighs, from all sides, were sent him, as he passed
> along, which, mixed with the soft music, made such a murmuring, as gentle
> breezes moving yielding boughs: I am assured, he won that day more
> hearts, than ever he had gained with all his toils of love and youth before.
> (III, pp. 397–400)

Two poems by Behn bring out the homoerotic element in an
androgynous ideal of beauty. 'Our Cabal', discussed briefly in the
previous chapter, includes among its large cast of assorted lovers the
bisexual Lycidas, who takes pleasure in breaking female hearts, and
the naive young Philander. Lycidas (identified in the poem as Mr.
J. H., or John Hoyle), very much aware of the 'power' of his
'Charms' over both sexes (157), reserves his 'Tenderness' for young
Philander, where with women, he is interested only in 'Conquest'
without emotional involvement (170).

> With him *Philander*, who nere paid
> A Sigh or Tear to any Maid:
> So innocent and young he is,
> He cannot guess what Passion is.
> But all the Love he ever knew,
> On *Lycidas* he does bestow;
> Who pays his Tenderness again,
> Too Amorous for a Swain to a Swain.   (181–8)

Amorous entanglements are seen in 'Our Cabal' as fundamentally
comic, a game of mismatching. Philander, yet another beautiful
youth of indeterminate sexuality, is presented as somehow un-
formed, the innocent plaything of eros, rather than as in any sense
the embodiment of an overwhelming transformative force. Any
amorous exchange here is limited to the eyes alone, rather than, as in

many of the passages we have been discussing, being a prelude to imagined bodily delights:

> A softer Youth was never seen,
> His Beauty Maid; but Man, his Mein:
> And much more gay than all the rest;
> And but *Alexis* finest Dress'd.
> His Eyes toward *Lycidas* still turn,
> As sympathizing Flowers to the Sun.　　　　(189–94)

In the more complex 'To the fair Clarinda, who made Love to me, imagin'd more than Woman', Behn raises the question of whether love can ever be 'Innocent', in exploring the possibility of a sexual relationship between two women. As the title suggests, the poem concerns the role of the imagination in erotic attraction and the instability of any definitions of gender. In a variant on the familiar cross-dressing motif, where the clothing heightens desire by the mystery it poses, the 'fair Clarinda' is presented as woman and man at once, someone for whom any 'Name' assigned can only be an outer garment:

> Fair lovely Maid, or if that Title be
> Too weak, too Feminine for Nobler thee,
> Permit a Name that more Approaches Truth:
> And let me call thee, Lovely Charming Youth.　　　　(1–4)

Modern critics, appropriating 'To the fair Clarinda' as a lesbian manifesto, have seen it as a poem which 'unmistakably celebrates lesbian love', 'clear evidence of a strong homosexual interest' on the author's part.[37] But this reading, besides being reductively biographical, underestimates the poem's wit and its presentation of sexual arousal as problematic and embarrassing. Behn's poem, like a number of her writings, emphasises the 'constraint' which conventional attitudes inculcated by society impose upon the expression of emotion, the 'Blushes' which indicate ambivalence of feeling. Clarinda's androgynous appearance sets free the imagination of the beholder, who can respond both to the 'Youth' and the 'beauteous Woman' in the enigmatic spectacle Clarinda presents, without feeling guilty:

> This last will justifie my soft complaint,
> While that may serve to lessen my constraint;
> And without Blushes I the Youth persue,
> While so much beauteous Woman is in view,

> Against thy Charms we struggle but in vain
> With thy deluding Form thou giv'st us pain,
> While the bright Nymph betrays us to the Swain.   (5–11)

Paradoxically, it is only because Clarinda is *not* 'more than Woman', that the love she engenders is free of danger. The poem raises the question of whether beauty is no more than a mask for aggressiveness, a bait to catch the unsuspecting, and suggests that love need not inevitably mean betrayal. Immediately preceding 'To the fair Clarinda' in the miscellany volume in which it initially appeared is 'To Mrs B. from a Lady who had a desire to see her, and who complains on the ingratitude of her fugitive Lover'. Though the 'Lady' calls herself Cleone rather than Clarinda, in all other respects the two poems make up a literary exchange, in which the language of love is used for reciprocal compliments and for reflections on the deceitfulness of men. The highly circumstantial title of 'To the fair Clarinda, who made Love to me, imagin'd more than Woman', as with such poems as 'To Lysander, on some Verses he writ, and asking more for his Heart than 'twas worth', would suggest an occasional origin to Behn's poem, an element of dialogue.

> Send me your pity, bounteous Shepherdess . . .
> Know this it yet remains in your fair breast,
> To render me the happy or unblest.
> You may act miracles if you'l be kind,
> Make me true joys in real sorrows find . . .
> Accept the heart I here to you present,
> By the ingratitude of *Strephon* rent.   ('To Mrs B.')[38]

At no point does 'To Mrs B.' suggest the possibility of sexual union between the two women, and 'To the fair Clarinda' observes the same decorum of courtly praise, preserving a certain distance. 'Kind', 'happy' and 'blest' are purged of the traditional connotations of sexual conquest and surrender, redefined, in a context of literary compliment, to express an ideal of female friendship. Yet, unlike Behn's poem, 'To Mrs B.' never breaks free from the postures of dependency which it seeks to disavow:

> No more to Treasons subject as before
> To be betray'd by a fair tale no more,
> As large as once, as uncontroul'd and free,
> But yet at your command shall always be.

Where 'To Mrs B.' views the two sexes as distinct and incompatible, presenting friendship between women as refuge for a 'wounded
heart', 'To the fair Clarinda' is one of a number of poems by Behn
which make manifest the ability of the imagination to dissolve the
customary boundaries of gender. Recent critics who interpret
Behn's poem as a declaration of lesbian passion forcing its way
through 'a culturally formulated discourse that cannot escape
heterosexual paradigms' misrepresent a poem which rejects any
such polarity. Shakespeare's sonnet 20 states a similar paradox in
praising an androgynous 'master mistress' able to exert a powerful
erotic appeal over 'men's eyes and women's souls'.[39] Both Behn's
poem and Shakespeare's sonnet are based on (and partially dissent
from) what Thomas Laqueur calls the 'one-sex model' of male and
female sexuality prevalent in the Renaissance, in which there is 'no
inherent gendering of desire' and woman is represented as 'a lesser
version of man along a vertical axis of infinite gradations', rather
than as 'an altogether different creature along a horizontal axis
whose middle ground was largely empty'.[40] To be 'more than
Woman' is, quite literally, to possess a penis.

> And for a woman wert thou first created,
> Till Nature as she wrought thee fell a-doting,
> And by addition me of thee defeated,
> By adding one thing to my purpose nothing.
>   But since she prick't thee out for women's pleasure,
>   Mine be thy love, and thy love's use their treasure.[41]

Where Behn, like Shakespeare, departed from the view, widely
held in the Renaissance and classical antiquity, that 'the standard of
the human body and its representations is the male body', is in
wittily presenting the 'addition' of a bodily appendage as descent
from, rather than as ascent toward, an ideal of beauty.[42] In 'To the
fair Clarinda', man is presented as both more than and less than
woman:

> In pity to our Sex sure thou wer't sent,
> That we might Love, and yet be Innocent:
> For sure no Crime with thee we can commit;
> Or if we shou'd – thy Form excuses it.
> For who, that gathers fairest Flowers believes
> A Snake lies hid beneath the Fragrant Leaves.   (12–17)

Like sonnet 20, the lines distinguish between 'love' and 'love's use':
love between man and woman can never be 'Innocent' because of

the aggressiveness inherent in sexuality, the drive to possess which consumes and commodifies the object of desire. Katherine Philips in her poems celebrating female friendship similarly constructs an ideal of love which can endure precisely because it does not find physical expression, sublimating bodily desires:

> Then let our Flames still light and shine,
>   And no false fear controul,
>   As innocent as our Design,
>   Immortal as our Soul . . .
>
> We wear about us such a charm,
>   No horrour can be our offence;
> For mischief's self can do no harm
>   To Friendship or to Innocence.[43]

But Behn differs from Philips in refusing to allow erasure of the body or make an absolute distinction between the sexes. Where Philips in her poems is confident that 'Innocence' can neither do nor receive harm, Behn equivocates. 'Crime' is what Behn in 'The Golden Age' calls 'Sin', those actions which law and custom, though not nature, forbid and penalise (in this case, with loss of reputation or diminished market value as damaged goods):

> Those vain those Politick Curbs to keep man in,
> Who by a fond mistake Created that a Sin;
> Which freeborn we, by right of Nature claim our own . . .
>   Honour! that hindred mankind first,
> At Loves Eternal Spring to quench his amorous thirst.   (112–21)

In line 15 of 'To the fair Clarinda', the unexpected, mischievous qualification 'Or if we shou'd' calls into question the assurance of the three previous lines, suggesting that women can feel sexual desire for women as well as men, and that this can take active as well as contemplative form. As Behn argues in 'To Amintas', a 'lovely shape', male or female, will 'excuse' anything, dissolving all moral compunctions. The hidden 'Snake', emblem here as in 'The Golden Age' of fallen sexuality, both marks the anatomical distinction between the sexes and transcends it, since all beauty tempts, acting as pander for the predatory instincts present in women as in men.

In the closing lines of 'To the fair Clarinda', the image of the hermaphrodite both explains and shrouds in further mystery the enigma of the beautiful Clarinda, presented here as a prodigy or 'Wonder':

Thou beauteous Wonder of a different kind,
Soft *Cloris* with the dear *Alexis* join'd;
When e'r the Manly part of thee, wou'd plead
Thou tempts us with the Image of the Maid,
While we the noblest Passions do extend
The Love to *Hermes*, *Aphrodite* the Friend.   (18–23)

In a retelling of the Ovidian myth in which a reluctant swain and a lovelorn nymph are united into a single bisexual creature, Clarinda is presented as an image of recovered wholeness, who, as one critic puts it, 'can be both lover and friend'.[44] As the juxtaposition of the sinister 'tempts' with the more reassuring 'noblest' would suggest, the balance is an unstable one. In this respect, Behn is true to the original Ovidian tale, in which the strange creature, which to the eye seemed 'neither and yet both' of the sexes (neutrumque et utrumque videntur), is presented as warring opposites locked in close sexual embrace, an emblem of the ineradicable contradictions inherent in sexuality.[45]

Behn's myth of the androgyne, as explored in the works I have been discussing, assumes that creativity, rational persuasion, and the spirit which is capable of giving life to inanimate matter are, paradoxically, both male in their nature and equally distributed among men and women: 'the Manly part of thee', 'my Masculine Part the Poet in me', 'what in strong Manly verse I would express'. Such a view, consonant with a dominant ideology which, as Laqueur has shown, identified the male seed with 'the very existence of civilization itself', both asserts the independence of women and entraps them within a paradigm where 'all difference is figured on the vertical scale of man' and 'Wommanish Tenderness' is perceived as a weakness.[46] Yet Behn in her poems, as we have seen, again and again calls into question the traditional boundaries of gender, rejecting the hierarchical assumptions which privilege one sex over another. Her plays, like her poems, chronicle the abuses of ineffectual tyrants and mount a sustained attack against a double standard which allowed men to engage freely in behaviour forbidden to women. Behn's translation of a philosophical dialogue by Fontenelle, *The Theory or System Of several New Inhabited Worlds*, undertaken in part to prove that 'an *English* Woman might adventure to translate any thing, a *French* Woman may be suppos'd to have spoken', illustrates her commitment as a professional writer to an ethos of competitive equality between men and women: 'What,

replied she, do you think me then incapable of all those Pleasures
which entertain our Reason, and only treat the Mind? I will
instantly show you the contrary.'[47] The 'double right' to the laurel
wreath she claims in her ambitious translation, over 1700 lines long,
of Cowley's Latin poem *Plantarum*, Book VI, states a descent both
from Apollo and Daphne. On the one hand, she holds, as Virginia
Woolf was to argue later, that 'in each of us two powers reside, one
male and one female',[48] and, on the other, her writings resist
domination and exclusion, the attempt to silence the voice of
imagination in a woman writer:

> I by a double right thy Bounties claim,
> Both from my Sex, and in *Apollo's* Name:
> Let me with *Sappho* and *Orinda* be
> Oh ever sacred Nymph, adorn'd by thee;
> And give my Verses Immortality.   ('Of Plants', VI, 590–4)

The tendency in recent feminist criticism to explore (or invent) an
exclusively female tradition, like the older critical habit, in studies of
Restoration literature, of treating dramatists or poets in isolation,
generalising freely from an excessively limited canon of works, has
produced some wildly contradictory assertions about Behn's
relationship to her contemporaries. Behn's plays have been treated
both as revolutionary in their 'systematic and persistent attack' on
conventional sexual attitudes and as themselves sexist, with 'values
and perceptions hardly distinguishable from those of the male
writers with whom she competed'.[49] One study claims that Behn's
plays simply replicated the beliefs of the audience they sought to
please: 'Had these comedies come to us unsigned, they would, I
suspect, be seen as no more or no less feminist than *The Country Wife*
. . . Her prejudices were those of her peers and her audience,
tempered by dramatic convention . . . These plays are "moral" or
even thematic only insofar as – and when – the audience wanted or
needed them to be.' Another critic, taking exactly the opposite view,
argues that Behn in her writings 'performs an extraordinary act in
frankly proclaiming female passion'.[50] The closest thing to an
authoritative study of the women dramatists of the period, Jacqueline Pearson's *The Prostituted Muse*, is far from clear in treating the
relationship between Behn and her male contemporaries. As I shall
show, Pearson's claim that 'almost all male dramatists accepted the
double standard' has no more validity than her assertion that 'Behn

is unusual in revealing how nakedly all social relationships . . . are simply slightly camouflaged struggles for power'.[51] It might therefore be useful to examine the treatment of female sexuality and the double standard in plays by Behn and some of her male contemporaries, to ascertain the extent to which they collude with patriarchal hegemony, or, in contrast, give serious consideration to the possibility of freedom for women, inside and outside the institution of marriage.

Several recurrent plot motifs in Restoration comedy turn on the problem of 'Resisting a Private Tyranny'.[52] All invoke a struggle for mastery, an assertion of an indecorous freedom against a conservative restraining force presented as unjust yet sanctioned by law and tradition. The first and most straightforward of these motifs, embodying the standard New Comedy conflict of crabbed, impotent age and impatient youth, shows an attempt by a parent or guardian to break the will of a young heroine, often by physical restraint, which is met with spirited, ingenious resistance. With rare exceptions, such as Nicholas Rowe's *The Fair Penitent* (1703), the sympathies of the audience, in comic and tragic versions of the *topos* by male and female dramatists alike, are directed toward the young rebel, since the forces of order (father, brother, duenna, foppish suitor) are presented as unnatural, mercenary, proud and foolish. Hippolita in Wycherley's *The Gentleman Dancing-Master* (1673) and Hellena in *The Rover* are variations on a single theme: witty, resourceful virgins, determined to 'take all innocent freedoms' and 'ramble', as men do:

To confine a Woman just in her rambling Age! take away her liberty at the very time she shou'd use it! O barbarous Aunt! O unnatural Father! to shut up a poor Girl at fourteen, and hinder her budding; all things are ripen'd by the Sun.

Nay I'm resolv'd to provide my self this Carnival, if there be e'er a handsom proper Fellow of my Humour above Ground, tho I ask first . . . Prithee tell me, what dost thou see about me that is unfit for Love – have I not a world of Youth? A Humour gay? A Beauty passable? A Vigour desirable? well shap'd? clean limb'd? sweet breath'd? And sense enough to know how all these ought to be employ'd to the best Advantage: yes, I do and will.[53]

Both passages, coming near the beginning of the respective plays, strongly hint through the choice of imagery and the evident liveliness of the heroines that the attempted confinement in a nunnery or a loveless marriage is not likely to succeed. The implicit ideology in these and similar plays is that of liberal contract theory: 'Disobedience' to 'unjust Commands' (*The Rover*, 1.i, p. 7) is justified, and the responsibility for fomenting rebellion rests with those who by their abuse of power have provoked it.[54] 'If you had not lock'd up your Daughter', comments the lover Gerrard in *The Gentleman Dancing-Master*, 'I am sure I had never cheated you of her' (III.i.592–3). Or as Hippolita says:

> Our Parents who restrain our liberty,
> But take the course to make us sooner free,
> Though all we gain be but new slavery,
> We leave our Fathers, and to Husbands fly.
>
> (*Gentleman Dancing-Master*, II.i.550–3)

When the young heroine is not an inquisitive virgin but an unhappy wife, married off in a mercenary transaction before the play begins, the act of rebellion is treated with somewhat more ambivalence, especially when it involves adultery and the deception of the husband, who may react violently to the affront to his honour. A recurrent theme in Restoration comedy is that cuckolds make themselves; the attempts by Pinchwife in *The Country-Wife* and Sir Feeble Fainwou'd in Behn's *The Lucky Chance* to secure exclusive possession of the young wives they treat as chattels, like the behaviour of Hippolita's father and Hellena's brother, rebound on them, bringing about what they most fear. In these plays, much is made of the impotence or failing powers of the elderly husband, as contrasted with the ripe and juicy youthfulness of the mismatched wife and the virility of potential rivals.

I find *Sir Feeble* we were a Couple of old Fools indeed, to think at our Age to couzen two lusty young Fellows of their Mistresses; 'Tis no wonder that both the Men and the Women have been too hard for us, we are not fit Matches for either, that's the truth on't.

> *That Warrior needs must to his Rival yield,*
> *Who comes with blunted Weapons to the Field.*
>
> (*The Lucky Chance*, v.ii, p. 69)[55]

The very names of the characters – Sir Feeble Fainwou'd, Sir Cautious Fulbank, Sir Davy Dunce, Pinchwife – direct audience response by suggesting impotent, grasping folly. Here again there is no significant difference between Behn and contemporary male dramatists in their treatment of this motif: in a competitive society, those with '*blunted Weapons*', physical or mental, will come out second-best. The implicit political principle underlying the cuckolding action at the centre of *The Lucky Chance*, Otway's *The Souldiers Fortune* and other plays of the period is once more a version of liberal contract theory: the sovereign who fails to fulfil his responsibilities, by anarchical incompetence or by tyrannous designs, forfeits his right to allegiance.

Behn in *The Lucky Chance* carries the critique of mercenary values considerably further than most of her contemporaries by presenting the young, attractive rake Gayman, the principal male figure in the play, as colluding in or tainted by these values. 'Money-less' (i.i, p. 4) and at the outset of the play reduced by his straitened circumstances to living in a garret 'about the largeness of a Pantry Bin, or a Usurer's Trunk' (i.ii, p. 10), Gayman is in two separate episodes led to prostitute himself, selling his sexual services for a cash payment, once to his ugly, foul-smelling landlady and once to a disguised benefactress who has sent him a bag of gold (ii.i, pp. 18–19). His moral obtuseness, as compared with Julia's generosity and resourcefulness, is indicated by his failure to recognise that Julia is the source of this gift of 'Love and Fortune' (ii.i, p. 20) and by his treatment of sex as a purely material transaction, with no feeling other than a degree of nausea. Gayman is tested, but unlike Valentine in *Love for Love* (also played by Betterton), he is found wanting:

> Some Female Devil old and damn'd to Ugliness,
> And past all Hopes of Courtship and Address,
> Full of another Devil called Desire,
> Has seen this Face – this – Shape – this Youth
> And thinks it worth her Hire. It must be so.
> I must moyle on in the damn'd dirty Road,
> And sure such Pay will make the Journey easie;
> And for the Price of the dull drudging Night,
> All Day I'll purchase new and fresh Delight.   (ii.i, p. 20)[56]

In the gambling scene of *The Lucky Chance*, the climax of the play's action, the satire is directed at all three men participating, the young and virile Gayman as well as the two old cuckolds, engaged in a conspiracy against the blameless, unsuspecting Julia, who is treated by all three as 'Moveables . . . Goods – Commodities', an object to be bargained over (iv.i, p. 51).[57] Later in the play, Julia (played, like so many Behn heroines, by Elizabeth Barry) explicitly equates Gayman's behaviour with that of Sir Cautious, when she accuses him of making her 'a base Prostitute' in collusion with her 'barbarous' husband:

L.FUL. If he cou'd be so barbarous to expose me,
Cou'd you who lov'd me – be so cruel too!
GAY. What – to possess thee when the Bliss was offer'd,
Possess thee too without a Crime to thee? (v.ii, pp. 65–6)

Though the main object of satire in the gambling scene is the callous materialism of husbands willing to prostitute their wives if they could 'do't discreetly', indifferent to the wife's feelings and to considerations of honour, the lover Gayman, for all his fine phrases of courtship towards her, treats Julia in no less selfish and calculating a way.

SIR CAUTIOUS. What loose my Wife, for three hundred pounds!
GAYMAN. Loose her Sir – why she shall be never the worse for my wearing Sir – The old covetous Rogue is considering on't I think – What say you to a Night? I'll set it to a Night – There's none need know it Sir.
SIR CAUTIOUS. Hum – a Night! three hundred pounds for a Night! Why what a lavish Whoremaster's this: we take Money to marry our Wives, but very seldom part with'em, and by the Bargain get Money – for a Night say you? gad if I should take the Rogue at his word, 'twould be a pure Jest. (*Aside*)
SIR FEEBLE. You are not Mad Brother.
SIR CAUTIOUS. No, but I'm wise – and that's as good; let me consider –
SIR FEEBLE. What whether you shall be a Cuckold or not?
SIR CAUTIOUS. Or loose three hundred pounds – consider that; a Cuckold! Why, 'tis a Word – an empty Sound – 'tis Breath – 'tis Air – 'tis nothing – but three hundred pounds – Lord, what will not three hundred pounds do! You may chance to be a Cuckold for nothing Sir –
SIR FEEBLE. It may be so – but she shall do't discreetly then. (IV.i, p. 52)

Julia, treated by all three men here as a passive object, to be passed from hand to hand, shows herself consistently as honest, forthright and generous. Lines addressed to a husband who has already sold her sexual favours to Gayman establish her moral superiority and, in the dramatic context, her vulnerability.

> I'll not change my Freedom and my Humour,
> To purchase the dull Fame of being Honest . . .
> I value not the Censures of the Crowd . . .
> We cannot help our Inclinations Sir,
> No more than Time, or Light from coming on –
> But I can keep my Vertue Sir intire. (v.ii, p. 61)

There is a hint in the gambling scene of a darker possibility also touched on in Hippolita's lines quoted above: it is possible that the heroine, seeking freedom, may simply exchange one tyrant for another. But this particular variation on the *topos* of the heroine fleeing from confinement by a mercenary, authoritarian society is not fully explored before *Clarissa*.

The heroine subject to unjustified restraint in these plays attracts the sympathies of the audience for several other reasons. Nearly always, she is innocent, trusting, as yet uncorrupted in a society where feeling is generally stifled. Margery Pinchwife in *The Country-Wife* even manages to preserve her pastoral innocence after committing adultery. In several plays the heroine is described as a 'wit', ingenious and resourceful, able to improvise and react quickly to changing circumstances – in Willmore's phrase in *The Rover*, 'one that has Wit enough to manage an Intrigue of Love'. Hellena, characterised like a number of these heroines as a 'mad Wench', is determined to choose for herself: 'I don't intend every he that likes me shall have me, but he that I like' (*The Rover*, III.i, p. 40; III.ii, p. 74). The wit combat between prospective lovers always contains an element of competition, as each strives to retain a degree of independence and gain a temporary advantage over the other: in some plays (*The Rover*, *The Way of the World*), the two recognise one another as fellow spirits and as equals, where in others (*The Gentleman Dancing-Master*, *The Lucky Chance*, Ravenscroft's *The London Cuckolds*) the woman is considerably more quick-witted than the man. But in all these plays the evidence of inventiveness, spontaneity, independence and high spirits in the heroine predisposes the audience, like her chosen partner, to look with favour on her. Willmore says to Hellena, whose 'Courage' he praises a few lines later: 'Thou has one Virtue I adore, good Nature . . . By Heaven, both the *Indies* shall not buy thee from me. I adore thy Humour and will marry thee, and we are so of one Humour, it must be a Bargain' (*The Rover*, v, pp. 97, 98, 102).

A further reason for condoning adultery in a number of plays in which the heroine is trapped in a loveless arranged marriage is the complication of a prior betrothal, a plot device which renders that marriage morally dubious and in some cases legally bigamous. This is a favourite motif in Restoration drama: G. S. Alleman, in his useful study *Matrimonial Law and the Materials of Restoration Comedy*, has identified ninety-one instances of clandestine marriages, betrothals in the presence of witnesses and elopements in plays written between 1663 and 1714, nearly all attempts by young lovers to choose for themselves rather than bow to the will of guardians.[58] The theme is particularly prominent in the plays of Behn, who treats resistance to a forced marriage in nine plays, nearly always emphasising the injustice of being treated as disposable property and deprived of 'free choice'. In Behn's *The False Count, The Lucky Chance* and *The Town-Fopp*, the existence of a prior contract in the form of a witnessed 'spousal', entered into before the action of the play begins (or in *The Town-Fopp*, presented in an early scene), means that sexual intercourse with a new spouse, imposed in a forced marriage, becomes adulterous, where any adultery with the returned lover is 'innocent'.[59] Sexual consummation in these plays becomes a means of asserting ownership. In *The Lucky Chance*, Sir Feeble, who has fabricated a report of Belmour's death, looks forward with lip-licking avidity to consummating his marriage with Leticia, thus triumphing over the 'rampant young dogs' who, like the disguised Belmour, may try to cheat him out of his newly purchased wife.

BELMOUR. And do you think this Marriage lawful Sir?
SIR FEEBLE. Lawful; it shall be when I've had Livery and Seisin of her
   Body – and that shall be presently Rogue – quick. (III.i, p. 29)

The equally unpleasant old merchant Antonio, in *The False Count*, after being exposed to public humiliation, can take consolation in having cuckolded the man who has cuckolded him, since in this case the heroine has been enjoyed by both her husbands.

Enforced marriage in Behn's plays is thus regularly seen as 'Prostitution in the lewdest manner, without the Satisfaction'.[60] This equation is explicit in *The Town-Fopp*, with its brothel scenes and its two arranged marriages for 'Interest' parting a betrothed couple – Celinda to the cynical whoremonger Sir Timothy Tawdrey and Bellmour, the play's principal character, to the deceived Diana, whom he mistreats after marriage. In his relationships with women, the fop Sir Timothy ('I love to buy my pleasure') is ruled by the 'pow'rful God', Money, accepting with alacrity an arranged marriage with a woman he has never seen in order 'to purchase a Mistress', the mercenary Betty Flauntit. In the following exchange, the contrast is plainly marked between the worldly, arrogant Lord Plotwell and his idealistic, self-pitying nephew Belmour, too weak to resist his uncle's commands or to contest 'that law/Which gives you

Power, and orders me Obedience', even though he knows that to succumb would be immoral:

> BELMOUR. If I must marry any but *Celinda*,
> I shall not, Sir, enjoy one moments bliss!
> I shall be quite unmann'd, Cruel and Brutal!
> A Beast, unsafe for Woman to converse with,
> Besides, Sir, I have given my Heart and Faith,
> And my second Marriage is Adultery.
> LORD. Heart and Faith, I am glad 'tis no worse; if the Ceremony of the
>   Church has not past, 'tis well enough.[61]

Lord Plotwell is presented as behaving tyrannously, using his economic power to enforce his will and 'dispose of' his nephew as he pleases:

> Why, what's in *Diana*, that you shou'd not love her? . . . Love me this Lady, and marry me this Lady, or I will teach you what it is to refuse such a Lady . . . Very fine! where is the Priest that durst dispose of you, without my order? Sirrah, you are my Slave – at least your whole Estate is at my mercy – and besides, I'll charge you with a Action of 5000 l. for your ten Years maintenance: Do you know that is in my pow'r too? (II.iii, p. 18)

Unlike several of the female victims of arranged marriages in Behn's plays, Belmour caves in under pressure, and then behaves unjustly himself. After surrendering to *force majeure*, Belmour rejects his new wife's sexual advances, characterising their life together as 'one continued Sin' and, wallowing in self-loathing, sets out to prove his sinfulness in the brothel. Tormented by an overwhelming sense of guilt at his betrayal of Celinda, he rejects all sexuality, comes to see all women as whores, and, like Castalio in Otway's *The Orphan*, finds an outlet for his emotions in misogynist railing:

> Gods! what an odious thing mere Coupling is!
> A thing which every sensual Animal
> Can do as well as we – but prithee tell me,
> Is there nought else between the nobler Creatures? (IV.ii, p. 41)

A happy ending is eventually brought about when Lord Plotwell, still behaving as an absolute monarch, decides to use his 'Interest or Estate' to 'purchase' a divorce (or annulment) for Belmour and Diana: 'I now think fit to unmarry 'em' (v.ii, p. 47). Belmour can then be reunited with Celinda, and since Diana, through no fault of her own, has remained a virgin, she can then be conveniently married off to a former suitor.

There are very few instances of plays in which the constraining forces of order and authority are treated sympathetically. In Rowe's *The Fair Penitent*, the heroine Calista inveighs against an 'Imperious' masculine rule which has abridged 'the native Freedom of her Will' (III.i.11–15), soliloquising in terms familiar in the feminist polemic of the period:

> How hard is the Condition of our Sex,
> Thro' ev'ry State of Life the Slaves of Man?
> In all the dear delightful Days of Youth,
> A rigid Father dictates to our Wills,
> And deals out Pleasure with a scanty Hand;
> To his, the Tyrant Husband's Reign succeeds
> Proud with Opinion of superior Reason,
> He holds Domestick Bus'ness and Devotion
> All we are capable to know, and shuts us,
> Like Cloyster'd Ideots, from the World's Acquaintance,
> And all the Joys of Freedom; wherefore are we
> Born with high Souls, but to assert our selves,
> Shake off this vile Obedience they exact,
> And claim an equal Empire o'er the World?   (III.i.40–53)

But, as the hedonist associations of the words 'Pleasure', 'Joys of Freedom' and 'the World's Acquaintance' suggest, Calista's position is severely compromised, and in their dramatic context her words are to some extent hypocritical. Rather than being imprisoned and forced into marriage, 'the yielding Fair' (I.i.166), after surrendering her virginity to the libertine Lothario, has agreed to a marriage with a man she does not love. Her father Sciolto, treated as a tragic figure, is noble and benevolent, and the clandestine liaison of Calista and Lothario is presented as an instance of 'Anarchy and Uproar', designed 'to break through Law, and spurn at Sacred Order' and resulting in a stageful of corpses, 'Horror, Blood, and Ruin' (II.ii.74; IV.i.245; V.i.154). Rowe is careful in the opening scene to establish an atmosphere of filial virtue, 'Goodness innate' (I.i.76), pervading Sciolto's household – suffocating in its own way, perhaps, but a positive image of family life and parental care very different from the petty tyrannies which the heroines of the comedies seek to resist or circumvent. Any 'generous Pity' the audience may feel for the misguided Calista comes not from any harsh treatment by her father or her deceived husband, but from her betrayal by Lothario, the play's least sympathetic figure, who in characteristic libertine fashion loses interest in her once he has gained her 'easie Heart', his passion diminishing after enjoyment (Preface, p. 305; 1.i.143).

In a number of plays by Behn, female characters are able to gain an unaccustomed momentary freedom of action by a change of costume. This familiar dramatic convention, as Pearson and other critics point out, has the 'potential simultaneously to support and to subvert the *status quo*'.[62] In Behn's *The Dutch Lover*, where the wronged Hippolyta, condemned by her family as 'fallen from Honour, and from Vertue' and as living 'in whoredom', dons men's clothing to wreak vengeance on her seducer, any criticism of the double standard is muted by the exigencies of the comic plot, with its obligatory happy ending. Sexual stereotypes are reinforced rather than challenged when Hippolyta, fortified in her resolution by her male dress, soliloquises 'My soul too is all man:/Where dwells no tenderness, no womanish passions' (especially since, even in male dress, she keeps showing her 'tenderness' by weeping).[63] The conventional, largely unmotivated repentance of the heartless seducer Antonio and the round of forgiveness which follows again undercut the criticism, earlier in the play, of a society in which lovers and parents alike treat women as a 'commodity' and place a disproportionate value on chastity (iv.ii, p. 66).

MARCEL. Pray, Sir, forgive them, your honour being safe,
Since *Don Antonio* has by marrying her
Repair'd the injury he did us all,
Without which I had kill'd him. (v.i, p. 90)

A similar ambivalence, in which the action of the play seems both to criticise and give tacit approval to conventional male attitudes toward female sexuality, can be found in Behn's *The Feign'd Curtezans* (1679). In this play, where Behn again uses the disguise motif in much the same way as her male contemporaries, Cornelia and her sister Marcella free themselves temporarily from the chains of convention and from patriarchal domination by pretending, in a spirit of adventure, to be courtesans.

CORNELIA. 'Life Sister thou art beautifull, and hast a Fortune too, which before I wou'd lay out upon so shamefull a purchase as such a Bedfellow for life as *Octavio*; I would turn errant keeping Curtizan, and buy my better fortune.
MARCELLA. That word too startles me.
CORNELIA. What Curtizan, why 'tis a Noble title and has more *Votaries*

then Religion, there's no Merchandize like ours, that of Love my sister! – And can you be frighted with the vizor, which you your self put on?[64]

As in the disguises of Hellena in *The Rover*, taking advantage of the authorised 'divertissements of a Carnival' to put on gypsy dress (I.i, p. 178), the masquerade is all innocent fun, a device enabling the witty heroine to behave provocatively while retaining her 'fixt resolves for Virtue'. Though Cornelia can say of the life of a courtesan, 'to give it its due, there are a thousand satisfactions to be found, more than in a dull virtuous life', she is a libertine in her words only (*The Feign'd Curtezans*, II.i, p. 15; IV.i, p. 51).[65] There are risks in such a strategy, since her rakish suitor Galliard has no such compunctions, and is fully prepared to turn Cornelia into a whore when she tells him she is not one:

CORNELIA. Stay, do you take me then for what I seem!
GALLIARD. I'me sure I do! and wou'd not be mistaken for a Kingdome!
But if thou art not! I can soon mend that fault, And make thee so, – come – I'm impatient to begin the Experiment. (IV.i, p. 50)

Predictably, the play ends in marriage, with Cornelia promising 'to be the most Mistriss like wife', taming her libertine suitor, who decides to 'trust good Nature' and abandon his 'past loose way of living' (v.i, p. 70).

Few plays of the period, by Behn or any of her male contemporaries, use cross-dressing and disguise in a way which is genuinely subversive. 'The breeches part', in which an actress assumes male dress, was one of the most common theatrical devices in Restoration drama, occurring in well over a hundred plays.[66] An element of sexual titillation is frequently present in these conventional transgressions of convention, expressed in a crude form in Wycherley's stage direction '*Pulls off her Peruke, and feels her breasts*', as Fidelia in *The Plain-Dealer* reveals herself as 'a very unfortunate woman' to the villainous Vernish, or in the many knowing comments in prologues and epilogues, addressed collusively to a male audience, advertising the physical charms of sexually experienced actresses:

What e're she was before the Play began,
All you shall see of her is perfect man.
Or if your fancy will be farther led
To find her Woman, it must be abed.[67]

Cross-dressing in itself therefore is as likely to pander to dominant patriarchal values as to challenge them: self-sacrificing heroines, like

Fidelia, willing to play the doormat, may differ in their strategy
from the more active and resourceful Cornelia, but each seeks to
'finde' and to secure a husband, and the assumed identity is primarily a means to that end.

> He would have look'd on me
> Amongst the sooty *Indians*; and I cou'd,
> To choose there live his Wife, where Wives are forc'd
> To live no longer, when their Husbands dye:
> Nay, what's yet worse, to share 'em whil'st they live
> With many Rival Wives.   (*The Plain-Dealer*, 1.i.541–6)

Yet a few plays of this period, by Behn and by other dramatists,
employ the cross-dressing motif to offer a more radical critique of
conventional attitudes toward female sexuality and toward the
sanctioned inequality privileging one sex over another. In Behn's
The Widdow Ranter (1690), the Duchess of Newcastle's *Bell in Campo*
(1662), Shadwell's *The Woman-Captain* (1680) and, the most original
of these plays, Thomas Southerne's *Sir Anthony Love* (1691), received
notions of sexual identity are destabilised, as they are in the poems of
Behn to androgynous master/mistresses discussed earlier in this
chapter. In each of these plays, the central character is a genuinely
androgynous figure, a woman whose male dress is not a temporary
disguise but expresses her inward nature, with all its contradictions,
freeing capacities and feelings which in other circumstances would
have remained hidden.

In Southerne's play, Sir Anthony's real name is Lucia, but she is
rarely called by that name: in the dramatis personae, she is listed as
'Sir Anthony Love', and she dons female clothing only for two brief
scenes (both times under an assumed identity). Neither her lover
Valentine nor the wealthy fool Sir Gentle Golding, the 'Keeper'
who 'bought' her from an aunt, and from whom she has absconded,
recognises her in the male guise by means of which, with complete
success, she violates all the conventional rules governing women's
behaviour in society. Sir Anthony is an expert swordsman, and has
acquired the 'Reputation of a Whoremaster, as the errant'st Rake-
hell of 'em all'. In a conversation early in the play with the one man
to whom she confides the secret of her identity, she is presented as
combining the characteristics of both sexes and, by implication, as
able to love and be loved by men and by women:

WAITWELL. You're a pretty proficient indeed, and so perfectly act the
Cavalier, that cou'd you put on our Sex with your Breeches, o' my
Conscience you wou'd carry all the Women before you.

SIR ANTHONY. And drive all the Men before me; I am for Universal
   Empire, and wou'd not be stinted to one Province; I wou'd be fear'd,
   as well as lov'd: As famous for my Action with the Men, as for my
   Passion for the Women.[68]

The polymorphous nature of sexual attraction as the play presents it
is emphasised in scenes involving two religious hypocrites, a Pilgrim
who, suspecting Sir Anthony may be a woman, is willing to make
love to her in 'any Sex', and a sodomite Abbé who abandons an
attempted seduction of the beautiful youth, recoiling in comic
horror when she reveals she is a woman (III.i.110–15; v.iv.43–113).[69]
Even after Sir Anthony reveals her identity to Valentine, she is
willing to share him with another woman for the sake of the 'Jest'. In
this way she can continue to enjoy the satisfactions of cameraderie,
retaining the status as wit and rake allowed her by her male dress:
the more refined pleasures of 'diverting . . . Roguery', it is suggested, give more delight than the physical 'Enjoyment' of sexual
consummation.

VALENTINE. 'Tis a whimsical Undertaking methinks, to support another
   Woman's Intrigue at your Expence –
SIR ANTHONY. There's no buying such a Frolick to dear.
VALENTINE. And to part with your Lover to oblige her!
SIR ANTHONY. So long, I can part with you; to provide for your pleasure
   as well as my own: Besides, 'tis a diverting piece of Roguery; and will
   be a Jest as long as we know one another. (v.iii.3–9)

The ending of the play, in which Sir Anthony's love of 'Roguery'
still predominates, is highly unconventional, since rather than
capitulating to marriage Sir Anthony retains her freedom of
action.[70] Throughout the play Sir Anthony is caustic at the expense
of marriage and its confinements, injurious to both partners: 'In all
plays, one side must be the looser; but Marriage is the only Game,
where nobody can be the winner . . . There's nothing but cheating
in Love' (IV.iv.111–19). In the characteristic manner of the libertine, she praises the challenge of an 'Intrigue' where 'the danger
doubles [one's] delight'. Not all Sir Anthony says can be taken at
face value, since she is always playing a role, seeking to maintain her
'Reputation' as a rake. But as wit and lover, male and female, Sir
Anthony never departs from an aggressive stance, expressing a
Hobbesian ethos of competition without quarter: 'Reputation must
be had: And we young Men generally raise ours out of the Ruine of

the Womens . . . We naturally covet, what we are forbid; for very often 'tis the bare pleasure of breaking the Commandment, that makes another Man's Wife more desirable than his own' (IV.iv.32–3, 67–72). At the end of the play, rather than marrying Valentine, she arranges two prudential, loveless marriages of convenience, one between herself and the contemptible Sir Gentle Golding, who immediately agrees to pay 'a Rent-charge of Five hundred' pounds a year to be divorced from her (v.vii.135–6), and one between Valentine and her rival Floriante.

VALENTINE. You continue your Opinion of Marriage.
SIR ANTHONY. *Floriante*, I grant you, wou'd be a dangerous Rival in a
   Mistress –
VALENTINE. Nothing can Rival thee.
SIR ANTHONY. And you might linger out, a long liking of her, to my
   uneasiness, and your own, but Matrimony, that's her security is mine:
   I can't apprehend her in a Wife. (IV.ii.76–82)

The play concludes with lines of breathtaking cynicism, as Sir Anthony recommends a fool as the ideal husband and 'sep'rate Maintenance', an agreed separation involving a financial settlement, as a recipe for preserving love:

SIR ANTHONY. Thus Coxcombs always the best Husbands prove
When we are faulty, and begin to rove,
A sep'rate Maintenance supplies our Love. (v.vii.143–5)

Another androgynous figure, though of a different type, plays a prominent role in Behn's tragicomedy *The Widdow Ranter*. Ranter, the principal female figure in the comic sub-plot, contrasted throughout with the Indian queen Semernia, who dies for love with exquisite passivity in elevated heroic language, is a virago, a roaring girl, an Amazon figure.[71] Liberated from the usual expectations of demure womanly behaviour by wealth ('We rich Widdows are the best Commodity this Country affords', I.iii, p. 12), the status of a widow and the primitivist setting of a pastoral North America where the characters dine on buffalo steak, the Widow Ranter violates all the normal proprieties: she swears, smokes a pipe and drinks punch copiously. Like Sir Anthony, she prefers to wear trousers and loves a jest, and she courts the 'mad Fellow . . . who has my heart and soul' in an aggressive way (IV.ii, pp. 42–3), not simply seizing the initiative but engaging in knockabout physical combat.

RANTER. Pox on't no, why should I sigh and whine, and make myself an
　　Ass, and him conceited, no, instead of snevelling I'm resolved –
JENNY. What Madam?
RANTER. Gad to beat the Rascal . . .
JENNY. Beat him Madam? What a Woman beat a Lieutenant General.
RANTER. Hang 'em, they get a name in War, from command, not
　　courage; how know I but I may fight, Gad I have known a Fellow
　　kickt from one end of the Town to t'other, believing himself a Coward,
　　at last forc'd to fight, found he could, got a Reputation and bullyed all
　　he met with, and got a name, and a great Commission.
JENNY. But if he should kill you Madam?
RANTER. I'll take care to make it as Comical a Duel as the best of 'em, as
　　much in Love as I am, I do not intend to dy it's Martyr. (IV.ii,
　　pp. 42–3)[72]

Like Sir Anthony, Ranter challenges the assumption that physical
courage is a masculine prerogative, behaving courageously in battle,
'fighting like a Fury' side by side with her lover, the equally blunt
and forthright Daring, who praises her in the end as 'a fit Wife for a
Souldier' (v.i, p. 48; v.iv, p. 55). Their scene of comic courtship, in
which they exchange insults in a parody of a proviso scene ('Gad I'd
sooner marry a She Bear, unless for a Pennance for some horrid Sin,
we should be eternally challenging one another to the Field, and ten
to one she beats me there; or if I should escape there, she would kill
me with Drinking'), ends, as the convention dictates, with expressions of mutual affection as they 'conclude a Peace': 'Give me thy
hand Widow, I am thine – and so intirely, I will never – be drunk
out of thy Company'. Less predictably, Daring suggests they marry
while she remains in trousers, suggesting that it was precisely those
qualities 'the Fashion of the World' considers masculine that attracted him to her.

DARING. Prithee let's in and bind the bargain.
RANTER. Nay, faith, let's see the Wars at an end first.
DARING. Nay, prithee, take me in the humour, while thy Breeches are on
　　– for I never lik'd thee half so well in Petticoats.
RANTER. Lead on General, you give me good incouragement to wear
　　them. (IV.iii, pp. 44–5)

　　The Amazon or virago, combative and courageous man-woman,
is a relatively common figure in Restoration drama, but normally, as
Pearson says, introduced to conservative effect, presenting 'fantasies
of powerful women ultimately subdued by men'. As the Amazon

queen says in Edward Howard's *The Womens Conquest* (1671), leading a choreographed demonstration of 'Love, and obedience':

> And Women, here divest
> Your selves of Arms with me . . .
> And let your Conquests henceforth be to love,
> And give Men sole supremacy.[73]

Rochester's dramatic fragment *The Conquest of China* is closer to *The Widdow Ranter* in presenting a positive model of unsubdued female courage, though the decorum is that of heroic drama rather than slapstick comedy. Remarks about the natural inferiority of women here are left to the cowardly and villainous Lycungus ('When she's my Slave, I'll set her Empire free . . . In stead of mee ruine and death shall reigne'), while the warrior Empress demonstrates in action her belief in the equality of the sexes, challenging the tyranny of custom:

> The day I'le prove the Injustice of that scorne
> Men treat our Sex withall, Woman is borne
> With equall thirst of Honour and of Fame
> But treacherous man misguides her in her aime
> Makes her believe that all her Glories lye
> In dull Obedience, Truth and Modesty,
> That to be Beautifull is to be Brave
> And calls her Conquerer when she's most his Slave
> Forbidding her those noble Paths to tread,
> Which through bold daring Deeds to Glory lead.[74]

Yet in the closing words of the scene, when the virtuous Hyachian pays tribute to the fair warrior, it is precisely the mixture of the 'Beautifull' and 'Brave' which he praises: blood and wounds ('like Rubies' on 'her faire neck', 241–2) make her sexually attractive, enhancing her appeal as a potential bedmate:

> Noe more shall Nations in distress and thrawll
> On helpless man for Aid in Battails call:
> This Woman's Valour is above us all –
> Where ere she fights, Beauty and Ruine joyne
> Rage on her Arme, While in her Eyes they shine.   (262–6)

No such element of sexual titillation is present in the sprawling, unstageable closet dramas of Margaret Cavendish, Duchess of Newcastle, which as Hobby says are 'a series of fantasy sketches' presenting 'idealised role-models' of feminine achievements. A recurrent theme in her plays, as in *The Conquest of China* and *The Widdow Ranter*, is the natural equality of men and women, obscured by inequalities in education. Masculine rule in these allegorical, didactic plays is almost invariably destructive.

FOURTH VIRGIN. Why we are not Fools, we are capable of Knowledge, we only want Experience and Education, to make us as wise as men . . .

THIRD VIRGIN. Certainly, if we had that breeding, and did govern, we should govern the world better than it is.

FOURTH VIRGIN. Yes, for it cannot be govern'd worse than it is.[75]

Lady Victoria in *Bell in Campo*, equally adept with her oratory and her sword, leads an army of women into battle, where they easily outperform the men: like most of the characters in the Duchess of Newcastle's plays, she speaks with the voice of the author: 'Shall only Men in Triumphant Chariots ride, and Women run as Captives by? shall only men be Conquerors, and women Slaves? shall only Men live by Fame, and women dy in Oblivion?'[76]

A triumphant female warrior is the principal figure in Shadwell's *The Woman-Captain*, written at the height of the Exclusion Bill crisis, one of a number of plays which explore the idea of the right of revolution as an excuse for seeking to escape from an unhappy marriage. The explicitly political vocabulary of this 'play about liberty cast in domestic terms' may possibly reflect Shadwell's staunch Whig allegiances, though Behn and Otway, both Tories, use similar analogies at roughly this time. Gripe, the old miser to whom the heroine is married, is constantly described as a tyrant, who treats his wife as a possession at his absolute disposal, and Mrs Gripe demands 'Christian Liberty . . . the liberty of a She-subject of *England*'.[77] In the course of the play, Mrs Gripe (yet another spirited heroine played by Elizabeth Barry) takes her deliverance into her own hands, enacting the doctrines of contract theory: when a ruler, civil or domestic, fails to perform his part of the covenant but instead 'by force invades the Right of another', the obligation to obey ceases and resistance is justified.[78]

The Woman-Captain, like *Sir Anthony Love* and *The Widdow Ranter*, uses the conventions of cross-dressing to question accepted gender roles, as Mrs Gripe, assuming male dress at the end of act III and thereafter, exposes, chastises and physically humiliates not only her husband but a series of male pretenders, showing them that 'there's more than roaring goes to true Valour' (V, p. 64). When she puts on

the costume of Captain, matching her language to her dress, Mrs
Gripe is transformed, bringing out a hitherto unrealised potential
which enables her not only to triumph over her husband, but to
become all-conquering. In a series of farcical scenes, the women all
succumb to her imagined virile charms (with much kissing and
'tousing') and the men, including her husband, are beaten, tied neck
and heels and marched about the stage, with the stated aim of
making 'an example' of them, revenging the wrongs done to her sex
by the play's epicures, bullies and would-be tyrants, all brought
abjectly under her domination:

MRS. GRIPE. Faith, I'll have him under my Command now, or press him
   for *Flanders* . . . I'll teach Husbands to provoke their own Flesh . . . I'll
   make him such an example. I'll make all Husbands have a care, how
   by Injuries they sower their Wive's love into revenge, or their meek-
   ness into rage. (III.iii, p. 39; V, p. 58)

Here, as in the play's closing lines, addressed directly to the audience, Shadwell explicitly draws a moral applicable to 'all
Husbands'.

MRS. GRIPE. Now all ye Husbands, let me warn ye!
If you'd preserve your Honours, or your Lives,
Ne'r dare be Tyrants o're your Lawful Wives. (V, p. 72)

The argument here, implicit in such titles as *The Provok'd Wife* and
The Wives Excuse: Or Cuckolds Make Themselves, is one we have seen in
the writings of Astell and Behn: not that rebellions *should* occur, but
that under sufficient provocation, they do occur. Vanbrugh in his
pamphlet *A Short Vindication of the Relapse and the Provok'd Wife* (1698)
makes a similar point: 'I therefore think that Play has a very good
End, which puts the Governor in mind, let his Soldiers be never so
good, 'tis possible he may provoke 'em to a Mutiny.'[79]

The dissolution of an unhappy marriage which ends *The Woman-
Captain*, as it does in Shadwell's *Epsom-Wells* (1673), Farquhar's *The
Beaux Stratagem* (1707) and several other plays of the period, is in
some ways pure wish-fulfilment. Mrs Gripe, having by a combination of 'Force' and 'Strategem' secured a separate maintenance
from her husband, only reveals her identity when she has gained her
'Liberty', financial as well as emotional.

MRS. GRIPE. And now good Mr. *Gripe*, your much abus'd Wife is free, and
   thanks you for her Liberty.
GRIPE. O Devil! Is it she all this while?
LADIES. A Woman!

MRS. GRIPE. Yes Ladies, I am; but wish my self a Man, for your sakes, and my own. (v, p. 72)

In the androgynous Utopia of the final scene of *The Woman-Captain*, as in the improvised unmarrying ceremony which concludes *The Beaux Stratagem*, there is an element of fantasy, providing a neat and clear resolution more common in art than in life. Tyrannous husbands, like kings, do not give up their power as easily as Mr Gripe, Squire Sullen or the doddering Sir Feeble and Sir Cautious at the end of *The Lucky Chance* – though it is striking that Sir Cautious, admitting he has been overmatched, retains control to the end, assuming he can dispose of Julia as part of his property: 'If I dye Sir – I bequeath my Lady to you – with my whole Estate' (v, p. 69). Southerne's *The Wives Excuse* (1691) ends more equivocally, with an agreement to separate in which the husband is free to enjoy the pleasures of the town, where the abused Mrs Friendall remains trapped in her own bitterness and in the conventions of an 'unjust' society, condemned 'to a slavery for life': 'I must be still your Wife, and still unhappy' (v.iii.305–8, 326). In the concluding scene of *The Woman-Captain*, there is a hint that the established, unjust order will reassert itself once the licence of carnival is over: Mrs Gripe's transformation lasts only so long as she is able to maintain her assumed identity, and she is left wishing she were a man, to enjoy in the flesh the pleasures which, in ordinary circumstances, she can merely contemplate. The epilogue, spoken in her own person by Elizabeth Barry, the actress for whom Shadwell, Behn, Vanbrugh and Southerne created a series of provoked wives, further emphasises the illusory nature of Mrs Gripe's triumph, collusively assuring the male audience that they need not feel unduly troubled by a 'Low' farce meant for their entertainment. Cross-dressing in this epilogue is used entirely for sexual badinage, in lines which, evoking the female body under the male dress, project 'satisfaction' of a more intimate kind:

> 'Sdeath, I'll not fear the briskest of ye all:
> No, though ye Rant and Roar, and sometimes Fight,
> I've that which never fails to do me right.   (Epilogue, Sig. A4)[80]

The pursuit of sexual pleasure by women, claiming in this respect full equality with men, is a central issue in at least three plays by Behn, the two parts of *The Rover* and *The City-Heiress*. All three of these plays emphasise the problematical aspects of libertine ideology and implicitly or explicitly criticise the double standard. Though adulterous liaisons form part of the action of several plays by Behn (*The Lucky Chance, Sir Patient Fancy*), projected or anticipated adultery, sex in the head, as with Lady Brute in *The Provok'd Wife*, is more common than actual consummation in plays by Restoration dramatists, and this is equally the case with Behn. In *The Rover*, Part II, Ariadne, scorning marriage as a sordid commercial transaction – 'Death, who wou'd marry, who wou'd be chaffer'd thus, and sold to slavery' – is thwarted in repeated attempts to arrange an assignation with the priapic Willmore.

ARIA. Faith no, I saw you, lik'd ye, and had a mind to ye.
WILL. Ay child –
ARIA. In short, I took ye for a man of Honour.
WILL. Nay, if I tell the Devil take me.
ARIA. I am a Virgin in distress.
WILL. Poor heart.
ARIA. To be marry'd within a day or two to one I like not.
WILL. Hum – and therefore wou'dst dispose of a small Virgin Treasure (too good for silly Husbands) in a friends hands.[81]

In an earlier scene, attracted by forbidden fruit, she expresses characteristic libertine sentiments – commonplace in a male speaker, but highly unusual in a female speaker – in badinage with Willmore: 'I love a man that scorns to impose dull truth and constancy on a Mistriss . . . New Lovers have new vows and new Presents, whilst the old feed upon a dull repetition of what they did when they were Lovers; 'tis like eating the cold meat ones self, after having given a friend a Feast' (II.i, p. 19). Yet in the end of the play Ariadne has to settle for the mercenary and selfish 'formal Matrimonial Fop' (II.ii, p. 30) chosen by her parents, unconvincingly agreeing, after five acts of mutual aversion, to a match which, as Willmore points out in the play's closing lines, lacks the excitement and challenge that 'Love and Gallantry' offer (V.ii, p. 85).

The principal female character in *The Second Part of The Rover*, played by Elizabeth Barry, is the courtesan La Nuche, who in contrast with Ariadne, is shown to be free of the artificial societal restraints hampering that 'poor sneaking thing an honest Woman', married or single: 'And if we chance to Love still there's a difference, your hours of Love are like the deeds of darkness, and mine like chearful Birds in open day' (IV.i, p. 54). Both parts of *The Rover* contain sympathetic portraits of courtesans, strong independent women who seek to control their own destinies and who, as outcasts, are able to see through the hypocrisies which govern respectable men and women in their customary behaviour. Thus, Angelica Bianca retorts, when Willmore accuses her of being 'infamous' and mercenary:

ANGELICA. Pray tell me, Sir, are you not guilty of the same mercenary Crime? When a Lady is proposed to you for a Wife, you never ask, how fair, discreet, or virtuous she is; but what's her Fortune – which if but small, you cry – She will not do my business – and basely leave her, though she languish for you. – Say, is this not as poor?
WILLMORE. It is a barbarous Custom, which I will scorn to defend in our Sex, and do despise in yours. (*The Rover*, II.ii, pp. 36–7)

The attack on the double standard, surprisingly, is even stronger in the equivalent passage in Behn's source, Thomas Killigrew's *Thomaso, or The Wanderer* (1664): here as in *The Rover*, the courtesan acts as advocate for all women, seeking 'some satisfaction for the slavery we suffer':

ANGELLICA. After all this severe truth, what are we guilty of that you have not confess'd? . . . You men are strangely partial to your selves, you would not despise us else; Is the fault single in us? If not, why should we lose our Honours in the Act, when you think it an Honour to be the Actors? Who made the Law against Love? Or where will you find it obligeth women only? If the Law be general, must not the crime be too?[82]

Yet in both parts of *The Rover*, the freedom of the courtesan is associated with 'Interest', the calculated withholding of a commodity to increase the price, and with the exercise of power. In the exchanges between Willmore and the two highly articulate courtesans, Angelica Bianca and La Nuche, neither of the two speakers is wholly right or wholly wrong, and each presents cogent criticisms of the ideological assumptions of the other:

WILLMORE. Thou'rt one who lazily workst in thy Trade, and sell'st for ready money so much kindness . . .
LA NUCHE. What, you would have a Mistriss like a Squirrel in a Cage, always in Action – one who is as free of her favours as I am sparing of mine. (*The Second Part of The Rover*, I.i, pp. 13–14)

Both La Nuche and Angelica Bianca, successful in their chosen profession, are aware that their ability to retain mastery over besotted male clients depends on vigilance in resisting the 'Inclinations' they may feel (III.i, p. 39), never allowing their defences to be breached by the emotion of love. Angelica Bianca surrenders to romantic impulse, rejecting the practical counsel of her worldly bawd: 'a No-Purchase, No-Pay Tatterdemalion, an *English* Picca-roon; a Rogue that fights for daily Drink, and takes a Pride in being loyally lousy . . . This is the fate of most whores' (*The Rover*, II.ii, p. 39). Yet after giving herself to Willmore in defiance of self-interest, Angelica Bianca finds that the only roles left her are 'a mean submissive Passion . . . content to've worn my Chains' or jealous rage directed at the inconstant Willmore once, predictably, he has lost interest in her:

> Had I remained in innocent Security,
> I should have thought all Men were born my Slaves.
> And worn my Pow'r like Lightning in my Eyes,
> To have destroyed at Pleasure when offended.   (v, pp. 91–2)

La Nuche, like Hellena in Part I, retains her freedom of manoeuvre as long as possible, taunting Willmore with the more 'substantial' claims of his rival, the wealthy Beaumond: 'Look ye, Sir, will not these Pearls do better round my Neck than those kind Arms of yours? these Pendants in my Ears than all the tales of Love you can whisper there?' (*The Second Part of The Rover*, v.i, p. 69).

The 'bargain' struck by Hellena and Willmore at the end of Part I and by La Nuche and Willmore at the end of Part II, though in neither case taking the form of a proviso scene, envisages the possi-bility of a relationship between men and women not based on ownership or domination. Conventional marriage and the cash transactions of prostitution, consistently equated in Behn's work, are contrasted with the free union of equals, 'of one humour' (*The Rover*, III.i, p. 45; v, p. 98) in their love of liberty, their scorn of convention, their willingness 'to live and starve by turns as fortune pleases': 'Now here's a bargain made without the formal foppery of Marriage' (*The Second Part of The Rover*, v.ii, p. 81). This 'bargain' is one which the proud and passionate Angelica Bianca, unlike her fellow courtesan La Nuche, can never bring herself to make, threatening to kill Willmore because he 'must, like chearful Birds, sing in all Groves,/ And perch on every Bough' (*The Rover*, v, p. 93). Hellena, like La Nuche in the sequel, accepts the hedonist assumptions on which Willmore consistently acts: that 'one hour of right-down Love is worth an Age of living dully on', and that 'inconstant Fortune' can never be mastered (*The Second Part of The Rover*, v.i, pp. 68–9). To 'Hellena the Inconstant', determined to 'lose no time', to catch love 'upon the Wing' and enjoy it 'whilst it lasts', the fickleness of the elusive Willmore is his greatest attraction: 'How this unconstant Humour makes me love him' (*The Rover*, iv.i, p. 68; v, pp. 97, 99).[83]

It is striking that in these supposedly equal unions, whether sanctioned by the 'bug words' of 'Hymen and priest . . . portion and jointure' or not, the double standard continues to operate, since the man retains a freedom of action which the woman surrenders. La Nuche, 'reform'd', may choose love over 'powerful Interest', but the proof of love is her agreement to 'follow' Willmore wherever he chooses to go (*The Second Part of The Rover*, v.i, p. 68; v.ii, p. 81). Hellena, conveniently killed off between the two parts of the play, to be dismissed jokingly 'with a Sham sadness' in a brisk exchange between young predatory males, has followed him to her death, expiring in an excess of 'kindness':

BEAU. I think thou hadst her but a month, prithee how dy'd she?
WILL. Faith, e'ne with a fit of kindness, poor soul – she would to Sea with me and in a Storm – far from Land she gave up the Ghost – 'twas a loss, but I must bear it with a Christian Fortitude.
BEAU. Short happiness vanish like to dreams.
WILL. Ay faith, and nothing remains with me but the sad remembrance – not so much as the least part of her hundred thousand Crowns. (i.i, p. 5)

The ambivalence with which female sexuality and libertine attitudes toward women are treated in *The Rover* is exemplified by the prominent role of attempted rape in the play's action. As Howe has shown, rape or the prospect of rape is extremely common in Restoration drama, and often is cynically exploitative, a means of 'exposing naked female flesh' as part of the stage spectacle, in which 'the actress's body [is] offered to the audience as a piece of erotic entertainment'. In narratives of projected or perpetrated rape, male and female members of the audience can indulge their sadomasochistic fantasies without feeling guilty: like Rochester's shepherdess Chloris, masturbating in her sleep, 'the Woman' in such scenes 'is suppos'd to remain innocent, and to be pleas'd without her Consent'.[84] Though Behn's plays are occasionally collusive in this way, with female characters shown 'in undress' and presented as erotic objects to the scrutiny of the male audience, Behn characteristically uses scenes of attempted rape to expose the violence and 'deliberated Malice' (*The Rover*, IV.iii, p. 80) implicit in the libertine ideology.

In several scenes of *The Rover*, Florinda, the heroine of the subplot, is threatened with sexual assault not only by the maladroit and foolish Blunt but by Willmore and his friend Frederick. Because of its crude aggressiveness, presented explicitly as compensation for Blunt's own inadequacy and previous failures with women, the near-rape by Blunt seems particularly threatening and unpleasant. Behn makes it clear that any sexual desire on Blunt's part is almost wholly sadistic in nature: humiliated in an encounter with the whore Lucetta (a parody version of Angelica Bianca, whose sole motivation is the desire for 'Booty'), stripped of his clothes and dumped into a 'Common Shore' (sewer) – Rochester's misogynist symbol for the stain of sexuality – Blunt seeks revenge on all womankind, and Florinda has no individual identity for him (III.iii, pp. 51–2).[85]

BLUNT. Come, no Resistance. *Pulls her rudely.*
FLORINDA. Dare you be so cruel?
BLUNT. Cruel? adsheartlikins, as a Gally-slave, or a *Spanish* Whore: Cruel, yes, I will kiss and beat thee all over: kiss, and see thee all over; thou shalt lie with me too, not that I care for the Injoyment, but to let thee see I have ta'en deliberated Malice to thee, and will be revenged on one Whore for the Sins of another . . . No, young one, no Prayers or Tears shall mitigate my Rage; therefore prepare for both my Pleasures of Enjoyment and Revenge, for I am resolved to make up my Loss here on thy Body, I'll take it out in kindness and in beating. (IV.iii, pp. 80, 81)

Behn is careful to show that Blunt's behaviour here is no mere aberration, but a product of the dominant ideology. His companion Frederick, no fool, is all too willing to join in, assuming, as does Willmore in an earlier scene, that any unattached woman is fair game. He desists from gang-rape on 'the Bed within' only when he discovers that she may be a 'Maid of Quality', an assault on whom would be punished, where the two men could 'ruffle a Harlot' safely.

BLUNT. We'll both lie with her, and then let me alone to bang her.
FREDERICK. I'm ready to serve you in matters of Revenge, that has a double Pleasure in't. (IV.iii, pp. 81–2)[86]

Earlier in the play, Willmore, the play's libertine hero, behaves in much the same way toward Florinda, though here the misunderstanding is comic, without the overt verbal and physical violence.

When Willmore, half-drunk, stumbles on Florinda, he immediately jumps to the conclusion that she is 'a very Wench', 'an errant Harlot', suitable for casual fornication (III.iii, p. 53; III.iv, p. 57).[87] His assumption, which he shares with the brutal Blunt (whom he despises), is that all women are sexually available, crying 'Rape' as provocation, pretending reluctance in order to increase desire.

> WILLMORE. For look you, Child, there will be no Sin in't, because 'twas neither designed nor premeditated: 'tis pure Accident on both sides ... Indeed should I make love to you, and you vow Fidelity, and swear and lye till you believ'd and yielded – that were to make it wilful Fornication, the crying Sin of the Nation – thou art, therefore (as thou art a good Christian) oblig'd in Conscience to deny me nothing. Now, come be kind, without any more idle prating.
>
> FLORINDA. Oh, I am ruin'd – wicked Man, unhand me.
>
> WILLMORE. Wicked! Egad, Child, a Judge, were he young and vigorous, and saw those Eyes of thine, would know 'twas they gave the first blow – the first provocation – Come, prithee let's lose no time, I say – this is a fine convenient place.
>
> FLORINDA. Sir, let me go, I conjure you, or I'll call out ... I'll cry Murder, Rape, or any thing, if you do not instantly let me go.
>
> WILLMORE. A Rape! Come, come, you lye, you Baggage, you lye: What, I'll warrant you would fain have the World believe now that you are not so forward as I. No, not you, – why at this time of Night was your Cobweb-door set open, dear Spider, but to catch Flies? (III.iii, p. 54)[88]

Though Willmore in this scene uses persuasion more than force, relying like other libertine rovers on 'the lucky minute', accepting without premeditation whatever windfalls fortune may bring, his attitude no less than that of Blunt and Frederick is dismissive of women, devaluing them to a mere object, to be enjoyed and then discarded. Even in this comic scene, violence is not far below the surface.[89]

A farcical yet unsavoury intended rape, in which the 'whining' Sir Charles Merriwill, his customary inhibitions removed by drink, strips to his drawers and pulls the heroine Lady Galliard about the stage, is the climax of the action of Behn's *The City-Heiress*, a particularly disturbing and problematical play in its treatment of female sexuality. The inept Sir Charles is at all points contrasted with his dashing friend and rival Tom Wilding (played by Betterton, where Lady Galliard was played by that specialist in sexually liberated, passionate heroines, Elizabeth Barry). In this scene of courtship his grotesque boorishness displays Sir Charles in the most unflattering light imaginable:

> *He begins to undress.*
> LADY GALLIARD. Hold, Sir, what mean you?
> SIR CHARLES. Onely to go to bed, that's all.
> *Still undressing . . .*
> LADY GALLIARD. What Imposition's this! I'll call for help.
> SIR CHARLES. You need not, you'll do my business better alone.
> *Pulls her.*
> LADY GALLIARD. What shall I do! how shall I send him hence! . . .
> SIR CHARLES. Come, come, no pausing; your promise, or I'll to bed.
> *Offers to pull off his Breeches, having pull'd off almost all the rest*
> *of his Clothes.*
> LADY GALLIARD. What shall I do, here is no Witness neer! And to be rid of him, I'll promise him, he'll have forgot it in his sober Passion. Hold, I do swear I will–
> *He fumbling to undo his Breeches.*
> SIR CHARLES. What?
> LADY GALLIARD. Marry you.
> SIR CHARLES. When?
> LADY GALLIARD. Nay, that's too much – Hold, hold, I will tomorrow – Now you are satisfi'd, you will withdraw?[90]

As a wealthy widow, Lady Galliard can to an appreciable extent exercise control over her actions and her estate. Wilding, scornful of the institution of marriage in characteristic libertine fashion ('Cou'd you be jealous of a woman I marry? Do you take me for such an Ass, to suspect I shall love my own Wife?'), points out to Lady Galliard the advantages of her free, unmarried state: 'Unless being sensible you have not discretion enough to manage your own affairs your self, you resolve, like other Widows, with all you're worth to buy a Governour, commonly called a Husband. I took you to be wiser' (IV.i, p. 39). For Lady Galliard, spirited and passionate, to be married off to Sir Charles at the end of the play, while still overwhelmingly in love with Wilding, is not only the acceptance of the second-best, but a conscious renunciation, bidding farewell both to love and freedom.

> LADY GALLIARD. Here, be as happy as a Wife can make ye – One last look more, and then – be gone fond Love.
> *Sighing and looking on Wilding, giving Sir Charles her hand.* (V.v, p. 61)

The irony of her surrender to the persistent, unromantic Sir Charles is even more pronounced because his drunken entrance comes immediately after an extended love scene between Lady Galliard and Wilding, ending with an offstage consummation: the stage direction concluding the scene is 'Exeunt into the Bedchamber, Wild. leading her with his arms about her' (iv.i, p. 42). The sexual explicitness of the play, and of this scene in particular, was notorious during Behn's lifetime:

> *The City Heiress,* by *chast Sappho* writ,
> Where the lewd *Widow* comes with brazen face,
> Just reeking from a *Stallion*'s rank embrace.[91]

Like Hellena and Willmore, Lady Galliard and Wilding are presented as kindred spirits, sexual equals. The promptings of the heart, as with a number of Behn's heroines, prove stronger in Lady Galliard than prudence or concern with 'Vertue':

> What heart can bear distrust from what it loves?
> Or who can always her own Wish deny?
> My Reason's weary of the unequal strife;
> And Love and Nature will at last o'ercome.
>
> (*The City-Heiress,* iv.i, pp. 41–2)

Wilding's carpe diem arguments thus meet a sympathetic response – 'Love bends my Soul that way' (iv.i, p. 39) – even though she is aware of the possible damaging consequences of giving in to desire and, soon rejected by a man grown 'weary' of her, becoming 'infamous, despis'd, loath'd, pointed at' (iv.i, pp. 39–40). In her awareness, even in the heights of passion, that the transports of the moment are sure to pass, Lady Galliard resembles other Behn heroines: Hellena in *The Rover,* who tartly answers Willmore's injunction to 'love and enjoy' with 'what shall I get? A Cradle full of Noise and Mischief, with a Pack of Repentance at my Back' (v, p. 98) or Sylvia in *Love-Letters Between a Nobleman and His Sister,* who at the moment of her surrender to impulse, is able to reflect, proleptically: 'But oh, *Philander,* if (as I've been told) possession, which makes women fond and doting, should make thee grow cold and indifferent – if nauseated with repeated joy, and having made a full discovery of all that was once imaginary, when fancy rendered every thing much finer than experience, oh, how were I undone!'[92]

Like Willmore in both parts of *The Rover* ('Poor as I am, I would not sell my self . . . My Purse shall never be my Pimp'), Wilding equates marriage 'for interest' with prostitution, contrasting it with the intense pleasures of fulfilling 'the desires of mutual Love':

Beauty shou'd still be the Reward of Love,
Not the vile Merchandize of Fortune,
Or the cheap Drug of a Church-Ceremony.
She's only infamous, who to her Bed,
For interest, takes some nauseous Clown she hates:
And though a Joynture or a Vow in publick
Be her price, that makes her but the dearer whore.

(The City-Heiress, iv.i, pp. 39–40)[93]

The argument is a powerful one, yet Lady Galliard, in a moment of revulsion, sees the promise of sexual freedom not as fulfilment but as imprisonment, turning her into an object to be used and exploited by a man with no regard for her feelings. Julia in *The Lucky Chance*, full of post-coital remorse, is similarly angry at her lover Gayman who, having 'seiz'd [his] Right of Love' has made her, in her own opinion, 'a base Prostitute, a foul Adultress' (v.ii, p. 65).

And have I promis'd then to be
A Whore? A Whore! Oh, let me think of that!
A Man's Convenience, his leisure hours, his Bed of Ease,
To loll and tumble on at idle times,
The Slave, the Hackney of his lawless Lust!
A loath'd Extinguisher of filthy flames,
Made use of, and thrown by – Oh infamous!

(The City-Heiress, iv.i, p. 41)

Again and again in Behn's plays, as in her poems, what is advertised as mutual, shared delight – 'Can Heaven or Man be angry that you please/Your self and me, when it does wrong to none?' (*The City-Heiress*, iv.i, p. 40) – turns out to be pleasure for the man, guilt and repentance for the woman. Though men and women are shown in Behn's writings to have 'equal desires', the libertine ideology, in which the sex act is an assertion of power, entails a fundamental inequality, with one partner reducing the other to a 'Convenience' or a 'Slave'.[94] In an early scene of *The City-Heiress*, Wilding presents the joys of sexual adventure as entirely one-sided: not only is the sought-for pleasure enhanced by 'Fear' and resistance, but all sexual enjoyment is accommodated to the model of violent rape. The distance between the charming libertine and the brutal, unimaginative fool is suddenly, disturbingly lessened:

WILDING. For, Widow, know, hadst thou more Beauty, yet not all of 'em were half so great a Charm as thy not being mine . . .

> The stealths of Love, the Midnight kind admittance,
> The gloomy Bed, the soft-breath'd murmuring Passion;
> Ah, who can guess at Joys thus snatcht by parcels!
> The difficulty makes us always wishing,
> Whilst on thy part, Fear still makes some resistance,
> And every Blessing seems a kind of Rape.　　　　　　(1.ii, p. 8)

In Behn as in Rochester, the libertine ideology leads to a cul de sac: one must be a predator to avoid being preyed upon. According to the Hobbesian ideology implicit in the lines just quoted, as in many plays and poems of the Restoration period, restless desire, spurred on by 'difficulty', must, as soon as it has overcome 'resistance', pass on to a new object, a new potential conquest. Behn's poem 'The Reflection' is typical in presenting desire as inherently unstable:

> For as my Kindling Flames increase,
> Yours glimeringly decay:
> The Rifled Joys no more can Please,
> That once oblig'd your Stay.　　　　　　(45–8)

Sylvia, the heroine of *Love-Letters*, is as committed as any male rake to the hedonist psychology and ethics characteristic of Restoration libertinism: adultery, even incest, are in her view 'no crime to heaven till man made laws', and marriage is 'a trick, a wise device of priests, no more – to make the nauseated, tired-out pair drag on the careful business of life, drudge for the dull-got family with greater satisfaction, because they are taught to think marriage was made in heaven; a mighty comfort that, when all the joys of life are lost by it'.[95] And yet, like all the female figures in Behn's writings who desire to be 'unconfin'd, and free', Sylvia in the course of the novel finds herself limited to one of two roles chosen for her by the ideology to which she adheres. On the one hand, as passive victim, she can 'caress and welcome [her] despair', luxuriating in self-abasement and castigating herself as 'useless' and 'despis'd'.[96] On the other hand, perpetuating the cycle of betrayal and abandonment, 'fatally instructed . . . in an art she ever after practic'd', she can apply the lessons taught her to make victims of her own: 'Yet since she found she had not a heart that any love, or loss of honour, or fortune could break; but, on the contrary, a rest of youth and beauty, that might oblige her, with some reason, to look forward to new lovers, if the old must depart . . . she resolved . . . she would make the best of her youth.'[97] The choice is a bleak one, and very remote from the androgynous ideal of equality for which Behn argues elsewhere: either, as with Angelica Bianca in *The Rover*, to allow oneself to become disarmed, her 'fancy'd Power' destroyed by surrendering to desire, to find that nothing she could offer afterwards was 'worth/ The Conqueror's Care or Value' (v, p. 93) or, accepting the role of a whore and the hardening of the heart it entails, to make sure she remains her own paymaster in the ceaseless hunt for 'new prey', fresh conquests.[98]

Conclusion

A central paradox of Restoration libertinism, as this study has shown, is that the principles of conduct it advocates are in some fundamental respects incompatible. Libertinism tends to equate freedom with mastery, reducing all sexual relations to 'new Conquests' in an endless war: as a rather battered, disreputable rake says in Sir Charles Sedley's *Bellamira* (1687), paraphrasing Hobbes: 'In matter of Women, we are all in the State of Nature, every man's hand against every man. Whatever we pretend.'[1] The courtesan heroine Bellamira, fiercely independent and generous of spirit, like the heroines of *The Lucky Chance*, *The Rover*, *The City-Heiress* and other plays by Behn, contests the assumption, implicit in the lines just quoted, that women serve primarily as objects of desire, rather than as desiring agents; and indeed the women in *Bellamira* consistently behave better than the men, a middle-aged, pox-ridden collection of 'Whore-masters, Gamesters, Drunkards, Bullies' (v.i.623), who illustrate the darker side of libertine hedonism.[2] Both Behn and Rochester in their writings frequently project an equality of desire, in which men and women alike are subject to the transgressive force of Eros. In poem after poem, Behn and Rochester argue much the same libertine doctrines, treating 'affected Rules of Honour' with contempt, and contrasting the 'holy Cheats, and formal Lyes' imposed by fearful tyrants, domestic and political, on 'their fellow *Slaves*' with a natural freedom 'kind Nature' offers to all, of either sex, who are bold enough to grasp the offered opportunity.[3] Behn's 'The Golden Age', like *The Rover*, contrasts the free play of desire with the cold usurping hand of force, in a fallen world where the only available roles are tyrant and slave:

> Fond Idol of the slavish Crowd,
> Thou wast not known in those blest days
> Thy Poyson was not mixt with our unbounded Joys:

214

> Then it was glory to pursue delight,
> And that was lawful all, that Pleasure did invite,
> Then 'twas the Amorous world injoy'd its Reign;
> And Tyrant Honour strove t'usurp in Vain.
>
> ('The Golden Age', 77–83)

In Dryden's *Marriage à la Mode* (1673), the characters exhibit a degree of sexual equality, as husbands and wives, fleeing boredom, engage in amorous intrigues and flirtations, following the libertine principles of conduct embodied in Doralice's song, which begins the play.

> Why should a foolish Marriage Vow
> Which long ago was made,
> Oblige us to each other now
> When Passion is decay'd? . . .
> If I have Pleasures for a Friend,
> And farther love in store,
> What wrong has he whose joys did end,
> And who cou'd give no more?[4]

As John Traugott has remarked, each of the play's principal characters, male or female, is treated as a 'free moral agent', in a 'never-ending game' in which, as in the many poems of the period 'against fruition', sexual consummation is infinitely deferred, retained in the imagination as a delightful prospect.

> DORALICE. We might upon trial have lik'd each other less, as many a man and woman, that have lov'd as desperately as we, and yet when they came to possession, have sigh'd, and cri'd to themselves: Is this all? (*Marriage à la Mode*, v.i.280–5)[5]

When, toward the end of the play, Doralice, her husband Rhodophil and her lover Palamede consider ways of resolving their triangular relationship, they explore, through the free play of wit, a possible accommodation in which marriage would not be imprisoning. The ideal society of sexual equals they project, in political metaphors drawn from the liberal tradition of contract theory, is far removed from the savage domestic warfare depicted in plays like *The Wives Excuse* and *The Way of the World*, or the crude misogyny with which, in Otway's *The Atheist*, Courtine expresses his aversion to his wife Sylvia: 'By this good day, she has kiss'd me till I am downright sick; I have had so much of her, that I shall have no stomach for the Sex again this fortnight.'[6] Significantly, Doralice,

the wittiest of the characters in *Marriage à la Mode*, has the last word
in the exchange, reminding the two men that the women involved
are not objects for barter or food cooked up for the jaded male
appetite, but independent rational creatures whose emotional needs
and preferences must be taken into account:

PALAMEDE. What dost think of a blessed community betwixt us four, for
   the solace of the women, and relief of the men? Methinks it would be a
   pleasant kind of life: Wife and Husband for the standing Dish, and
   Mistris and Gallant for the Desert.
RHODOPHIL. But suppose the Wife and the Mistris should both long for
   the standing Dish, how should they be satisfi'd together? . . . then I
   think, *Palamede*, we had as good make a firm League, not to invade
   each other's propriety.
PALAMEDE. Content, say I. From henceforth let all acts of hostility cease
   betwixt us; and that in the usual form of Treaties, as well by Sea as by
   Land, and in all Fresh waters.
DORALICE. I will adde but one proviso. That who ever breaks the
   League, either by war abroad, or by neglect at home, both the Women
   shall revenge themselves, by the help of the other party. (v.i.397–417)[7]

Rochester, in an unfinished 'Satire on Men', one of several poems
he wrote in the persona of a woman, projects as comic hypothesis a
world in which neither sex required the other, either for physical
pleasure or for companionship:

> What vaine unnecessary things are men
> How well we doe with out 'em, tell me then
> Whence comes this meane submissivness wee finde
> This ill bred age has wrought on womankinde
> Fall'n from the rights their sex and beautyes gave
> To make men wish despaire and humbly crave.[8]

The female speaker, unlike Rochester's Artemiza with her praise of
the 'gen'rous passion' Love, is unable to conceive of any mode of
human relationship not based on exploitation and dominance.
'Things must goe on in their Lewd naturall way' (32), in which,
within any relationship, one partner, male or female, must dominate, with the other reduced to subservience.[9] Where in 'former
dayes' women ruled unchallenged – 'When if my Lady frown'd
th'unhappy Knight/was faine to fast and lye alone that night'
(23–6) – the 'Arrogant pretending' men are now able to exercise
absolute power. On the Mall and in the playhouse, 'Women Cour-
sers' shop for their merchandise with brutal insolence, 'to chaffer,

chuse and ride theire bargains home', judging the 'good lipps and teeth' of women as of horses (8–15). To escape this humiliation, the female narrator suggests retreat to a solitary hedonism explicitly equated in both men and women with the pleasure of masturbation:

> E're beare this scorne, I'de bee shutt up at home
> Content with humoring my selfe alone . . .
> Besides the Beastly men wee dayly see
> Can Please themselves alone as well as wee.   (21–2, 33–4)

As a poem by a man imagining what it might be like to be a woman, addressing, through an unreliable narrator, a male and female audience whose characteristic attitudes it satirises, Rochester's 'Satire on Men', with its multiple ironies, undercuts the sexual separatism it purports to endorse. What it suggests, along with other works by Rochester and Behn considered in this study, is that freedom is a necessary illusion, nurturing the imagination by its very unattainability.

As Harold Weber has pointed out, Rochester's poetry is characterised by a 'violent movement between extremes', with one of its components, along with an idealisation of the erotic, an expressed contempt for women, seemingly 'grounded on . . . hatred and fear':[10]

> Love a *Woman!* y'are an *Ass,*
>   'Tis a most insipid Passion,
> To choose out for your happiness
>   The idlest part of *Gods Creation!*
>   ('Song': 'Love a Woman', 1–4)

Rochester's poem in answer to a poem by Lady Betty Felton is breezily patronising, relegating women to a mindless existence, flat on their backs: nothing could be more remote from Behn's pleas for female autonomy and equality with men:

> Were it not better far your Arms t'employ,
> Grasping a Lover in pursuit of Joy,
> Than handling Sword, and Pen, weapons unfit:
> Your Sex gains Conquest, by their Charms and Wit . . .
> So slain, I mean, that she should soon revive,
> Pleas'd in my Arms to find herself Alive.   (6–9, 12–13)

And yet, in 'A Letter from Artemiza to Chloe', Rochester creates a series of female speakers to present what one critic has described as his 'most positive vision . . . of the redemptive potential inherent in the satirist's role'.[11] As in Behn's 'To Lysander, on some Verses',

wholehearted surrender to 'Passion' (63), a 'gen'rous' giving of
oneself (40), 'a Heart Unfeign'd and True', is contrasted with
mean-spirited calculation, the contamination of the ideal in a universe of remorseless competition and universal distrust, 'as if they
came to spye, not to admire' (107). Like Behn, Rochester's Artemiza
attacks 'Love-Merchants' who turn love into a 'Trade':[12]

> This onely Joy, for which poore Wee were made,
> Is growne like play, to be an Arrant Trade;
> The Rookes creepe in, and it has gott of late
> As many little Cheates, and Trickes, as that.   (50–3)

Where Behn in the final stanzas of 'To Lysander, on some Verses',
allows for the possibility of reciprocity and equality in sexual
relationships, 'love upon the honest Square' (49), Rochester in 'A
Letter from Artemiza to Chloe', as in 'The Fall', 'Absent from thee'
and Lucina's plea in *Valentinian* to remain in her 'Dear solitary
Groves where Peace does dwell,/Sweet Harbours of pure Love and
Innocence' (III.ii.1–2), projects a state of unfallen, undivided sexuality tantalisingly beyond reach, a 'safe . . . refuge' (41–2) no longer
available in a universe where the physical and the spiritual are
irreparably sundered:

> But how, my dearest Chloe, shall I sett
> My pen to write, what I would faine forgett,
> Or name that lost thing (Love) without a teare
> Synce soe debach'd by ill-bred Customes here? . . .
> To an exact perfection they have wrought
> The Action Love, the Passion is forgott.
> 'Tis below witt, they tell you, to admire,
> And e'ne without approving they desire.
>   ('Artemiza to Chloe', 36–9, 62–5)

Behn's characteristic tone of amused, worldly tolerance, 'A joyful
looker on,/Whilst Love's soft Battel's lost and won',[13] is very different from the guilt-ridden pessimism of Rochester, in 'Artemiza to
Chloe' and in other poems, for whom even an idealised love, the
'onely Joy' (50) in an otherwise meaningless, mechanical existence,
is inseparable from pain:

> That Cordiall dropp Heav'n in our Cup has throwne,
> To make the nauseous draught of life goe downe,
> On which one onely blessing God might rayse
> In lands of Atheists Subsidyes of prayse.
>   ('Artemiza to Chloe', 44–7)

The impulse of rebellion, as we have seen, is central to the imaginative universe of Behn and Rochester, and is associated for both with the transgressive force of Eros, presented in their writings as naturally hostile to, and threatening to, the established institutions of church, family and state. This force, to which their writings again and again pay tribute, seeks to break down walls, and has no more room for the self-denial of asceticism than for practical considerations and man-made law. Yet Rochester, trapped in a dualism he seeks in the *Satyr against Mankind* and his dialogue with Burnet to disavow, is never able to treat the disruptive energies of the erotic impulse without a certain distaste, presenting libertine freedom – '*Cupid*, and *Bacchus*, my Saints are,/May drink, and Love, still reign' – both as irresistibly attractive and as 'the Readyest way to Hell'.[14] Behn, on the other hand, tends to embrace such an amoral force wholeheartedly as a fact of nature which renders moral judgement otiose, presenting it as a universal principle, more readily understood by women than by timorous or self-aggrandising men, by which the warring elements in divided human nature are capable of being reconciled. Behn's 'To Amintas, Upon reading the Lives of some of the Romans' is one of many works by her which celebrate this transgressive libidinal force:

> Had *Pompey* lookt like thee, thô he had prov'd
> The vanquisht, yet from *Egypts* faithless King
> He had receiv'd the vows of being belov'd,
> In stead of Orders for his murdering.   (33–6)

Yet Behn as well as Rochester sees the libertine promise of freedom from all restraint as deeply problematical, especially when, hardened into dogma, it becomes reactionary and conventional, a licence for exploitation, a ready-made ideology which men use to construct the prisons in which they enclose both women and themselves.

Notes

INTRODUCTION: THE IMPERFECT ENJOYMENT

1 Felicity Baker, in 'The Radical Poetry of *Don Giovanni*', reads Mozart's opera as a 'transgressive . . . destructuring' of 'the cruelly primitive religious morality of the Don Juan myth': *Cross-References: Modern French Theory and the Practice of Criticism*, ed. David Kelley and Isabelle Llasera (Leeds, 1986), pp. 123–35.

2 On the creation of the categories of normal and deviant sexuality, see Michel Foucault, *The History of Sexuality, Volume 1: An Introduction*, tr. Robert Hurley (Harmondsworth, 1981), esp. pp. 39–46. Ideas of hegemony underlie Guido Ruggiero's highly interesting study, *The Boundaries of Eros: Sex Crime and Sexuality in Renaissance Venice* (New York and Oxford, 1985), though the view there of sexuality as a force naturally opposed to and finally uncontrollable by law is very unlike that of Foucault.

3 Foucault, *History of Sexuality*, 1, pp. 97, 100–1, 157.

4 Claude Reichler, *L'age libertin* (Paris, 1987), p. 53 (my translation); cf. pp. 8–10. On the theme of 'incompleteness' as characteristic of libertinism, cf. James Grantham Turner, 'The Culture of Priapism', *Review*, 10 (1988), 1–34.

5 See *Symposium*, 200–12, *The Collected Dialogues of Plato*, ed. Edith Hamilton and Huntington Cairns (New York, 1961).

6 'Against Constancy', 17–20, *The Poems of John Wilmot Earl of Rochester*, ed. Keith Walker (London, 1984). All quotes from Rochester are, except as noted, from Walker's text, which is generally preferable to the modernised texts of the poems in *The Complete Poems of John Wilmot Earl of Rochester*, ed. David M. Vieth (New Haven and London, 1968).

7 Otto Rank, 'The Don Juan Figure', tr. Walter Bodlander, in Oscar Mandel, *The Theatre of Don Juan* (Lincoln, Neb., 1963), p. 627. Cf. 'On the Universal Tendency to Debasement in the Sphere of Love', *The Standard Edition of the Complete Psychological Works of Sigmund Freud*, tr. James Strachey *et al.* (24 vols., London, 1966–74), XI, 189 (subsequent references to *SE*).

8 *The Country-Wife*, 1.i.197–201, *The Plays of William Wycherley*, ed. Arthur

Friedman (Oxford, 1979). On the association between libertinism and the flourishing trade in pornography in the later seventeenth century, see David Foxon, *Libertine Literature in England, 1660–1745* (London, 1964) and Roger Thompson, *Unfit for Modest Ears* (London, 1979).

9 *Between Men: English Literature and Male Homosocial Desire* (New York, 1985), pp. 1–2, 49–66.

10 All the play's male figures, for all their differences in other respects, share the same casual misogyny implicit in the competitive model: the passages quoted above are spoken by Pinchwife, Horner, his friend Dorilant and Harcourt, the play's romantic lover. On the relationship between Horner's values and those of the other characters, see Sedgwick, *Between Men*, pp. 51–9.

11 Macpherson, *The Political Theory of Possessive Individualism: Hobbes to Locke* (Oxford, 1962), esp. pp. 45–68; 'The Statue in Stocks Market', 21–4, Andrew Marvell, *Poems and Letters*, ed. H. M. Margoliouth, rev. Pierre Legouis and E. E. Duncan-Jones, 3rd edn (2 vols., Oxford, 1972).

12 On the ending of *The Country-Wife*, see Robert Markley, *Two Edg'd Weapons: Style and Ideology in the Comedies of Etherege Wycherley and Congreve* (Oxford, 1988), pp. 177–8.

13 *The Novel of Worldliness* (Princeton, 1969), p. 21.

14 *SE*, xi, 185; Andrea Dworkin, *Intercourse* (London, 1988), p. 73. The argument that a 'violent and death-haunted sexuality' associated with phallocentric domination encourages 'a state of covert warfare between the sexes in which, while not all men are rapists, every woman is a potential victim' is advanced in essays by Benoîte Groult, Luce Irigaray and others, in *New French Feminisms; An Anthology*, ed. Elaine Marks and Isabelle de Courtivron (London, 1981), pp. 68–110; and in Joan Smith, *Misogynies* (London, 1989), esp. p. 154.

15 Angela Carter, *The Sadean Woman* (London, 1979), pp. 24, 141–2.

16 For discussions of the china scene, see Markley, *Two Edg'd Weapons*, pp. 172–5 and Sedgwick, *Between Men*, pp. 57–9.

17 Rochester's 'scepter lampoon' contains a similar passage, in which the woman, assuming the active role, both 'enjoys' and is enjoyed: 'Whilst she employes, hands, fingers, mouth and thighs,/E're she can raise the Member she enjoys' ('A Satire on Charles II', 30–1). For good discussions of the 'Song', see Carole Fabricant, 'Rochester's World of Imperfect Enjoyment', *Journal of English and German Philology*, 73 (1974), 343–4; and Sarah Wintle, 'Libertinism and Sexual Politics', in *Spirit of Wit: Reconsiderations of Rochester*, ed. Jeremy Treglown (Oxford, 1982), pp. 156–9.

18 Reichler, *L'age libertin*, p. 87; Foxon, *Libertine Literature in England*, p. 48.

19 The poem is discussed in Ken Robinson, 'The Art of Violence in Rochester's Satire', *Yearbook of English Studies*, 14 (1984), 93–4, and in

Reba Wilcoxon, 'The Rhetoric of Sex in Rochester's Burlesque', *Papers in Language and Literature*, 12 (1976), 277–9.

20 'Crazy Jane talks with the Bishop', 15–16, *The Collected Poems of W. B. Yeats* (London, 1950).

21 'To a Lady', 179–80, Jonathan Swift, *Complete Poems*, ed. Pat Rogers (Harmondsworth, 1983).

22 Cf. 'Epistle to a Lady', 95–100, 219–48. There is an excellent discussion of 'On Mistress Willis' in Robinson, 'The Art of Violence', pp. 106–7.

23 For a feminist analysis of the double standard as ideology in which 'a woman's body incarnates shame, her genitals especially signifying dirt and death', see Dworkin, *Intercourse*, pp. 198–229, esp. p. 214. A useful survey of the element of misogyny in satires written during the period of this study is Felicity A. Nussbaum, *The Brink of All We Hate: English Satires on Women, 1660–1750* (Lexington, Ky., 1984).

24 The relationship between Rochester's poem and Scroope's is discussed in David M. Vieth, *Attribution in Restoration Poetry* (New Haven and London, 1963), pp. 231–8.

25 *The Man of Mode*, II.ii.290; V.ii.390, 396, *The Dramatic Works of Sir George Etherege*, ed. H. F. B. Brett-Smith (2 vols., Oxford, 1927).

26 Thomas Hobbes, *Leviathan*, ed. Michael Oakeshott (Oxford, 1960), XIII, p. 83.

27 For further discussion, see chapter 4. The structure of 'A Letter from Artemiza to Chloe', with its plurality of voices, is discussed in Harold Love, 'Rochester and the Traditions of Satire', in *Restoration Literature: Critical Approaches*, ed. Harold Love (London, 1972), pp. 164–72; and Anne [Righter] Barton, *John Wilmot Earl of Rochester* (Chatterton Lecture, British Academy; London, 1967), pp. 55–6.

28 *English Works*, ed. Sir William Molesworth (11 vols., London, 1839–45), IV, 33 (subsequent references to *EW*).

29 'The Disappointment', 1, 3, 12, 42, 61–2, 97, 101–15, *The Works of Aphra Behn*, ed. Janet Todd, *Vol. I: Poetry* (London, 1992). Subsequent quotations from Behn's poetry are taken from this edition except where, as noted, a better text can be found in Behn's *Poems upon Several Occasions*, 2nd edn (London, 1697) – as *Poems* (1697), a reprint of separate volumes published in 1684 and 1688. 'The Disappointment' was first published, wrongly attributed to Rochester, in *Poems on Several Occasions: By the Right Honourable, the E. of R——* (Antwerp, 1680), with a number of textual variants.

30 Marvell's 'Damon the Mower' provides a striking parallel: 'To Thee the harmless Snake I bring,/Disarmed of its teeth and sting . . ./On me the morn her dew distills/Before her darling Daffadils' (35–6, 43–4). The similarity may be fortuitous or may reflect a common classical source, since the first publication of Behn's poem in 1680 predates Marvell's *Miscellaneous Poems* (1681).

31 'L'occasion perdue recouverte', in [Benech de Cantenac], *Poesies*

nouvelles du sieur de C. . . (Paris, 1662). The French source is discussed in Richard E. Quaintance, 'French Sources of the Restoration "Imperfect Enjoyment" Poem', *Philological Quarterly*, 42 (1963), 190–9, which calls attention to another contemporary translation published in *Wit and Drollery* (London, 1682), pp. 1–16.

32 *Wit and Drollery*, p. 16. For a good comparison of the conclusions of the Behn and Cantenac poems, see Quaintance, 'French Sources', pp. 198–9.

33 'On the Universal Tendency to Debasement in the Sphere of Love', *SE*, XI, 183. The concluding section of Rochester's poem imitates, at some distance, Ovid, *Amores* III, vii.

34 *The Rakish Stage: Studies in English Drama, 1660–1800* (Carbondale, Ill., 1983), pp. 138–75. Useful attempts to define a libertine tradition in the literature of this period include Dale Underwood's *Etherege and the Seventeenth-Century Comedy of Manners* (New Haven and London, 1957), pp. 10–40, still in many ways the best introduction, and James Grantham Turner's wide-ranging and carefully argued 'The Properties of Libertinism', in *Unauthorized Sexual Behaviour during the Enlightenment*, ed. Robert P. Maccubbin (*Eighteenth-Century Life*, 9, 1985), pp. 75–87.

35 On the authorship of 'To the Post Boy' and *Sodom*, see chapter 2.

36 *The Atheist*, v.430–1, *The Works of Thomas Otway*, ed. J. C. Ghosh (2 vols., Oxford, 1932); Nicholas Rowe, *The Fair Penitent*, III.i.50–3, *Five Restoration Tragedies*, ed. Bonamy Dobrée (Oxford, 1928).

37 Mary Astell, *Reflections upon Marriage*, 3rd edn (London, 1706), Sig. b2ᵛ. Cf. *The History of the Nun*, in Behn, *Oroonoko and Other Stories*, ed. Maureen Duffy (London, 1986), pp. 152–3: 'The women are taught, by the lives of men, to live up to all their vices.'

38 Behn, *Sir Patient Fancy* (London, 1678), Preface to the Reader, Sig. A1ᵛ.

39 Behn, 'To Mr. *Creech*', *Poems* (1697), pp. 51–2; Astell, *A Serious Proposal to the Ladies* (London, 1694), p. 4.

1 HOBBES AND THE LIBERTINES

1 The standard account of Restoration libertinism, to which all later studies must be indebted, is Underwood, *Etherege and the Comedy of Manners*, esp. pp. 10–40, 72–80. Later studies of Restoration drama tend to assume, rather than analyse or substantiate, the influence of Hobbes: for example, Harold Weber's *The Restoration Rake-Hero: Transformations in Sexual Understanding in Seventeenth-Century England* (Madison, Wis., 1986) attempts to distinguish between 'the Hobbesian libertine of Wycherley and the philosophical libertine of Congreve' (p. 52), without defining either term of this simple binary opposition.

2 Collier, *A Short View of the Immorality, and Profaneness of the English Stage* (London, 1698), Preface, Sig. A5; Tenison, *The Creed of Mr. Hobbes Examined* (London, 1670), p. 2. For an excellent study of Hobbes's

contemporary reputation, see Samuel Mintz, *The Hunting of Leviathan* (Cambridge, 1962).

3 Thomas Creech, *T. Lucretius Caro the Epicurean Philosopher, His Six Books De Natura Rerum Done into English Verse* (Oxford, 1682), Sig. b3^v.

4 Gay, *The Enlightenment: An Interpretation. Vol I: The Rise of Modern Paganism* (New York, 1968), p. 99; Creech, *Lucretius . . . Six Books*, (1682), Sig. b3. The anonymous editor of the 1714 edition of Creech's translation, *T. Lucretius Caro, Of the Nature of Things* (2 vols., London, 1714), provides copious 'Notes and Animadversions' intended 'to shew the Weakness, and to expose to . . . Readers the Insufficiency' of Lucretius's atheist principles (1, Sig. B2^v).

5 Thomas Shadwell, *The Virtuoso* (London, 1676), Act 1, p. 1; Creech, *Lucretius . . . Six Books* (1682), p. 3. Cf. Rochester's translation from Seneca's *Troades* ('After Death, nothing is'), 5: 'Let Slavish Soules lay by their feare' (in *Poems*, ed. Walker).

6 Cf. *Leviathan*, XII, pp. 73–5; and XXXVII, pp. 289–91; and see the careful discussion of Hobbes's religious views in Mintz, *Hunting of Leviathan*, pp. 41–5.

7 Sir Charles Wolseley, *The Unreasonableness of Atheism* (London, 1669), p. 196, as quoted in Mintz, *Hunting of Leviathan*, pp. 39–40; Burnet, *Some Passages of the Life and Death of the Right Honourable John Earl of Rochester* (London, 1680), pp. 72–3, 100.

8 'The Advice', 9–20, *The Poems of Charles Sackville Sixth Earl of Dorset*, ed. Brice Harris (New York and London, 1979).

9 William Hazlitt, *Lectures on the English Poets* (London, 1818), p. 164, quoted in *Rochester: The Critical Heritage*, ed. David Farley-Hills (London, 1972), p. 214. The phrase 'poet of unbelief', frequently applied to Rochester, was originally used by Vivian de Sola Pinto: see Pinto's biography of Rochester, *Enthusiast in Wit* (Lincoln, Neb., 1962), p. 114.

10 Burnet, *Some Passages*, pp. 100–1, 39.

11 Edward Ward, *The Libertine's Choice: Or the Mistaken Happiness of the Fool in Fashion* (London, 1704), pp. 11–12. Underwood's *Etherege and the Comedy of Manners*, to which I am greatly indebted, makes considerable use of contemporary anti-libertine satires such as the 'Satyr against Vertue', *The Libertine* and *The Libertine's Choice* in defining the parameters of libertinism during this period.

12 *The Anxiety of Influence: A Theory of Poetry* (New York, 1975), pp. 5, 30.

13 Mintz, *Hunting of Leviathan*, p. 23. In Walker's text of *Satyr* the adversarius's lines are printed in italics.

14 *Human Nature*, VII, par. 1, in *EW*, IV, 31. Cf. *Leviathan*, VI, p. 31: 'For although unstudied men do not conceive any motion at all to be there, where the thing moved is invisible, or the space it is moved in is, for the shortness of it, insensible; yet that doth not hinder, but that such motions are.'

15 Burnet, *Some Passages*, p. 52. The passage in Burnet is discussed in Reba Wilcoxon, 'Rochester's Philosophical Premises: A Case for Consistency', *Eighteenth-Century Studies*, 8 (1974), 183–4 and Ken Robinson, 'Rochester's Dilemma', *Durham University Journal*, 40 (1979), 227, 230. Further evidence of the status of these lines from Lucretius as libertine creed is their presence in Shadwell's *The Virtuoso*, declaimed by the play's model *honnête homme* in the opening lines (Act I, p. 1).

16 *De Cive*, xv, par. 5, 7, *EW*, II, 207, 209. For discussion of Hobbes's theory of political obligation, see Quentin Skinner, 'The Ideological Context of Hobbes's Political Thought', *Historical Journal*, 9 (1966), 286–317.

17 Edward Earl of Clarendon, *A Brief View and Survey of the Dangerous and Pernicious Errors to Church and State, in Mr. Hobbes's Book, Entitled Leviathan* (Oxford, 1676), p. 230. The more orthodox passage about 'the life to come' is from *Behemoth*, Dialogue I, ed. Ferdinand Tönnies (London, 1889), p. 54, as cited in M. M. Goldsmith, *Hobbes's Science of Politics* (New York, 1966), p. 119.

18 *De Cive*, VI, par. 16, *EW*, II, 86; cf. *ibid.*, XIV, par. 17, *EW*, II, 195–7; and *Leviathan*, XXVI, p. 174; XXVII, p. 188.

19 James Tyrrell, *A Brief Disquisition of the Law of Nature, According to the Principles and Method laid down in the Reverend Dr Cumberland's Latin Treatise on the Subject* (London, 1692), p. 285; Richard Cumberland, *A Treatise of the Laws of Nature*, tr. John Maxwell (London, 1727), p. 39. The most influential revisionist study of Hobbes is Howard Warrender, *The Political Philosophy of Hobbes* (Oxford, 1957).

20 Cumberland, *Treatise*, p. 90.

21 The 'ethical hedonism' of Epicurus and his followers is distinguished from the 'psychological hedonism' of Hobbes in Wilcoxon, 'Rochester's Philosophical Premises', pp. 196–7. Wilcoxon sees a divergence from Hobbes's behaviourism in the emphasis here on the 'reforming will', while Ken Robinson in 'Rochester and Hobbes and the Irony of *A Satyr against Reason and Mankind*', *Yearbook of English Studies*, 3 (1973), pp. 110–13, finds this passage more compatible with Hobbesian materialism.

22 Walter Charleton, *Epicurus's Morals*, 2nd edn (London, 1670), pp. 1, 17. Defenders of Epicureanism in the seventeenth century, like Charleton and Pierre Gassendi, emphasised its ethical dimension, seeing it as a consolatory wisdom-philosophy.

23 In *De Cive*, v, Hobbes contrasts the natural sociability of animals with the contentiousness of man, in a passage which in some ways resembles Rochester's argument in the *Satyr against Mankind* that man is 'the *Basest Creature*' (128):

> But among men the case is otherwise. For, first, among them there is a contestation of honour and preferment; among beasts there is none: whence hatred and envy, out of which arise sedition and war, is among men; among

beasts no such matter. Next, the natural appetite of bees, and the like creatures, is conformable, and they desire the common good, which among them differs not from their private. (*EW*, II, 66–7)

But where Rochester's contrast of men and beasts is consistently normative, aimed at humbling man's pride, Hobbes's is more dispassionate, and its primary aim is to refute the conventional Aristotelian view that man 'is a creature born fit for society' (*De Cive*, I, *EW*, II, 2). At no point does he admit any distinction between man and beast in the operations of the 'animal motion' of appetite and aversion, deliberation and will: see, e.g., *De Corpore*, xxv, *EW*, I, 406–10.

24 Tyrrell, *Brief Disquisition*, p. 309. My account of the ethical relativism of Hobbes is substantially indebted to Mintz, *Hunting of Leviathan*, pp. 23–31.

25 'The Fall', 5–8, *Poems on Several Occasions*, which provides a better text than either Walker or Vieth. I quote from the Scolar Press facsimile (Menston, 1971).

26 Holy Sonnet XVII, 8, John Donne, *The Divine Poems*, ed. Helen Gardner (Oxford, 1952); 'Peace', 1–2, *The Works of Henry Vaughan*, ed. L. C. Martin (Oxford, 1914); 'The Pulley', 16–20, *The Works of George Herbert*, ed. F. E. Hutchinson (Oxford, 1941).

27 See, e.g., Charleton, *Epicurus's Morals*, pp. 24–5:

When we say that Pleasure in the General is the . . . Chiefest Good, we are very far from understanding those Pleasures, which are so much admired, courted and pursued by men wallowing in Luxury, or any other pleasures that are placed in the meer motion or action of Fruition, whereby, the sense is pleasantly tickled . . . but only this . . . Not to be pained in Body, nor perturbed in Mind.

28 *Human Nature*, IX, *EW*, IV, 53. Macpherson, *Political Theory of Possessive Individualism*, argues that the model of society underlying Hobbes's discussion of the state of nature is a 'possessive market society': 'The innate striving of all men for unlimited power over others is not a self-evident physical postulate in the way the desire for continued motion is . . . Only in a society in which every man's capacity to labour is his own property, is alienable, and is a market commodity, could all individuals be in this continual competitive power relationship' (pp. 45, 59).

29 *Human Nature*, *EW*, IV, 53.

30 *The Way of the World*, I.i.101–2; II.i.73, 79–80, 271–2, *The Comedies of William Congreve*, ed. Anthony G. Henderson (Cambridge, 1982).

31 *Human Nature*, *EW*, IV, 53.

32 For an interesting treatment of the presentation of 'Vice under characters of advantage' in *The Man of Mode*, see Harriet Hawkins, *Likenesses of Truth in Elizabethan and Restoration Drama* (Oxford, 1972), pp. 79–97.

33 Hobbes's account of human motivation and the origin of civil society in *De Cive* places particular emphasis on fear:

We must therefore resolve, that the original of all great and lasting societies consisted not in the mutual good will men had toward each other . . . I comprehend in this word *fear*, a certain foresight of future evil; neither do I conceive flight to be the sole property of fear, but to distrust, suspect, take heed, provide so that they may not fear, is also incidental to the fearful . . . It is through fear that men secure themselves. (*De Cive*, I, *EW*, II, 6)

34 The animal imagery recurs throughout the poem, presenting a consistently reductive view of sexuality and of human motivation generally: for further discussion, see chapter 2.

35 See the interesting commentary on 'A Ramble in Saint James's Parke' in Ken Robinson's 'The Art of Violence', pp. 97–100.

36 A similar view of the play is argued in Richard Braverman, 'Capital Relations and *The Way of the World*', *ELH*, 52 (1985), 133–58, which sees Fainall and Mirabell as representing 'two conflicting orders of power, one essentially patriarchal and the other based on new relations of trust'.

37 Etherege, *She wou'd if she cou'd*, v.i.482–4. Cf. Lee, *The Princess of Cleve* (London, 1689), II.iii, p. 24.

38 Dramatis personae, Sig. A4^v; Act II, p. 23. For a parallel, see *Leviathan*, XIII, p. 83: 'It is consequent also to the same condition [the state of nature], that there be no propriety, no dominion, no *mine* and *thine* distinct; but only that to be every man's, that he can get; and for so long, as he can keep it.' Another speech by Ramble more or less paraphrases Rochester's *Satyr against Mankind*, 106–10: 'The order of Nature! the order of Coxcombs; the order of Nature is to follow my appetite: am I to eat at Noon, because it is Noon, or because I am hungry? to eat because a Clock strikes, were to feed a Clock, or the Sun, and not myself: let dull grave Rogues observe distinction of seasons' (*The Countrey Wit*, Act II, p. 22).

39 Robert Jordan, 'The Extravagant Rake in Restoration Comedy', *Restoration Literature*, ed. Love, pp. 69–90, calls attention to the presence of carnivalesque 'airy' and 'wild' protagonists in a number of plays of the period. But Jordan's essay casts its net somewhat too widely, making few distinctions among these characters.

40 Ravenscroft, *The London Cuckolds*, I.i, p. 7; *The Constant Couple*, I.i.133–6, *The Works of George Farquhar*, ed. Shirley Strum Kenny (2 vols., Oxford, 1988).

41 Behn, *The Rover; Or, The Banish'd Cavaliers*, ed. Bill Naismith (London, 1993), v, pp. 91, 100. Twentieth-century critics have responded to Willmore with varying degrees of admiration and hostility: for further discussion, see chapter 5.

42 *The London Cuckolds*, 'Actors Names', Sig. A2^v; Behn, *The Lucky Chance, or an Alderman's Bargain* (London, 1687), II.i, p. 20; II.ii, p. 21.

43 III.i, pp. 28b, 33; IV.i, p. 35.

44 *The London Cuckolds*, II.ii, p. 24; IV.i, p. 35. The convention of the 'lucky minute' or unforeseen sexual encounter in Restoration poetry is discussed by Treglown in *Spirit of Wit*, pp. 86–90.

45 A number of sermons by Tillotson and Barrow are explicitly directed

against the Hobbesian doctrine of universal self-interest. See, e.g., Tillotson's sermon 'Of Forgiveness of Injuries' (1689): 'So far is it from being true, which Mr. *Hobbes* asserts as the fundamental *Principle* of his *Politicks, that Men are naturally in a State of War and Enmity with one another*; that the contrary Principle, laid down by a much deeper and wiser Man, I mean *Aristotle*, is most certainly True, *That Men are naturally a-kin and Friends to each other*' (*Works*, 9th edn, 3 vols., London, 1728, I, 305).

46 See Macpherson, *Political Theory of Possessive Individualism*, pp. 194–262; and Richard Ashcraft, '*The Two Treatises* and the Exclusion Crisis: The Problem of Lockean Political Theory as Bourgeois Ideology', in J. G. A. Pocock and Richard Ashcraft, *John Locke* (Los Angeles, 1980), pp. 25–114. The best treatment of the conventional and innovative elements in Locke's political theory is James Tully, *A Discourse on Property: John Locke and his adversaries* (Cambridge, 1980).

47 *Amendments of Mr. Collier's False and Imperfect Citations, Complete Works of William Congreve*, ed. Montague Summers (4 vols., London, 1923), III, 200. This aspect of *Love for Love* is discussed in Hawkins, *Likenesses of Truth*, pp. 109–14; and in Paul and Miriam Mueschke, *A New View of Congreve's Way of the World* (Ann Arbor, 1958), pp. 71–9.

48 Further echoes of Hobbes, overt or indirect, can be found in several of Scandal's speeches (e.g. 1.i.367–9), and in the extended scene between the mutually distrustful sisters Mrs Frail and Mrs Foresight (II.i.449ff.), which ends in a pact for their common advantage; see esp. 468–70: 'How can anybody be happy, while they're in perpetual fear of being seen and censur'd.'

49 Richard Braithwait, *The English Gentleman* (London, 1630), p. 65: 'the *Noblest* and most *generous Disposition*' can be 'known by certain infallible markes', which include '*Munificence*' and '*Fortitude*' (p. 61). Both he and Henry Peacham in *The Compleat Gentleman* (London, 1622), see the quality of noble generosity as instinctive and uncalculating: 'For that's the best and noblest bountie, when our *Liberalitie* is on *such* bestowed, by whom there is no hope it should be requited' (Braithwait, p. 68). According to Peacham, 'wildnesse or unstaiedness' in youth often characterise those of generous disposition (pp. 33–4). See also Ruth Kelso, *The Doctrine of the English Gentleman in the Sixteenth Century* (Urbana, Ill., 1929), pp. 18–20, 88–91: '*Generosity*, when differentiated from *nobility*, had reference . . . to personal qualities rather than dignities and honors, and when differentiated from *gentility*, to merit rather than birth' (p. 20).

50 The exceedingly pietistic reading of the play in Aubrey L. Williams, *An Approach to Congreve* (New Haven and London, 1979), pp. 157–75, sees Angelica, living up to her name, as divine minister securing Valentine's conversion to a state of grace.

51 Accounts of the influence of Locke on *Love for Love* include Norman N.

Holland, *The First Modern Comedies* (Bloomington and London, 1959), pp. 164–5 and W. H. Van Voris, *The Cultivated Stance: The Design of Congreve's Plays* (Dublin, 1965), pp. 88–101. Susan Staves, *Players' Scepters: Fictions of Authority in the Restoration* (Lincoln, Neb. and London, 1979), pp. 278–83, 306–14, comments on the 'movement from the libertine rake to the good-natured hero' in plays of the 1690s in terms of the contrast between Hobbesian and Lockean theories, though she does not discuss *Love for Love* in any detail.

52 John Locke, *Two Treatises of Government*, ed. Peter Laslett, 2nd edn (Cambridge, 1970), I.9, p. 166. Filmer and Hobbes agree in seeing sovereign power as absolute and unlimited, but disagree in their theories of its origin, which to Hobbes was contractual – a contract made at the institution of a commonwealth to the terms of which all subjects are irrevocably bound, with no possibility of withdrawing consent, unless the commonwealth itself is dissolved by conquest (*Leviathan*, XVIII, pp. 113–20; XXIX, p. 218).

53 *Leviathan*, XXIV, p. 161; *De Cive*, XII, *EW*, II, 157.

54 *Two Treatises*, II.57, p. 324.

55 *Ibid.*, I.52, p. 196. Tully argues that this 'workmanship' theory of the relationship between man and God is central to Locke's treatment of property; for a clear account of the differing views of Locke and Filmer, see *Discourse on Property*, pp. 55–61.

2 THE TYRANNY OF DESIRE: SEX AND POLITICS IN ROCHESTER

1 *Enthusiast in Wit* is an only slightly revised version of Pinto's *Rochester: Portrait of a Restoration Poet* (London, 1935). *Lord Rochester's Monkey* (London, 1974), written in the 1930s, was rejected by its original publisher, possibly on the grounds that it might be open to prosecution for obscenity, and remained unpublished (and unrevised) for forty years.

2 *The Letters of John Wilmot Earl of Rochester*, ed. Jeremy Treglown (Oxford, 1980) (subsequent references to *Letters*). The *Letters* also contains a good, crisply written biographical introduction.

3 Burnet, *Some Passages*, Sig. A7^v. Critics who have expressed doubts about the reliability of Burnet include Dustin H. Griffin, *Satires against Man: The Poems of Rochester* (Berkeley and Los Angeles, 1973), p. 13; and David Farley-Hills, *Rochester's Poetry* (London, 1978), p. 173.

4 Burnet, *Some Passages*, pp. 30–1; Greene, *Lord Rochester's Monkey*, p. 208. For a similar view of Burnet, see Ken Robinson, 'Rochester's Dilemma', p. 230.

5 Burnet, *Some Passages*, p. 13; p. 12.

6 Cf. *Letters*, p. 8 and Greene, *Lord Rochester's Monkey*, pp. 13–26, 72–5, on the influence on Rochester of his mother.

7 Robert Parsons, *A Sermon Preached at the Funeral of the R^t Honorable John Earl of Rochester* (Oxford, 1680), pp. 8–9.

8 *Ibid.*, pp. 4, 3, 6. There is no doubt that, as Vieth and Anne Barton argue, the epigram 'To the Post Boy' is a highly polished satire, rather than an impromptu dashed off in the heat of the moment: see Vieth, *Attribution in Restoration Poetry*, pp. 199–203 and Barton, *John Wilmot*, pp. 51–3. Rochester may be the author: he is certainly capable of directing a satire at himself as prototypical rake, and of 'mythologizing his own life and personality' (Barton, p. 53). Yet the specific charges against Rochester in this poem, particularly allegations of cowardice and murder, are so severe that it strains credulity to think any author would accuse himself of such things in public:

> Frighted at my own mischeifes I have fled
> And bravely left my lifes defender dead.
> Broke houses to break chastity and died
> That floor with murder which my lust denyed. (9–12)

Violent death occasioned in pursuit of lust is common enough in rakes' progresses (cf. the death of the Commendatore in the first scene of *Don Giovanni*), but lines 9–10 refer to a specific, discreditable incident in 1676 in which Rochester ran away from an affray in which a friend was mortally wounded. Though Vieth (pp. 200–2) cites six MS attributions to Rochester, these are not necessarily to be trusted and four are ambiguous in identifying Rochester as the author or as purported speaker and object of the satire.

9 Parsons, *Sermon Preached*, p. 8.

10 Anthony Hamilton, *Memoirs of Count Grammont*, ed. Sir Walter Scott (London, 1905), p. 293. Cf. Johannes Prinz, *John Wilmot Earl of Rochester* (Leipzig, 1927), pp. 58–60 and Pinto, *Enthusiast in Wit*, pp. 71–2.

11 *Lord Rochester's Monkey*, pp. 86–8.

12 *Poems*, ed. Walker, p. 122; for the impromptu 'Here's Monmouth the witty', see *Complete Poems*, ed. Vieth, p. 135.

13 K. H. D. Haley, *William of Orange and the English Opposition 1672–4*, pp. 60–1, quoted in *Complete Poems*, ed. Vieth, p. 60; Gilbert Burnet, *History of His Own Time*, ed. M. J. Routh (6 vols., Oxford, 1833), I, 486. See also David Vieth, 'Rochester's "Scepter" Lampoon on Charles II', *Philological Quarterly*, 27 (1958), 424–32. All quotations from the 'scepter' lampoon are taken from *Complete Poems*, ed. Vieth.

14 'The History of Insipids', printed as Rochester's in *Poems by John Wilmot Earl of Rochester*, ed. Vivian de Sola Pinto (London, 1953), but rejected in Vieth's edition, has been proved to be by John Freke, an associate of Shaftesbury and Locke: see Frank H. Ellis, 'John Freke and the History of Insipids', *Philological Quarterly*, 44 (1965), 472–83. It is included in *Poems on Affairs of State: Augustan Satirical Verse, 1660–1714* (New Haven and London, 1963–), I, as is the 'Satire' by John Lacy, another false

attribution to Rochester. 'Portsmouth's Looking-Glass' is in *Works* (1709), pp. 153–7; its authorship, along with that of 'The Royal Angler', is discussed in *The Gyldenstolpe Manuscript Miscellany*, ed. Bror Danielsson and David M. Vieth (Stockholm, 1967), pp. 266–71. 'The Royal Angler' (title from *The Works of the Earls of Rochester and Roscommon*, London, 1709) is printed in *Poems on Affairs of State*, ii, pp. 189–91.

15 See Ken Robinson, 'Rochester's Income from the Crown', *N&Q* (February 1982), 46–50; and Greene, *Lord Rochester's Monkey*, pp. 87, 195–6.

16 Not all MS versions place these lines at the end of the poem: because of the unusually 'divergent and corrupt' texts of this widely circulated poem (*Poems*, ed. Walker, p. 185), there is no poem by Rochester for which it is more difficult to produce a definitive version. On the political dimension of the poem, see Ronald Paulson, 'Rochester: The Body Politic and the Body Private', in *The Author in His Work*, ed. Louis L. Martz and Aubrey Williams (New Haven and London, 1978), pp. 105–7.

17 Lacy, 'Satire', 7–8, 10, 71–2, *Poems on Affairs of State*, i, 425–8; 'Portsmouth's Looking-Glass', *Works* (1709), p. 156; 'The Royal Angler', 1–20, *Poems on Affairs of State*, ii, 190.

18 'Tunbridge Wells', 166–75; Lacy, 'Satire', 88; 'The Royal Angler', 31–4; 'Portsmouth's Looking-Glass', *Works* (1709), pp. 156–7; 'The History of Insipids', 157–68 (*Poems on Affairs of State*, i, 251).

19 'The Royal Angler', 21–2; Lacy, 'Satire', 33–4.

20 Evidence for the authorship of *Sodom*, attributed to Rochester in three of the eight extant MSS, is inconclusive, but the balance of probability favours Rochester's authorship. In his recent edition of Rochester, *Complete Poems and Plays* (London, 1993), Paddy Lyons comments that 'current scholarship prefers to endorse the attribution to Rochester' and that 'it has not proved possible to sustain alternative claims' of authorship (p. 314). Lyons's edition, which accepts *Sodom* as authentic, provides readily accessible texts of *Sodom* and *Valentinian*. The most extensive recent study, J. W. Johnson, 'Did Lord Rochester Write *Sodom*?', *Publications of the Bibliographical Society*, 81 (1987), 119–53, assigns the play to Rochester, as does Larry Carver in 'The Texts and the Text of *Sodom*', *PBSA*, 73 (1979), 19–40. A. S. G. Edwards, in 'The Authorship of *Sodom*', *PBSA*, 71 (1977), suggests a hypothesis of multiple authorship, pointing out that the play exists in two widely different versions; on the relationship of the various MSS of *Sodom*, see also Carver, 'Texts'. Edwards and Carver convincingly refute the argument, advanced by Rodney Baine, 'Rochester or Fishbourne: A Question of Authorship', *Review of English Studies*, 22 (1946), 201–6, that the author of the play is the otherwise obscure Christopher Fishbourne. Johnson overstates the case when he claims to have demonstrated 'as fully as it is epistemologically possible that John Wilmot was the writer responsible for *Sodom* as it has come down to us' (p. 120), since he treats his evidence with insufficient scepticism. But it seems reasonable to

conclude that Rochester is either sole author or principal author of *Sodom*.

21 British Library MS. Harl. 7312, Act I, p. 123; further references to *Sodom* are to this MS. I am indebted to Keith Walker and Michael Miller for providing transcripts of this MS and the two versions of *Sodom* in Princeton MS. Am. 14401.

22 *Sodom*, Act I, pp. 123–4. The element of political satire in *Sodom* has been pointed out by several critics: Richard Elias, 'Political Satire in *Sodom*', *Studies in English Literature*, 18 (1978), 423–38; Carver, 'Texts', pp. 21–2; and *Complete Poems and Plays*, ed. Lyons, pp. xv–xvi.

23 *Valentinian: A Tragedy* (London, 1685), v.v, p. 76. In Rochester's adaptation, the luxurious emperor, like the tyrant Bolloximian in *Sodom*, is presented as bisexual. The lines are addressed to his catamite, the eunuch Lysias, with whom he is 'discover'd on a Couch' at the beginning of the scene: 'Oh let me press these balmy Lips all day,/And bathe my Love-scorch'd Soul in thy moist Kisses' (p. 74).

24 The extended scene between Valentinian and the virtuous Lucina from which these lines are quoted has no counterpart in Fletcher's *Valentinian*. But the critique of authoritarian rule is present in Fletcher's play as well: Rochester retains the scene following the rape of Lucina virtually unchanged, including Valentinian's powerful line 'Justice shall never hear ye, I am justice'.

25 Basil Greenslade, 'Affairs of State', in *Spirit of Wit*, ed. Treglown, p. 96. Treglown also sees Charles as serving for Rochester as 'proxy' for his dead father: see *Letters*, p. 27.

26 On the character of Rochester's mother, see Greene, *Lord Rochester's Monkey*, pp. 17–18, 163–6; and *Letters*, pp. 7–8, 20–1, 64, 81, 94–5, 142, 248–55.

27 Burnet, *History of His Own Time*, 1, 486.

28 George Savile, Marquess of Halifax, *Complete Works*, ed. J. P. Kenyon (Harmondsworth, 1969), pp. 255, 257–9, 262–3.

29 Robert Wolseley, Preface to *Valentinian* (1685), Sig. A2ᵛ.

30 *Works* (1709), Sig. a8.

31 A variant for 'idlest' in some MSS is 'silliest'. On Rochester's bisexuality, see *Letters*, pp. 25–6, 160; Marianne Thormählen, *Rochester: The Poems in Context* (Cambridge, 1993), pp. 20–7; and an excellent essay by Harold Weber, '"Drudging in Fair Aurelia's Womb": Constructing Homosexual Economies in Rochester's Poetry', *Eighteenth Century: Theory and Interpretation*, 33 (1992), 99–117.

32 'On a False Mistress', in *Works* (1709), p. 103; 'An Allusion to Horace', 120; 'A Satire against Marriage', 5–8, *Works* (1709), p. 42. Cf. Weber, '"Drudging in Fair Aurelia's Womb"', pp. 110–14. The obscene farce, *Sodom*, probably by Rochester, provides a close parallel, in which sodomy is seen as an alternative to the 'drudgery' of heterosexual copulation. The two speakers are the King of Sodom and a courtier.

BOLLOXIMIAN. Borastus! I no longer Cunt Admire
> The drudgery has worn out my desire.
BORASTUS Your Grace may soon to humane Arse retire. (Act I, 26–8,
> p. 123)

33 *Aubrey's Brief Lives*, ed. Oliver Lawson Dick (Ann Arbor, 1962), p. 321;
Burnet, *Some Passages*, p. 15.

34 On Rochester's state of health after 1677, see *Letters*, pp. 33–6, 155–6,
158, 202–3; and, on his last illness, Greene, *Lord Rochester's Monkey*,
pp. 215–20.

35 See *Leviathan*, VI, p. 32; and Wilcoxon's valuable study, 'Rochester's
Philosophical Premises'. Rochester, in Wilcoxon's view, 'was psychologically unable to attain that state of imperturbability toward which
his philosophical sympathies, both metaphysical and ethical, should
have led' (p. 198).

36 Cf. 'The Fall', 3–4; the lines translated from Seneca's *Troades*; and
Leviathan, XXXVII, pp. 294–6.

37 The attribution to Dorset rests on an anecdote in a letter from Godfrey
Thacker to the Earl of Huntington (Huntington MS. HA 12525), cited
in Lucyle Hook, 'Something More about Rochester', *Modern Language
Notes*, 75 (1960), 478–80; and Vieth, *Attribution in Restoration Poetry*,
pp. 168–72, 411–12:

> My Lord Buckhurst and Lord Rochester being in company, a suddaine Malan-
> cholly possest him Rochester inquiring the reason hee answered hee was
> troubled at Rochesters lude way of living, and in the verses over the leafe
> exprest it
>> you rise at Eleaven
>> And dine at two
>> you get drunk at seaven
>> And have nothing to doe
>> you go to a wentch but for feare of a clapp
>> you spend in your hand or spue in her lapp.

Harris, in *The Poems of Charles Sackville*, rejects Dorset's authorship as
'highly improbable', seeing the incident as 'almost certainly apocryphal', a bit of gossip manufactured for Huntington's amusement
(pp. 186–7). Walker, who in his edition includes 'I rise at eleven'
among the doubtful poems, is similarly sceptical of the ascription to
Dorset: his conclusion is that 'in technique and point of view the poem
is eminently Rochesterian' (*Poems*, p. 311). Both Vieth (pp. 83–9) and
James Thorpe in his edition of *Rochester's Poems on Several Occasions*
(Princeton, 1950), pp. xxx–xxxi, point out that the 1680 edition consists of two distinct sections: one (the first thirty-three poems according
to Thorpe, the first thirty-seven poems according to Vieth) consisting of
poems by or about Rochester, and the other consisting of miscellaneous
poems by other authors. By Vieth's own principles, 'I rise at eleven'
(the twentieth poem in the collection and the sixth in a subsection of
songs) is thus likely to be authentic, since the only poems in the first part

of the collection not by Rochester are those demonstrably written as satires on him or directly linked with poems by him. Four poems fit into these categories: 'The Argument' (p. 34) is a rather tedious pornographic poem in which Lord R— figures as insatiable lecher (*Attribution in Restoration Poetry*, pp. 174–7), while 'In Defence of Satyr' and 'The Answer' are items in a satiric exchange between Rochester and his enemy Sir Carr Scroope, as is the Song 'I cannot change as others do'. Though Vieth rejects both 'I rise at eleven' and 'In the fields of Lincoln Inn' (the sixteenth poem in the collection and the second song), these two poems fall into a separate category, since there is no real evidence that either is another author's satire on Rochester. (For 'In the fields of Lincoln Inn', see *Attribution in Restoration Poetry*, pp. 172–4; there are two conflicting MS attributions of this poem, to Rochester and to Sir Charles Sedley.) If, with the exceptions noted, all the rest of the first thirty-three poems in the 1680 volume are to be accepted as authentic, I see no reason to exclude either 'I rise at eleven' or 'In the fields of Lincoln Inn'.

38 The poem is quoted in the text of *Poems on Several Occasions* (1680).

39 In quoting 'The Fall', I follow the text of *Poems on Several Occasions*.

40 Harold Love, 'A Restoration Lampoon in Transmission and Revision: Rochester's (?) "Signior Dildo"', *Studies in Bibliography*, 46 (1993), 250–62, has argued that though the poem has been accepted as Rochester's by Vieth and Walker, 'the evidence for his authorship is not particularly strong' and is by no means conclusive.

41 Cf. *The Country-Wife*, v.iv.19–175. On topical satire in 'Signior Dildo', see Thormählen, *Rochester*, pp. 285–95.

42 MS. Harl. 7312, p. 120.

43 See *An Outline of Psychoanalysis*, *SE*, xxxiii, 188–91 and 'Ejaculatio Praecox', *Selected Papers of Karl Abraham* (London, 1949), pp. 287–95. For a psychoanalytical reading of Rochester, see Griffin, *Satires against Man*, pp. 120–9.

44 MS. Harl. 7312, p. 148. I have not been able to identify the insatiable 'Canthes'; there may be an allusion to the aphrodisiac Cantharides, but this seems unlikely. The same reading appears in *Complete Poems and Plays*, ed. Lyons, p. 322, which uses another manuscript as copy-text.

45 See 'A Special Type of Choice of Object made by Men' and 'On the Universal Tendency to Debasement in the Sphere of Love', *SE*, xi, 166–72, 180–3.

46 Burnet, *Some Passages*, p. 25.

47 For other examples, see Sir Thomas Wyatt, 'My lute awake', 21–35, *Collected Poems*, ed. Joost Daalder (Oxford, 1975); John Donne, 'The Apparition', *Poems*, ed. Sir Herbert Grierson (London, 1912); and Sylvia Plath, 'Daddy', *Collected Poems* (London, 1981).

48 Pinto, *Enthusiast in Wit*, p. 80.

3 ABSENT FROM THEE

1 'The Answer', 6, *Poems*, ed. Walker, p. 115. Though their interpretations differ to some extent, both Lucien Goldmann, *The Hidden God*, tr. Philip Thody (London, 1969) and Norbert Elias, *The Court Society*, tr. Edmund Jephcott (New York, 1983), emphasise the symbolic role of ritual for an aristocracy declined 'from being *noblesse d'epée* to being *noblesse de cour*' (Goldmann, *The Hidden God*, p. 26).

2 'The Sense of Nothing', *Spirit of Wit*, ed. Treglown, p. 3.

3 Jean-Paul Sartre, *What is Literature?*, tr. Bernard Frechtman (London, 1967), p. 112. Cf. Goldmann, *The Hidden God*, p. 17, arguing that in any historical period writers and philosophers 'achieve the maximum possible awareness of the social group whose nature they are expressing'.

4 Sartre, *What is Literature?*, pp. 58, 60.

5 On definitions of libertinism, see Turner, 'The Properties of Libertinism', pp. 75–87. As Turner points out, the *OED* gives religious libertinism priority over sexual libertinism, though the two strands cannot be disentangled.

6 *The Hidden God*, p. 37.

7 Blaise Pascal, *Pensées*, ed. Louis Lafuma (Paris, 1962), par. 418, p. 178; Pascal, *Pensées*, tr. A. J. Krailsheimer (Harmondsworth, 1966), p. 152.

8 *Pensées*, par. 110, p. 66; par. 410, p. 173. Jacques Vallée, Seigneur Des Barreaux, whose view of man Pascal argues against (par. 410), was a *libertin* poet of the seventeenth century notorious for his atheism and debauchery. Several of his sonnets, praising the senses over 'la sotte raison' which alienates man from the happiness enjoyed by 'les bestes sauvages', may have directly influenced Rochester's *Satyr*: see Griffin, *Satires against Man*, pp. 176–9 and Frederic Lachèvre, *Disciples et successeurs de Théophile de Viau* (Paris, 1911), pp. 6, 241–6.

9 *Pensées*, par. 427, 428, pp. 182, 187–8; par. 156, p. 94.

10 *Ibid.*, par. 410, p. 173; Lachèvre, *Disciples et successeurs*, pp. 227–38.

11 *Pensées*, par. 597, p. 267; par. 421, p. 180; par. 617, p. 272. A similar view of Rochester is argued in Robinson, 'Rochester's Dilemma', pp. 223–31.

12 Melanie Klein locates such feeling in early infancy, where Freud associates the sense of guilt and unworthiness with the Oedipal triangle: see *SE*, XIX, 30–7; XXI, 127–33 and Klein, 'On the Theory of Anxiety and Guilt', *Envy and Gratitude and other Works* (London, 1975), pp. 25–42. It is probably significant that both Pascal and Rochester lost a parent at an early age and were brought up under conditions of some insecurity as precocious children of whom a great deal was expected by the surviving parent. In both cases, a distrust of emotional attachments and a deep-rooted sense of guilt have their genesis in the author's childhood.

13 *Pensées*, par. 449, p. 196; par. 114, p. 67.
14 See Lachèvre, *Disciples et successeurs*, p. 246; the parallel is pointed out in Griffin, *Satires against Man*, p. 179.
15 On the structure of the *Satyr*, see Griffin, *Satires against Man*, pp. 202–6 and Eric Rothstein, *Restoration and Eighteenth-Century Poetry 1660–1780* (London, 1981), pp. 31–2.
16 *Poems*, p. 285.
17 On the status of the two versions and the date of the 'Addition', see Kristoffer F. Paulson, 'The Reverend Edward Stillingfleet and the "Epilogue" to Rochester's *A Satyr against Reason and Mankind*', *Philological Quarterly*, 50 (1971), 657–63. With the exception of Pinto, who interprets the poem in narrowly biographical terms (*Enthusiast in Wit*, pp. 157–8 and *Poems*, pp. 214–15), critics tend to underplay the differences between the 'Addition' and the original version of the poem: see, e.g. Griffin, *Satires against Man*, pp. 239–43; Farley-Hills, *Rochester's Poetry*, pp. 179–86; and Thormählen, *Rochester*, pp. 225–9, 235–9.
18 Paulson, 'Stillingfleet', p. 659.
19 The closest parallel is Montaigne, *Essais*, 1.42, cited by Walker (*Poems*, p. 285): 'il y a plus de distance de tel à tel homme, qu'il n y a de tel homme à telle beste'. For other similar passages, see Farley-Hills, *Rochester's Poetry*, p. 185.
20 '*Avarice, Pride, Sloth*, and *Gluttony*' (203), Lust (205) and envy (195); the seventh may well be implied in the words 'chide' and 'raile' (197). The treatment of abuses in church and state in the epilogue resembles the contemporaneous satires of Marvell in attitude and tone, especially 'Last Instructions' and *The Rehearsal Transpros'd*. Rochester echoes Marvell explicitly in attacking the ambitious prelate Samuel Parker in 'Tunbridge Wells', 68–81, and the two men are known to have admired one another's satiric writings.
21 *Pensées*, par. 198, p. 102.
22 Rochester's translation of Lucretius ('The *Gods*, by right of Nature'), 2.
23 *Pensées*, par. 148, p. 86 (cf. par. 136, pp. 79–80); par. 136, p. 78.
24 *Ibid.*, par. 148, p. 86. Pascal is in this respect more pessimistic than Rochester, because his severe, uncompromising asceticism led him to reject all human attachments: 's'il y a un Dieu il ne faut aimer que lui et non les créatures passagères' (par. 618, p. 273). In par. 198 he speaks of his own inability to form emotional relationships ('Quelques objets plaisants s'y sont donnés et s'y sont attaché', p. 102), and in par. 795 he refers to the sexual act as a sign of man's 'faiblesse' and 'servitude' (p. 313).
25 The epilogue, included in the opera's first performance in Prague, is generally believed to have been omitted by Mozart in the Vienna performance of 1788. According to Wolfgang Hildesheimer, *Mozart*, tr. Marion Faber (New York, 1982), pp. 231–2, the '*scena ultima* of *Don Giovanni* has repeatedly been attacked over the years'. Theodor Adorno

in 1967 considered it a 'letdown' after 'the grandeur of the Commen-
datore-scene', arguing that its retention in performance can only be the
result of 'a neoclassical . . . love of convention' (*Süddeutsche Zeitung*, 24
February 1967, in Hildesheimer, pp. 231–2).

26 Søren Kierkegaard, *Either/Or*, tr. David F. Swenson, Lilian Marvin
   Swenson and Howard A. Johnson (Princeton, 1971), I, p. 98.

27 Burnet, *Some Passages*, pp. 22, 38; cf. *Satyr against Mankind*, 98–111.

28 Burnet, *Some Passages*, pp. 45, 47–8.

29 Cf. Wilcoxon, 'The Rhetoric of Sex', pp. 274–6.

30 Burnet, *Some Passages*, pp. 43–6.

31 *Paradise Lost*, VIII, 167–97, in John Milton, *Complete English Poems, Of
   Education, Areopagitica*, ed. Gordon Campbell (London, 1990). The
   parallel is noted in Underwood, *Etherege and the Comedy of Manners*,
   pp. 32–4. Thomas Fujimura, in 'Rochester's "Satyr against Mankind"':
   An Analysis', *Studies in Philology*, 55 (1958), 578–83, sees the contrast of
   speculative and practical reason as central to the *Satyr*, stressing the
   poem's traditional elements.

32 Satire VIII, in Nicolas Boileau-Despréaux, *Oeuvres Complète*, ed. Fran-
   çoise Escal (Paris, 1966), pp. 42, 44; cf. p. 47. The clearest account of
   the differences in approach between Rochester and Boileau is John F.
   Moore, 'The Originality of Rochester's *Satyr against Mankind*', *PMLA*,
   58 (1943), 393–401. See also Wilcoxon, 'Rochester's Philosophical
   Premises', pp. 190–1.

33 Satire VIII, pp. 41, 47. The contrast between the beasts, whose 'Teeth,
   and Claws' are their means of survival, and man, who kills his fellow
   man gratuitously (*Satyr against Mankind*, 133–40), is a commonplace in
   the tradition of theriophily, though Rochester's version of a universal
   war in the animal kingdom is indebted to *Leviathan*, XIII. See Moore,
   'Originality', pp. 394–6; and Griffin, *Satires against Man*, pp. 165–7,
   171–3.

34 The only critic who has pointed out Rochester's deliberate sophistry in
   his syllogistic reasoning here is Charles A. Knight, 'The Paradox of
   Reason: Argument in Rochester's "Satyr against Mankind"', *Modern
   Language Review*, 65 (1970), 258–9.

35 Robinson, 'Rochester's Dilemma', pp. 224–5, 227. The 'syntactic dislo-
   cations' in the passage are discussed in a rather leaden commentary by
   Griffin, *Satires against Man*, pp. 207–9.

36 Satire VIII, p. 41.

37 The passage, from the comic playwright Menander, is cited in Moore,
   'Originality', pp. 399–400; cf. Griffin, *Satires against Man*, pp. 159–60.
   Rochester probably knew the passage in translation, and Moore,
   without giving examples, says it was often quoted by Renaissance
   writers.

38 As Fujimura has noted, the shifting meaning of 'reason' in the poem
   'opens the door to misinterpretation' ('Rochester's "Satyr"', p. 579).

Howard Erskine-Hill, in 'Rochester: Augustan or Explorer', *Renaissance and Modern Essays*, ed. G. R. Hibbard (London, 1966), pp. 52–6, carefully distinguishes between Rochester's treatment of 'human pride' in the *Satyr* and that of Pope and the fideist Montaigne.

39 *Paradise Lost*, IX, 634, *Complete English Poems*, ed. Campbell. Walker has called attention to the lines by Quarles, to which Rochester is evidently indebted for several verbal details: see *Poems*, p. 283. Griffin, in a generally helpful discussion, points out parallels with Spenser, Milton, and Bunyan, as well as other authors (*Satires against Man*, pp. 209–16).

40 See Griffin, *Satires against Man*, p. 211.

41 *Paradise Lost*, XII, 648; and preface ('The Verse'), *Complete English Poems*, ed. Campbell, p. 148; cf. Griffin, *Satires against Man*, pp. 210–11.

42 *The Oracles of Reason* (London, 1693), pp. 117–18, quoted in *Poems*, ed. Walker, p. 255.

43 Blount, who considered Hobbes 'the great Instructor of the most sensible Part of Mankind in the Noble Science of Philosophy', in his letter to Rochester advanced the argument, derived ultimately from Hobbes, that the idea of the soul's immortality was a convenient fiction: 'lawgivers considering the proneness of Men to evil, and themselves aiming at the Public Good, establish'd the Immortality of the Soul, perhaps, at first, not so much out of a regard to Truth, as to Honesty, hoping thereby to Induce Men to Virtue' (*Oracles*, pp. 104–5, 123). In a second letter, he argues another quasi-Hobbesian position congenial to Rochester: 'that a Temporal Interest was the great Machine upon which all human Actions moved; and that the common and general pretence of *Piety* and *Religion*, was but like Grace before a Meal' (p. 156).

44 *Troades*, 397–408, Seneca, *Tragedies*, tr. Frank Justus Miller (London, 1968). It has long been assumed that Rochester's translation can be dated 1680, the year of his death, when he sent it to Blount, but Paul Hammond has shown convincingly, on the evidence of Bodleian MS Don.b.8, that it was written before February 1675, and thus is roughly contemporaneous with the shorter version of the *Satyr* ('The Dating of Three Poems . . .', *Bodleian Library Record*, 11 (Nov. 1982), 58–9): see *Poems*, ed. Walker, p. 254.

45 Seneca, *Troades*, 399–400. Critics who point out differences in emphasis between Rochester's poem and the Senecan original include Wilcoxon, 'Rochester's Philosophical Premises', pp. 184–8; and Erskine-Hill, 'Rochester', p. 58.

46 There are several good discussions of 'Upon Nothing', most of which include comparisons with the Senecan translation: see especially Everett, 'The Sense of Nothing', pp. 36–7; Barton, *John Wilmot*, pp. 66–7; Robinson, 'Rochester's Dilemma', pp. 225–6; and Farley-Hills, *Rochester's Poetry*, pp. 173–8.

47 *Some Passages*, pp. 53–4. Here and elsewhere in the conversations with Burnet, Rochester shifts his position on the mortality of the soul:

> He thought the Soul did not dissolve at death . . . He thought it more likely that the Soul began anew, and that her sense of what she had done in this Body, lying in the figures that are made in the Brain, as soon as she dislodged, all these perished, and that the Soul went into some other State to begin a new Course. (pp. 53–4, 65–6)

48 On the psychology of conversion, see William James, *The Varieties of Religious Experience* (London, 1902), Lectures vi–x, 127–258.

49 *Some Passages*, pp. 33, 35–6.

50 *Ibid.*, p. 20.

51 'Reas'ning *Engine*' (*Satyr against Mankind*, 29) is an allusion to Descartes's theory that beasts were essentially automata, differing from men by the absence of reason: see George Boas, *The Happy Beast in French Thought of the Seventeenth Century* (Baltimore, 1933), pp. 82–91; and Griffin, *Satires against Man*, pp. 217–18. On the relationship between yearning and imagined 'felicity' in Traherne, see *The First Century*, pars. 22, 41–5, in Thomas Traherne, *Poems, Centuries, and Three Thanksgivings*, ed. Anne Ridler (London, 1966): 'It is of the Nobility of Mans Soul that He is Insatiable . . . Want being the Parent of Celestial Treasure'.

52 Burnet, *Some Passages*, p. 7.

53 The passage, for which there is no equivalent in Fletcher's original play, is divided into five-line stanzas in British Library MS. Add. 28692, printed in *Poems*, ed. Pinto, pp. 71–2. Fletcher's Maximus is far less sympathetic.

54 Cf. Burnet, *Some Passages*, p. 52: 'He could not think the World was made by chance, and the regular Course of Nature seemed to demonstrate the Eternal Power of its Author.'

55 *The London Stage 1660–1800, Part I: 1660–1700*, ed. William Van Lennep (Carbondale, Ill., 1965), pp. 238, 325–6. ·

56 John Bunyan, *Grace Abounding to the Chief of Sinners*, ed. Roger Sharrock (Oxford, 1962), par. 53, p. 19; par. 84, p. 27.

57 Burnet, *Some Passages*, pp. 71, 76–7.

58 *Ibid.*, pp. 68–9. Cf. *Leviathan*, xxvii, p. 188; xxxix, p. 306; and Blount, *Oracles*, pp. 121–4.

59 Pinto, the first to print 'Sab: Lost' from Rochester's MS (Nottingham MS Portland PwV. 31), finds biographical significance in it, on very little evidence (*Poems*, p. 183); see Vieth, *Attribution in Restoration Poetry*, pp. 223–4. The title is incomprehensible, but the general drift of the poem, as far as it goes, is clear enough.

60 The passage, in a variant version, 'Lucina's Rape or the Tragedy of Valentinian', British Library MS. Add. 28692, is included in *Poems*, ed. Pinto, p. 70. In line 10, I have emended 'found' (Pinto's reading is 'Footsteps! found', with no full stop at the end of the line) to 'sound',

and, following the MS, have removed a superfluous full stop in the penultimate line.

61 Cf. 'Absent from thee', 16. In the pastoral imagery and the general situation of Lucina, exposed to tempters by the absence of her spouse, there are echoes of *Paradise Lost*, Books IV and IX.

62 This element of conflict is present in Fletcher's play in the characters of Maximus and Æcius, but it is more pronounced in Rochester's Maximus, untainted by political ambition.

63 Cf. *Valentinian*, V.v, p. 75, where the second stanza of this 'Song' is printed as two quatrains. A variant reading of the final line 'And makes the Slave grow pleas'd again', is printed in several early editions (1680, 1682, 1685, 1691, 1696) and by Pinto and Vieth (in their editions).

64 Vieth, *Attribution in Restoration Poetry*, pp. 204–12; *Poems*, ed. Walker, pp. 21, 233. Thorpe in his edition of *Rochester's Poems on Several Occasions*, p. 178, has argued that the existence of a version of 'The Answer' in Lady Rochester's hand is no proof of her authorship. But the existence of drafts of four other lyric poems by Lady Rochester (printed in the appendix to *Poems*, ed. Pinto, pp. 143–7, 228–9) and the fact that the MS of 'The Answer', like these other poems, shows marks of revision, strongly suggest that Lady Rochester is the author at least of the first two stanzas of 'The Answer'. The draft (Nottingham MS Portland PwV. 31) is of two stanzas only, leaving the authorship of the final stanza uncertain. Paul Hammond comments that 'the five stanzas were at some stage put together to form a single poem', included in at least five manuscript miscellanies of the period under the overall title 'To Thirsis' ('The Robinson Manuscript Miscellany . . .', *Proceedings of the Leeds Philosophical and Literary Society*, 18, Dec. 1982, p. 305). It seems to me likely that Rochester wrote the final stanza and was responsible for the final version of the two-part poem.

65 In the draft, line 12 of 'The Answer' reads 'Kindness you would soon abuse', with 'My' deleted before 'Kindness' (*Poems*, ed. Pinto, p. 172).

66 In the last line, Pinto prints 'kill', the reading in some early texts. Walker's emendation to 'fell' provides the best reading: 'sell', the most common early reading, must originate in a simple scribal error.

67 The draft reads 'Your love fond fugitive to gain' in line 16 (*Poems*, ed. Pinto, p. 172). Several of Lady Rochester's poems seem to explore a similar situation, berating Thirsis for 'tedious absence and unjust disdain':

> Such conquering charms contribute to my chain
> And ade fresh torments to my lingering pain
> That could blind Love judge of my faithfull flame
> He would return the fugitive with shame
> For haveing bin insenceable to Love
> That does by constancy its merrit prove (*ibid.*, p. 143)

But one should be cautious about reading biographical significance into such conventional verse; several of the drafts in Lady Rochester's hand employ a male persona, and all are traditional in their language and material.

68 As Griffin points out (*Satires against Man*, pp. 272–3), the lines allude to the episode of Sin and Death, *Paradise Lost*, II, 648–870.

69 On ambivalence in 'Upon Nothing', cf. Barton, *John Wilmot*, p. 66 and Robinson, 'Rochester's Dilemma', p. 226.

70 There are three independent versions of the poem included in *Poems*, ed. Walker, pp. 39–42, designated by Walker as versions a, b and c. The title 'To A Lady, in A Letter', which I cite for convenience, appears only in version c. Quotations are taken from all three versions, since the poem underwent considerable revision, and none can be considered a 'final' text: see the discussion in Vieth, *Attribution in Restoration Poetry*, pp. 222–3. Passages quoted above are version c, 3; version a, 4, 2; version b, 1; version c, 28; and version a, 5–8.

71 Version c, 4, 33–4, 1; version a, 21–4. The stanza quoted appears in all three versions, with minor verbal variants, 'pleasure' instead of 'Passion' in version c, and 'the Juice of Lusty Men' in versions b and c.

72 See *Poems*, ed. Pinto, p. 143.

73 'A Song', 16, Richard Crashaw, *Poems*, ed. L. C. Martin (Oxford, 1957); cf. also Donne, 'A Hymn to Christ, at the Authors last Going into Germany' and Vaughan, 'They are all gone into the world of light'.

74 *Some Passages*, pp. 145–6.

4 PLAYING TRICK FOR TRICK: DOMESTIC REBELLION AND THE FEMALE LIBERTINE

1 Though Otway wrote a succession of excellent parts for Elizabeth Barry, including Monimia and Belvidera in *Venice Preserv'd*, helping to establish her as the leading actress of the day, she refused to return his love and, indeed, while he was courting her, had a child by Rochester. The letters were originally printed in *Familiar Letters: Written by the Right Honourable John late Earl of Rochester, and several other Persons of Honour and Quality* (2 vols., London, 1697), and are reprinted in *Works*, ed. Ghosh, II, 474–81. On the relationship of Barry and Otway, personal and professional, see Elizabeth Howe, *The First English Actresses: Women and Drama 1660–1700* (Cambridge, 1992), pp. 113–21.

2 See Eric Rothstein, *Restoration Tragedy* (Madison, Wis., 1967), pp. 139–44 and Howe, *First English Actresses*, pp. 147–8, 156–70. Though Barry made her reputation in the pathetic roles of Belvidera, Monimia, Teraminta and Isabella, in the 1690s she regularly played proud and lustful villainesses against Anne Bracegirdle, who specialised in beleaguered innocence. The phrase 'Ravish'd Virgin' comes from William Mountfort's *The Injur'd Lovers* (1688), the first play which teamed the two actresses in this way.

3 *SE*, XI, 170; on the archetypal figures of virgin and whore in literary tradition, see the suggestive remarks of Leslie Fiedler, *Love and Death in the American Novel*, 2nd edn (New York, 1969), pp. 49–52, 294–306.

4 *Samson Agonistes*, 230.

5 Gould, *Love Given O're* (London, 1683), Sig. A2, p. 12; John Oldham, 'A Satyr upon a Woman, who by her Falshood and Scorn was the Death of my Friend', *The Works of Mr. John Oldham, Together with his Remains* (4 vols., London, 1692), I, 143. For a full discussion of Gould's satire against women, the responses it evoked and other poems of the period on similar themes, see Nussbaum, *Brink of All We Hate*, pp. 8, 21–42.

6 Richard Ames, *The Female Fire-Ships. A Satyr against Whoring* (London, 1691), p. 3; Gould, *Love Given O're*, pp. 2, 7.

7 [Sarah Fyge], *Female Advocate*, Sig. A2ᵛ. Ames, as Nussbaum has shown, is the author of poems on both sides, including, besides that already mentioned, *Sylvia's Revenge* (1688), *The Pleasures of Love* (1691) and *The Folly of Love* (1693); see *Brink of All We Hate*, pp. 34–41.

8 *Female Advocate*, pp. 23, 15; cf. *Paradise Lost*, III, 95–134.

9 *Female Advocate*, p. 10; *Sylvia's Complaint, of her Sexes Unhappiness*, pp. 4, 6, 12.

10 The poems on the other side of the debate share many of the same libertine assumptions – 'What we may at any time enjoy,/Does ev'n the relish of the Bliss destroy' (*Folly of Love*, p. 17) – but show no sympathy for the women they depict.

11 The statement first appears in *The Review*, 15 September 1711, and recurs in *Moll Flanders* and *Colonel Jack*: see *Selected Writings of Daniel Defoe*, ed. J. T. Boulton (Cambridge, 1976), p. 15.

12 Otway, *The Atheist*, v.430–1, *Works*, ed. Ghosh, II; Shadwell, *Bury-Fair* (London, 1689), II.i, p. 36; Behn, 'The Golden Age', 114, *Poetry*, ed. Todd. For an excellent account of the use of 'political language to talk about marriage' in Restoration drama, see Staves, *Players' Scepters*, pp. 111–89, esp. 128–35.

13 On the patriarchal legal system under which 'the husband and wife are one, and the husband is that one', see Lawrence Stone, *The Family, Sex and Marriage in England 1500–1800* (abridged edn, Harmondsworth, 1979), pp. 136–42, 164–8, 222.

14 *The Ladies Defence: or the Bride-Woman's Counsellor Answer'd: A Poem. In a Dialogue between Sir John Brute, Sir William Loveall, Melissa, and a Parson. Written by a Lady*, p. 3. Published anonymously, it is a response to a particularly reactionary sermon on wifely obedience by John Sprint; for her representative domestic tyrant and misogynist in the dialogue, she uses the name of Sir John Brute, after Vanbrugh.

15 The term 'Passive Obedience' had particular currency at this time as the watchword of High Church Tories and crypto-Jacobites, who considered the Revolution of 1688 to be an illegal act and gave de facto

allegiance to the reigning monarch, while considering his title to the throne questionable. See J. P. Kenyon, *Revolution Principles: The Politics of Party 1689–1720*, 2nd edn (Cambridge, 1990), pp. 4, 64–5, 129–30.

16 Astell, *Reflections upon Marriage*, p. 84; Chudleigh, *Essays upon Several Subjects in Prose and Verse* (London, 1710), Sig. A4–A4^v.

17 pp. 31, 45. On the relationship between Astell and Chudleigh, see the biographical introduction to the selection of Chudleigh's poems in *Eighteenth-Century Women Poets*, ed. Roger Lonsdale (Oxford and New York, 1990), p. 1 and Ruth Perry, *The Celebrated Mary Astell: An Early English Feminist* (Chicago and London, 1986), pp. 106–8, 490–2. According to Perry, Astell shows 'a simultaneous belief in authority and recognition of its incompatibility with justice in domestic life. She unequivocally believed that a hierarchical system of power was necessary and right in church and in state; but when it came down to it, in private life, she could not abide the tyranny that men exercised over women' (p. 165).

18 Astell, *A Serious Proposal to the Ladies, for the Advancement of their True and Greatest Interest. In Two Parts. By a Lover of her Sex* (London, 1697), pp. 38–40, 90; *Reflections upon Marriage*, pp. 89–90. For an excellent discussion of the themes of chastity and female friendship in Astell's writings, see Perry, *Celebrated Mary Astell*, pp. 120–48. Kate Lilley, 'Blazing Worlds: Seventeenth-Century Women's Utopian Writing', in *Women, Texts and Histories 1575–1760*, ed. Clare Brant and Diane Purkiss (London, 1992), pp. 114–18, sees Astell's arguments for 'separatism' in her Utopian tract as 'compromised' by a degree of inconsistency as to whether her seminary is to be 'a permanent withdrawal or a temporary respite from, and preparation for, the world of men'.

19 Chudleigh, *Poems on Several Occasions* (London, 1703), p. 40. According to Hilda L. Smith, *Reason's Disciples: Seventeenth-Century English Feminists* (Urbana, Ill. and London, 1982), the poem argues that 'only single women could freely pursue intellectual interests' (p. 169).

20 *The Provoked Wife*, 1.i.62–7, Sir John Vanbrugh, *Four Comedies*, ed. Michael Cordner (Harmondsworth, 1989); Defoe, *True-Born Englishman*, 804–13, *Selected Writings*, ed. Boulton, p. 72. Cf. Kenyon, *Revolution Principles*, pp. 57–9, 102–27.

21 *Reflections upon Marriage*, Preface (unpaginated), p. 90. A different view of the relationship between Astell's feminism and Whig constitutional theory is argued in Carole Pateman, *The Sexual Contract* (Cambridge, 1988), pp. 90–5, 120–5 and Ruth Perry, 'Mary Astell and the Feminist Critique of Possessive Individualism', *Eighteenth-Century Studies*, 23 (1989–90), 444–57. Rather than seeking to extend the principles of 'Native Liberty' to the domestic sphere, Perry argues, Astell attacks such doctrines as hypocritical, a mask for privilege. Pateman goes further, arguing in a powerful critique of contract theory that the idea of the social contract, as set forth by Locke and others, explicitly

excludes women, denying them the status of 'individuals' and relegating them to a status of permanent subordination in 'a theoretical strategy that justifies subjection by presenting it as freedom' (p. 39).

22 *Reflections upon Marriage*, pp. 90–1. The view that the responsibility for rebellion lies with the would-be tyrant and oppressor is a commonplace in Locke and other Whig contract theorists: 'If any *mischief* come in such Cases, it is not *to be charged* upon him, who defends his own right, but *on him* that *invades* his *Neighbours*' (*Two Treatises*, II.228, p. 435).

23 On the tradition of Ovidian complaint, poems by male authors assuming the persona of a seduced and abandoned woman, see Lawrence Lipking, *Abandoned Women and Poetic Tradition* (Chicago and London, 1988); and John Kerrigan, ed., *Motives of Woe: Shakespeare and 'Female Complaint'* (Oxford, 1991).

24 *Reflections upon Marriage*, Sig. b2^v.

25 *Ibid.*, Sig. A1, A2, A4^v, a1, b3–b3^v. Most recent critics of Astell, including Perry, place greater emphasis than I do on the political conservatism underlying Astell's warnings against rebellion in the face of domestic tyranny: see, e.g., Perry, *Celebrated Mary Astell*, pp. 151–215; and 'Mary Astell and the Feminist Critique', pp. 445–52. Lilley, in contrast, argues that 'Astell claims to leave existing patriarchal power relations intact, not out of respect but out of scorn' ('Blazing Worlds', p. 117).

26 Otway, *The Atheist*, II.136–7.

27 p. 27. On the legal position of women under the law of coverture, see Stone, *Family, Sex and Marriage*, p. 222 and Pateman, *Sexual Contract*, pp. 90–2, 119–21. Margaret J. M. Ezell, *The Patriarch's Wife: Literary Evidence and the History of the Family* (Chapel Hill and London, 1987), a revisionist study, argues that 'the image of patriarchalism as an umbrella overshadowing the entire span of a woman's life' during this period is overstated (p. 16). But evidence that mothers as well as fathers arranged marriages hardly justifies abandoning the term 'Patriarchal' and replacing it with 'parental', as Ezell suggests (p. 34).

28 'The Emulation', *Poems on Several Occasions . . . By Mrs. S. F.* (London, 1703), p. 108, which is the source of the quotations of Fyge's poems.

29 A selection of Fyge's poems, with a useful biographical introduction, is included in *Kissing the Rod: An Anthology of Seventeenth-Century Women's Verse*, ed. Germaine Greer, Susan Hastings, Jeslyn Medoff and Melinda Sansone (London, 1988), pp. 345–53 and in *Eighteenth-Century Women Poets*, ed. Lonsdale, pp. 26–32.

30 *Gentleman's Magazine*, 51 (March 1781), pp. 121–2; *Secret Memoirs . . . from the New Atalantis, The Novels of Mary Delariviere Manley*, ed. Patricia Köster (2 vols., Gainesville, Fla., 1971), I, 429–35. The biographical notice in *Gentleman's Magazine* includes excerpts from Fyge's letters. See also Jeslyn Medoff, 'New Light on Sarah Fyge (Field, Egerton)', *Tulsa Studies in Women's Literature*, 1 (Fall 1982), 155–75 and *Kissing the Rod*, ed. Greer, pp. 345–6.

31 The first passage is spoken by the figure based on Egerton in *New Atalantis*, ed. Köster, I, 431; the second is a letter by Egerton included in *Gentleman's Magazine*, p. 121.

32 Chudleigh, *The Ladies Defence*, Preface to the Reader; cf. Astell, *Reflections upon Marriage*, pp. 83, 92: 'Superiors don't rightly understand their own interest when they attempt to put out their Subjects Eyes to keep them Obedient. A Blind Obedience is what a Rational Creature should never Pay, nor wou'd such an one receive it did he rightly understand its Nature. For Human Actions are no otherwise valuable than as they are conformable to Reason . . . A peaceable Woman . . . will neither question her Husband's Right nor his Fitness to Govern; but how? Not as an absolute Lord and Master, with an Arbitrary and Tyrannical sway, but as Reason Governs and Conducts a Man, by proposing what is Just and Fit'. On the ideal of rationality in Astell's writings, see Catherine Gallagher, 'Embracing the Absolute: The Politics of the Female Subject in Seventeenth-Century England', *Genders*, I (1988), 33–7 and Ruth Perry, 'Radical Doubt and the Liberation of Women', *Eighteenth-Century Studies*, 18 (1984–5), 490–3.

33 The 'unequal Strife' between instinct and repression is a recurrent theme in Fyge's writings.

34 Other poems in which Fyge presents her life as a succession of disasters, with hopes for freedom constantly raised and then thwarted, include 'On my leaving London', 'On my leaving S——y' and 'The Fatality'.

35 For a similar attack on 'stupid ignorance . . . impos'd by men' on women, see the lines by Damaris, Lady Masham, the daughter of Ralph Cudworth and friend and correspondent of Locke, *Kissing the Rod*, ed. Greer, p. 321.

36 'The Emulation', *Triumphs of Female Wit, in Some Pindaric Odes. Or, The Emulation*, pp. 1–2. In all probability, 'The Emulation' is by a male author, using a female persona: in *Kissing the Rod*, Greer and her co-editors present arguments for male authorship of a poem they see as 'a competent catalogue of . . . commonplaces' (p. 309). A version of 'The Emulation', with a number of variants, is included in *Sylvia's Complaint* (1692); this may be evidence of common authorship, or at least male authorship.

37 'The Emulation', *Triumphs of Female Wit*, Sig. B1ᵛ, p. 3. *The Ladies Defence* similarly urges the 'Ingenious Ladies' to whom it is addressed to 'moderate their Desires' and never 'entertain an Aversion for things that 'tis not in their Power to avoid' (Epistle Dedicatory).

38 The Duchess of Newcastle, characterising herself as 'Ambitious as ever any of my Sex was, is, or can be', makes a similar point in the preface to *The Description of a New World, called The Blazing-World* (London, 1668): 'Rather than not be Mistress of a World, since Fortune and the Fates would give me none, I have made One of my own . . . thus believing, or, at least, hoping, that no Creature can, or will, Envy me

for this World of mine' (cited in Gallagher, 'Embracing the Absolute', p. 27).

39 Mary Ann O'Donnell, *Aphra Behn: An Annotated Bibliography of Primary and Secondary Sources* (New York and London, 1986), lists among Behn's works published during her lifetime or shortly after her death seventeen plays, seven volumes of poetry, twenty-two separately published poems, mostly occasional, and over twenty substantial prose works, published separately or in collected volumes, in the overlapping categories of 'Histories, Novels, and Translations'. The British Library catalogue lists fifty-nine works by Behn and two by Sarah Fyge.

40 *A Satyrical Epistle to the Female Author of a Poem, call'd Sylvia's Revenge* (London, 1691), pp. 5, 22, with '*Poesie*' corrected to '*Poetess*', after the 1709 edition of Gould's *Works*. 'Sapho' in this passage is Behn and 'Ephelia' the pseudonymous author of *Female Poems* (1679). For further instances during this period of the claim that 'a woman author was almost by definition sexually immoral', see Jacqueline Pearson, *The Prostituted Muse: Images of Women and Women Dramatists 1642–1737* (New York and London, 1988), pp. 9–14.

41 Jane Spencer, *The Rise of the Woman Novelist* (Oxford, 1986), pp. 28–9; *Kissing the Rod*, ed. Greer, pp. 25–8 (quoting *The Athenian Mercury*, 1694). As 'a Young Lady of Quality' puts it delicately in a funeral elegy to 'The Incomparable Astraea', ''Twas pity that she practis'd what she taught' (*Kissing the Rod*, p. 269).

42 'The Description of a Poetress', British Library Harleian MS 6913, fol. 251–2; Spencer, *Rise of the Woman Novelist*, pp. 42–3; Behn, *Poems* (1697), Sig. A7^v–A8; *Athenian Mercury*, 27 November 1694, in *Kissing the Rod*, ed. Greer, p. 27. 'The Description of a Poetress', cited by Angeline Goreau in *The Whole Duty of a Woman: Female Writers in Seventeenth Century England* (Garden City, NY, 1984), p. 221, as an attack on Behn, may be satirising another contemporary woman poet (references to the name *Porter* and 'her elder sister' do not seem to fit Behn), but its overall tone is characteristic of attacks on 'that lewd harlot' Behn: for further instances of such attacks, see Maureen Duffy, *The Passionate Shepherdess*, 2nd edn (London, 1989), pp. 259, 288.

43 'A Session of the Poets', 73–80, in Rochester, *Poems*, ed. Walker, p. 135. Recent feminist critics have argued that Behn in her writings turned the association of female author and prostitute to her own advantage, treating female sexuality as 'a commodity to be turned to profit by women': see Catherine Gallagher, 'Who was that masked woman? The prostitute and the playwright in the comedies of Aphra Behn', *Women's Studies*, 15 (1988), 23–42, esp. 25–9.

44 Angeline Goreau, *Reconstructing Aphra: A Social Biography of Aphra Behn* (Oxford, 1980), pp. 165, 272–3; Sara Heller Mendelson, *The Mental World of Stuart Women: Three Studies* (Brighton, 1987), pp. 159–72; Duffy, *The Passionate Shepherdess*, pp. 187, 214. In the introduction to

Behn's *Poetry*, Todd perpetuates the view that Behn's erotic poems are based on 'personal experience', interpreting the poems biographically (p. xxiv). Elaine Hobby in *Virtue of Necessity: English Women's Writing 1646–1688* (London, 1988), pp. 152–5, similarly emphasises Behn's 'pro-woman' radicalism, but does not treat the poems as autobiography.

45 Duffy, *Passionate Shepherdess*, p. 142; Mendelson, *Mental World*, pp. 166, 167; Goreau, *Reconstructing Aphra*, pp. 165, 194–5, 204.

46 Mendelson, *Mental World*, p. 169; Goreau, *Reconstructing Aphra*, pp. 271–3. Though Goreau overstates the 'revolutionary' aspects of 'The Golden Age', her discussion of the poem is in many ways perceptive. Lilley sees it in terms of Utopian writing of the period, and is far more aware of Behn's 'expansion and rewriting of Tasso', as well as the poem's ideological ambivalence and complexity ('Blazing Worlds', pp. 124–7).

47 'The Golden Age', stanzas i–v, in *Poetry*, ed. Todd. Behn describes her poem as 'A Paraphrase on a Translation out of French'; her immediate source is probably *L'Aminte du Tasse* (Paris, 1676), a close translation of the Italian original. Quotations from Tasso are from *Tasso's Aminta. A Pastoral Comedy, in Italian and English*, 2nd edn (Oxford, 1650). The tradition of libertine naturalist poetry inaugurated by Tasso's poem is discussed in Frank Kermode, 'The Argument of Marvell's "Garden"', *Essays in Criticism*, 2 (1952), 225–41.

48 *Reconstructing Aphra*, p. 272.

49 Though Locke did not publish his *Two Treatises* until 1689, other liberal theorists anticipated his treatment of a natural right of every man to 'a *Property* in his own *Person* . . . the *Labour* of his Body, and the *Work* of his Hands' (*Two Treatises*, ii.27, and see Laslett's note, p. 305). Gallagher argues, without particular reference to 'The Golden Age', that Behn in her writings endorsed 'the possessive individualism of Locke and Hobbes, in which property in one's self both entails and is entailed by the parcelling out and serial alienation of one's self' ('Who was that masked woman?', p. 29).

50 Tasso writes of '*Honor* . . . che di nostra natura 'l feo tyranno', contrasting it with the 'legge aurea, e felice,/Che Natura scolpi, s'ei piace, ei lice' (18–19, 25–6).

51 Cf. Chudleigh, *The Ladies Defence*, p. 3 and Astell, *Reflections upon Marriage*, pp. 90–1.

52 There is no reason to doubt the authenticity of the letters, of which no manuscript version survives, though the 'Memoirs of the Life of Mrs. Behn', probably by Gildon, prefixed to *Histories and Novels*, is a tissue of fabrications. On the psychology of the letters, see Goreau, *Reconstructing Aphra*, pp. 203–5.

53 Another work in the same genre by Behn is 'A Paraphrase on Oenone to Paris', included in Dryden's collection *Ovid's Epistles, Translated by several Hands* (1680), and reprinted in *Poetry*, ed. Todd, pp. 12–19. On

the relationship between the Ovidian heroic epistle and the *Portuguese Letters*, see Lipking, *Abandoned Women*, pp. 35–6, 199–202.

54 Among several parallels in Roger L'Estrange's English translation of *Lettres portugaises*, *Five Love-Letters from a Nun to a Cavalier* (London, 1678), cf. Letter IV: 'But Alas! I have not the heart to give it over. When I write to you, methinks I speak to you: and our letters bring us nearer together' (p. 78). For an interesting account which treats the letters as though they were a work of fiction 'which closely imitates the *Portuguese Letters*', see Marilyn L. Williamson, *Raising their Voices: British Women Writers, 1650–1750* (Detroit, 1990), pp. 212–14.

55 In the *Portuguese Letters*, just as Mariana is characterised by her spontaneity, impulsiveness and incessant longings to be heard, the unresponding Chamilly is characterised by his refusal to speak, which the reader, like Mariana, is led to see as coldness and selfishness. There is an excellent account of the *Portuguese Letters*, emphasising its psychological complexity, in Peggy Kamuf, *Fictions of Feminine Desire* (Lincoln, Neb., and London, 1982), pp. 55–66.

56 Dorothy Mermin, 'Women Becoming Poets: Katherine Philips, Aphra Behn, Anne Finch', *ELH*, 57 (1990), 335–55, compares Philips and Behn as 'coterie poets' who 'write in and of small private worlds', addressing poems to 'a group of friends . . . who provided both subjects and audience for verses . . . circulated in manuscript', and emphasises in both poets a 'revisionary' response to 'existing poetic conventions' (pp. 341–5). See also Ezell, *Patriarch's Wife*, pp. 68–71, 85–7; and Harold Love, *Scribal Publication in Seventeenth-Century England* (Oxford, 1993), pp. 56–7.

57 Goreau, *Reconstructing Aphra*, pp. 203–4.

58 Most modern criticism of these poems limits itself to fruitless biographical speculation, largely concerned with whether 'Lysander' is or is not John Hoyle. Mendelson spends several pages trying to work out Lysander's identity from evidence gleaned from Behn's writings (*Mental World*, pp. 166–8); Duffy, whose account of these poems is no less relentless in its biographical emphasis, claims that 'Amyntas', 'Lysander' and 'Lycidas' in the poems can all at various times be identified with Hoyle (*Passionate Shepherdess*, pp. 140–2, 146–7).

59 Cf. Judith Kegan Gardiner, 'Aphra Behn: Sexuality and self-respect', *Women's Studies*, 7 (1980), 67–78: 'The innate psychology of both sexes is identical . . . Because there is no emotional distinction between the two sexes in Behn's writing, she can describe her characters in androgynous terms' (pp. 72–3). Williamson, who briefly discusses the treatment of female sexuality in 'On Desire', argues that Behn 'tends to use a traditional male vocabulary to convey women's emotions' (*Raising their Voices*, pp. 149–50).

60 'Against Fruition' I, 19–20; 'Against Fruition' II, 15–16, *The Works of Sir John Suckling*, ed. L. A. Beaurline and Thomas Clayton (2 vols.,

Oxford, 1971); 'Against Fruition', 27–8, Abraham Cowley, *Poems*, ed.
A. R. Waller (Cambridge, 1905); Suckling, 'Against Fruition' II, 19.

61 As Walker points out, the poem is a free imitation of Petronius's
celebrated lines 'Foeda est in coitu et brevis voluptas' (*Poems*, p. 236),
only applied, untraditionally, to a female speaker. Greer compares
Rochester's poem to Behn's in *Kissing the Rod*, p. 260.

62 *Miscellany*, p. 128, in *Poems* (1697). Behn's answer poem immediately
follows in the *Miscellany*, and echoes or reinterprets several passages in
Alexis's poem, e.g., 'What with much care we gain and skill/An empty
nothing find, or real ill' (p. 127).

63 Hobby, *Virtue of Necessity*, p. 154; Chudleigh, 'To the Ladies', *Poems*
(1703), p. 40.

64 *The Younger Brother: or, The Amorous Jilt*, v.i, p. 47. On the 'needful
Perjury' of the libertine, cf. Dorimant in *The Man of Mode*, II.ii.216–18:
'What we swear at such a time may be a certain proof of a present
passion, but to say truth, in Love there is no security to be given for the
future.'

65 Durfey, *Madame Fickle: Or the Witty False One* (London, 1677), II.ii,
p. 20; III.ii, p. 34; IV.i, p. 49; v.iii, p. 64. Cf. *The Constant Couple*,
v.iii.181–221, in *Works*, ed. Kenny.

66 Southerne, *The Maid's Last Prayer; or, Any Rather Than Fail*, III.242–5,
The Works of Thomas Southerne, ed. Robert Jordan and Harold Love
(2 vols., Oxford, 1988).

67 In an interesting example of casting against type, Lady Trickitt was
played by Bracegirdle, who normally played virtuous heroines. There
are interesting discussions of the play, emphasising its 'grim' presentation of 'universal corruption' in the society depicted, in Peter
Holland, *The Ornament of Action: Text and Performance in Restoration
Comedy* (Cambridge, 1979), pp. 154–6 and Howe, *First English Actresses*,
pp. 138–42, 182.

68 *Oroonoko*, ed. Duffy, pp. 161, 206.

69 Janet Todd, *The Sign of Angellica: Women, Writing and Fiction, 1660–1800*
(London, 1989), p. 77; Staves, *Players' Scepters*, pp. 247, 248; Hobby,
Virtue of Necessity, pp. 98–101. Williamson in *Raising their Voices* presents
Behn as unable in her novellas to 'resolve the conflict . . . between
romance structures and the moral themes that she tried to graft onto
them' (p. 216).

70 See Hobby, *Virtue of Necessity*, p. 100. Jacqueline Pearson, 'Gender and
Narrative in the Fiction of Aphra Behn', *Review of English Studies*, 42
(1991), 40–56, 179–90, finds in both works 'an ambiguity that disrupts
conventional moralizing', simultaneously implying two 'different and
contradictory code[s] of values' (pp. 49, 51).

71 The equivalent passage in *Love-Letters Between a Nobleman and His Sister*,
ed. Maureen Duffy (London, 1987) has many close verbal resemblances:

She had wit enough to have made these eternal observations, that love once
gone is never to be retrieved, and that it was impossible to cease loving, and
then again to love the same person . . . When once one comes to love a new
object, it can never return with more than pity, compassion, or civility for the
first: this is a most certain truth which all lovers will find, as most wives may
experience, and which our *Sylvia* now took for granted, and gave him over for
dead to all but her revenge. (p. 220)

72 See Thompson, *Unfit for Modest Ears*, pp. 132–57, for an account of nuns
and nunneries in erotic and pornographic writings of the seventeenth
century, evoking 'fantasy situations within a taboo area' (p. 152).

73 *Venus in the Cloister; or, The Nun in her Smock* (London, 1725), p. 89; for
further discussion, see Thompson, *Unfit for Modest Ears*, pp. 151–4.

74 Instances of such biographical speculation include Duffy, *Passionate
Shepherdess*, pp. 100–1; Duffy's introduction to *Oroonoko*, pp. 15–19; and
Mendelson, *Mental World*, pp. 117–21.

75 Enforced marriages are presented here and in Behn's plays both as the
social norm and as morally indefensible – in the words of one study,
'the use of women as exchangeable . . . symbolic property for the
primary purpose of cementing the bonds of men with men' (Sedgwick,
Between Men, pp. 25–6).

76 Hobby, *Virtue of Necessity*, p. 99. Michael McKeon, *The Origins of the
English Novel, 1600–1740* (Baltimore, 1987), p. 238, sees Miranda as a
variant on the traditional 'corrupt aristocrat', as oppressor and
seducer, only female rather than male.

77 In such poems as 'To Lysander at the Musick-Meeting' and 'To
Amintas, Upon reading the Lives of some of the Romans', Behn similarly subverts conventional expectations of gender by voluptuously
celebrating male beauty. For further discussion, see chapter 5.

78 Miranda's behaviour in threatening the 'life and honour' of Henrick
after he rebuffs her advances has familiar literary precedents, notably
Racine's Phèdre. Behn's more comic variant on this motif resembles
Racine's tragedy in presenting naked desire as overcoming the normal
restrictions governing conduct.

79 As Laura Brown has noted in 'The Romance of Empire: *Oroonoko* and
the Trade in Slaves', *The New Eighteenth Century*, ed. Felicity Nussbaum
and Laura Brown (New York and London, 1987), the power of the
gruesome conclusion to *Oroonoko* depends on 'a fascination with the
brutality depicted' (p. 60).

80 Behn, *Oroonoko*, ed. Duffy, p. 96; Delariviere Manley, *The Power of
Love; in Seven Novels* (London, 1720), p. 206. 'The Wife's Resentment' is
closely based on a novella by Bandello included in William Painter's
sixteenth-century collection of tales, *The Palace of Pleasure*. Though the
plot follows Painter in its general outlines, in Manley's version the
killing is eroticised, and she also adds a number of references to the
unthinking and selfish libertinism of Count Roderigo, who in the
closing pages is killed and dismembered.

81 The highly theatrical scene of the killing of Imoinda, with its echoes of *Othello* and *Venice Preserv'd*, is quite explicit in linking eros and death:

> All that love could say in such cases, being ended . . . the lovely, young and ador'd victim lays her self down before the sacrificer; while he, with a hand resolved, and a heart-breaking within, gave the fatal stroke, first cutting her throat, and then severing her yet smiling face from that delicate body, pregnant as it was with the fruits of tenderest love . . . But when he found she was dead, and past all retrieve, never more to bless him with her eyes, and soft language, his grief swell'd up to rage; he swore, he rav'd, he roar'd like some monster of the wood, calling on the lov'd name of Imoinda . . . He had not power to stir from the sight of his dear object, now more beloved, and more ador'd than ever. (p. 94)

82 *Three Essays on Sexuality*, *SE*, VII, 158. The dismemberment of Oroonoko which ends the narrative explicitly includes castration and equates the executioner's knife with the 'fatal knife' with which Oroonoko killed Imoinda (pp. 94, 98–9).

83 *Reflections upon Marriage*, Sig. b3–b3ᵛ.

84 Astell, *An Impartial Enquiry into the Causes of Rebellion and Civil War in this Kingdom* (London, 1704), p. 61. 'Of Plants' is Behn's free translation of a Latin poem by Cowley, but similar Tory sentiments can be found in a number of poems by her attacking 'the Lawless People's rage' and 'the frantick Croud': see, e.g., 'A Poem to Sir Roger L'Estrange', 41 and 'A Pastoral to Mr. Stafford', 88.

85 'A Pindaric Poem to the Reverend Doctor Burnet, on the Honour he did me of Enquiring after me and my Muse', 49–56. Cf. 'A Congratulatory Poem to her Sacred Majesty Queen Mary', which similarly presents the poet as 'sullen with Stubborn Loyalty' to 'an Unhappy dear Lov'd *Monarch*', and thus unable to join the 'eager Homage' of other poets (4, 38–9).

86 For a discussion of the 'Pindaric Poem', emphasising the irony of its 'back-handed compliment' to Burnet, see Duffy, *Passionate Shepherdess*, pp. 287–93. I am grateful to Stella Revard for her comments about the 'Pindaric Poem' in relation to the tradition of Pindaric odes.

87 Another poem by Behn (among many) using similar motifs is 'The Reflection', in which the 'Betray'd' Serena mourns fruitlessly on the 'Melancholy Shore' (54–8). For further discussion of the *Heroides* and its imitators, see Lipking, *Abandoned Women*, pp. 33–41, 67.

5 MY MASCULINE PART: APHRA BEHN AND THE ANDROGYNOUS IMAGINATION

1 'To Mrs. W[harton] on her Excellent Verses', 31; 'To Mr. *Creech* (under the Name of *Daphnis*) on his Excellent Translation of Lucretius', *Poems* (1697), p. 55. Other Behn poems in praise of Rochester include the Prologue to *Valentinian* and 'On the Death of the late Earl of Rochester'.

2 *Sir Patient Fancy*, Preface to the Reader, Sig. A1ᵛ; letter to Lord Arlington, 3 November 1666, *Calendar of State Papers, Domestic* (1666–7), p. 236; letter to Jacob Tonson (1683), *Gentleman's Magazine*, new series, 5 (1836), 481–2. The most reliable biographical account of Behn is Duffy, *Passionate Shepherdess*.

3 Letters to Arlington and Thomas Killigrew, 4 September, 3 November and 26 December 1666, *Calendar of State Papers* (1666–7), 97, 236, 371; letter to Killigrew, 1668 (undated), *ibid.* (1668), p. 127. The last is quoted in Duffy, *Passionate Shepherdess*, p. 99, in a slightly different text.

4 *Gentleman's Magazine* (1836), 481–2; Katherine Philips, *Poems* (London, 1667), Preface, Sig. A1ᵛ. On Philips's view of publication, 'more closely tied toward attitudes toward print than toward gender', see Ezell, *Patriarch's Wife*, pp. 85–9. The 'Island' in Behn's letter refers to 'A Voyage to the Isle of Love', a long poem translated from the French, which concludes the 1684 edition of her *Poems*, as *Davideis* is placed after shorter poems in the 1668 edition of Cowley's *Works* and two plays translated from the French conclude Philips's 1667 *Poems*.

5 See Howe, *First English Actresses*, pp. 80–1, 113–19, 129–36, 178–80 and *The London Stage 1660–1800, Part 1*, ed. Van Lennep, *passim*.

6 Sig. A2–A2ᵛ.

7 See O'Donnell, *Aphra Behn: Bibliography*, for further details.

8 William Wycherley, 'To the *Sappho* of the *Age*, suppos'd to Ly-in of a Love-Distemper, or a Play', *Miscellany Poems* (London, 1704), p. 192. These lines, which equate female authorship with both venereal disease and childbirth ('Your easiest Offsprings of your Wanton Brain'), provide a virtual thesaurus of sexist insults directed at Behn. Howe, who shows what a shrewd businesswoman Elizabeth Barry was, makes the excellent point that the attacks on Barry as mercenary prostitute 'represent, above all, a dislike of a remarkable female professional success' (*First English Actresses*, pp. 27–31).

9 Howe, *First English Actresses*, pp. 27–31, esp. 30; cf. Pearson, *Prostituted Muse*, pp. 143–4, 277. The quotations above all come from works by presumably sympathetic twentieth-century critics, accepting unfounded allegations uncritically as fact: see Holland, *Ornament of Action*, p. 228; *Poetry*, ed. Todd, p. xviii; Behn, *Oroonoko, The Rover and Other Works*, ed. Janet Todd (Harmondsworth, 1992), p. 7; and Philip H. Highfill, Jr., Kalman A. Burnim and Edward A. Langhans, eds., *A Biographical Dictionary of Actors, Actresses . . . in London, 1660–1800* (Carbondale and Edwardsville, Ill., 1973), I, 316–22.

10 For further discussion of Behn's 'confidence in her own authority as a woman writer', as expressed in her prefaces and other writings, see Spencer, *Rise of the Woman Novelist*, pp. 42–52.

11 *The Forc'd Marriage, or The Jealous Bridegroom*, Prologue, Sig. A3. The prologue is discussed in Gallagher, 'Who was that masked woman?', pp. 24–7. Behn uses the phrase 'Brother of the Pen' satirically in her

poem 'A Letter to a Brother of the Pen in Tribulation', full of jokes about whores and sweating tubs.

12 'Leave this gawdy guilded Stage', *Poems*, ed. Walker, p. 25. Rochester's poem is generally thought to have been addressed to Elizabeth Barry.

13 On the varying ways in which the tradition of the Amazonian warrior is put to use in the drama of the period, see Pearson, *Prostituted Muse*, pp. 87–92, 125, 130.

14 'The Emulation', stanza II, *Triumphs of Female Wit*, p. 3.

15 'Who was that masked woman?', pp. 23, 27–31.

16 *The Dutch Lover*, 'An Epistle to the Reader', Sig. A3ᵛ, A4.

17 'To Mr. *Creech*', *Poems* (1697), pp. 51–2. Another poem to Creech, suggesting a close and long-standing friendship between the two writers, is 'A Letter to Mr. *Creech* at *Oxford*, Written in the last great Frost'.

18 For Creech's revisions, see *Poetry*, ed. Todd, pp. 29, 383. In her letter to Tonson, discussed earlier in this chapter, Behn expresses some 'resentment' at Creech for tampering with her text (*Gentleman's Magazine*, 1836, p. 481).

19 Prologue to *Valentinian*, 39–42, *Poetry*, ed. Todd; 'To Mr. *Creech*', in *Poems* (1697), pp. 54–5. Behn's 'On the Death of the late Earl of Rochester' praises the 'instructing Rage' of Rochester's 'sharp Pen' in satires, but again emphasises 'the charms of Poetry, and Love' (8, 29–30).

20 Preface to *Fables Ancient and Modern*; 'To the Memory of Mr. Oldham', 3; 'To my Dear Friend Mr. Congreve', 44, *The Poems of John Dryden*, ed. James Kinsley (4 vols., Oxford, 1958), pp. 389, 853, 1445. For an ironic version of 'Lineal Descent', see 'MacFlecknoe'.

21 'On the Death of the late Earl of Rochester', 19, 51. Behn's remarks about 'Toils of Sickness' are accurate, according to Duffy, *Passionate Shepherdess*, pp. 259, 264–5: in her letter accompanying the poem she speaks of herself as 'very ill and have been dying this twelve month'. Dryden presents himself in similar terms in the closing lines of 'To Mr. Congreve', as 'worn with Cares and Age' (66).

22 'On the Death of the late Earl of Rochester', 38–44, 48. *Ibid.*, lines 7–10 resemble the opening lines of *Absalom and Achitophel* (1681) and the echo may well be deliberate (see esp. line 10 of Dryden's poem). Behn's poem was written in 1680, and Dryden might have seen it before its publication in 1685.

23 *The Lucky Chance*, Preface, Sig. A1. Rochester's friend Robert Wolseley, in a poem to Anne Wharton, included in Behn's miscellany *Lycidus* (1688), pp. 96–101 (in *Poems*, 1697), presents Anne Wharton, more conventionally, as inheritor of her uncle's poetic gifts, with her 'noble blood' inspiring equally 'noble thoughts' (p. 101). There is an excellent account of Behn's poem to Wharton in Margaret Anne Doody's review of the Todd edition, *London Review of Books*, 22 April 1993, p. 3.

24 Duffy, *Passionate Shepherdess*, pp. 202–5 and Todd, *Poetry*, pp. 390–1, both see Wharton's poem to Behn as critical of the supposed immorality of Behn's poems, but this seems to me a misreading, and entirely ignores Behn's stated discipleship and the identification in Behn's poem of the deceased poet with his niece. Wharton's poem 'To Mrs. A. Behn, On what she Writ on the Earl of Rochester' is included in the miscellany volume *The Temple of Death . . . Together with several other Excellent Poems . . . To which is added several Poems of the Honourable Madam Wharton*, 2nd edn (London, 1695), pp. 242–4.

25 A substantial proportion of the love poems in the Greek Anthology, especially those in Book XII, *Musa Puerilis*, are addressed by a male to a male; see the excellent discussion of this subject in K. J. Dover, *Greek Homosexuality* (London, 1978), esp. pp. 9–15, 57–68, 111–24.

26 See the remarks on this poem in Doody, *London Review of Books*, p. 3, comparing it with other elaborate descriptions in Behn's poems and fiction of 'the beauty of both men and women'.

27 *The Rover*, ed. Naismith, II.i, p. 27; Doody, *London Review of Books*, p. 3.

28 *Literary Fat Ladies: Rhetoric, Gender, Property* (London and New York, 1987), pp. 131, 154.

29 Mermin, 'Women Becoming Poets', esp. pp. 345–6, 351. The poem is discussed and compared with the Horatian original in *Kissing the Rod*, ed. Greer, pp. 248–9.

30 Cf. stanza 1 of Cowley's imitation, in *Poems*, ed. Waller, p. 37.

31 Horace, *Odes*, I.v.12–13, in *The Odes and Epodes*, ed. C. E. Bennett (London and New York, 1918); Milton, 'The Fifth Ode of Horace, lib. 1', 12–13. Cowley after his version of these lines adds: 'But there's no danger now for Me' (p. 38).

32 Horace, *Odes*, I.v.9; Milton, 'Fifth Ode', 9; *Kissing the Rod*, ed. Greer, p. 249. Cf. Horace, *Odes*, I.v.13–16: 'me tabula sacer/votiva paries indicat uvida/suspendisse potenti/vestimenta maris deo'.

33 Hobby, *Virtue of Necessity*, p. 153; cf. 'On Desire', 103–4, 108 and, for a similar conceit by a male libertine poet, 'A Rapture', 115–46, *The Poems of Thomas Carew*, ed. Rhodes Dunlap (Oxford, 1949).

34 The version printed in *The Muses Mercury* (1707) has the title 'To Mr. H—le [Hoyle], being belov'd by both Sexes': see *Poetry*, ed. Todd, p. 433.

35 *Love-Letters*, ed. Duffy, II, pp. 115–25, 117–18. For a discussion of transvestism in *Love-Letters*, see Pearson, 'Gender and Narrative', pp. 181–2.

36 The passage is discussed in Todd, *Sign of Angellica*, p. 83.

37 Duffy, *Passionate Shepherdess*, p. 285; Bernard Duyfhuizen, '"That Which I Dare not Name": Aphra Behn's "The Willing Mistress"', *ELH*, 58 (1991), 78.

38 *Miscellany* in *Poems* (1697), pp. 172–5.

39 Duyfhuizen, '"That Which I Dare not Name"', pp. 78–9; sonnet 20, lines 2, 8, *Shakespeare's Sonnets*, ed. Stephen Booth (New Haven and

London, 1977). Cf. the discussion of sonnet 20 in Joseph Pequigney, *Such Is My Love: A Study of Shakespeare's Sonnets* (Chicago and London, 1985), pp. 30–41.

40 *Making Sex: Body and Gender from the Greeks to Freud* (Cambridge, Mass. and London, 1990), pp. 32, 52, 148.

41 Sonnet 20, 9–14, *Shakespeare's Sonnets*, ed. Booth.

42 Laqueur, *Making Sex*, p. 62; on the classical ideal of male beauty, see Dover, *Greek Homosexuality*, pp. 64–81.

43 'To my Excellent Lucasia, on our Friendship' and 'A retir'd Friendship, To Ardelia', Philips, *Poems*, pp. 29, 52. See also 'Friendship's Mystery, To my dearest Lucasia', pp. 21–2.

44 Duyfhuizen, '"That Which I Dare not Name"', p. 79.

45 Ovid, *Metamorphoses*, IV.379, tr. Frank Justus Miller (London, 1916). On the hermaphrodite as 'erotically irresistible effeminate boy' in the Renaissance, see Lisa Jardine, *Still Harping on Daughters: Women and Drama in the Age of Shakespeare* (London and New York, 1989), pp. 17–19.

46 *The Lucky Chance*, Preface, Sig. a1; 'To Mr. *Creech*', in *Poems* (1697), p. 51; Laqueur, *Making Sex*, pp. 58, 110.

47 'An Essay on Translated Prose', p. 1 and *The Theory or System*, p. 5, in *Histories, Novels, and Translations* (London, 1700).

48 Virginia Woolf, *A Room of One's Own* (Harmondsworth, 1975), p. 97.

49 Goreau, *Reconstructing Aphra*, pp. 228–30; Katherine M. Rogers, *Feminism in Eighteenth-Century England* (Brighton, 1982), pp. 98–9.

50 Frances M. Kavenik, 'Aphra Behn: The Playwright as "Breeches Part"', in *Curtain Calls: British and American Women and the Theater, 1660–1820*, ed. Mary Anne Schofield and Cecelia Macheski (Athens, Ohio, 1991), p. 190; Duyfhuizen, '"That Which I Dare not Name"', p. 64.

51 pp. 54, 150.

52 Astell, *Reflections upon Marriage*, p. 27.

53 *The Gentleman Dancing-Master*, I.i.1–5, *Plays*, ed. Friedman; *The Rover*, I.i, p. 8 (text corrected from the 1677 edition to provide one omitted word). There is no significant difference between the male and female dramatists Wycherley and Behn in their presentation of this conventional motif.

54 See Locke, *Two Treatises*, II.226–8, pp. 433–5. For similar arguments by sixteenth-century political theorists, see the discussion in Quentin Skinner, *The Foundations of Modern Political Thought* (2 vols., Cambridge, 1978), II, 239–41, 326–9.

55 Cf. the exchange between Horner and Pinchwife, in *The Country-Wife*, I.i.385–6: 'If she be silly, she'll expect as much from a Man of forty nine, as from him of one and twenty.'

56 For a somewhat different view of this episode, emphasising the ways in which money in *The Lucky Chance* is used to represent 'bodies or their

sexual use', see Gallagher, 'Who was that masked woman?', pp. 35–9. Gallagher interprets Julia's gift as an attempt 'at once to gratify her sexual desire and preserve her honour'.

57 Gallagher sees the gambling scene and the play in general as a subtle exploration of the possibility of female autonomy in a male-dominated society, in which, paradoxically, 'the danger of becoming a piece of someone else's property is at once asserted and denied' ('Who was that masked woman?', pp. 31–4, 39–41).

58 Alleman, *Matrimonial Law* (Philadelphia, 1942), pp. 5–59, 84–92. Cf. Robert L. Root, Jr., 'Aphra Behn, Arranged Marriage, and Restoration Comedy', *Women and Literature*, 5 (1977), 1–14; and Hume, *Rakish Stage*, pp. 176–213.

59 *Sir Patient Fancy*, i.i, p. 1. On 'spousals', see Stone, *Family, Sex and Marriage*, p. 31; and Alleman, *Matrimonial Law*, pp. 5–30.

60 Behn, *The Younger Brother*, i.i, p. 2; quoted in Pearson, *Prostituted Muse*, p. 161.

61 *The Town-Fopp: or, Sir Timothy Tawdrey*, 2nd edn (London, 1699), i.i, pp. 2–3; i.ii, p. 8; ii.iii, p. 70. It is an adaptation of George Wilkins's *The Miseries of Enforced Marriage* (1607), in which the heroine kills herself and the hero descends into total debauchery and prodigality before repenting at the end, under the influence of an Oxford divine. There is a good discussion of *The Town-Fopp* in Staves, *Players' Scepters*, pp. 171–3.

62 Pearson, *Prostituted Muse*, p. 103; cf. pp. 108–9, and, on Behn, pp. 157–60. Howe, *First English Actresses*, discussing the 'breeches role' in Restoration drama, argues that most plays, rather than being 'subversive', show 'an unwillingness to seriously challenge the male status quo' (pp. 56–62, esp. 59).

63 *The Dutch Lover* (London, 1673), i.ii, p. 8; iv.iii, p. 65.

64 *The Feign'd Curtezans, Or, A Night's Intrigue*, ii.i, p. 14. As in *The Rover*, one of the sisters is fleeing from an arranged marriage, and the other from confinement in a convent.

65 Hellena maintains the masquerade throughout her scenes with Willmore, appearing in a variety of disguises, male and female, and only tells him her name after he agrees to marry her: see *The Rover*, v.i, pp. 98–9, 100. The parts of Hellena and Cornelia were both played by Elizabeth Barry.

66 See Howe, *First English Actresses*, pp. 56–9; and Pearson, *Prostituted Muse*, pp. 100–18. Howe makes a strong case for the breeches roles as 'yet another means of displaying the actress as a sexual object' (p. 59).

67 *The Plain-Dealer*, iv.ii.362, *Plays*, ed. Friedman; Dryden, Prologue to *The Tempest*, 35–8, *Poems*, ed. Kinsley.

68 *Sir Anthony Love; or The Rambling Lady*, i.i.6–14, 46, 505, *Works*, ed. Jordan and Love.

69 There is of course a degree of sexual titillation in these scenes, as in the

spectacle of the popular, attractive actress Susannah Mountfort, involved in one after another provocative situation. Mrs Mountfort particularly specialised in breeches roles, and *Sir Anthony Love* was her greatest success: Southerne writes in his dedicatory epistle, 'As I made every Line for her, she has mended every Word for me; and by a Gaiety and Air, particular to her Action, turn'd every thing into the Genius of the Character' (*Works*, I, 171). Where Pearson, *Prostituted Muse*, sees the play as a satire on 'a brutal society' and as seriously concerned with 'the oppression of women' (pp. 115–17), Howe, *First English Actresses*, argues that *Sir Anthony Love* 'offers no real threat to the established social order' (pp. 59–62, and on Mountfort's popularity in the role, pp. 82–5).

70 On the ending, see Pearson, *Prostituted Muse*, p. 117 and Weber, *Restoration Rake-Hero*, pp. 168–71. In their edition of Southerne, Jordan and Love compare *Sir Anthony Love* with the tradition of rogue literature (*Works*, I, 165). The relationship between the libertine, male and female, and the picaresque rogue is explored in Maximillian E. Novak, 'Freedom, Libertinism, and the Picaresque', *Studies in Eighteenth-Century Culture*, 3 (1973), 35–48.

71 On the tradition of the virago or female warrior in seventeenth-century drama, see Simon Shepherd, *Amazons and Warrior Women: Varieties of Feminism in Seventeenth-Century Drama* (Brighton, 1981), pp. 67–106; and Pearson, *Prostituted Muse*, pp. 87–92. In the original production, which was not a success, Ranter was played by Betty Currer, Semernia by Anne Bracegirdle and Daring by Samuel Sandford, who usually played villains.

72 There is an excellent discussion of *The Widdow Ranter*, discussing parallels and contrasts between main plot and sub-plot, in an unpublished Ph.D. thesis by Eva Simmons, 'Virtue Intire: Aphra Behn's contribution in her comedies to the marriage debates of the seventeenth century' (University of London, 1990).

73 Pearson, *Prostituted Muse*, pp. 87–92; Howard, *The Womens Conquest*, v.i, pp. 85, 87.

74 *The Conquest of China*, 189, 193; 8–17, in *Poems*, ed. Pinto, pp. 67, 62; all references are to Pinto's text. Rochester's fragment was intended for a play by Sir Robert Howard (the brother of Edward Howard): see Pinto's note, pp. 183–4.

75 *The Unnatural Tragedy*, Margaret Cavendish, Duchess of Newcastle, *Playes Written by the Thrice Noble, Illustrious and Excellent Princess, the Lady Marchioness of Newcastle* (London, 1662), p. 332. There are good discussions of the Duchess of Newcastle's plays in Hobby, *Virtue of Necessity*, pp. 105–11; and Pearson, *Prostituted Muse*, pp. 125–33.

76 *Playes*, p. 609.

77 Staves, *Players' Scepters*, p. 169; Shadwell, *The Woman-Captain*, I.ii, p. 11. Cf. the heroine's praise of 'Liberty' in Otway's *The Atheist*, v.430–4: 'Do not our Fathers, Brothers and Kinsmen often, upon

pretence of it, bid fair for Rebellion against their Soveraign; And why ought not we, by their Example, to rebel as plausibly against them?' Hume lists *The Woman-Captain* as one of several 'amusing' plays which treat domestic discord as material for farce: 'in none of these cases is *marriage* considered seriously, the institution or the laws regulating it criticized, or the emotions of the participants analyzed with any real feeling' (*Rakish Stage*, pp. 185–6).

78 Cf. Locke, *Two Treatises*, II.149, 222–4, pp. 384, 430–3. Southerne uses a similar political analogy in *The Wives Excuse*, II.ii.78–82: 'In a marry'd State, as in the publick, we tye our selves up, indeed; but to be protected in our Persons, Fortunes and Honours . . . for few will obey, but for the Benefit they receive from the Government.'

79 Sir John Vanbrugh, *A Short Vindication of the Relapse and the Provok'd Wife, from Immorality and Profaneness*, p. 51. Vanbrugh's pamphlet, arguing that 'the Business of Comedy is to shew People what they shou'd do, by representing them upon the Stage, doing what they shou'd not' (p. 45), is an answer to Jeremy Collier's *A Short View of the Immorality, and Profaneness of the English Stage* (London, 1698).

80 For similar passages in prologues and epilogues, see Howe, *First English Actresses*, pp. 58–62.

81 *The Second Part of The Rover* (London, 1681), IV.i, p. 57. The role of Ariadne was played by Betty Currer, who as Howe shows frequently played whores and women of the world (e.g., Aquilina in *Venice Preserv'd*), though she also played more conventional young heroines, usually as a second lead: see *First English Actresses*, pp. 78–9, 101–2, 184.

82 *Comedies, and Tragedies* (London, 1664), Part I, II.iv, p. 339. John Barton's 1986 adaptation of *The Rover*, abandoning Behn's text for a rewritten version of Killigrew in this passage, makes the attack on the double standard clumsily explicit:

ANGELICA
> You men are strangely partial to yourselves.
> What crime is mine that you would not now commit?
> Who made the laws by which you judge me? Men!
> Men who would rove and ramble, but require
> That women must be nice.

See Aphra Behn and John Barton, *The Rover* (London, 1986), Scene 7, p. 38. Killigrew's Angellica Bianca in later scenes is more conventionally grief-stricken and less independent in her attitudes than the character in Behn or in Barton's adaptation: 'Can you tell your heart I am yours, and not remember I might have been any bodies? . . . Have you kindness and good nature enough to hide such a stain? . . . oh! that such a stream [of tears] could make me as pure a Virgin as I am now a perfect Lover; then I would beg to be thy wife; but that must not be' (*Thomaso*, Part I, II.iv, pp. 340–1).

83 At another point Hellena says of Willmore 'I am as inconstant as you'

(*The Rover*, III.i, p. 45). The roles of Hellena and La Nuche were both played by Barry. Pearson, who has an interesting discussion of the treatment of female 'sexual outlaws' in the plays of Behn, sees the behaviour of both La Nuche and Angelica Bianca as displaying 'generosity' (*Prostituted Muse*, pp. 164–5). For another view of the ending of Part II, see Holland, *Ornament of Action*, pp. 67–8.

84 Howe, *First English Actresses*, pp. 43–6; John Dennis, *Original Letters, Familiar, Moral and Critical* (London, 1721), pp. 63–4, cited in Howe, p. 45. On the treatment of rape in Restoration drama, with its 'titillating combination of violence and eroticism', see also Pearson, *Prostituted Muse*, pp. 95–9.

85 Cf. Rochester's 'On Mistress Willis', with its equation of 'Cunt' and 'Common shore', discussed in my Introduction; and cf. the discussion of Blunt and Lucetta in Pearson, *Prostituted Muse*, p. 154. In the parallel scenes in Killigrew's *Thomaso*, Part II, II.iv, pp. 409–12, Edwardo's motivation of being 'reveng'd on all the sex' is similar, but much less is made of the equivalence of kissing and beating, and the virtuous Serulina is sufficiently unruffled to express sympathy for the Englishman 'abus'd' by a whore: 'I confess I do not wonder to finde you thus enrag'd' (p. 412). There is more actual violence in *Thomaso* than in *The Rover* (Edwardo cuts Lucetta's face, disfiguring her, Lucetta and another whore plot to kill Thomaso and their hired bravos kill another man by mistake), but it is treated far less critically.

86 Frederick's behaviour here is closely based on a scene in *Thomaso*, where Ferdinando rather than Edwardo says 'we'll both ly with her, one will be enough to beat her' (Part II, II.iv, p. 411). But Killigrew's Ferdinando, a fool like Edwardo, is equally motivated by revenge, and Thomaso, rather than acting similarly, upbraids them as 'horrid beasts' for their 'barbarous' assault on 'oppress'd innocence' (Part II, III.iv, p. 417).

87 In Killigrew's *Thomaso*, Part I, IV.ii, pp. 357–9, the foolish Edwardo rather than Thomaso is the drunken aggressor in this scene, which Behn follows in a number of verbal details. Here as elsewhere, Killigrew makes the distinction between gallant cavalier and foolish pretender much more clear-cut than Behn does.

88 The text is corrected in accordance with the original edition (1677): the modern reprint here and in one other passage follows Montague Summers's 1915 collected edition in omitting several words.

89 One recent critic, Nancy Cotton, in 'Aphra Behn and the Pattern Hero', sees Willmore as 'not criticized' in any way, but as a straightforward model for imitation, exemplifying the 'good qualities' of the cavalier tradition: 'The play implies not that whoring is foolish, but that Blunt is simply not the man that Willmore is, that he can't measure up' (*Curtain Calls*, ed. Schofield and Macheski, p. 215). Hobby, in contrast, is extremely severe on the 'feckless', 'insensitive' Willmore as

potential rapist, seeing him as in no significant ways different from Blunt: according to Hobby, in Behn's writings 'rape or the threat of it is shown to be an almost routine masculine threat to bully and manipulate women' and Willmore is 'wholly incapable of understanding the viewpoint of the women [he has] sex with' (*Virtue of Necessity*, pp. 122–7).

90 *The City-Heiress: Or, Sir Timothy Treat-all* (London, 1682), ii.ii, p. 19; iv.ii, p. 47. There is a good discussion of the 'grim comedy' of this scene in Howe, *First English Actresses*, p. 136.

91 Robert Gould, 'A Satyr against the Play-House', *Poems* (London, 1689), p. 173. I am indebted to Paddy Lyons for his discussion of this scene in *The City-Heiress* in an unpublished lecture at an Aphra Behn conference, University of London Extra-Mural Studies, 30 May 1987. See also Pearson, *Prostituted Muse*, pp. 161–2; and Howe, *First English Actresses*, pp. 134–5.

92 *Love-Letters*, ed. Duffy, Part i, p. 85. A letter from Sylvia's sister makes a similar point in harsher terms: 'And when, my sister, thou hast run thy race, made thyself loathed, undone and infamous as hell, despis'd, scorn'd and abandon'd by all, lampoon'd, perhaps diseas'd; this faithless man, this cause of all will leave thee too, grow weary of thee, nauseated by use' (*ibid.*, Part i, p. 72).

93 Cf. *The Rover*, ii.ii, p. 35 and *The Second Part of The Rover*, v.i, p. 69. Both La Nuche and Angelica Bianca are faced with a choice between 'interest' and love; on the treatment of a similar conflict in Congreve's *Love for Love*, see chapter 1.

94 Cf. the closing lines of *The Dutch Lover*, v.i, p. 88: 'The Ladies too in blushes do confess/Equal desires, which yet they'l not confess'. *Love-Letters* similarly presents men and women as equally susceptible to desire, as do such poems as 'The Disappointment', 'On Desire' and 'On a Juniper-Tree, cut down to make Busks'.

95 *Love-Letters*, ed. Duffy, Part i, pp. 107–9.

96 See 'On the first discovery of falseness in Amintas', 5–6, 28–9, one of several poems by Behn in the voice of a seduced and abandoned woman.

97 *The History of the Nun*, p. 152; *Love-Letters*, ed. Duffy, Part iii, p. 372.

98 *Love-Letters*, ed. Duffy, Part iii, p. 461.

CONCLUSION

1 'The Answer', 17, Rochester, *Poems*, ed. Walker, p. 21; *Bellamira, or The Mistress, The Poetical and Dramatic Works of Sir Charles Sedley*, ed. V. de Sola Pinto (2 vols., London, 1928), ii.iv.115–17. Cf. *Leviathan*, xiii, p. 82.

2 There is a good account of *Bellamira* in Pearson, *Prostituted Muse*, pp. 94–5.

3 Rochester, *Satyr against Mankind*, 177–8; 'To Corinna', 11–12.
4 I.i.4–7, 12–15, *Four Comedies*, ed. L. A. Beaurline and Fredson Bowers (Chicago and London, 1967).
5 Traugott, 'The Rake's Progress from Court to Comedy: A Study in Comic Form', *Studies in English Literature*, 6 (1966), 381–407, esp. 392–6.
6 *The Atheist*, IV.94–7, *Works*, ed. Ghosh. For an account of the treatment of marital discord in *The Atheist*, see Hume, *Rakish Stage*, pp. 97–100.
7 The idea that an 'Original Community of all things' in the state of nature should be, for reasons of enlightened self-interest, voluntarily surrendered in favour of a contractual 'league, not to invade each other's propriety' is a central tenet of Locke's political theory: 'Though in the state of Nature he hath such a right, yet the Enjoyment of it is very uncertain, and constantly exposed to the Invasion of others' (*Two Treatises*, I.40; II.123, pp. 187, 365).
8 'Fragment of a Satire on Men', 1–6. The fragment, in Rochester's hand, can be found in Nottingham Portland MS PwV. 31.
9 Cf. the relationship between the 'Fine Lady' and the 'humble Knight' her husband in 'A Letter from Artemiza to Chloe': 'Telling the Knight, that her affayres require,/Hee for some houres obsequiously retire./I thinke, shee was asham'd, to have him seene' (74, 80–2).
10 Weber, '"Drudging in Fair Aurelia's Womb"', p. 102.
11 Carole Fabricant, 'The Writer as Hero and Whore: Rochester's *Letter from Artemisia to Chloe*', *Essays in Literature*, 3 (1976), 152–66, esp. 154. For a similar view of the poem, see Farley-Hills, *Rochester's Poetry*, pp. 204–12.
12 Behn, 'To Lysander, on some Verses', 9, 3–4.
13 'On a Juniper-Tree, cut down to make Busks', 92–3, in *Poetry*, ed. Todd.
14 'Upon his Drinking a Bowl', 21–2; 'To the Post Boy', 2.

Index